Essays

in

Sociological

Explanation

NEIL J. SMELSER
Professor of Sociology
University of California, Berkeley

PRENTICE-HALL, INC., *Englewood Cliffs, New Jersey*

Prentice-Hall Sociology Series

NEIL J. SMELSER, *Editor*

LIBRARY OF CONGRESS CATALOG CARD NO.: 68-24430

Current Printing (*last number*):

10   9   8   7   6   5   4   3   2   1

PRINTED IN THE UNITED STATES OF AMERICA

PRENTICE-HALL INTERNATIONAL, INC., *London*
PRENTICE-HALL OF AUSTRALIA, PTY. LTD., *Sydney*
PRENTICE-HALL OF CANADA, LTD., *Toronto*
PRENTICE-HALL OF INDIA PRIVATE LTD., *New Delhi*
PRENTICE-HALL OF JAPAN, INC., *Tokyo*

Preface

In reviewing the essays I have composed during the past half-dozen years, I have been able to group them conveniently according to two of my continuing sociological interests. The first is an interest in codifying the distinctive scope of sociology as a discipline, specifying the character of sociological explanation, and tracing the relations between sociology and the other social and behavorial sciences. Part I of this book consists of essays on these topics. The second is an interest in generating explanations for processes of social change, and establishing interrelations among these processes. Part II focuses on these issues.

Part I begins with a general essay on the character of the sociological enterprise, and the relations among this enterprise and the other social sciences. In this essay I contrast six disciplines according to four criteria—the subject matter of each, the determinants stressed by each, the logical structure of each, and the research methods of each—and attempt to outline the potential for interdisciplinary exchanges among them. This essay grew from a session I chaired on "The Uses of Sociology by the Other Social Sciences" at the annual meetings of the American Sociological Association in Washington in 1962. At that session I was greatly stimulated by the ideas presented in papers by Asa Briggs, Alfred H. Conrad, and Daniel J. Levinson. My essay, completed more than two years after the meetings, was first published as Chapter I of *The Uses of Sociology,* edited by Paul F. Lazarsfeld, William H. Sewell, and Harold L. Wilensky.

Each of the next four chapters selects a theme from Chapter One and presses its analysis further. Chapter Two—"The Optimum Scope of Sociology"—considers sociology as a distinctive discipline once again, outlining its contours and subdivisions, and attempting to evaluate what appear to be the broad current trends in the discipline. This essay was first presented at a conference entitled "A Design for Sociology," held in Philadelphia in December 1967, and sponsored by the American Academy of Political and Social Science. It will appear within the next few months, along with several other papers and discussions, in a special publication of the Academy.

Though many of the essays in this volume are methodological in emphasis, Chapter Three is most explicitly so. It is an essay on a method of research widely employed in the social sciences—the "comparative method," which is used in comparing complex social units that are few in number (for example, nations) and do not readily lend themselves to experimental or statistical analysis. Using economic institutions as a concrete example, I attempt to outline some of the methodological problems associated with comparative analysis, and to suggest a few research strategies for the comparative study of societies. The paper was originally submitted to the working group on "Economics and Sociology" at the Sixth World Congress of Sociology at Evian in 1966. It was published in the *Transactions of the Sixth World Congress of Sociology.*

Chapter Four takes up the relations between sociology and history, but from an angle different from that of Chapter One. In this essay I attempt to delineate the sometimes subtle similarities and differences in the approaches of sociological and historical investigators. Rather than frame these similarities and differences in the abstract, however, I try to arrive at them by reviewing some of the issues that arose from my empirical work on economic and social changes during the British Industrial Revolution. The paper was originally delivered at the annual meetings of the American Sociological Association in Los Angeles and at the Pacific Coast Meetings of the American Historical Association in San Francisco, both in August of 1963. It has been published recently in Volume I of the *Journal of Social History.*

Chapter Five—"Social and Psychological Dimensions of Collective Behavior"—focuses on the relations between sociology and psychology. Like Chapter Four, however, it does so not in general terms but in relation to the explanation of particular empirical phenomena. In my earlier book, *Theory of Collective Behavior,* I considered collective outbursts and collective movements mainly from the standpoint of sociological factors, though the work contained many implicit psychological assumptions and assertions. In this essay, composed several years after the appearance of that book, I make an effort to evaluate the respective potential of sociological and psychological explanations of collective episodes. I use the psychoanalytic literature as the main springboard for investigating the psychological approach. The paper was first presented to members of the Ad Hoc Research Committee of the San Francisco Psychoanalytic Institute, and has not been published before.

In Part II, I have included two essays on the modernization of traditional societies and one general essay on social change. Chapter Six is an account of the main structural changes that accompany economic and social development, and some of the social disturbances that typically arise. The paper was first delivered at the North American Conference on the Social Implications of Industrialization and Technological Change, held in Chicago in 1960 under the sponsorship of the Department of Social Sciences of UNESCO. It was published subsequently in *Industralization and Society*, edited by Bert F. Hoselitz and Wilbert E. Moore. Chapter Seven, written jointly with Seymour Martin Lipset, explores the implications of rapid economic development for the forms and rates of social mobility. The essay concerns both broad theoretical issues and research problems that arise in comparing national units with respect to mobility. The paper was first presented at the Conference on Social Structure, Social Mobility, and Economic Development, held in San Francisco in 1964 under the sponsorship of the Committee of Economic Growth of the Social Science Research Council. It was later published in *Social Structure and Mobility in Economic Development*, edited by Lipset and myself.

The origins of Chapter Eight—"Toward a General Theory of Social Change"—are diverse. My earliest interests in sociology concerned the systematic analysis of processes of social change, and several times during my teaching career at the University of California, Berkeley, I have offered general courses on social change, in which I developed many of the ideas that appear in this paper. Two more specific occasions, however, led to the actual composition of the essay. First, in 1965 the staff of Human Sciences Research, Inc., McLean, Virginia, commissioned me to prepare a working paper on the implications of theories of social change for the short-term and long-term consequences of a social catastrophe such as nuclear attack on the United States. Limited as it was, this topic proved impossible to address without opening up almost every issue involved in the analysis of social change. Second, also in 1965, I undertook to prepare a general chapter on social change in the text under my editorship, *Sociology*, published in 1967. Chapter Eight is an effort to synthesize these several sources into a general theoretical essay on social change. Parts of the essay derive from the working paper. A small part has been adapted from the chapter in the text. But the largest part of the material has not been published before.

BERKELEY, CALIFORNIA   NEIL J. SMELSER

Contents

PART I: Sociology as a Scientific Enterprise

ONE: Sociology and the Other Social Sciences *

An inquisitive layman will often ask a sociologist: "What is sociology, anyway?" The question is not an easy one. Moreover, after the sociologist replies—usually haltingly and in general terms—the layman may pose a second question, such as, "Well, how is that different from social psychology?" or "Isn't that what anthropologists do?" These, too, are likely to yield vague, unsatisfactory answers. Sociology seems to defy simple definition of itself and clear demarcation from related endeavors.

Somehow it seems more appropriate to ask the question of sociology than it does of some of her sister social sciences. *What Is Sociology?* seems a reasonable title for a recent introductory text.[1] The title *What Is Economics?* would appear more to signify a critical treatment of the foundations of economics than to introduce the field that has crystallized in the mid-twentieth century. *What Is History?* would signify more a foray into the philosophy of historical inquiry than an introduction to the field. In short, the query "What Is ———?" when applied to a discipline betokens an effort to locate the distinctive focus of a field still in search of its identity, one which has only recently achieved solid institutional support.

In this essay I aim to explore the distinctive character of sociology and its relations to the other social sciences. I shall proceed by opening four topics in sequence:

1. The criteria by which the various social-science disciplines can be described and related to one another.

* This essay appeared originally in *The Uses of Sociology*, edited by Paul Lazarsfeld, William H. Sewell, and Harold L. Wilensky (New York: Basic Books, Inc., 1967).

[1] Alex Inkeles, *What Is Sociology? An Introduction to the Discipline and Profession* (Englewood Cliffs, N.J.: Prentice-Hall, Inc., 1964).

2. The contours of sociology according to these criteria.

3. The contours of several neighboring fields according to the same criteria—the fields of economics, political science, anthropology, history, and psychology.[2] Some might object to the inclusion of the last two on grounds that history is in the humanities and that psychology is scientific but not social, but I think that much can be learned by comparing sociology with these two fields.

4. Some possibilities of theoretical and empirical articulation between sociology and the other disciplines.

My emphasis will be conceptual. I am interested in the theoretical and empirical relations among the social sciences as they stand today. I shall not trace how these relations have developed in the history of thought. Nor shall I discuss, except by way of occasional illustration, the consequences of the institutional relations among sociology and the other social sciences: for example, the fact that sociology is departmentally linked here with anthropology, there with political science, and elsewhere with economics.

CRITERIA FOR DESCRIBING AND COMPARING THE SOCIAL SCIENCES

The simplest way to characterize a discipline is to depict its subject matter concretely. Economists may be said to study businessmen and organizations, as they produce and market commodities, and consumers as they buy and use these commodities. Other social sciences are not so specific in their focus. Upon being asked to define anthropology, Malinowski is reported to have replied that anthropology is "the study of man, embracing woman." Likewise, sociology is very diffuse, covering behavior in families, hospitals, educational institutions, street-corner gangs, experimental small groups, armies, and religious revivals, to name only a few settings. To describe a social science concretely, however, does not yield a very scientific account, since it usually refers to the list of topics that, over a long period, have interested those who call themselves economists or sociologists or whatever. Such a description is likely to change, moreover, as new problems make their appearance in society—problems such as imperfect competition, race relations, mental illness, and poverty.

A more analytic way of describing and comparing disciplines is to ask how knowledge is generated, organized, and verified in each. This, in turn, breaks down into a number of criteria:

---

[2] These five fields, plus sociology, are those which Bernard Berelson also classifies as "social sciences." "Introduction to the Behavioral Sciences," in Bernard Berelson, ed., *The Behavioral Sciences Today* (New York: Basic Books, Inc., 1963), p. 1.

First, it is necessary to specify what aspect of the concrete subject matter preoccupies the investigator. Economists are not interested in every aspect of the behavior of businessmen; they wish to discover specifically why businessmen produce different quantities of commodities at different times, why they charge different prices at different times, why they hire more or fewer workers under different conditions, and so on. Sociologists are not interested in every aspect of the family; they focus on patterns of rights and obligations of family members, changes in the rates of family formation and dissolution, differences in fathers' and sons' career patterns, and so on. By asking such questions, we identify the distinctive *scientific problems, phenomena to be explained,* or *dependent variables* of a discipline.

Second, it is necessary to specify what each discipline treats as the distinctive causes (or determinants, or factors, or conditions) of variation in the dependent variables. In determining how much of a given commodity will be produced at a given price, the economist asks how much of the commodity the consumers are demanding, how much the businessman has to pay for raw materials and labor to produce the commodity, and how his competitors are behaving. In accounting for variations in divorce rates, the sociologist turns to the society's degree of urbanization and industrialization; its levels of interreligious, interethnic, and interclass marriage; and its laws affecting divorce. In this search for associated conditions, the social scientist attempts to identify distinctive *independent variables.*

The focus of a scientific discipline, then, can be specified by listing the dependent and independent variables that preoccupy its investigators. But these lists of variables do not tell the whole story. It is necessary, third, to specify the ways in which a discipline imposes a *logical ordering* on its variables. Indeed, merely by distinguishing between dependent and independent variables, we elicit one instance of logical ordering—that is, specifying which variables are to be viewed as causes and which as effects. On the basis of this ordering, various *hypotheses*—statements of the conditions under which dependent variables may be expected to vary in certain ways—can be formulated. A more complex kind of ordering results when a number of hypotheses are combined into an organized system (often called a *model*). Suppose, for example, the economist is equipped with three hypotheses: that private investment influences aggregate employment in specific ways, that government spending influences employment in other ways, and that foreign trade influences it in still other ways. A model is created when the economist states the interactions among these determinants, all in relation to employment, in a logically rigorous way (for example, in the form of simultaneous equations). An example of a cruder model is provided by psychoanalytic theory. Slips of the tongue are determined primarily by the strength of repressed instinctual conflicts. But in addition they occur more frequently when an individual is fatigued and thus inattentive. If it were possible to single out the precise strength of these two determinants—repressed conflict and fatigue—and combine them into a more complex form, a model would be at hand.

Logical ordering does not end with complex models. These models are embedded in a number of definitions, assumptions, and postulates. The hypothesis that investment creates a higher level of employment, for example, rests on the assumption that laborers are motivated to respond positively to wage offers made by employers. The hypothesis linking repressed conflict and slips of the tongue rests on a complex set of assumptions about instincts and their manifestations, the defensive operations of the repressing psychic agency, and the relations between psychic conflict and motor activity. Such definitions, assumptions, and postulates constitute the *theoretical framework* of a scientific discipline. Within this framework the specific hypotheses "make sense." To put it more strongly, the hypotheses and models should be *derived,* as rigorously as possible, from the theoretical framework.

Fourth, it is necessary to specify the *means employed to accept or reject statements* in the various scientific disciplines. These include the methods of scientific inquiry—such as the experimental—as well as specific techniques and instruments for collecting, measuring, and processing data. The several social sciences vary considerably in the research methods they can and do utilize.

In this essay I shall use these four criteria—dependent variables, independent variables, logical ordering, and research methods—to describe, compare, contrast, and suggest ways of integrating the several social sciences. I shall digress momentarily, however, to comment on one additional way to characterize disciplines: to list their component "schools of thought."

Generally the term *school* refers to an indefinite number of scholars who stress a particular aspect of or approach to a discipline. The term also implies that its proponents are emotionally committed to their approach and are prepared to defend it from attack and to deprecate different or competing schools. A school, then, is simultaneously a subdivision of a field and a species of cult or sect.

Schools in the social sciences can be classified according to the four criteria for describing a field:

1. What aspects of social life are to be studied? The "symbolic interactionist" school, for example, focuses on relatively microscopic units of social action and emphasizes various psychic processes that accompany acts; this contrasts, for example, with the "structuralist" approach, which

studies institutional patterns without explicit reference to the social psychological aspects of discrete acts.

2. What are the determinants of social behavior? Schools clustering around independent variables may be quite specific in focus, as in the case of the "overconsumption" approach to the business cycle; or they may be quite general, as in the case of the schools of "geopolitics" or "economic determinism."

3. What are the most appropriate models or theoretical perspectives? The "organicist," and more recently the "functionalist," schools rest in part on a view of society as functioning like a biological organism; the "cultural relativist" school is based on scientific notions of how social units may be compared with one another as well as on moral notions of how legitimate it is to claim that one society is superior to another; the "phenomenological," "nominalist," and "realist" positions are based on different philosophical views regarding the nature of reality.

4. What are the methods by which propositions are accepted or rejected? One feature of the "positivist" school, for example, concerns the procedures necessary to consider a statement verified; this school contrasts with the "verstehen" and "intuitionist" approaches to inquiry. Sometimes schools are named after specific methodological procedures, as in the case of the "experimentalist," "statistical," or "survey" approaches to inquiry.

When a school is named after a man, this usually involves some distinctive combination of several criteria. For example, the Marxian approach is characterized by an emphasis on distinctive aspects of social life (economic and related institutional structures and processes), distinctive determinants ("economic determinism"), a distinctive theoretical and philosophical perspective ("dialectical materialism"), and a method of validating arguments (based mainly on logical demonstration and comparative historical analysis).

The presence of numerous "schools" in a discipline generally betokens a relative scientific immaturity (though certainly not an immaturity in all kinds of scholarship). As it achieves scientific maturity, it more nearly attains consensus on the scientific problems to be posed, the relevant independent variables, a theoretical and philosophical perspective, and appropriate research methods. Simultaneously it witnesses a decline of distinctive schools; a decline in the quantity of polemic about the "nature" of the field and the value of different "approaches" to the field; a decline in propaganda, proselytization, and defensiveness; and an increase in discussion of findings in relation to accepted criteria of validation. The existing disciplines may be ordered according to the degree to which they currently manifest these several concomitants of this aspect of scientific maturity. At one extreme are mathematics and physics, and at the other are humanistic disciplines such as literary and art criticism. The social sciences occupy an intermediate position, with sociology manifesting more signs of this kind of immaturity than economics, but perhaps fewer than political science.

SOCIOLOGY [3]

Sociology, like many of its sister social sciences, is characterized by a proliferation of schools—such as functionalism, social behaviorism, symbolic interactionism, historicism, and so on [4]—and consequently great disagreement among sociologists about the fundamental problems, concepts, theories, and methods in the field. Moreover, the field displays an increasing number of subdivisions—sociology of the family, stratification, religion, medicine, leisure, law, deviance, collective behavior, for instance —each of which differs in one or more respects from the other. Because of this internal diversity, it is difficult, even presumptuous, to try to present a single view of the character of the field. Necessarily, then, my characterization of sociology will have to be approximate; it will overemphasize some aspects of the field and underemphasize others; and it will gloss over many disagreements concerning fundamental features.

Dependent Variables

Sociological analysis begins with a problem. Posing a problem means identifying some variation in human behavior and framing a "why" question about this variation. Such variation becomes the dependent variable —that which is to be explained. This variation may involve a single event (Why did violence erupt in the Congo when it did?); it may involve presumed regularities in the occurrence of events (Why are colonial societies that are emerging from domination prone to outbursts of hostility?); or, at a higher level, it may involve questions of structural variation in large classes of events (Why do feudal land patterns arise and persist? Why do they break down, sometimes in one way and sometimes in another?).

After isolating a certain problem, the sociologist specifies concrete units that identify the dependent variable.[5] In the field of sociology these

---

[3] Part of this section, as well as the following section on economics, is an elaboration of material originally presented in Neil J. Smelser, *The Sociology of Economic Life* (Englewood Cliffs, N.J.: Prentice-Hall, Inc., 1963), pp. 24–31.

[4] There are numerous ways to classify these schools, differing according to the descriptive criteria chosen. For two different efforts to classify schools, see Don Martindale, *The Nature and Types of Sociological Theory* (Boston: Houghton Mifflin Company, 1960), and Helmut R. Wagner, "Types of Sociological Theory: Toward a System of Classification," *American Sociological Review*, XXVIII (1963), 735–42.

[5] In practice the operation of posing problems and the operation of specifying concrete units proceed simultaneously and interact with each other.

concrete units are most commonly found in the *units of social structure* and in *variation of human behavior oriented to social structure.*[6] This common focus obtains in spite of the facts that (1) the types of social groupings in which structure is observed vary greatly—small face-to-face groups, formal organizations, voluntary associations, and diffuse collectivities such as ethnic groups; (2) the types of institutional settings in which social structure is observed vary greatly—familial, political, religious, medical, and educational.

"Social structure" is a concept used to characterize recurrent and regularized interaction among two or more persons. The basic units of social structure are not persons as such, but selected aspects of interaction among persons, such as roles (for example, businessman, husband, church member) and social organization, which refers to structured clusters of roles (such as a bureaucracy, an informal clique, a family). The important defining feature of social structure is that interaction is selective, regularized, and regulated by various social controls.

In connection with these social controls, three basic concepts are particularly important:

1. *Values* legitimize the existence and importance of specific social structures and the kinds of behavior that transpire in a given social structure. The value of "free enterprise," for instance, endorses the existence of business firms organized around the institution of private property and engaged in the pursuit of private profit.

2. *Norms* are standards of conduct that regulate the interaction among individuals in social structures. The norms of contract and property law, for instance, set up obligations and prohibitions on the agents

---

[6] To characterize the field in this manner excludes, at first glance, several of its subfields: (1) those subfields at the "cultural" boundary of social behavior—the sociology of literature, art, music, ideology, and mass culture—which cannot be classified as units of social structure proper; (2) those subfields at the "physical" and "biological" boundaries of social behavior—specifically demography, ecology, and some parts of urban and rural sociology—where the units of behavior are not social-structural but rather events and situations classified in terms of biological processes and spatial location; (3) those subfields at the "personality" boundary of social behavior—for example, socialization, some aspects of deviance and collective behavior, and the catchall field of social psychology. Despite this difference from other fields that focus on social structure itself, the reason for including them in sociology is that the analysis of these kinds of behavior social structure appears as an important independent variable. For example, in the sociology of knowledge, the major focus is on those kinds of social structures that give rise to distinctive cultural productions; in some parts of demography, the focus is on those kinds of structure (family systems, the rural-urban balance, stratification) that give rise to, say, differential fertility rates; and in the analysis of the differential occurrence of attitudes and opinions, explanatory variables are frequently social-structural in character (age, sex, socioeconomic position, and religious affiliation).

in economic transactions. As the examples show, at any given level of analysis norms are more specific than values in their control of interaction in social structures.

3. *Sanctions*—including both rewards and deprivations—involve the use of various social resources to control the behavior of personnel in social structures. Aspects of this control include the establishment of roles, the inducement of individuals to assume and perform the roles, and the control of deviance from expected role performance. Examples of sanctions are coercion, ridicule, appeal to duty, withdrawal of communication, and so on.

A concept which unifies the elements of social structure—including roles, collectivities, values, norms, and sanctions—is the concept of *institutionalization*. This refers to distinctive, enduring expectations whereby these elements are combined into a single complex. When we speak of the institutionalization of American business, for instance, we refer to a more or less enduring pattern of roles and collectivities (such as businessmen and firms), values (for instance, free enterprise), norms (laws of contract and property, informal business codes), and sanctions (profits, wages).

Many questions about dependent variables in sociology are stated as follows: Why are the elements of social structure patterned the way they are? Another class of dependent variables is specified in terms of systematic variations in human behavior oriented to social structure. Given some structure, when can conformity be expected? What are the consequences of conformity for the social structure? When can deviance from social structure be expected? What are the different forms of deviance, and why does one type of deviance rather than another arise? What are the consequences for the social structure of different kinds of deviance? Specifying the possible "consequences" of conformity or deviance involves identifying a further range of dependent variables—reactions to deviance (social control), changes in social structure, persistence of structural patterns, collective outbursts.

What are the major types of social structure? This question is usually answered by turning to some notion of the basic functions, or directional tendencies, of social systems. These functions concern the general orientations of social life. Or, as the question is often put: What are the exigencies that must be met in order for the social unit to continue functioning? Analysts who attempt to identify the basic directional tendencies of social units speak of "functional exigencies." Typical exigencies include:

1. Creation and maintenance of the cultural values of a system. For some systems, such as societies, this involves long periods of socialization and complex structures such as families, churches, schools, and training institutes.

2. Production, allocation, and consumption of scarce goods and services (sometimes called the economic function). Typical structures that specialize in this function are firms, banks, and other agencies of credit.

3. Creating, maintaining, and implementing norms governing interaction among units in the system (sometimes called the integrative function), such as the law and its enforcement agencies.

4. Coordination and control of the collective actions of the system or a collectivity within it, in modern societies by the state, political parties, and associated agencies (sometimes called the political function).

The usual basis for classifying social structures is to indicate the main functions they serve: political, economic, familial, religious, educational. The classification of social structures in this way involves assigning *primacy* of function only. Even though religious structure is a concept applied to a clustering of rites or an organized church, the social significance of this bundle of activities is not exhausted by this concept. Analytically, the concrete religious structure has a political aspect, an economic aspect, and so on. The notion of structure, then, is used to identify theoretically significant properties of concrete clusters of activities devoted primarily, but not exclusively, to meeting a particular social exigency.

This presentation of the central dependent variables in the field of sociology may convey the impression that there is uniform consensus as to these variables and the ways to describe and classify them. I do not mean to convey this impression. Much of contemporary sociological inquiry and debate does not involve systematic efforts to establish connections between these and other variables—in short, efforts to explain variations in dependent variables. Rather, it involves a search for descriptive and classificatory languages for identifying various dependent variables, as well as a continuing debate about what the dependent variables of the field *should* be.

Independent Variables

The sociological concepts listed thus far—that is, those revolving around the notion of social structure—are used mainly to identify dependent variables and to frame scientific problems. As such they do not provide hypotheses to account for variation or to explain processes of social adjustment, maladjustment, and change. To generate these additional ingredients of sociological analysis, one must take account of several classes of independent variables.

For any given dependent variable in sociology, the number and kinds of conditions that potentially affect its variation are, at first sight, discouragingly great. An individual's ability to perform a simple task in a small-group setting is influenced most immediately by his intelligence, training, and motivation. These three immediate factors are further conditioned by his social-class background, his ordinal position in his family, the presence or absence of others in the same room when he is performing the task, the behavior of the person assigning him the task, and many other factors. When we turn to the search for conditions influencing social aggregates, such as changes in the divorce rate over the past century, the number and kinds of potentially operative conditions are even more complex. The initial picture, then, is one of a *multiplicity* of operating conditions, a *compounding* of their influences on the dependent variable, and an *indeterminacy* regarding the effect of any one condition or several conditions in combination. The corresponding problem facing the scientific investigator at this stage is to *reduce* the number of operating conditions, to *isolate* one condition from another, and thereby to *make precise* the role of each condition. How are these problems faced?

The general answer to the question is that the sociologist, by virtue of his disciplinary commitments, tends to opt for social-structural conditions as explanatory variables. But, in addition, the investigator must impose some sort of *organization* on the conditions. One of the simplest ways of organizing conditions is seen in the distinction between *independent* and *intervening* variables. A classic example will show the power of this distinction. Robert Michels, in his comparative study of political parties and trade unions,[7] was preoccupied with the problem of why large-scale organizations, even those with liberal and socialist ideologies, tend universally to develop oligarchical authority systems. For Michels this problem constituted the dependent variable, or that which demanded explanation. According to Michels' account, three sets of independent variables produce oligarchy. The first are found in the technical and administrative characteristics of organizations themselves—the impossibility of direct communication and coordination of decisions by the many, with the consequence that responsibility falls into the hands of the few. The second are found in the psychological propensities of the masses to adulate and venerate leaders. The third are found in the superior oratorical, intellectual, and cultural skills of the leaders themselves.[8]

Oligarchy, once established, itself has consequences. In particular, Michels pointed out the tendency for leaders, once in power, to gain access to resources, to come to think of themselves as indispensable, and to regard their right to office as necessary and sacred. These by-products of oligarchical leadership, moreover, feed back and further consolidate the original tendencies for power to become centralized.[9] The several classes of varia-

---

[7] *Political Parties: A Sociological Study of the Oligarchical Tendencies of Modern Democracy*, trans. Eden and Cedar Paul (New York: Dover Publications, 1959).
[8] *Ibid.*, Part I.
[9] *Ibid.*, Part II, Chapters 1 and 2.

bles identified by Michels thus constitute a set of independent, intervening, and dependent variables, as shown in Figure 1. The picture of the variables, thus organized, is much simpler than a picture of the lengthy list of associations among every combined pair of variables.

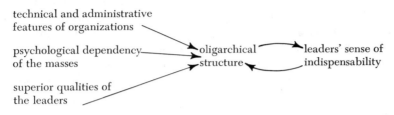

technical and administrative
features of organizations

psychological dependency
of the masses

superior qualities of
the leaders

oligarchical
structure

leaders' sense of
indispensability

FIGURE 1

The example also reveals that the distinction among independent, intervening, and dependent variables is a relative one and that the status of any given variable may change according to the analytic purposes at hand. For example, the variable "oligarchical structure" is dependent with respect to "technical and administrative features"; it is independent with respect to "leaders' sense of indispensability"; and it is intervening with respect to the relation between "technical and administrative features" and "leaders' sense of indispensability." Furthermore, "leaders' sense of indispensability" is both independent and dependent if we consider its feedback to the power structure. In sociological investigation, then, no given substantive variable can be considered as inherently independent, intervening, or dependent.

When we proceed from more or less static accounts of variation to the analysis of processes of adjustment and change, different sets of explanatory variables must be brought to bear. Among the most important of these variables in sociology are the concepts of strain, reactions to strain, and attempts to control reactions to strain.

1. Strain refers to various kinds of malintegration in the relations among elements of a social system. Among the many types of strain that arise in a social system are ambiguity in role expectations, role conflict, discrepancies between expectations and actual social experiences, and conflicts of values.

2. The initial responses to situations of strain tend to be disturbed reactions which are frequently, but not always, deviant and malintegrative from the standpoint of the social system. A variety of specific social problems arise from deviance: crime, alcoholism, hoboism, suicide, addiction, mental disorders, and social movements, to name a few.

3. Attempts to control reactions to strain may involve either structuring the initial situation so as to minimize strain or attempting to control reactions to strain once they have arisen.

By arranging these three variables into different patterns, social investigators attempt to account for the persistence and change of behavior oriented to social structures. By way of qualification, however, it should be noted that these three sets of variables are not inherently independent variables, but may themselves be the subject of explanation; for example, the investigator of the social conditions underlying strain makes strain the dependent variable and various social-structural categories the independent variables.

Relations Among Different Classes of Variables

In discussing the hypotheses relating independent and dependent variables, I have already opened the discussion of the relations among variables. Indeed, most research activity in sociology is directed either toward the discovery or establishment of empirical generalizations (which are not hypotheses as such, but rather data bearing on hypotheses)[10] or toward the establishment of quite specific and discrete relations between an independent variable and a dependent variable. The field still suffers from shortage of full-scale explanatory models. Those models that do exist may be classified into three types:

1. Static models that organize a number of different variables to account for structural characteristics. The work of Michels is an example.
2. Process models, which refer to changes of variables *within* a social structure. Process models are used, for example, in analyzing rates of social mobility, voting rates, and certain types of social control (for instance, psychotherapy, which often "rehabilitates" persons considered to be "disturbed"). In these examples the social structure is assumed to remain unchanged.[11]
3. Change models, which refer to changes of the structure itself. For example, when attempts to control strain fail, new structural arrangements may result. The movement to the new structure may be *controlled* (as

[10] An example of this kind of research is the preoccupation with the factual question of whether social mobility is increasing, decreasing, or remaining constant in recent American history. For a summary of recent research on this question, see Elton F. Jackson and Harry J. Crockett, Jr., "Occupational Mobility in the United States: A Point Estimate and Trend Comparison," *American Sociological Review,* XXIX (1964), 5–15.

[11] An example of a model applied to voting behavior is the discussion of panel analysis in Patricia L. Kendall and Paul F. Lazarsfeld, "Problems of Survey Analysis," in Robert K. Merton and Paul F. Lazarsfeld, eds., *Continuities in Social Research* (New York: The Free Press of Glencoe, Inc., 1950).

when a new law is passed by the constituted authorities to meet a pressing social problem) or *uncontrolled* (as when a revolutionary party overthrows the authority and sets up a new constitution and government). The new equilibrium, moreover, may be precarious; changes may necessitate further changes. Repeated failure of social control mechanisms may result in the disintegration of the system. All these examples involve changes in the social structure.[12]

Most sociological models are framed in nonmathematical language. Mathematical models, rare in sociology, are employed mainly in the analysis of population movements and small-group processes, and occasionally in the analysis of voting behavior and social mobility.[13]

Sociology also displays a certain amount of systematic effort to formalize the various ingredients of scientific explanation—variables of several types and their organization into definite relationships—into comprehensive theoretical frameworks. These efforts are most conspicuously identified with the names of Talcott Parsons and his associates, who have attempted to specify the nature of systems of social action and to state in very general terms the relations among the elements of these systems—relations which presumably form the basis for a great number of formal models.[14] Despite these efforts at formalization of theory, most models and theories in sociology rest on assumptions and postulates that are vaguely formulated and unexamined. For example, models of social mobility generally rest on the psychological postulate that individuals in a system of stratified positions and rewards are, other things being equal, more or less uniformly motivated to move to as high a point as possible in the hierarchy. Such an assumption, while perhaps necessary for generating manageable models and specific hypotheses, is certainly open to doubt on empirical grounds and may contain hidden implications that would, if made explicit, lead investigators to modify their theoretical formulations. To choose another set of examples, theories of alienation, anomie, and conflict frequently rest on a variety of implicit assumptions about human nature, what sorts of experiences degrade the person, and how the person

12 Models of this kind may be found in Neil J. Smelser, *Theory of Collective Behavior* (New York: The Free Press of Glencoe, Inc., 1963).

13 For an example of the application of mathematical models to the explanation of structural variation, see Harrison C. White, *An Anatomy of Kinship: Mathematical Models for Structures of Cumulated Roles* (Englewood Cliffs, N.J.: Prentice-Hall, Inc., 1963); for an example of the application of mathematical models to nonexperimental processes of collective behavior, see William N. McPhee, *Formal Theories of Mass Behavior* (New York: The Free Press of Glencoe, Inc., 1963).

14 See especially Talcott Parsons, Robert F. Bales, and Edward Shils, eds., *Working Papers in the Theory of Action* (New York: The Free Press of Glencoe, Inc., 1953), and Marion J. Levy, Jr., *The Structure of Society* (Princeton: Princeton University Press, 1952).

typically reacts to these experiences.[15] The field of sociology—as contrasted with economics, as we shall see presently—is notable for its extraordinary diversity of underlying assumptions concerning social and psychological phenomena. This diversity, more than any other single factor, probably leads to the frequently expressed view that sociology is not a unified field and to the frequent and not always well informed disputes about fundamental principles in the field.

Research Methods [16]

Sociology's diversity of dependent variables, independent variables, and theoretical frameworks is matched by a corresponding diversity in research methods. Before proceeding to illustrate this point, I shall introduce a distinction by which the various methods of drawing inferences in the social sciences can be compared with one another. This distinction is between determinants treated as *parameters* and determinants treated as *operative variables*. Parameters are determinants that are known or suspected to influence a dependent variable, but in the investigation at hand, are made or assumed not to vary. Operative variables are conditions that are known or suspected to influence a dependent variable and, in the investigation, are made or allowed to vary in order to assess this influence. By making variables into parameters for purposes of analysis, most of the potentially operative conditions are made not to vary, so that the operation of one or a few conditions may be isolated and examined. The distinction between parameters and variables is, of course, a relative one. What may be treated as a parameter in one investigation may become a variable condition in another.

The field of sociology displays a plethora of research methods designed to accomplish the continuous and systematic transformation of conditions into parameters and variables in order to refine and generalize explanations. The *experimental method,* for example, which involves the direct manipulation of situations to create parameters and variables, finds widespread use in social-psychological and small-group experimentation. Most often experimentation is conducted by establishing two groups—the

[15] For an examination of some of the implications of the "Marxian" and "Durkheimian" views of the human conditions as manifested in research in industrial sociology, see Louis Schneider and Sverre Lysgaard, " 'Deficiency' and 'Conflict' in Industrial Sociology," *American Journal of Economics and Sociology,* XII (1952–1953), 49–61.

[16] In this section I shall be concerned with only one aspect of research methodology: the ways in which data are manipulated to permit the investigator to draw relatively valid inferences. These ways include the experimental, statistical, comparative, and clinical methods, as well as the method of heuristic assumption. I shall not be able to discuss particular methods of measurement, such as content analysis or attitude surveys; nor will I discuss particular statistical techniques, such as the analysis of variance.

experimental and the control—that are identical in respect to many known or suspected sources of variation, such as age, sex, intelligence, educational level, socioeconomic background, and the like. The conditions that are shared by the two groups are established as parameters. Then, with regard to the operative condition under investigation, the experimental group is stimulated, the control group not. This condition, not shared by the two groups, is thereby established as the operative variable.

The *statistical method,* applying mathematical techniques to populations and samples of events containing large numbers, attempts to achieve the same manipulation of parameters and operative conditions as does the experimental method. The main difference between the two is that experimentation does so by situational manipulation, whereas statistical analysis does so by conceptual (mathematical) manipulation, which holds constant or cancels out sources of variation or shows them to be actually inoperative. An example of this type of analysis is found in the sociological analysis of intergenerational mobility. Over an intergenerational period, some social mobility (defined as differences in occupational status between father and son) is required simply by virtue of long-term structural changes in the occupational structure itself. If the tertiary sector is expanding, for example, more sons will necessarily move into service industries from other backgrounds. Investigators of mobility frequently wish to inquire into other determinants than changing industrial structure—determinants such as family size, ordinal position in family, or achievement motivation, for example. In order to isolate these other determinants, the investigator calculates some sort of mobility rate that is to be expected solely on the basis of structural changes alone, subtracts this rate from the gross mobility rate, and analyzes the difference in terms of the other suspected independent variables. In this way the effect of structural changes is held constant or made into a parameter for purposes of further analysis.[17]

Using this method to rule out spurious relations and thus isolate genuine ones is best illustrated in multivariate analysis as it is practiced in survey research. Suppose that in a national survey it is found that age is positively correlated with intolerance. Suppose also that level of education is found to be negatively correlated with intolerance. Since age and educational level are themselves correlated (above the age of completed education, young people are more educated than old people), it is impossible to know, on the basis of the two correlations taken alone, if either or both or neither is a determinant of intolerance. To gain this knowledge, a method

[17] For an example of a research on social mobility using this kind of statistical manipulation, see Natalie Rogoff Ramsøy, "Changing Rates of Mobility," in Neil J. Smelser and Seymour Martin Lipset, eds., *Social Structure and Mobility in Economic Development* (Chicago: Aldine Press, 1966).

of partial correlation is applied: Holding education constant, what is the apparent influence of age? And holding age constant, what is the apparent influence of education? By carrying out a succession of such operations, both on the two variables in question and on other variables that are associated with them, the investigator makes parameters out of a number of possibly and apparently operative conditions and arrives at a truer picture of the actually operative conditions.[18]

The method of statistical manipulation of historical data finds widespread use in sociology, both when the data are "given"—as in census reports—and when they are measured specifically for research purposes—as in attitude surveys. Sometimes, however, the number of cases is too small to permit manipulation by statistical methods; for example, when research involves the comparison of large, complex nation-states. Under such conditions the sociologist has recourse to the *comparative method.* Because of the restricted number of cases, the investigator is forced to rely on the method of *systematic comparative illustration.* Despite this unique restrictive feature of the comparative method, its logic is identical to the methods just reviewed in that it attempts to yield scientific explanation by the systematic manipulation of parameters and operative variables. A classic example will show this identity. One of Durkheim's central findings in his study of suicide was that Protestants persistently display higher rates of suicide than Catholics.[19] The variable he employed to explain this finding was differential integration of the two religious groupings: Protestants, with their antiauthoritarian, individualistic traditions, are less integrated than Catholics and hence less protected against self-destruction. On examining the countries on which his religious data were available, however, Durkheim noticed that the Catholics were in the minority in every case. Could it not be, he asked, that minority status rather than religious tradition is the operative variable in the genesis of lower suicide rates among Catholics? To throw light on this question, he examined regions such as Austria and Bavaria, where Catholics are in the majority; in these regions he discovered some diminution of the religious differences between Protestants and Catholics, but Protestant rates were still higher. On the basis of this examination, he concluded that "Catholicism does not . . . owe [its protective influence] solely to its minority status." [20] In this

[18] For an extended exercise that used the variables of age, education, and various measures of intolerance, cf. Samuel A. Stouffer, *Communism, Conformity, and Civil Liberties: A Cross-section of the Nation Speaks Its Mind* (Garden City, N.Y.: Doubleday & Company, Inc., 1955), pp. 89–108. Stouffer actually found both age and education correlated with intolerance, even after correcting for the influence of each on the other. For a brief general discussion of this method as applied to the wartime researches on the American soldier, cf. Kendall and Lazarsfeld, *op. cit.*

[19] Emile Durkheim, *Suicide,* trans. John A. Spaulding and George Simpson (New York: The Free Press of Glencoe, Inc., 1951), pp. 152–56.

[20] *Ibid.,* p. 157.

operation Durkheim used no statistical techniques; yet he was approximating their use through systematic comparative illustration. He was making minority status into a parameter in order to isolate the distinctive influence of the religious variable.

A fourth research method that finds wide application in sociology is the *case study,* in which a single social unit becomes the focus of intensive description and analysis with respect to certain variables. Examples of this kind of research are found in the classic study of the Bank Wiring Room in the Hawthorne studies; [21] the studies of behavior related to social class in a single local community; [22] and the studies of behavior and interaction in a single mental hospital. [23] The case study is methodologically inferior to the other methods just reviewed because, being based on a single case, it presents no basis for the systematic control of conditions by the manipulation of parameters and operative variables. Nevertheless, the case study has proved to be of great value in discovering and illustrating important new variables in sociological investigation. A further characteristic of the case method is that it is commonly—though by no means necessarily—associated with participant observation and with using relatively few informants as sources of data.

A further method of transforming potentially operative variables into parameters is the crude but widely employed method of *heuristic assumption.* For example, in an experimental small-group setting in which the influence of different leadership structures on morale is being investigated, the investigator makes use of a number of important but unexamined heuristic assumptions—that the subjects speak the same language, that they operate under many common cultural assumptions, that they are more or less uniformly motivated to participate in the experiment, and so on. All these variables, if treated as variables, would certainly influence the outcome of the experiment; but they are implicitly assumed not to be variables—that is, to be parameters—for purposes of the analysis. To mention another example, it is a convenient heuristic assumption that individuals in a stratification system are motivated to move upward. [24] Necessary as such assumptions are, and widely as they are employed, this method is inferior to the methods of experimentation, statistical analysis, and comparative analysis because it rests on no situational or conceptual manipulation other than making a simplifying or convenient assumption. Seldom if ever are serious attempts made to establish the empirical validity of the

[21] F. J. Roethlisberger and William J. Dickson, *Management and the Worker,* 2nd ed. (Cambridge: Harvard University Press, 1947), Part IV.

[22] W. Lloyd Warner and Associates, *Democracy in Jonesville* (New York: Harper & Row, Publishers, Inc., 1949).

[23] Erving Goffman, *Asylums* (Garden City, N.Y.: Doubleday & Company, Inc., 1961).

[24] Above, p. 16.

assumption or to correct for the degree to which the assumption is not valid. The method of heuristic assumption accomplishes by making believe what the other methods accomplish by situational or conceptual manipulation in the light of some known or suspected empirical variation. Nevertheless, despite these shortcomings, the method of heuristic assumption provides the investigator a service that is logically the same as the experimental, statistical, and comparative methods: systematic manipulation of operative conditions and parameters to permit the isolated investigation of a limited number of selected independent variables.

In sociology no single method of research just reviewed can be said to predominate; sociology is relatively hybrid in this respect. As we shall see later, many of the other social sciences can be more readily characterized by a typical or favorite method of organizing data and drawing inferences.

ECONOMICS

The following "informative introductory description" of economics appears in Paul A. Samuelson's *Economics,* the best known text on the subject: "Economics is the study of how men and society *choose,* with or without the use of money, to employ *scarce* productive resources to produce various commodities over time and distribute them for consumption, now and in the future, among various people and groups in society." [25] From this definition we may build a description of economics in terms of the ingredients of a scientific theory—dependent variables, independent variables, and relations among these variables in economics.

Dependent Variables

A first set of dependent variables is found in the term *commodities.* What is the level of the total production of goods and services in a society? What different kinds (shoes, guns, butter) are produced, and in what proportions? Economists thus attempt to account for variations in the level and composition of production.

A second set of dependent variables is found in the term *scarce productive resources.* Goods and services are produced by the application of the following factors of production: (1) land, or the state of the natural resources, cultural values, and technical knowledge; (2) labor, or the level of motivation and skill of human beings; (3) capital, or the level of resources available for future production rather than immediate consumption; and sometimes (4) organization, or the principles of combination and recombination of the other factors. Organization involves the operation of institutions such as property and contract as well as the activity

[25] Paul A. Samuelson, *Economics: An Introductory Analysis,* 5th ed. (New York: McGraw-Hill Book Company, 1961), p. 6.

of entrepreneurs. Economists are thus interested in explaining the levels and relative proportions of these resources in productive use and the techniques by which they are combined.

A third set of dependent variables is indicated by the term *distribute.* Which individuals and groups receive the goods and services generated in the productive process? Or, to put it in terms of payments, what is the distribution of income generated in the economic process?

The basic dependent variables in economics, then, are production, techniques of organizing resources, and distribution of wealth. In the Keynesian system, the basic dependent variables are the volume of employment (or the proportion of available labor in productive use at any given time) and the national income (or the total level of production).[26] Even in small subfields of economics the specific problems posed turn out to be instances of the basic dependent variables. In the study of wages in labor economics, for instance, the following elements generally need explaining:

> (*a*) the general level of wages in the nation and its movements during past decades, (*b*) the wage spread between occupations and changes in the spread from time to time, (*c*) wage differentials between regions and areas and alterations in such differentials over the course of time, (*d*) interindustry differentials and shifts in them, (*e*) interfirm differentials in a locality and changes therein, and (*f*) differentials between persons working in the same occupation within a plant.[27]

Independent Variables

How are the level and composition of production, the allocation of resources, and the distribution of wealth determined? In the broad comparative sweep these may be determined by political regulation, custom, religious decree, and so on. Formal economic analysis, however, has traditionally stressed supply and demand in the market as the immediate independent variables. For any given commodity, such as shoes, a person will be willing to buy much if it costs little, little if it costs much. The producer of this commodity will be willing to supply much if the price is high, little if the price is low. The price of the commodity falls at that point where the demand curve and the supply curve intersect.

This supply-demand principle is used to account for the behavior of all the dependent variables. The level and composition of production depend on the existing supply and demand conditions for products; the level and composition of the factors of production depend on the same kinds of

---

[26] J. M. Keynes, *The General Theory of Employment, Interest and Money* (New York: Harcourt, Brace & World, Inc., 1936), p. 245.

[27] Richard A. Lester, *Labor and Industrial Relations: A General Analysis* (New York: The Macmillan Company, 1951), p. 53.

condition for them; and finally, the proportions of income received by different individuals and groups depend on the supply and demand conditions governing the relations among economic agents.

Relations Among Variables

By constructing various combinations of these dependent and independent variables, economists have created a whole variety of equilibrium models to explain price levels, business cycles, economic growth, and other economic phenomena. One of the most famous models in economics concerns the prediction of the quantity of a given commodity that an individual firm will produce under conditions of perfect competition. Given a certain level of demand, the firm can expect to receive a given price (revenue) for each item it produces. But the firm itself has to pay for the factors it utilizes in production. These costs determine the conditions of supplying its commodity to consumers. By a series of constructions, economists have built a model that predicts that the firm will produce that quantity of a commodity at which the *cost* of producing the extra unit of the commodity (marginal cost) equals the *revenue* that it will receive for that extra unit (marginal revenue). Basically, this model says that the value of the dependent variable (quantity of the commodity produced by a firm) is a function of the value of two sets of independent variables (demand and supply).

Turning to the analysis of aggregates, the Keynesian model identifies the independent variables—in the first instance—as the propensity to consume, the schedule of the marginal efficiency of capital, and the rate of interest.[28] The propensity to consume is a demand category; the marginal efficiency of capital rests on expectations about profits to be returned for investments; and the rate of interest rests on the supply of money and the demand for liquidity. By manipulating the values of these independent variables, Keynes established a set of predictions leading to unemployment of a society's resources and reduction of its national product (dependent variables).

In these illustrative economic models the behavior of various dependent variables—prices, level of production, and so on—rests on the operation of the economic forces of supply and demand. But as a matter of empirical fact, many dozens of variables—economic, political, legal, religious—affect prices and production, and if a complete picture of economic life were to be given, many of these kinds of variables would have to be incorporated into the theoretical framework of economics. How do economists deal with these noneconomic variables? A common method is to realize that while they affect supply and demand conditions, it is necessary *for*

---

[28] *Ibid.*, p. 245.

purposes of analysis to assume that they do not change. This is the meaning of Samuelson's statement that economic analysis takes institutions and tastes as given; [29] by "given" he means that potential sources of influence are assumed to be constant.

To illustrate: In constructing his equilibrium system, Keynes considered several things as given: the existing skill of the labor force, the existing equipment, the existing technology, the existing degree of competition, the existing tastes of the consumer, the existing attitudes of people toward work, and the existing social structure.[30] All these, if they varied, would affect the independent variables (for example, the propensity to consume and the marginal efficiency of capital) and through them the dependent variables (employment and national income); but they are assumed not to vary.

One of the most important givens in traditional economic analysis is that of economic rationality: if an individual is presented with a situation of choice in an economic setting, he will behave so as to maximize his economic position. As an investigative device, however, economic rationality allows the economist to proceed *as if* the only independent variables were measurable changes in price and income. By employing givens such as those just reviewed, the economist simplifies the theoretical framework within which he operates. His world thus simplified, he is enabled to create elegant theoretical solutions, often expressed in mathematical language, to economic problems.

Research Methods

Several of the research methods that receive wide application in sociology find much more limited use in economics. The experimental method is seldom if ever employed by economists. The comparative method is limited mainly to its use by economic historians and those interested in the development of the emerging nations.[31] And finally, the case-study method is restricted to accounts of single firms, industries, banks, and so on.

The main research methods in economics, then, are the statistical method and the method of heuristic assumption. As an example of the former, let us say we wish to trace the influences on the long-term trend of potato prices. It is known that potato prices vary seasonally as well as year by year, but it is necessary to remove these influences. So the average

[29] Samuelson, *op. cit.*, 2nd ed., 1951, p. 15. In later editions Samuelson omitted this observation.

[30] Keynes, *op. cit.*, p. 245.

[31] For an example of the quite systematic use of the comparative method by an economic historian, see H. J. Habakkuk, *American and British Technology in the Nineteenth Century: The Search for Labour-Saving Inventions* (London: Cambridge University Press, 1962).

seasonal variation for fifty years is calculated, and seasonal fluctuations for each individual year are canceled out by adding or subtracting the average seasonal variation from the actual prices. In this way one influence on prices is removed by statistical manipulation, and a truer picture of uncontaminated long-term price trends emerges. This sort of statistical analysis, as well as various tests of association, receives wide application in economics. The multivariate analysis of survey data, however, is found much less frequently in economics than in sociology, being limited, by and large, to surveys of consumers' and investors' attitudes.[32]

As indicated in the discussion of the economists' theoretical framework, the typical method in economics is the method of heuristic assumption. The most familiar version of this method is the famous explanatory strategy of *ceteris paribus*—other things equal. By assuming tastes and institutions to be given for purpose of analysis, and by assuming that certain factors do not change during a given time period, economists make parameters out of variables. By using this method to simplify sources of variation, economists have been able to reduce the number of operative variables to a manageable number and to create relatively simple and elegant models of economic variables.

Relations Between Sociology and Economics

From the accounts of the central concerns of sociology and economics reviewed thus far, it would appear that the two disciplines have little in common. Their concerns with dependent variables diverge: economics is concerned especially with variations in the level of production, techniques of production, and distribution of goods and services; sociology is concerned with variations in social structure and behavior oriented to this structure. Even when sociologists focus on economic behavior and institutions, as in the subfield of industrial sociology, they choose different aspects of these phenomena than do economists. Furthermore, there is little overlap in independent variables. And finally, the characteristic economic models are built on vastly different assumptions and logical ordering than are sociological models.

Despite these differences, two disciplines can and should articulate at a number of critical points, to the profit of each. The most evident contribution that sociological analysis can make to economics is in the area of "givens." The various simplifying economic assumptions about human motivation and social structure are subject to widely divergent degrees of empirical accuracy; some persons "economize" much more than others, and some societies display much more economic rationality than others.

---

[32] For assessments of some of the problems of using the survey method in economics, see George Katona and Eva Mueller, *Consumer Expectations, 1953–1956* (Ann Arbor: Survey Research Center, Institute for Social Research, University of Michigan, n.d.), pp. 7–11.

The degree to which persons can be described in terms of the postulate of economic rationality, moreover, is dependent on their social-structural moorings (for example, their religious doctrines and memberships), their position in the stratification system, and their past and present family involvements. Insofar as sociological theory and empirical research are sound in these areas, sociology can begin to provide more informed bases for the simplifying noneconomic assumptions that economists necessarily make in their discipline.[33] The need for systematic sociological supplementation of economic theory and research is especially evident in certain subbranches of economics: consumption theory, which is so obviously influenced by family and class memberships; labor economics, which is so clearly influenced by family and voluntary organization memberships; comparative economic structure, in which it becomes obviously unfeasible to assume tastes and institutional structure constant from one society to another; and economic development, in the analysis of which it becomes progressively less permissible to treat tastes and institutions as constant when the periods of time and magnitudes of change considered involve vast social and psychological reorganization.

In a number of areas economists have begun systematically to introduce noneconomic variables. To illustrate, organizational decision-making theorists have explicitly challenged the traditional economic assumptions that firms are free from internal conflict and that they possess full information about the market;[34] game theorists see organizations (such as firms, trade unions, and government agencies) standing in political as well as economic relation to one another;[35] consumption theorists have begun systematically to introduce considerations of imitation, race, age, and marital status into their formal models;[36] and theorists of imperfect competition see firms standing in political relations to one another and to government agencies.

Likewise, sociological theories, insofar as they involve assumptions about economic life, can be systematically informed by economic theory and research. If, for example, an investigator of the family is interested in the impact of unemployment on a society's family system, he can inform

---

[33] See Talcott Parsons and Neil J. Smelser, *Economy and Society* (New York: The Free Press of Glencoe, Inc., 1956), Chapter 4.

[34] James G. March, "Some Recent Substantive and Methodological Developments in the Theory of Organizational Decision-Making," in Austin Ranney, ed., *Essays on the Behavorial Study of Politics* (Urbana: University of Illinois Press, 1962), pp. 191–208.

[35] Martin Shubik, *Strategy and Market Structure* (New York: John Wiley & Sons, Inc., 1959).

[36] James Duesenberry, *Income, Savings, and the Theory of Consumer Behavior* (Cambridge: Harvard University Press, 1949); Milton Friedman, *A Theory of the Consumption Function* (Princeton: Princeton University Press, 1957); Guy H. Orcutt, Martin Greenberger, John Korbel, and Alice M. Rivlin, *Microanalysis of Socioeconomic Systems: A Simulation Study* (New York: Harper & Row, Publishers, Inc., 1961).

himself of the magnitude of unemployment by reference to trade-cycle theory, investment theory, and theory of economic development. In general, however, the codification of sociologists' assumptions about economic behavior and institutions is neither simplified nor systematic enough to permit specification of the precise points of contribution from economics to sociology, as it is the other way around.

In addition to gaining substantively from economic theory and research, sociology stands to profit in a formal sense from economics. Of all the behavioral sciences, economics has reached the highest point of theoretical development, with the possible exception of certain branches of psychology, such as learning theory. It has done so by simplifying the number of variables via the method of heuristic assumption, combining these variables into simplified models, expressing these models in mathematical terms, and representing variables in quantifiable terms. Difficult as these operations are to perform in some branches of sociology, the field is in need of reducing the scatteration of variables and creating simpler, more concise models. In meeting this need, sociologists probably can profit more from studying the formal aspects of economic theory than from studying the formal aspects of psychology, biology, and the physical sciences, since economics, among all these possibilities, deals with social systems of one type, and social systems are the stuff of sociological analysis.[37]

Unfortunately, contemporary academic arrangements in universities are not the best for encouraging active collaboration between economists and sociologists. Departments of economics and sociology are infrequently conjoined, and few joint courses are given. Also, there is a subtle tendency for economists to view sociology as soft and for sociolgists to be frightened away from using economics by the technical aspects of economic theory and research. The main points of contact between the two disciplines are in various professional schools and institutes, such as schools of business administration and institutes of industrial and labor relations; in addition, a number of promising points of active collaboration between economists and sociologists have appeared in the past two decades with the establishment of various interdisciplinary centers and institutes concerned with economic development.

POLITICAL SCIENCE

In principle, political science should be amenable to formulation in as theoretically elegant terms as economics. Its focus on the creation, organization, distribution, and utilization of power parallels is potentially as specific as economics' focus on the production, distribution, and consumption

[37] Parsons and Smelser, *op. cit.*, Chapter 2.

of wealth. Models concerning the principles by which the components of power—legitimacy, public support, administrative skill, financial resources, and so forth—are combined conceivably could parallel models of market equilibrium so typical in economics. In practice, however, theoretical formulation in scientific terms has not reached anything near the proportions in political science it has in economics. Only in recent decades can the study of political life—despite its traditional name of political science —be said to be becoming a social science at all, in the sense that it possesses the ingredients of a scientific framework as outlined earlier in this essay. Therefore, while I shall use the same list of scientific ingredients I used in characterizing sociology and economics, I shall have to indicate those areas of activity in political science to which they do not apply.

Dependent Variables

I have already indicated the central substantive focus of political science: behavior and institutions that are concerned primarily with the creation and exercise of power. The ways in which political scientists define and describe this behavior and those institutions, however, vary greatly.

One tradition of political science is concerned with describing formal political institutions at different political-geographical levels. American government, for example, customarily has been taught as an account of how American political institutions work, according to the Constitution, statutory law, and customary practice. The same could be said for traditional treatments of state government, federal-state relations, and county and municipal government. The same applies to the traditional approach to international relations, except that it has also been characterized in part by an emphasis on diplomatic history. In these traditional areas of political science, the literature also displays some concern with policy implications—for example, the pros and cons of various forms of city government, such as mayor, city council, and city manager. An offshoot of this historical-descriptive tradition in political science is one type of comparative government, preoccupied, by and large, with Western constitutional governments and large-scale political institutions such as legislatures, civil services, and judiciary systems.

In recent decades a new emphasis in political science has emerged: the behavioral approach. Given impetus by the conceptual frameworks and research methods of the other behavioral sciences, this approach has given quite a different definition to the subject matter of political science.[38] One contrast with the traditional approach [39] is that the behavioral

---

[38] See, for example, Evron M. Kirkpatrick, "The Impact of the Behavorial Approach on Traditional Political Science," in Ranney, *op. cit.*, pp. 1–29.

[39] I do not wish to convey the impression in my necessarily abbreviated account that the distinction between "traditional" empirical political science and the "be-

emphasis concentrates more on the behavior of individuals in political situations and less on the formal structure of political institutions. The behavioral approach, moreover, is relatively more interested in explaining behavior in terms of social and psychological determinants and less in simply describing behavior. Moreover, the behavioral approach leans toward quantitative measurement and statistical manipulation and away from qualitative accounts of political phenomena. In addition, especially insofar as the behavioral approach has invaded comparative politics, it not only has concentrated more on the dynamics of political behavior than on the structure of institutions, but also has enlarged the kinds of settings in which political behavior occurs to include tribes, clans, quasi-developed parties, and so on, as well as formal systems of representative government and bureaucracy.[40] Finally, the language associated with the behavioral approach, in both its noncomparative and comparative aspects, is considerably more abstract and analytic—employing terms like "political socialization" and "interest articulation"—than the language specific to the particular political institutions under study.

Independent Variables

Insofar as the traditional approach to empirical political science is descriptive of the history, workings, and effectiveness of various formal political institutions, it can be said that there is very little explicit interest in explanation via the use of independent variables. From time to time explanations are given—for instance, the paralysis of the political process in the French Fourth Republic may be attributed to the fragmentation of parties or to the French electoral system—but such explanations tend to be based on *ad hoc* and historically specific considerations, rather than on systematic specification of factors making for political effectiveness.

Investigators using the behavioral approach to politics are concerned explicitly with the determinants of political behavior. A list of these determinants, moreover, reads very much like a general catalogue of determinants in sociology and psychology. Voting behavior, for example, has been shown to be influenced by race, education, socioeconomic level, religion, and family, as well as by various psychological variables.[41] Indeed, it is

---

havioral" approach to political life is clearly set off in two distinct divisions or that there is no internal diversity within each approach.

[40] See Gabriel Almond and James S. Coleman, eds., *The Politics of the Developing Areas* (Princeton: Princeton University Press, 1960); Harry Eckstein and David E. Apter, eds., *Comparative Politics: A Reader* (New York: The Free Press of Glencoe, Inc., 1963).

[41] For reviews of this literature, see Heinz Eulau, *Recent Developments in the Behavior Study of Politics* (Stanford: Stanford University Press, 1961), and Herbert Hyman, *Political Socialization* (New York: The Free Press of Glencoe, Inc., 1959).

somewhat arbitrary to assign this new tradition of research to either political science, sociology, or psychology, since variables from all three disciplines are liberally intermingled, and very similar research is conducted by those who call themselves sociologists, political scientists, and psychologists.

Relations Among Variables

Political science shows great diversity with respect to models and theories. In the essentially descriptive tradition of empirical political study, models and theories as I have characterized them can scarcely be said to exist, since the major thrust of the study is historical and descriptive, rather than formally explanatory. In addition, what has gone by the name of political theory in political science is usually not theory in the scientific sense of the word, but rather the study of the moral and political philosophy. This type of traditional political theory is more akin to the study of intellectual history or the study of ethics than it is to any of the social sciences.

The growth of scientific theory proper in political science is very recent and is also associated with the behavioral revolution in the field. To choose only a few illustrations, Harold Lasswell's early efforts at accounting for the distribution of power in a political system possess the embryonic ingredients of a formal theory; [42] Anthony Downs' endeavors to create a theory of democracy are considerably more formal—in fact, his model of political behavior imitates economic theory by postulating a version of political rationality and building a theory of political process on this and other simplifying assumptions; [43] David Easton, building mainly on the work of social-systems analysts in sociology, has developed a comprehensive and methodologically self-conscious theory of the political system; [44] and a number of analysts have attempted to systematize the structure and processes of international relations into a variety of theoretical frameworks.[45] In varying degrees of completeness, these models and theories contain the ingredients of formalized statements of relations among variables, explicit attention to guiding assumptions, and (to a lesser extent) derivation of testable hypotheses.

[42] Harold D. Lasswell, *Politics: Who Gets What, When, How* (New York: McGraw-Hill Book Company, 1936).

[43] Anthony Downs, *An Economic Theory of Democracy* (New York: Harper & Row, Publishers, Inc., 1957).

[44] David Easton, *The Political System* (New York: Alfred A. Knopf, Inc., 1953); *A Framework for Political Analysis* (Englewood Cliffs, N.J.: Prentice-Hall, Inc., 1965); *A Systems Analysis of Political Life* (New York: John Wiley & Sons, Inc., 1965).

[45] Morton Kaplan, *System and Process in International Relations* (New York: John Wiley & Sons, Inc., 1957); Thomas C. Schelling, *The Strategy of Conflict* (Cambridge: Harvard University Press, 1960).

Research Methods

In most of the traditional branches of political science, the research methods resemble those of the historian and philosopher more than those of the other social scientists. These methods include the examination and qualitative description of formal constitutional documents, laws, and historical events and an attempt to draw from these sources adequate characterizations of institutional political structures; also the examination and textual analysis of the writings of political philosophers in an effort to interpret, criticize, and synthesize their views on the broader philosophical aspects of politics and ethics. In the newer branches of political science that have been grouped loosely under the heading of the behavioral approach, the methods of research are, except for relative emphasis, almost indistinguishable from the methods of sociology and social psychology. Experimental research finds little use in political science,[46] but political scientists have employed a vast array of methods of data gathering, statistical manipulation, and comparative methods that are also commonly used in sociology.[47]

Relations Between Sociology and Political Science

In reviewing the relations between sociology and economics, I emphasized the differences in dependent variables, independent variables, and theoretical models and frameworks.[48] Given these differences, the appropriate relations between the fields appeared to be *complementary articulation*. With respect to political science—and now I refer only to the behavioral approach—the story is different. Political sociologists and political scientists often study the same empirical phenomena: voting behavior, political attitudes, the structure of political parties, social mobility through political channels, social and political unrest, and so on. As we have seen, they explain these phenomena by using very similar types of independent variables. Research methods in the two fields also show striking resemblances. And insofar as formal models of behavior have been developed by political scientists, they tend often to resemble the theoretical frameworks employed by sociologists.[49] Correspondingly, the relations between the two fields have not been so much those of complementary articulation

[46] The relevance of small-group research for political science has, however, been examined by Sidney Verba in *Small Groups and Political Behavior* (Princeton: Princeton University Press, 1960).

[47] For a brief sketch of common approaches and techniques, see Seymour Martin Lipset, "Sociology and Political Science: A Bibliographical Note," *American Sociological Review*, XXIX (1964), 730–34.

[48] Above, p. 24.

[49] Despite a considerable number of different emphases, the overall formal similarities between the social-system models of Parsons and Easton are notable. See Easton, *A Systems Analysis*, and Parsons and Smelser, *op. cit.*

as those of *overlapping of common preoccupations.* Indeed, it strikes me that were it not for the historical fact that the behavioral approach to politics grew up in the context of existing academic departments of political science, there is little reason to believe that it would not be a special subdivision of sociology, similar to social stratification or the sociology of religion.

One exception to this general characterization of the two disciplines as overlapping should be noted. As formal theories of the political system continue to develop in political science, they will undoubtedly come to resemble formal economic theories, insofar as they will deal with the creation and exercise of power and will rest on a relatively formal series of assumptions regarding the givens within which political processes occur. As this type of analysis of specialized social processes advances, the need for mutual articulation will grow correspondingly, and the relations between sociology and political science will come to resemble more those that now obtain between sociology and economics.

In terms of academic arrangements, the linking of departments of sociology and political science is probably no more frequent than the linking of sociology and economics. The spirit of collaboration on both sides of the disciplinary boundaries, however, is more congenial than is the case with sociology and economics, and it seems safe to predict that the next few years will see the growth of joint courses and seminars and joint appointments in departments of sociology and political science. Other areas of interaction between the two fields are in survey research centers, area study programs (especially those dealing with nations with totalitarian governments), and various comparative study centers, such as the Center for the Study of Internal War at Princeton University and the Center for the Comparative Study of New Nations at the University of Chicago.

ANTHROPOLOGY

If we leave physical anthropology, archaeology, and the anthropological study of linguistic systems aside, we may be very brief in our treatment of anthropology. The reason for this is that the similarities between social and cultural anthropology on the one hand and sociology on the other vastly outweigh the differences; and the differences are frequently matters of shading.

By and large, sociology and anthropology are preoccupied with the same classes of dependent variables: social structure and behavior oriented toward social structure. Within this basic similarity, however, it is possible to discover some different emphases. Because of the important personality and culture subdivision in anthropology, it is probable that anthropologists focus more on socialization and personality than sociologists; but even this generalization is subject to question, particularly in the light of the growing interest in socialization and personality in the sociology of the family and the sociology of mental health and illness. It is also probable that the influence of Freudian psychology is more marked in anthropology than it is in sociology, but it is by no means absent in the latter. Again, anthropologists—particularly American anthropologists influenced by the work of scholars like Ruth Benedict and Clyde Kluckhohn—focus on cultural values and meaning systems more than do sociologists; but the existence of sociological interest in art, literature, religion, and mass culture qualifies this generalization. And finally, anthropological research has centered more on certain institutional sectors—especially kinship, magic, and religion—that have been thought to infuse the simpler societies they have studied; but these subjects are not without interest to sociologists, and, especially in modern times, anthropologists have interested themselves in economic structure, political structure, stratification, economic development, and other aspects of social life.

Anthropologists and sociologists traditionally have studied social life in different settings. Anthropologists have concentrated on small, simple, often nonliterate societies, whereas sociologists have chosen to study large, complex, literate civilizations. Particularly in the past two decades this distinction has been breaking down, as sociologists and anthropologists alike study caste in Indian villages, as anthropologists take up investigations of places like East London, and as sociologists broaden their comparative scope.

Perhaps the most pervasive difference between the two fields resides in divergent styles of conceiving societies. Both anthropologists and sociologists tend to think of societies as interrelated systems; the solid place of structural-functional thought in each discipline testifies to this commonality. Within this broadly similar framework, however, certain differences emerge. Anthropologists tend more to think in unique-pattern ways about society. Perhaps this tendency results from the historical fact that they have concentrated on small, relatively undifferentiated societies; perhaps it stems from the dominance of the relativistic viewpoint during the interwar period, in which "[emphasis] was placed . . . on the unique and the contextual. The search for internal coherence between institutions, or coherence between individual psychology and social form, or the coherence between belief and behavior all within a single and often arbitrarily defined unit was the fashion of the period." [50] This characterization must be qualified, however, by mentioning the considerable body of anthropological cross-cultural analysis that focuses on connections between a few sets

---

[50] Cora DuBois, "Anthropology: Its Present Interests," in Berelson, *op. cit.*, p. 31.

of variables in a wide range of cultural settings.[51] By contrast with the anthropologist's predominantly unique-pattern approach, the sociologist's preoccupation with the interrelatedness of social phenomena tends to be—but is not always—characterized more by a search for aggregated connections between a limited number of variables and less by a focus on totality of patterns as such.

Related to these different styles of interpreting social interrelations are further differences in research methods and outlook. Anthropology tends to be characterized mainly by the case-study method, in which the investigator actually immerses himself in the single culture to be studied.[52] In many cases he becomes a participant observer and more often than not relies on informants for much of his data about the culture. One outgrowth of this kind of involvement is that the anthropological investigator comes to appreciate the richness and complexity of social life in the culture under study; he tends to focus more on the broader meaning context of social behavior. At the same time and for the same reasons, he is likely to be unfriendly to objective methods of measurement that pull items of behavior from this meaning context. He therefore has a predilection to represent behavior in the same meaning context as that of the culture under study.[53] By contrast, the comparative sociologist (as well as the comparative economist and political scientist), being more concept- and variable-centered, tends to be more willing to apply objective comparative measures and to lift items of behavior from their unique cultural contexts.[54]

So much for some of the contrasts in substance, method, and style between anthropology and sociology. In all cases these contrasts appear to be subtle shadings rather than clear-cut differences. We might conclude this brief section by suggesting the ways in which these two quite similar fields might interchange usefully with each other. Certainly the possibilities of mutual interchange of *empirical data* are great, since anthropologists and sociologists still tend to study different types of society and different institutional contexts within these societies. In particular, the comparative analysis of social structure and the study of social change can profit as sociologists inform themselves better on the character of social life in relatively undifferentiated societies and anthropologists on the

---

[51] A notable work in the tradition of cross-cultural analysis is George P. Murdock, *Social Structure* (New Haven: Yale University Press, 1948).

[52] Again this statement must be qualified by reference to the considerable amount of systematic comparative analysis conducted by anthropologists.

[53] Marcel Mauss stated this predilection very directly in characterizing his own comparative methodology. *The Gift: Forms and Functions of Exchange in Archaic Societies* (New York: The Free Press of Glencoe, Inc., 1954), pp. 2–3.

[54] As we shall see (below p. 39), this difference between the clinical and the aggregated-variable emphases is paralleled in psychology.

character of social life in more complex societies. The opportunities for *complementary theoretical articulation,* however, are considerably less, simply because the variables and theoretical frameworks of the two disciplines are so fundamentally similar. The tendency, therefore, would seem to be one of consolidation of the theoretical frameworks of sociology and anthropology rather than complementary articulation of distinct frameworks, as is the case between sociology and economics. In fact, it is not unreasonable to suggest that as theoretical refinement and codification advance in the social sciences, the differences between anthropology and sociology will be the first to be absorbed into a common theoretical framework.

HISTORY

During the past century many opinions have been ventured on the general relations between history and sociology (or the social sciences in general). These notions range widely. At one extreme is the view of a number of German writers toward the end of the nineteenth century that sociology is a generalizing science in search of uniform laws of social life and that history is a particularizing study dealing with the unique occurrences of human life, and, as a consequence of this distinction, the two enterprises are completely separate from each other. At the other extreme is the recent view expressed by S. D. Clark that "nothing today would appear to set off [sociology and history] from one another other than the biases and prejudices inherited from the past. The . . . explanation of what occurs by comparing a particular occurrence with other occurrences is the task which the historian performs and it is a task which must be performed by the sociologist the moment he turns to examine the processes of change in society." [55] Writers on the philosophy of science and the sociological study of change take various positions between these two extremes. [56]

In treating history as a social science, it is possible, as with anthropology, to be quite brief, though for a different reason. History, more than any of the disciplines here considered in this essay, lacks the ingredients of a formal scientific method, so it would be inappropriate to attempt a point-by-point comparison with sociology in terms of these ingredients. Nevertheless, it is possible to compare the two disciplines from the stand-

[55] S. D. Clark, "Sociology, History, and the Problem of Social Change," *Canadian Journal of Economics and Political Science,* XXV (1959), 400.
[56] For a variety of views on the relations between history and scientific explanation, see Patrick Gardiner, ed., *Theories of History* (New York: The Free Press of Glencoe, Inc., 1959).

SOCIOLOGY AND THE OTHER SOCIAL SCIENCES   35

point of the data to be explained, the approach to causal explanation, the interpretative frameworks employed, and the research methods used.

History and sociology share a catholicism with respect to data that may legitimately be studied within their respective disciplines. It is literally true that there can be a history of anything: industrial capitalism, French doorknobs, or misspellings in New England cookbooks. And because the range of sociological variables is so great—including social structure and behavior oriented to social structure—it is virtually true that there can be a legitimate sociology of anything, so long as it can be encompassed by these broad categories. Certainly there could readily be a sociological treatment of industrial capitalism, French doorknobs, and even misspellings in New England cookbooks. Thus, in principle, historians and sociologists are immersed in a common mass of raw material. In practice, however, their attention is directed toward data that have been recorded at different points in time. Most historians choose data that have been recorded in the relatively distant past, whereas most sociologists choose data that have been recently or are being currently recorded. Not all historians and sociologists behave this way, however, and there is no inherent reason in either discipline why they should do so.

Despite their common comprehensiveness of data, history and sociology are subdivided in ways so different that ready comparisons between the two fields are quite difficult. As a rule, historians use three criteria to subdivide their field—chronological time, cultural or national tradition, and aspects of social life. The familiar phrases, "British social history of the late nineteenth century" and "Western European intellectual history during the eighteenth century," exemplify these criteria. Sociologists tend to divide their field by somewhat more abstract terms: types of social structure, types of behavior oriented to social structure, types of social groupings, and so on. It is true that some sociologists are regional or area specialists and thus focus on a distinctive cultural or national tradition. It is also true that the familiar institutional subdivisions of sociology—religion, law, military, and so forth—correspond with some of the subdivisions of history—religious, legal, or military history, for instance—but these correspondences are only very approximate.

In their methods of identifying problems for study, sociologists and historians also display different, though overlapping, emphases. A historical problem, generally speaking, is rooted in and emerges from the logic of events of a given place and period; for example, why did the French monarchy and aristocracy become so unresponsive to demands for social reform during the eighteenth century? By contrast, a sociological problem, generally speaking, tends to be rooted in and is generated by some conceptual apparatus; for example, what are the relations between blocked social mobility and social protest, as illustrated in the eighteenth-century French case? This is not to say that the approach of the historian is inductive and that of the sociologists deductive. Both necessarily rely on preconceived concepts, assumptions, and suspected associations among historical happenings. The relative differences are in degree of explicitness of preconceptions and in degree of abstraction from a particular historical context.

In their concern with explanations, a similar difference in emphasis between sociologists and historians emerges. By contrast with a field like economics, both tend to be comprehensive and eclectic in their concern with causes (or independent variables). This eclecticism, however, stems from different sources. For sociologists, it arises not from any commitment to diversity or complexity of causes—as a rule sociolgists are as committed to determinate causal explanations as other social scientists—but rather because the field itself has not been able to specify these causes and hence displays a great proliferation of independent variables.[57] The eclecticism of historians stems from the fact that their historical problem is rooted in a particular place and historical period. A historical period itself, however, being quite indiscriminate in the way it unfolds, does very little by way of isolating, specifying, and organizing causes of events; it requires the machinations of human investigators—machinations that take the form of the experimental, statistical, and other methods of research— to manipulate causes and assess their general operation in a variety of different historical situations. The historian, attentive to a problem and period, interprets the causes of events as he finds them, as it were, and thus takes on the natural eclecticism of causation in an uncontrolled historical sequence of events. Thus, the historian is prepared to admit invasions, personality characteristics of kings, population increases, changes in landownership patterns, and social-protest movements as causes, if these appear to be important for his particular historical problem. The relatively more systematic social scientist, on the other hand, attempts to hold constant various of these events by diverse means of situational and conceptual manipulations, thus isolating, simplifying, and making less eclectic his concern with causes.

To summarize, a sociologist's approach to data, problems, and causes of events—in contrast to a historian's—tends to rest on a more formal, explicit conceptual apparatus that is more self-consciously selective of facts. Insofar as the historian adopts such an apparatus, and insofar as he adopts the relatively systematic methods of manipulating data utilized by the sociologist, the difference between the two disciplines tends to disappear.

Given these contrasting emphases, what types of interchange might

---

[57] Above, pp. 11–14.

prove profitable between history and sociology? A first type stems from the fact that sociologists and historians emphasize present and past, respectively, in their studies of society.[58] Particularly in comparative analysis and in the study of social change, each discipline stands to profit from examining the data produced and analyzed in the other. A second type of exchange involves the use of historical investigations to formulate sociological problems and vice versa. A careful reading of a historical monograph—even one on a subject remote from the sociologist's substantive interests—indubitably will reveal empirical connections between events that can inform his sociological preoccupations. Similarly, a careful study of sociological theory and research will instruct historians in new connections, new kinds of data to be sought, and new kinds of historical questions to be asked. As indicated above, historical problems have tended to be rooted in specific empirical contexts, and sociological problems have tended to be generated from conceptual frameworks, though this generalization does not apply unequivocally to either discipline. Insofar as it is correct, however, both sociologists and historians will gain from studying one another's problems, since the origins of their respective problems complement one another.

A third type of exchange involves the respective methods of research and data assessment in history and sociology. Historians, like archaeologists, often confront isolated historical fragments in their work, from which they must, in the absence of more complete data, draw inferences about the historical period in question. Clearly it is impossible to use formal research methods such as statistical analysis in these circumstances. Instead, historians have developed an art of seeking out and piecing together isolated items to delineate a picture of society's past structure and activities. By and large the skills involved in this art have remained implicit; indeed, the art is almost an intuitive one. Certainly it would be of enormous service to both historians and sociologists if a historical investigator would set down a definitive methodology of historical inference from fragmented data. In particular, the sociologist could profit from such a methodology, since it would better enable him to turn to empirical situations that are relevant and important for his investigations, but meager in their supply of data. Historians, on their side, stand to gain from adopting —to a greater extent than they already have—the formal research techniques of sociologists, particularly in their analyses of historical data that can be represented quantitatively. These techniques are especially appropriate for the study of modern history, which is so much more abundant in formal, written records of human transactions.

---

[58] This difference of emphasis is formally similar to the difference between anthropologists, who tend to concentrate on simple societies, and sociologists, who tend to concentrate on complex ones. Above, p. 32.

PSYCHOLOGY [59]

Despite the differences I have noted, it is correct to say that sociology, economics, political science, and anthropology are *social* sciences.[60] The reason for this is that the overarching focus of these disciplines is on interpersonal relations that emerge when two or more persons interact with one another. The units of analysis are the relations among persons—or roles, or structures—and behavior oriented to these relations. In this respect, all four disciplines contrast with psychology, which studies the same mass of behavorial data, but has a different analytic focus. The analytic focus of psychology is the individual person as a system of needs, feelings, aptitudes, skills, defenses, and such, or on one or more processes, such as the learning of skills, considered in detail. In all cases the organizing conceptual unit is the person. The four social sciences differ in various ways in the kind of social structures and systems they study; psychology differs from all of these in that it lies at a separate analytic level altogether. This fundamental contrast not only epitomizes the differences between psychology and the social sciences but also suggests the distinctive ways they may contribute to one another.

Within its overarching analytic focus on the individual person, psychology studies a number of different kinds of variables.[61] Among the most important of these are the concept of need, which is a construct referring to the internal motivational forces that give direction, intensity, and persistence to behavior; the concept of capacities, including intelligence and skills by means of which the individual arrives at some resolution of tensions resulting from these motivational forces; the concept of personality structure, which refers to the combination of patterns of needs and capacities into relatively enduring modes of adaptation to his environment; and various more dynamic concepts, including stress and psychic conflict, responses to stress and conflict, attempts to control these responses, and resulting processes of personality change. In attempting to account for variations in these, psychologists tend to focus on the psychic system itself; but they frequently do make use of social units as independent variables: for example, size of family, order of birth in family,

---

[59] Part of this section is an elaboration of material originally presented in the Introduction to the book edited by William T. Smelser and myself, *Personality and Social Systems* (New York: John Wiley & Sons, Inc., 1963).

[60] The same cannot be said of history, both because it does not focus so directly on systems of social interaction and because it does not rest on the use of scientific methods to as great a degree as the other disciplines.

[61] I am not here considering physiological psychology, animal experimentation, and cognition and learning, since these do not always rely on conceptions of the individual personality. My remarks apply more to personality psychology and social psychology.

socioeconomic status, ethnic and religious group memberships, and so on.

In this essay I shall not review the various ways in which psychologists organize their variables into models and systems, except to note in passing a contrast within psychology that parallels one of the contrasts between anthropology and sociology. I refer to the contrast between the clinical or unique-pattern approach versus the aggregated-variable approach.[62] Within psychology the clinical psychologist tends to focus on the single individual, interpreting his behavior in the meaning context of his personality pattern, whereas many experimental and social psychologists focus on a more limited number of personality variables and attempt to discover connections among these variables—connections manifested by an aggregate of individuals with different unique personality constellations—by using the formal research methods of experimental control and statistical analysis. It would be an instructive exercise in intellectual history to compare and contrast the tensions between anthropologists and sociologists, one the one hand, with the tensions between the clinical and experimental social psychologists, on the other.

In the light of this briefest of characterizations of psychology as a science, what can be said about the possibilities for exchange between it and sociology?[63] These possibilities are both formal and substantive; the substantive exchanges, in turn, break down into empirical and theoretical ones. With respect to formal interchanges, it is evident that many psychological variables are cognate with sociological variables at a different analytic level. For example, the concept of need parallels the concept of functional exigency of a social system in many ways; the concept of individual capacities parallels the concept of social resources; the concept of personality structure parallels the concept of social structure; the concept of ego control parallels the concept of social control; and so on.[64] Furthermore, various models of personality adjustment, growth, and disorganization parallel models of social change.[65] Careful study of psychological models by sociologists, and vice versa, is likely to produce new issues for both, since the analytic levels in which each have been generated are quite different.[66]

This formal interchange between variables and models at different

<hr />

[62] Above, p. 33.

[63] Though I shall speak only of the relations with sociology, my remarks will apply equally well to economics, political science, and anthropology.

[64] For an elaboration of these and other analogies, see Smelser and Smelser, *op. cit.*, pp. 5–12.

[65] For an effort to work out the parallels between personality development and social processes of structural differentiation, see Talcott Parsons, Robert F. Bales, *et al.*, *Family, Socialization, and Interaction Process* (New York: The Free Press of Glencoe, Inc., 1955).

[66] See the brief discussion of the possibilities of formal interchange between economics and sociology, above, p. 26.

levels should not be confused with psychological or social reductionism, which marks an attempt to translate, without loss, all statements at one analytic level into statements regarding the operations of variables at another level. An example of a reductionist statement would be: "Society is no more than the sum total of the psychological states of its members." The general consequence of reductionist reasoning, if pushed far enough, is to deny the independent conceptual status of one analytic level. In this respect reductionist reasoning is the opposite of reasoning by analogy. Analogy involves *no* claim of causal influence between two analytically independent levels, but only a claim of formal similarities between the levels; reductionism involves a claim of *total* determination of processes at one level by reference to variables at another level. The status of the reduced process is that of an epiphenomenal by-product with no causal feedback.

With respect to substantive exchanges, it is evident that social and psychological perspectives can be fruitfully combined into explanatory frameworks. For any given empirical problem—for example, the study of suicide rates in different settings—different social variables, such as religion, family structure, and ethnic group membership, can each account for some variation. If combined into a more complex interactive model of determinants, the explanatory power of these social determinants is even greater. After a certain point the continuous refinement of social variables becomes subject to diminishing returns. The investigator must ask how the various social influences are processed intrapsychically if he is to account for more variation and if he is to discover why some individuals do and others do not commit suicide under identical social conditions. Similarly, psychologists interested in the importance of early childhood experiences on personality development are able to enhance the adequacy of their explanations if they can be informed as to the influence of, say, family structure and social-class level on the probability of occurrence of diverse kinds of childhood traumas.

To appreciate the possibilities of substantive exchange between sociology and psychology at the theoretical level, we may refer to the problem of givens once more. As we have seen, sociological concepts, hypotheses, and theoretical frameworks always rest on a number of assumptions about human motivations, skills, and so on.[67] And psychological explanations inevitably rest on certain presuppositions regarding the kinds of social framework within which these explanations apply. Too often these underlying assumptions are vague, implicit, and unexamined appendages to the theory in question. Some of the most promising avenues of collaboration between sociologists and psychologists are through mutual enlightenment

[67] Above, pp. 6 and 15–16.

as to the psychological and sociological underpinnings of their respective theories, mutual instruction as to the questionable assertions these underpinnings may conceal, and mutual exchange of findings so that these assertions may be made more adequate theoretically.

I shall conclude this section with one observation on research methods in psychology. One distinguishing feature of psychology is that it makes much more extensive use of the experimental method than the other disciplines here considered. Another is that, because of its historical connection with psychotherapeutic and psychiatric practice, it makes very extensive use of the method of clinical case study. So pronounced is each of these features that research strategies in the field tend often to be thought of as either clinical approaches to depth variables or socioexperimental approaches to surface variables such as attitudes or overt behavior. I submit that psychologists would benefit greatly by giving careful study to the uses of the comparative method in sociology,[68] which stands between these two extreme alternatives in the sense that it does not deal with enough cases to permit elaborate statistical control but does deal with enough to permit approximations to such control even with depth variables. Adaptation of this method to intraindividual comparisons would do much, in my opinion, to permit more systematic investigation of variables now considered inextricable from the richness and complexity of a single clinical case and to reduce conflicts among psychological investigators, who now tend to opt exclusively for either the clinical or the socioexperimental approach.

SUMMARY AND CONCLUSION: INTEGRATION AND COLLABORATION AMONG THE SOCIAL SCIENCES

To pull together the various strands developed in this essay, let me summarize the interchanges that may be expected among the various social sciences. This summary should provide the reader with an indication of the several analytic uses of sociology for the other social sciences, but I shall present the summary as it should be presented—not in terms of a one-way flow, but as two-way interchanges.

1. Insofar as sociology and other social sciences take an interest in common data, each discipline should be able to provide a partial account of empirical variations in these data. With reference to sexual behavior and attitudes, for instance, sociological research can provide insight as to the types of class background and family structure associated with distinctive patterns of sexual behavior; psychological research can provide evidence as to how social and other variables are processed intra-

[68] Above, pp. 18–19.

psychically, thus contributing more microscopic kinds of insight; and historical and anthropological research can shed light on how these social and psychological determinants have worked out in diverse cultural contexts. These relations among the various disciplines, it must be stressed, are not competitive, but essentially complementary.

2. Insofar as every discipline necessarily restricts its range of inquiry and makes simplifying assumptions about—that is, treats as given—those areas outside this range, each discipline stands to be informed as to the adequacy of thee assumptions by referring to the empirical research and theoretical formulations of neighboring disciplines. These more general relations among the disciplines are also of a complementary character.

3. Insofar as common formal problems are faced by theorists in different disciplines, they stand to profit from studying formal solutions generated in neighboring disciplines. Equilibrium theory as formulated in biology and economics, for example, has proved of value in formulating principles of equilibrium in sociology and psychology. Great care must be taken, however, to avoid wholesale importation of theoretical models from other disciplines, and the social scientist should always temper analogous formulations with qualifications appropriate to new empirical and theoretical settings.

4. Insofar as the various disciplines face common problems of drawing inferences from data, they stand to gain from studying the diverse research methods employed in neighboring disciplines. Sociologists, for example, when they meet a problem that demands tracing the course of quantitative indices over time, would do well to turn to the well developed techniques of analyzing time series in economics. And, as indicated, psychologists can profit by developing research methods similar to the comparative method in sociology and anthropology.

These various types of interchange raise the more general problem of the integration of knowledge in the social sciences. This problem is a perennial one. Ever since the social sciences began to develop, scholars have repeatedly expressed apprehension about the increasing fragmentation of knowledge through specialization. Correspondingly, they have sounded the call for greater integration—even unification—of scientific knowledge. Justified as these demands are, they are not without their utopian elements; indeed, the hopes expressed for the unification of scientific knowledge often resemble the hopes for the unification of the world religions. The utopian element lies in the overemphasis on ends and the underemphasis on means.

During the past twenty years, scholars have expressed much misty-eyed enthusiasm about a number of words, all of which refer in one way or another to the end of unification: words such as codification, integration, cross-fertilization, interdisciplinary research, and the multidisciplinary approach. As is often the case, this proliferation of inexact synonyms signifies a search for something, the nature of which we are not aware. Moreover, a vague romanticism often seems to govern thinking about the means of attaining the end of unification. It appears to me that many of the numerous interdisciplinary arrangements of the past two decades—institutes, centers, regional study groups, seminars, conferences, and panels—have rested on the belief, even hope, that if only scholars from different specialties are placed in one another's presence, some process of integration will occur spontaneously. Unfortunately, the endeavors based on this hope are usually quite barren, yielding mainly general talk *about* integration rather than results *of* integration. Just as it is true that people of different nations will not reach sympathetic understanding of one another by virtue of being placed together in an international exchange program or seminar, so it is true that scholars will not integrate their specialized branches of knowledge merely by talking with one another about their subjects or even reading one another's books.

If spontaneous combustion is not the path to integration of scientific knowledge, what is? I hope I have indicated some guidelines in this essay. A major requirement of integration is that some common language be developed so that the elements of the different social sciences can be systematically compared and contrasted with one another. The language I have employed is the language of the ingredients of science: dependent variables, independent variables, theoretical frameworks, and research methods. Having developed this language, we may better see what kinds of integration are possible and what kinds are not. And in examining the relations between sociology and the other social sciences in terms of the scientific ingredients of each, we turned up a variety of types of integration. In the relations between sociology and anthropology, for example, we discovered an essential identity of scientific enterprise; in the relations between sociology and economics, we discovered possibilities of complementary theoretical articulation at the social level of analysis; in the relations between sociology and psychology, we discovered possibilities of complementary theoretical articulation at different analytic levels; in the relations between sociology and history, we saw possibilities of exchange mainly in terms of problems, data, and research methods; and in some cases—for example, in the relations between scientific sociology and traditional political theory—we discovered such a difference in approach and methods that the question of integration is probably irrelevant. In short, by employing this common language to compare and contrast the various social sciences, we have seen that integration of scientific knowledge is a complex and diversified, not a simple and unitary, thing.

This enterprise of comparing and contrasting the social sciences within a common language is a very laborious and disciplined one. So, also, is the process by which social scientists may actually profit from the theory and research of a neighboring social science. Unfortunately, it is not possible for a sociologist (or any other kind of social scientist), upon reaching a blind alley in his analysis, to ask, "How can, say, economics help me here?" and come up with a simple, satisfactory answer by reading a text in economics. In order to call upon the assistance of a sister discipline, he must become in some degree disciplined in that discipline, so that he may appreciate the context and significance of its contribution, rather than lift it from its disciplinary moorings and thus distort it. To insist upon this kind of continuing education as a precondition for successful interdisciplinary exchange is to insist upon a great deal of work for social scientists. But in the end this work is necessary, if interchanges between the disciplines are to be profound and rewarding, rather than simple and disappointing.

TWO: The Optimum Scope of Sociology *

INTRODUCTION

The word "optimum" in the title of this essay suggests two guidelines I shall follow.

First, the word implies that sociologists have a number of different ways to define the scope of the field, and that some ways are better than others. It suggests, therefore, that I should strike an evaluative note in this essay. My account of sociology's scope should not be only inductive; it should be neither a distillation of definitions from textbooks, nor a recapitulation of statements by giants of the sociological tradition, nor a descriptive survey of what sociologists do. Rather, my account should explore critically the relations between what sociologists are doing and what they ought to be doing. I am confident that this evaluative emphasis is acceptable, since even those who insist that sociology be value-free acknowledge by that very insistence that we may relax the taboo on evaluation when we converse about the values and norms around which our own inquiry should be organized.

Second, "optimum" implies that sociologists should conceive of themselves as agents who proceed deliberately if not always consciously in creating the scope, limits, and divisions of their field, not merely as passive "discoverers" of an aspect of social life that is given in nature and remains only to be recorded and studied. I shall elaborate this implication later.

* Paper presented at a conference, "A Design for Sociology," December 1967, in Philadelphia, sponsored by the American Academy of Political and Social Science. The paper is soon to appear in a special publication of The American Academy of Political and Social Science.

The word "scope" also has two connotations, both of which I shall consider in this essay.

The first connotation concerns the range of empirical subject matter of the field, and the ways in which this subject matter is subdivided.

The second connotation concerns the level of generality of propositions, models, and theories in sociology. At one extreme the scope may be bound closely to identifiable data and limited in theoretical relevance; at the other extreme the scope may be extended to abstract, comprehensive "grand theory"; or the scope may be pitched at some intermediate or "middle-range" level.

It should be evident from these introductory remarks that my emphasis will be on sociology as an academic discipline. I shall examine it as a social science, mentioning its uses in society and its applications to social policy only in passing.

THE CONCEPTUAL STATUS OF SOCIOLOGY

One Field, Many Frameworks   Sociologists frequently—though often implicitly—assume that their discipline, like other disciplines, covers a determinate range of empirical data. If this assumption were extended, the empirical world would be viewed as consisting of biological data (births, deaths, digestion, elimination), psychological data (gratification and frustration of needs, expression of emotions), economic data (investments, purchases), sociological data (interpersonal behavior in institutionalized roles), and so on. Following this kind of assumption, we would proceed to define the scope of sociology in an empirical way—that is, by identifying the appropriate range of data.

Even cursory examination reveals, however, that such an assumption is not warranted. To illustrate its vulnerability, let us consider a single empirical datum—the act of a man purchasing tickets for four to Hawaii, where he plans to spend two weeks on vacation. Clearly this act has *psychological* significance, since the man has motives for purchasing the tickets and for choosing Hawaii as a vacation spot. In addition, the act has *economic* significance, since the individual is spending his funds for tickets rather than other goods and services; moreover, his purchase, when aggregated with others, constitutes the economic demand for the airline industry. Finally, the act has *sociological* significance, in that the other three passengers are the purchaser's wife· and children, and in that his purchase was preceded by a decision-making ,process within the family that led to the choice of Hawaii. The datum itself, then, can be a datum for at least three disciplines, and it cannot legitimately be limited to only one.

From this it must be concluded that sociology does not deal with a special class of empirical data; instead, it deals with data *as interpreted within a special type of conceptual framework*. Sociology and the other behavioral sciences arise from a common body of empirical data rather than several separate classes of data. With respect to characterizing the subject matter of sociology, then, I hold the position that its subject matter is not in any natural way given in social reality, but is the product of a selective identification of aspects of the empirical world for purposes of scientific description, classification, and explanation. Without a conceptual framework, it is not possible to identify ranges of empirical variation that are scientifically problematical.

Given this epistemological position, the problem of defining the scope of sociology changes from a search for empirical boundaries to an effort to outline the distinctive conceptual frameworks to which empirical data are referred for assessment. What are the frameworks—or lines of conceptual abstraction—that are commonly found in sociology? In reviewing the common preoccupations of those who call themselves—or are called—sociologists, I have been able to locate at least five distinctive conceptual frameworks for identifying and describing the subject matter of the field (and these five might easily be multiplied by further subdivision).

The first framework is found mainly in the special fields of demography and ecology. It involves the interpretation of events as aspects of human organisms considered in their physical and biological environments and in relation to the coordinates of space and time, without reference in the first instance either to the psychological systems or to the social relations of the organisms. The preoccupation of demography and ecology is to explain regularities and variations in the size and composition of human populations, as well as regularities and variations in births, deaths, physical movements, and spatial arrangements. To be sure, investigators in these fields frequently have recourse to psychological and sociocultural variables in attempting to explain these regularities and variations. But at the present time I am considering the subject matter only as the phenomena to be explained.

The second framework is found mainly in the long-standing (if still sprawling and indefinite) special field of social psychology. It involves the interpretation of behavior in terms of its psychological significance to the individual considered as self or person. Stated another way, the conceptual framework used to organize the study of behavior is the psychological system of the human being—for example, his motives, his attitudes, his cognitions, his skills, and his sense of identity. Properly speaking, this framework is the focus of psychology, but it also has a solid place in academic sociology.

These two frameworks focus on the individual person, either in his significance as a biological organism or in his significance as a psychological system. A third framework—that which concerns the group—arises when we consider numbers of individual persons who become aggregated, more or less purposively, as members of a collectivity with some common orientation or orientations. When sociologists refer to primary groups, voluntary associations, or class groupings, for example, they usually think of them as being made up of numbers of persons considered as members. Sometimes sociologists study social groups as units in their own right, interacting with one another without reference to their individual members—as in the case of competition among political parties, conflict among racial groups, or status-striving among cliques.

A fourth and quite different perspective emerges when social life is considered, not from the vantage point of the persons involved, but rather from the vantage point of the relations between persons. The familiar concept of "role" characterizes these relations—the roles of husband and wife, politician and voter, employer and employee, businessman and consumer. The concept of person and the concept of role are analytically separate, even though both are based ultimately on a common body of behavioral data. The two concepts cut across one another. A person occupies many different roles; and a role cannot refer to a complete person, but only to selected aspects of his behavior. The equally familiar concept of social structure refers to identifiable patterns of roles that are organized primarily around the fulfillment of some social function or activity—for example, religious structure, educational structure, political structure.

The concepts of group and social structure, then, refer to different aspects of social data. Or, to emphasize the conceptual aspects, they are different ways of looking at social data. Furthermore, the same behavioral phenomena can be legitimately characterized according to both aspects. For example, a trade union can be described both as a group with individual members and as a system of interrelated roles—officers, shop stewards, representatives of locals, and the like. In the present state of sociology, both group analysis and structural analysis are widely employed; but it has not yet been settled whether either, both, or neither is the best basis for organizing sociological knowledge.

The fifth framework concerns a variety of cultural phenomena that regulate, legitimize, and lend meaning to all social behavior—whether this behavior be conceptualized according to the "person," "group," or "structural" perspectives. Norms, for example, refer to standards that regulate the interaction among persons and groups; values refer to standards that provide legitimacy for social arrangements and social behavior; ideologies and cosmologies provide a context within which values and norms themselves are grounded in meaning.

As a first approximation, then, we may affirm that the scope of the subject matter of sociology is found in the several conceptual frameworks

I have sketched. The sociological enterprise is to account for regularities, variations, and interdependencies among the phenomena that constitute these frameworks. By way of qualification, I should add that these several frameworks are not always neatly set off from one another conceptually, that in many studies the investigator operates within more than one of the frameworks, and that, occasionally, a sociologist may venture into still other conceptual territories than those mentioned.

This view of the conceptual scope of sociology yields evidence in favor of a conclusion many of us share—that sociology, by comparison with some other sciences, lacks a single, accepted conceptual framework. The field is diffuse and difficult to distinguish from others because it contains a diversity of frameworks, some of which it shares with other fields such as psychology and social anthropology. If anything, then, sociology is too comprehensive, diffuse, soft in the center, and fuzzy around the edges. These qualities make for a field that is enormously complex and engaging, but less scientifically adequate than might be optimal.

It follows that if sociology continues its movement toward scientific maturity, it must be expected that it will shed certain aspects of these frameworks and consolidate others. This is a natural consequence of the development of a specialized field of knowledge from a more diffuse tradition of thought. Unsettling as it may be for those of us who like sociology as we know it and practice it, this prospect seems to be in the historical cards. After all, sociology has already had a history of severing some of its connections with social philosophy, social policy, social problems, and social ideology—connections which are far from completely severed in the mid-twentieth century.[1] It also appears that some special subfields of sociology, such as demography, may now be heading toward separate disciplinary status, if we take as evidence the consolidation of a theoretical framework, the growth of a specialized literature not widely read by many other sociologists, the growth of a separate professional association, and the establishment of separate programs and even departments in institutions of higher learning. The future relations between the various social-psychological perspectives—such as symbolic interactionism, social behaviorism, and the new "ethnomethodology"—and the other frameworks of sociology seem uncertain; some may be assimilated in modified form to other disciplines, others may remain attached in modified form as parts of a discipline oriented primarily to the "group" and "social-structural" perspectives, while others may become specialties on their own. Despite some uncertainty about the precise lines of future development, it seems

[1] See Seymour Martin Lipset and Neil J. Smelser, "The Setting of Sociology in the 1950's," and Talcott Parsons, "Some Problems Confronting Sociology as a Profession," both in Lipset and Smelser, eds., *Sociology: The Progress of a Decade* (Englewood Cliffs, N.J.: Prentice-Hall, Inc., 1961), pp. 1–30.

evident that future generations will know many sociologies and will view the work of our own generation as hopelessly broad in its sociological preoccupations.

It may be correct to view the future of sociology as one of spinning off some frameworks and consolidating those that remain. But I do not view this pattern of growth, considered alone, as optimal. The growth of new specialities, however scientifically adequate they may be, always raises new questions about their relations with other bodies of knowledge. More specialization will aggravate the already pressing problem of the insulation of the various branches of the behavioral sciences from one another. Optimally, a new pattern of integrating knowledge should arise simultaneously, a pattern whereby the implications of one discipline or subdiscipline for the work of others becomes a subject of disciplined inquiry in itself. Even in the present state of specialization of the behavioral sciences, too little is known of the potentially profitable interchanges among the various disciplines.[2] As knowledge becomes more specialized, the need for new synthesis and coordination will become even greater. Without the growth—indeed the specialization—of intellectually synthesizing activities, it will become more likely that scientific specialities will tend to paint themselves into corners, exhausting their potentialities through excessive refinement rather than opening their assumptions to the theories and research of neighboring zones of inquiry. I would hope, then, that two processes will dominate the future growth of sociology: the inevitable fragmentation and consolidation into more specialities, and the intellectual coordination of these specialities on a new level of interdisciplinary integration.

I shall conclude this discussion of conceptual frameworks in sociology with a brief comment on some of the intellectual controversies within the discipline. Many of these derive in part from the fact that some sociologists have committed themselves to one framework or another, and have assumed a more or less polemic stance as regards its value for sociology as a whole. Ready examples could be provided for frameworks like the ecological, the psychological, and the structural-functional.[3] But I should also like to mention another controversy—perhaps the most widespread one in the field at the present time—in this context of commitment to different conceptual frameworks. I refer to the continuing and multifaceted controversy between those who tend to stress conflict and change in their

---

[2] For a review of some of these interchanges, see Chapter One, above.

[3] See, for example, the following sources: Otis Dudley Duncan and Leo F. Schnore, "Cultural, Behavioral, and Ecological Perspectives in the Study of Social Organization," *American Journal of Sociology*, LXV (1959), 132–46; George D. Homans, "Bringing Men Back In," *American Sociological Review*, XXIX (1964), 809–18; Robert K. Merton, *Social Theory and Social Structure*, revised and enlarged ed. (New York: The Free Press of Glencoe, Inc., 1957), Chapter 1.

approach and those who tend to stress integration and stability. The first position has historical roots in figures like Karl Marx and Georg Simmel, and its contemporary representatives are figures like Lewis Coser and Ralf Dahrendorf; the second position has historical roots in figures like Emile Durkheim and A. R. Radcliffe-Brown, and is most conspicuously identified with the name of Talcott Parsons at the present time. Many read this controversy in almost completely ideological terms—i.e., in terms of whether the theorist is assuming a radical or conservative stance toward the *status quo*. This interpretation may have some merit. But I should like to add that to identify the respective conceptual frameworks adopted by the representatives also contributes to an understanding of the roots of the controversy. One of the differences between these loosely defined approaches is that the "conflict" and "change" approach tends to rely more on the "person" or "group" perspective, and the "integration" and "stability" approach tends to rely more on the "social-structural" or "cultural" framework. Because of an initial emphasis on different frameworks, the two types of theorists become more capable of and more disposed to analyze situations of instability and stability, respectively. Indeed, it is individuals and groups that come into conflict, not relational qualities such as structures; it is persons and groups that have clashing interests, not roles and structures; and concepts like roles and normative expectations, by their very logic, refer to the ways in which persons and groups routinely—and in a regulated way—interact with one another.

To generalize this observation, commitment to a given conceptual framework tends to focus the attention of the social investigator on certain types of topics and scientific problems. Talcott Parsons has made a pertinent observation on this issue in a discussion of the study of dynamics in sociology:

> Dynamic analysis is not . . . possible in terms of the systematic treatment of institutional structure alone. [Dynamic analysis] involves the possibility of generalized treatment of behavioral tendencies of the human actors, in the situations in which they are placed and subject to the expectations of their institutionalized roles. In the most general terms such generalization depends on a theory of "motivation" of human behavior. The ultimate foundations of such a theory must certainly be derived from the science of psychology.[4]

I would add only that a theory of dynamics must be derived from a theory of group formation and action as well as from a theory of personality. In this connection it is interesting to note that in the thought of Karl Marx,

---

[4] "The Present Position and Prospects of Systematic Theory in Sociology," in *Essays in Sociological Theory*, revised ed. (New York: The Free Press of Glencoe, Inc., 1954), p. 233.

the forces that make for integration and resistance to change in society are found in the *relations* among the various elements of the economic structure and the social superstructure (for example, the temporarily stabilizing influences of law, religion, and the state during any given historical period); and the forces that make for conflict and change are found in *groups* of motivated individuals (class-conscious organizations, revolutionary parties). The relational structure provides the historical contradictions that give rise to conflict and change, but political groups actually enter into conflict and effect processes of change. Marx, in short, used both the "structural" and the "group" perspectives, depending on the issue he was addressing. The conclusion I draw from these various observations is that future advances in the study of social change depend in part on the attainment of a more profitable synthesis of these two perspectives than we have been able to effect in the past.

Subdivisions in Sociology   To this point I have considered sociology in terms of the several conceptual frameworks that constitute its subject matter. My account also suggests why the commonly listed subdivisions of the field frequently appear to be overlapping, inconsistent, and confusing. The difficulties in subdividing arise because, with a diversity of frameworks and approaches, many different principles of division are available. It is not surprising, therefore, that even a casual inspection of the subfields appearing in textbooks, catalogues, and programs of the annual meetings of the American Sociological Association reveals a number of cross-cutting bases of classification for the field:

1. Some subfields correspond more or less to the major conceptual frameworks listed above—for example, demography, social psychology, social organization, sociology of culture.

2. Additional subfields arise when the major conceptual frameworks are subdivided by empirical illustration. For example, in the "group" framework we find the sociology of small groups, voluntary associations, formal organizations, and so on. Within the "structural" framework, we find structures identified according to type of function—sociology of religion, medicine, law, education, and so on. Within the "cultural" framework we find the sociology of literature, knowledge, popular culture, and the like.

3. Some subfields arise when investigators focus on some relations between the major conceptual frameworks. The focus of the subfield of socialization and personality, for instance, is the relation between the sociocultural structure and the formation of individual personalities; the subfield of deviance and social control refers to the same relation, studied from the standpoint of degree of conformity to the sociocultural structure.

4. Still other subfields refer to analytic aspects of social life that cut

across the frameworks listed above. Stratification, for example, refers to the study of the hierarchical organization of roles, persons, and groups in social life; and political sociology refers to the generation, allocation, and utilization of power in social life.

5. Some subfields refer to a process, such as collective behavior or the sociology of economic development.

6. A few subfields refer to the study of the logic and techniques of conceptualization and empirical research—for example, theory and methodology.

7. Finally, some subfields arise as a result of sociology's historical tendency to focus on social problems that are pressing in the larger society —for example, the sociology of prostitution, mental illness, or poverty.

Since all these criteria of classification are used—and each used incompletely—in the internal division of sociology, the contemporary scene yields a bewildering patchwork of fields that is anything but scientifically optimal. Furthermore, it seems reasonable to expect that two basic shifts in the bases of classification will accompany the increasing scientific maturation of the field:

First, while sociology will undoubtedly continue to be called upon to address itself to society's moral, political, and social problems, it will approach them not by creating subfields around specific types of problems, but rather by bringing understanding to these problems from more general principles of social structure and group processes. Consider an analogy. Economics does not have subfields of "inflation" or "depression," but rather throws light on these phenomena by applying more general principles from the theories of consumption, production, and price. Similarly, insights on delinquency, civil disorder, and other social problems will, in the future, come not from concrete subfields of sociology named after these problems but from general knowledge concerning processes of deviance and social control. Indeed, sociology shows some signs that this kind of change has already occurred to a degree, as courses in principles of deviance have come to displace courses organized around a variety of "social problems" in many educational institutions.

Second—and related to the first point—the naming of subdivisions after specific groups and social structures will probably give way to more general characterizations of structures and processes. The main reason for this is that subdivisions identified with particular historical circumstances inhibit the development of a discipline with truly general principles. The subfield of race relations, for example, seems to be a very appropriate one for societies like the United States, South Africa, and Indonesia, where racial groupings play a salient role in society; but it does not seem to apply readily to racially and ethnically homogeneous societies like the

Scandinavian ones. Again, the sociology of law seems to be an appropriate subfield for societies like ours, where law is such an important social institution; but, for societies governed largely by unwritten mores, the sociology of law has little relevance. A more general, analytic characterization, such as social control, would be preferable, since it encompasses both legal and nonlegal types of social regulation.

The upshot of these observations is that sociological subdivisions will probably evolve toward fewer, more analytic areas concerning basic social structures and processes; and that this is desirable in the interests of developing a science that is genuinely theoretical and broadly comparative. But this kind of development will not occur without creating serious dilemmas for the discipline. I have been arguing for sociological subdivisions that are not tied to particular social problems or to concrete groups or structures. But it remains the case that most of the sociological data with which we must deal are recorded by and refer to concrete units, such as societies, communities, formal organizations, and individual persons. Governments conduct censuses, municipal or county agencies record most suicide and crime statistics, business firms keep records, and so on. Moreover, a preponderance of the data these units tend to emit, collect, and record is concerned with problems that preoccupy them in any given historical period. Because such units are the source of much of our necessary data, it is tempting to use them as the basis of our sociological framework. In comparative sociology, for example, most comparisons are made among national or societal units. In one way this makes sense, since most aggregated comparative data are generated by societies. But for many purposes "the society" may not be the best comparative unit. We may wish to organize our study around the comparison of regions with different religions, different languages, or different ethnic solidarities. Yet these kinds of regions scarcely produce data suitable for comparative analysis. These circumstances illustrate the fact that the conceptual framework which the sociological investigator may wish to use to generate insights may lie on a different analytic level from the sociocultural contexts within which his available data have been generated.[5] Furthermore, the more analytic his categories, the more remote they are likely to be from these contexts.

The lesson to be drawn from this dilemma, however, is not that sociology should restrict itself to concepts that correspond to the context within which social data are available. To argue this would be to argue for a sociology as concrete as the social units that produce the data on which it relies. Rather, the lesson is that sociologists must expect to con-

---

[5] In this regard, sociology differs from the experimental sciences, which can generate their own data in a contrived situation that more nearly meets the requirements for the theoretical concepts around which propositions are being tested.

tinue to be preoccupied with methodology—defined broadly as the canons by which theoretically relevant scientific statements are assessed in the light of empirical data. As sociological concepts become more comprehensive, new methods for relating these concepts to social data must be invented, and new ways of recording and representing data must be fashioned. It is sometimes asserted that a preoccupation with methodology signifies an immature scientific discipline in search of itself, and that this preoccupation will fade away as the science advances. I do not share this view. The peculiar relation between analytic sociological concepts and much of the data with which the discipline deals suggests that new levels of methodological concern must arise as the field becomes theoretically and empirically more sophisticated.

THE CHARACTER OF SOCIOLOGICAL EXPLANATION

Thus far I have attempted to delineate the optimum scope and the optimum subdivisions of sociology, indicating at the same time some problems and dilemmas that arise in striving for these optima. The second connotation of "scope" I wish to address refers to the kinds of activities that go into sociological explanation—that enterprise of accounting for regularities, variations, and interdependencies among the phenomena identified within the sociological frameworks. What should be the scope of these activities? At what level should they be pitched? Frequently two alternative strategies are debated: either to investigate relatively modest hypotheses that remain close to the empirical data or to deal with more comprehensive and abstract "theory" that is more remote from data. I shall argue, however, that this distinction is not the best way to frame the issue of the appropriate scope of sociological explanation; and simultaneously I hope to formulate a somewhat different "principle of legitimacy" that should govern the various activities that enter into sociological explanation.

Facts, Hypotheses, and Theories   The several sociological frameworks I outlined earlier were advanced as ways to characterize the major *dependent variables* of the discipline—those phenomena, variations in which are to be explained. Explanation itself, however, begins with the search for *independent variables* (or causes, or determinants, or factors, or conditions), to which variations in the dependent variables are referred.

What are the independent variables most frequently use by sociologists to explain variations in social phenomena? By and large, sociologists find their explanatory variables by turning to those very phenomena that, in other contexts, they may wish to explain. Variations in demographic behavior, such as fertility, are frequently explained by reference to attitudes, group memberships, positions in the social structure, or differential exposure to cultural values (for instance, religion). Similarly, variations in attitudes are frequently explained by turning to group, social-structural, and cultural variables. Certain types of social structures (for example, the isolated nuclear family) have been accounted for by referring to other structural variables (for example, industrial bureaucracy); and the persistence of extended family systems in spite of industrialization is often attributed to distinctive cultural traditions. Again, cultural productions such as art forms or ideologies are often accounted for by referring to conditions that obtain in different parts of the social structure. Sociological explanation, then, looks to variables within the same or neighboring frameworks to account for variations.[6]

The form of sociological explanation that appears least complicated is the simple hypothesis—a statement of the logically and presumably temporally prior conditions under which dependent variables may be expected to vary in certain ways. Two simple examples of sociological hypotheses are the following: (1) The size of the nuclear family is an inverse function of position in the stratification system. (2) The level of social violence of any group is a direct function of its level of economic privation. In the first case one structural variable is explained by reference to another structural variable; in the second case a certain type of behavior is explained by simultaneous reference to group membership and the group's position in the social structure.

Closer examination reveals, however, that even simple hypotheses of this sort involve a number of ancillary assertions, assumptions, and perspectives. Consider the second illustration from the preceding paragraph. If taken without qualification, the hypothesis implies that economic deprivation, measured by some objective criterion, has a direct effect on a group and its members. This assertion is questionable on psychological grounds, since different groups have different levels of susceptibility to economic hardship, depending on their cultural values and historical experience; and, within any group, individuals bring different meanings to economic deprivation and have different threshholds of tolerance for it. Furthermore, the hypothesis implies a number of psychological variables —affects such as rage, and processes by which these affects are converted into action—that intervene between the independent and dependent variables. Finally, the sociological investigator frequently finds the empirical relation between variables like deprivation and violence to be weak; and he wishes to refine the hypothesis by considering additional determinants of violence that may interact with deprivation, as well as additional responses to deprivation other than violence. For all these reasons, it turns

[6] Here I am excluding various "nonsociological" theories that rest more or less exclusively on biological, climatological, geographical, or other nonsociological factors.

out that a relatively simple and innocent hypothesis invariably involves a whole family of statements that stand in some implicit but relatively determinant relation to one another. Put another way, any single hypothesis is nestled in a system of hypotheses. Put still another way, any hypothesis implies a more complex *model* or *theory* of behavior. Furthermore, the roots of this model or theory are to be found, once again, in the various frameworks—ecological, psychological, group, structural, and cultural—that constitute the substance of sociology.

If this be the case, what is the distinctive character of model building or theory construction itself? This process often involves a number of activities, but as a first approximation it might be said that it consists in making explicit the variables and relations that are often only implicit in simple hypotheses, and setting these ingredients into some formal or logical—including mathematical—relation with one another. Taking a hypothesis as the initial point of reference, the specialist in empirical research looks in the direction of the world of facts, and proceeds according to the logic of locating, measuring, and recording data; assuring the reliability and representativeness of these data; and controlling for the operation of other possible independent variables by experimental, statistical, or other research techniques. The theorist looks in the direction of the world of concepts. He examines the conceptual rather than the empirical context of the hypothesis. He attends to such matters as the mutual exclusiveness and logical exhaustiveness of classes of variables and relations; the internal consistency of hypotheses, and their consistency with other bodies of knowledge; their economy of expression; and their power, when combined with other assumptions and assertions, to generate new hypotheses. By this characterization I do not mean to personify the specialist in empirical research and the specialist in theory as two separate breeds. The same investigator frequently attends to both empirical and theoretical issues. But the classes of activity are clearly distinguishable from one another.

From this characterization it becomes clear that sociological theory borders very closely on logic and epistemology, as well as on moral and political philosophy. Any sociological theory rests on definite epistemological foundations—indeed, my own presentation of the nature of a sociological fact and the character of sociological explanation implies a definite epistemological position. Furthermore, because the substance of sociology involves, above all, formulations of general assertions of man's relation to man, it overlaps with religious, moral, and political doctrines that focus on the very same classes of relations. One of the most common exercises in theoretical analysis is to relate the thought of a theorist to some ideological position or to some school of moral and political philosophy. In fact, some of the most heated controversies in sociology concern the ideological or philosophical foundations of a theory rather than its explanatory utility.

Before moving on, I should like to digress momentarily to examine a distinction employed in the preceding paragraphs—the distinction between theory and fact. In one form or another, this distinction is almost universally accepted by social and behavioral scientists. According to the distinction, the world may be divided into empirical facts (behavioral data) that are given in the "real world" and theory (concepts, constructs, models) that is in the "world of ideas"; and the core task of scientific inquiry consists in systematically generating explanations by bringing theory and fact into some appropriate relation with one another. I should like to raise some questions about this form of the distinction.

In a classic statement, Lawrence J. Henderson defined a fact as "an empirically verifiable statement about phenomena in terms of a conceptual scheme." [7] The important phrase for present purposes is "in terms of a conceptual scheme." I argued above that there is no such entity as a "sociological fact" apart from the conceptual framework to which it is referred. Even such apparently real and irreducible data as the birth of a child or a market transaction depend on the selective identification of aspects of empirical phenomena; notions of instance and class; and grammatical conventions—in short, a conceptual framework that serves to select from, identify, and organize experience. When we refer to facts or behavioral data, then, we actually refer to a universe of statements, the rules for the organization of which are commonly rooted in the unexamined structures of common language and common sense. There cannot be a fact without a conceptual framework.

As I have indicated, sociological explanation consists in bringing constructions such as hypotheses, models, and theories to bear on factual statements. But in what do these constructions consist? *They are also conceptual frameworks.* They are composed of concepts that are related to one another by a certain logic—that is, by rules of discourse that are usually more precise and rigorous than those governing the use of common language. Accordingly, sociological explanation has to be defined not as the relation between two different classes of things—theories and facts—but as *a relation between two conceptual frameworks.* It consists in comparing the linguistic and conceptual conventions by which we organize phenomena we call the empirical world with the linguistic and conceptual conventions by which we organize phenomena we call ideas. If a certain relation between the two frameworks is attained, we judge

[7] Quoted in Talcott Parsons, *The Structure of Social Action* (New York: McGraw-Hill Book Company, 1937), p. 41.

an assertion to be "valid" or "verified"; if another relation is attained, we judge the assertion to be "rejected" or "in need of modification." This formulation constitutes a kind of correspondence theory of scientific truth, but the correspondence is between different kinds of conceptual frameworks rather than between conceptual frameworks and facts. This kind of conclusion is somewhat disturbing to those of us who like to think of a "real world" that is separate from our ideas about it; but it is more in keeping with the ways in which experience is organized and scientific investigation proceeds.

This formulation underscores the principle that scientific innovation may arise from two principal sources: (1) It may arise from a modification of the conceptual framework by which we regard the "factual world." This may involve a new way of conceptualizing a fact (a "discovery"), a new way of measuring it, a new way of bringing it into relation with another fact. This change may then disturb a previous "correspondence" with an explanatory or theoretical framework, and lead to modifications of this framework, and its relations with the framework by which we organize the "factual world." (2) Scientific innovation may arise by virtue of a modification of the relations among theoretical constructs themselves, which may suggest new ways of looking at "facts," which in turn may generate new methods of organizing facts to correspond with the new theoretical relations. Scientific advance consists in a continuous feedback between these two ways of organizing experience.

Toward a Principle of Legitimacy for Sociological Activities   The history of social thought has witnessed the appearance and disappearance of many epistemological positions, each of which has advanced and defended a principle by which knowledge concerning human affairs can best be generated. Among these approaches are rationalism, positivism, and intuitionism. In the shorter history of the scientific investigation of social life, too, certain methods have been selected as favorite candidates in the race to advance scientific knowledge—for example, the experimental method, quantification, clinical observation.

Each of these approaches or methods possesses the characteristics of a value system, in that proponents of each have attempted to set up criteria to legitimize the scope and method of social inquiry. Unfortunately, they have manifested another feature of value-systems as well—the tendency to harden into doctrinal schools, which form the bases from which cadres of scholars launch out to combat other scholars about the relative legitimacy of their respective approaches to knowledge. These conflicts are probably inevitable features of the human condition, and will remain with us as long as we continue the effort to design the discipline. But the tendency to form schools around epistemological positions does exact a cost; it discourages the dispassionate examination of the synthetic relations that might obtain among the different approaches and methods.

The version of sociological explanation I have sketched—which is generally consistent with the method of empirical science that has evolved during the past several centuries—is also a value position. As such, it attempts to sketch the broad lines of legitimacy for a variety of sociological activities. Moreover, this version of sociological explanation envisions no single, royal road to scientific knowledge about society. It does not give any special priority to the quantification of data, speculation, or the creation of theory at a given level of abstraction. It legitimizes a wide range of activities—recording data, designing measures, setting up experiments, analyzing data, classifying variables and relations, deducing hypotheses, speculating freely, and tracing the moral and ideological implications of a theoretical system. All can contribute, indeed all are essential, to the sociological enterprise.

Such a catholic approach appears to have the merit of being inclusive, tolerant, and nonpolemic. By virtue of these very merits, however, it seems almost to lose its power of legitimizing. To legitimize so much is almost to legitimize nothing, since it appears that "anything goes" in sociology. The approach I have sketched seems to run the danger of intellectual anomie, bred by an excess of freedom and permissiveness.

A second, qualifying principle is therefore necessary. This is the principle that no investigative activity in sociology is scientifically legitimate unless it can be related directly to the core sociological enterprise: accounting for variations and interdependencies of data within a sociological framework. This criterion is a relational one. It implies that the legitimacy of a sociological activity cannot be determined by examining this activity in isolation; it must be examined in relation to the broader corpus of sociological theory and research. To illustrate:

1. A small-group experiment may be flawlessly designed, but it is without sociological merit unless it can be brought to bear in some way—by confirming, rejecting, suggesting modification, and so on—on theoretically relevant statements within a sociological framework.

2. A field study may be extraordinarily rich and interesting in its anecdotal material, but if the material is not related to some theoretically relevant proposition, it has no sociological merit.

3. A new method of estimating true crime rates may be ingenious, and useful for a community policy; but unless the new measure is incorporated into some theoretically relevant proposition, it has no sociological validity.

4. A new hypothesis may be elegantly derived from a complex set

of mathematical relations—or even produced by a computer—but unless the mathematics can be related to substantive sociological theory, and unless the hypothesis can be related to sociological data, it has no sociological merit.

5. The discovery of a valid comparative association between institutional complexes—say, authority systems and division of labor—may be impressive; but unless it can be incorporated into a system of sociological hypotheses, it is of no sociological utility.

6. A scholarly treatise tracing the history of the concept of social cohesion may be informative and engaging; but unless the work is related to the current sociological enterprise of theory and research, it is of no sociological value.

7. A critical examination of a theorist's system, which demonstrates convincingly that he falls into the neo-Marxist tradition or that he has a conservative bias, may be both scholarly and gratifying or irritating on ideological grounds, but unless it can assist in the evaluation of some theoretical scheme or empirical research, it has no sociological merit.

In short, to use adjectives like "flawless," "rich," "ingenious," "rigorous," "elegant," or "interesting" falls short of endowing sociological work with full legitimacy; the work must also be related to the central sociological enterprise—either by the perpetrator of the work or by someone else—before it can be said to constitute a contribution.

This assertion requires one major qualification, however. While I am convinced that the criterion is optimal for the growth of scientific sociology, it can be applied in only an approximate way. The reason for this is that the sociological frameworks and research procedures themselves are not final and fixed. They are in a continuous state of flux, and much disagreement obtains in the profession about the core of sociology itself. I see the application of the criterion of sociological legitimacy, then, not as something definitive. I see its application as part of the ongoing search of sociology, as a general guideline in the continuing evolution of the discipline.

To conclude, the two criteria of legitimacy I have suggested are an attitude of permissiveness for a variety of theoretical and empirical activities, combined with an obligation to relate these to the core of sociology. These criteria, like other optima suggested in this essay, constitute an effort to encourage the greatest specialization in the discipline, but simultaneously to guarantee the continuing effort to synthesize its knowledge.

THREE: The Methodology of
Comparative Analysis of
Economic Activity *

The objective of this essay is to throw light on a number of difficult and unresolved methodological issues that have plagued the comparative analysis of economic institutions and behavior—as well as other types of comparative analysis—for many decades. I shall first outline the issues, then mention a few efforts that scholars have made to solve them, and finally outline my own views on a methodological perspective and some research strategies that may improve on these suggested solutions.

THE ISSUES

The issues I shall address take the following forms:

1. In what ways is it appropriate to regard comparative economic analysis as the search for features of economic life that are universal in their incidence and in what ways as a study of variations? For example: Is the psychological propensity to economize to be considered universal? Is it profitable to search for similar institutional forms (e.g., the market) from society to society? Is it appropriate to ascertain the degree to which industrialization is correlated with the isolated nuclear family? In one respect the answers to these questions are empirical; however, I am posing them in terms of their methodological appropriateness.

2. How is it possible to compare economic institutions and activities

* Revised version of a paper delivered at the annual meetings of the American Sociological Association, Miami Beach, August 1966; and prepared for the Sixth World Congress of Sociology, Evian, September 1966. The paper was originally published in the *Transactions of the Sixth World Congress of Sociology* (Louvain: Éditions Nauwelaerts, 1968), Vol. II, pp. 101–17.

in diverse sociocultural contexts? This issue, which might be termed "the problem of comparability," arises at three distinct levels: (*a*) How can we be certain that the *events* and *situations* we wish to explain are comparable from one sociocultural context to another? How, for example, can we compare production rates a century ago with production rates today? Were not recording procedures different then from now? Was not the social meaning of a product different then from now? More generally, are not "the [economic] activity and the income . . . inseparable and . . . both embedded together in the customs and ways of thought which mold the social life of the community as a whole?" [1] (*b*) How can we be certain that the general *dimensions* used to compare societies crossculturally do not do violence to the events and situations we wish to study? In what sense is it appropriate to apply the concept "economic" to both the role of an African subsistence farmer and to that of a member of the board of directors of a large American corporation? In what sense are both roles economic? Certainly it appears that *some* general dimensions are necessary to engage in comparative analysis; otherwise the investigator would seem to be committed to a radical relativism that prohibits him from moving beyond the confines of a single social unit. But the truth of this general point does not solve the problem of what particular comparative dimensions do least violence to the distinctive sociocultural meaning of events and situations, yet at the same time provide a genuinely general basis for comparison. (*c*) How is it possible to compare very different *social units* (or social systems) with one another? Does it make any sense to compare a highly complex economy like those of the modern West or the Soviet Union with hunting-and-gathering tribes in Australia, when it is obvious that these economies differ from one another in almost every conceivable respect?

3. Should economic activity in different societies be described in terms of its meanings to the members of the societies themselves, or should it be measured by some objective index? Should we, at one extreme, be prepared to regard as economic any kind of activity that any culture happens to regard as economic? Or should we, at the other extreme, search for indices such as dollar equivalents to describe all economic activity everywhere, no matter what its sociocultural context? [2]

---

[1] S. Herbert Frankel, *The Economic Impact on Under-Developed Societies* (Cambridge: Harvard University Press, 1959), pp. 41–42.

[2] Claude Levi-Strauss has presented this distinction in terms of its relation to consciousness. "[The anthropologist] may have to construct a model from phenomena the systematic character of which has evoked no awareness on the part of the culture. . . . Or else the anthropologist will be dealing, on the one hand, with raw phenomena and, on the other, with the models already constructed by the culture to interpret the former." See "Social Structure," reprinted in Sol Tax, ed., *Anthropology Today: Selections* (Chicago: University of Chicago Press, 1962), p. 324.

4. If, indeed, we wish to investigate economic life in different contexts, how are we to define the various concepts to be used—concepts such as "economic" and "noneconomic" themselves, "capital," "savings," "production," and so on?

These several issues are closely interrelated. The degree of universality of a phenomenon depends in part on the way this phenomenon is defined. "Marketplace," which refers to a physical location at which exchange takes place, for example, is more nearly universal than "market," which in the economist's definition would involve not only exchange but also some generalized medium of exchange such as money, equilibrating mechanisms such as supply and demand, and perhaps some notion of economic rationality attributed to buyers and sellers.[3] Moreover, the degree of comparability of different units also depends on the choice and definition of concepts. To choose a noneconomic example, the concept of civil service is so intimately linked with a bureaucratic form that it is literally useless in connection with societies without a formal state or governmental apparatus. The concept of administration is somewhat superior, since it is not so closely tied to particular forms of bureaucracy, but even this term is quite culture-bound. Weber's concept of staff is even more helpful, since it can encompass, without embarrassment, various political arrangements based on kinship and other forms of particularistic loyalties.[4] Staff is more satisfactory than administration, then, and administration more satisfactory than civil service, because the former allow for a wider range of instantiation in principle. The questions of definition of concepts, adequacy of comparability, and universality of occurrence, then, appear to rest in large part on a single master question: how adequately does the investigator choose and use his comparative categories? To this question this essay is devoted.

APPROACHES TO THE ISSUE OF COMPARABILITY

In the area of comparative economics existing solutions to the master question I have posed tend to fall between two extremes—phenomenological subjectivism (and relativism) on the one hand, and positivistic objectivism on the other. With respect to the former, the investigator, conscious of the vast ranges of variability in economic activity and in meanings assigned to it in different sociocultural contexts, is pulled toward the

---

[3] For a discussion of the distinction between marketplace and market, and the empirical occurrence of both, see Paul Bohannan and George Dalton, "Introduction," in *Markets in Africa* (Evanston: Northwestern University Press, 1962), pp. 1–12.

[4] Max Weber, *The Theory of Social and Economic Organization*, trans. A. M. Henderson and Talcott Parsons (New York: Oxford University Press, 1947), pp. 329 ff.

position of representing the "economic" differently for each culture. This position is well stated by Marcel Mauss, who characterized his own comparative methodology as follows:

> . . . *since we are concerned with words and their meanings,* we choose only areas where we have access to the *minds of the societies* through documentation and philological research. This further limits our field of comparison. Each particular study has a bearing on the systems we set out to describe and is presented in its logical place. In this way we avoid that *method of haphazard comparison in which institutions lose their local colour and documents their value.*[5]

Presumably the research method most appropriate to this kind of definition is ethnographic work in the field, on the basis of which the investigator records the values, beliefs, and other cultural items as faithfully and accurately as possible. If pressed to its extreme, however, this position leaves the investigator in a state of paralysis. He soon ends in a position of radical relativism, at which he must treat everything as "economic" that any group happens to define thus; and, respecting "local color" in this way, he loses his grasp on any general concept of the economic whatsoever, and hence loses any ability to engage in comparative analysis.

The first rule of thumb in comparative analysis, then, is to avoid concepts that are so particularly tied to single cultures or groups of cultures that no instance of the concepts, as defined, can be found in other cultures. Some more general definition of the economic is required—for example, a definition based on the fact that all societies face the problem of scarcity of natural resources and human resources and skills, and that they must come to term in some institutionalized way with this problem. Such a definition would appear to have comparative potential, since all societies can be said to have a scarcity problem and display economic behavior; moreover, the definition would appear to avoid the conceptual paralysis associated with the extreme of phenomenological subjectivism. But it is necessary to proceed further and ask how economic behavior, defined thus, is identified empirically in different sociocultural contexts.

One convenient and widely used way of identifying the economic is to limit the empirical referents of the term, as did Alfred Marshall, to those aspects of men's attitudes and activities which are subject to measurement in terms of money.[6] From the standpoint of empirical pre-

---

[5] *The Gift: Forms and Functions of Exchange in Archaic Societies,* trans. Ian Cunnison (New York: The Free Press of Glencoe, Inc., 1954), pp. 2–3. Emphasis added.

[6] Alfred Marshall, *Principles of Economics,* 8th ed. (New York and London: The Macmillan Company, 1920), Book I, Chapter 2.

cision, this monetary index has clear advantages. From the standpoint of encompassing economic behavior on a uniform and universal basis, however, it is severely limited. Even in our own society, many activities that are economically significant—housewives' labor, lending a hand to a friend, etc.—are seldom expressed in monetary terms. In the case of economies based on subsistence farming and domestically consumed household manufacture, the limitations of the monetary index are even more marked, since the most fundamentally economic kinds of behavior—such as the production, distribution, and consumption of foodstuffs—never become monetized. In addition, the monetary index is limited from the standpoint of comparing a growing economic system with its own past, since one of the concomitants of economic growth is the entry of an increasing proportion of goods and services into the market context—and hence their increasing monetization; this means that if the monetary definition of *economic* is used, the rate of growth will be artificially inflated by the fact of the transformation of nonmonetized economic activity into monetized economic activity.[7] When used for international comparisons of wealth, such indices suffer not only from the fact of differential levels of monetization, but also from the frequent practice of translation of various currencies into dollar or some other equivalencies, usually on the basis of current international exchange ratios. Since many of these ratios are pegged artificially and do not represent true economic exchange ratios, additional bias creeps into the comparative estimates.

Another objective definition has been suggested in the work of Polanyi, Arensberg, and Pearson.[8] Reacting negatively to the tradition of formal economics—which distorts comparisons by imposing a market bias on nonmarket economies—they suggest that economic activity be defined as that instituted process which results in a "continuous supply of want-satisfying *material* means." This materialistic definition introduces a bias precisely opposite to that of the monetary definition of economic activity —a bias in favor of the primitive and peasant societies. In such societies, it appears (but is not necessarily the case) that economic activity is devoted to a sort of material subsistence based on food, clothing, and shelter. In advanced market societies, however, in which expressive behavior, ideas, personalities, and other nonmaterial items have economic value,

---

[7] It should be added that some definitions of economics do not limit economic activity to monetized activity. Thus Samuelson's textbook definition is "... the study of how men and society choose, *with or without the use of money,* to employ scarce productive resources to produce various commodities over time and distribute them for consumption, now and in the future, among various people and groups in society." Paul A. Samuelson, *Economics: An Introductory Analysis,* 5th ed. (New York: McGraw-Hill Book Company, 1961), p. 6. Emphasis added.

[8] Karl Polanyi, Conrad M. Arensberg, and Harry W. Pearson, *Trade and Market in the Early Empires* (New York: The Free Press and The Falcon's Wing Press, 1957).

the formula of the economic as the "supply of want-satisfying material means" collapses as an adequate comparative tool. It is as illegitimate to try to force a physical or material bias on all economic activity as it is to impose a fully developed model of the market on all economic activity.[9]

How, then, is the comparative analyst to steer a course between the Scylla of paralysis associated with culture-specific definitions and the Charybdis of distortion associated with more general definitions?[10] No ready solution exists in the literature, from my reading, and the approach I now propose is put forth as an indication of the general direction to be taken rather than as a final solution to this difficult dilemma.

Any encompassing definition and measure of economic activity must involve more than some convenient index of monetized activity, physical production, or some other objective phenomenon. It must involve a definition of the production, distribution, and consumption of scarce goods and services *in relation to individual and social goals*. Economists have long recognized this relational quality of economic activity in their preoccupation with the notion of utility as the basis of value. Yet their preoccupation has been predominately with the wants of individuals, despite the tradition of welfare economics that has pursued questions of interindividual comparability and community welfare.[11] Furthermore, economists have generally tended to treat wants as given and stable, and therefore subject to no further analysis. But in comparative analysis the question of wants as the ultimate defining basis for economic activity and

[9] For further development of this point, and further criticism of the formulation developed by Polanyi, *et al.*, cf. Neil J. Smelser, "A Comparative View of Exchange Systems," *Economic Development and Cultural Change*, VII (1959), 173–82.

[10] This tension between culture-specific and general measures has made its appearance in the general theoretical discussions of structural-functional analysis, in particular in the discussion of the "postulate of indispensability." In general terms, this postulate holds that there are certain universal functional exigencies (such as the socialization of the young, the integration of diverse groups in society) which society faces, *and* that there are *specific* social-structural forms which *alone* serve these functions (structural forms such as the nuclear family for socialization and organized religion for integration, for instance). Thus the postulate of indispensability links specific institutional or behavorial indices with general social functions, just as the monetary definition of economic activity links "measurement in terms of money" to the general concept of "economic." The formulations are parallel. Objecting to the postulate of indispensability, Merton has asserted that "just as the same item may have multiple functions, so the same function may be diversely fulfilled by alternative items. Functional needs are . . . taken to be permissive, rather than determinant, of specific social structures." Robert K. Merton, *Social Theory and Social Structure*, revised and enlarged ed. (New York: The Free Press of Glencoe, Inc., 1957), pp. 33–34. In line with this position, Merton goes on to insist on the importance of concepts like "functional alternatives," "functional substitutes," and "functional equivalents." Here Merton is opting for general comparative concepts (functions) that encompass a wide variety of empirical manifestations (items).

[11] See, for example, I. M. D. Little, *A Critique of Welfare Economics* (Oxford: The Clarendon Press, 1950); Jerome Rothenberg, *The Measurement of Social Welfare* (Englewood Cliffs, N.J.: Prentice-Hall, Inc., 1961).

measurement cannot be taken as a parametric given; [12] it must be treated in relation to variable societal values and goals.

To arrive at an appropriate comparative definition of economic activity, therefore, we first recognize that a society possesses a value system that defines certain goals as desirable for members and groups of the society at various levels. By a process of institutionalization, the appropriate channels for realizing these goals are specified. It is apparent, however, that all societies exist in an environment that does not guarantee automatically the complete and instantaneous realization of these goals. Hence an important part of the societal situation is that certain instiutionalized attention be given to the supply of various facilities to attain the valued goals. Part of this attention is economic activity. The goals—and the institutionalized means for attaining them—may vary considerably; they may concern perpetuation of kinship lines, attainment of a state of religious bliss, territorial expansion, or maximization of wealth. Economic activity in any society is defined as a *relation* between these goals and the degree of scarcity of goods and services. Indeed, the definition of the economic in any given society—and the structure of its economy—will be in large part a function of both the institutionalized values and goals and the availability (or scarcity) of human and nonhuman resources.

The investigator of comparative economic activity, then, must allow cultural values and meanings to intervene between his most general concept ("the economic") and its specific measurements. He must begin by comparing systematically the value systems of different societies, then identify and measure—using a different set of operational rules in each society—what classes of activity are economic (scarce) in relation to these values. This difficult and prolonged method of research is certainly more plagued with problems of operationalization than the simple comparison of market transactions. The difficulties of the comparative analysis of cultural values are only too well appreciated by anthropologists and comparative sociologists. But I am convinced that comparative analysis—both of economic activity in particular and social behavior in general—cannot proceed far without striving to introduce social values and meanings into the comparative identification and measurement of general constructs; if it does not undertake this task, it will be bedeviled by uncorrectable distortions from the very outset of study.

[12] Joseph S. Berliner, an economist, commenting on the anthropological method, states: "Economists do not as a rule search for regularities between the economic system and the kinship system or religious or political systems; the latter are assumed to be 'given'... The application of the cultural anthropological method... would involve the replacement of the shift parameter by a series of variables.... The economist's assumption of the stability of consumer preferences, at least with respect to cultural variables in the short run, is probably valid. For long-run prediction, however, the use of cultural variables may significantly improve the results." "The Feet of the Natives are Large: An Essay on Anthropology by an Economist," *Current Anthropolgy,* III: 1 (February 1962), 53–54.

From a methodological point of view, I am suggesting that some of the sources of cultural variability (values and goals) that obscure a neat correspondence between universal concept (the economic) and its specific manifestations (items of behavior) *be themselves systematically classified and brought to bear on the measurement process.* As I have indicated, past solutions to this methodological issue have tended either to ignore these sources of variability by treating them as given and nonvariable or to be discouraged from comparative analysis and driven into isolated case studies by them. The type of solution suggested here would incorporate the sources of cultural variability into the very process of comparative analysis. I see this solution as in keeping with the general method of scientific analysis, *viz.,* to make determinate those sources of variation that have hitherto been assumed to be so simple as to be nondeterminate or so complex as to be indeterminate.

SOME RESEARCH STRATEGIES FOR COMPARATIVE ANALYSIS

Thus far the discussion has concerned primarily general and conceptual means of coming to terms with the problems of sociocultural variability and complexity. In addition, there are a number of more concrete and specific strategies to be observed in posing research questions and conducting research—strategies also directed toward the problems of variability and complexity. In the remainder of this essay I shall outline these strategies, again using mainly the comparative study of economic activity for illustration.

Let us begin with a specific comparative problem: why does the gross national product of some societies grow at a faster rate than that of others? (Assume for the moment that adequate comparative measures for GNP have been devised.) The factors contributing to the answer to such a question are obviously very numerous. In the first instance, the several factors of production—land, labor, capital, and organization—and the characteristics of demand determine the level of production. Each of these determinants is, however, itself conditioned by a vast array of sociocultural factors—the kinship system, the educational framework, the stratification system, the political structure, and so on. How does the investigator deal with this array of determinants?

In general, the social scientist imposes some sort of conceptual organization on the conditions, for example, by distinguishing among independent, intervening, and dependent variables. In the illustration at hand, the supply of the various factors of production are considered to be dependent variables in relation to the sociocultural factors, independent with respect to the level of the gross national product, and intervening with respect to the relations between the sociocultural factors and the

GNP.[13] Further conceptual organization is often imposed on the conditions by combining them into various forms of explanatory models.[14]

Another fundamental way of organizing conditions is found in the distinction between conditions treated as *parameters* and conditions treated as *operative variables*. As indicated above,[15] parameters are conditions that are known or suspected to influence the dependent variable, but which, in the investigation at hand, are made or assumed not to vary. Operative variables are conditions that are known or suspected to influence the dependent variable and which, in the investigation at hand, are made or allowed to vary in order to assess this influence. By making variables into parameters for purposes of analysis, most of the potentially operative conditions are made not to vary, so that the operation of one or a few conditions may be isolated and examined.

The distinction between parameters and operative variables is a relative one. What is treated as a parameter in one investigation may become a variable condition in another. Suppose, for example, it is known that foreign trade is important in the determination of the national income of a society, but that calculation of the impact of foreign trade on the domestic economy is impossible unless certain internal relations—say, between private investment, government investment, and consumption—are already known. The economist may proceed by asuming that foreign trade is a parameter—i.e., that it does not exist, or that it occurs at a constant rate throughout the time period in question—and, by thus simplifying the picture of the determinants of income, may proceed to establish national income as some function of private investment, government investment, and current consumption. Having established these relations, he may then "relax" the restricting assumption about foreign trade, and "allow" it to vary, thus tracing its impact on the known relations internal to the economy. In the same operation he may very well have transformed domestic investment into a parameter—i.e., assumed it not to vary—in order to pinpoint the impact of foreign trade more precisely.

The several methods of inquiry in the social sciences may be characterized in terms of the ways in which parameters and operative variables are controlled, manipulated, combined, and recombined into explanatory accounts.[16] In this essay I am particularly concerned with the comparative method—or the method of systematic comparative illustration—which is employed for the scientific analysis of historical data which cannot be controlled experimentally and the number of cases of which is too small to

---

[13] For further illustrations of the use of independent, intervening, and dependent variables, see above, pp. 12–13.

[14] Above, pp. 14–16 and below, pp. 209–16.

[15] Above, p. 16.

[16] Above, pp. 16–20.

permit statistical analysis. I have already showed how Durkheim's analysis of suicide rates employed this method of systematic comparative illustration.[17] Max Weber's studies on religion and rational bourgeois capitalism provide another illustration.

Weber's starting-point was those societies in northwest Europe and North America that had developed rational bourgeois capitalism. He wished to establish the essential characteristics that these societies had in common. In doing so he was using the *positive* comparative method—identifying similarities in conditions associated with a common outcome. Then, turning to societies that had not developed this kind of economic organization (e.g., classical India, classical China), he asked in what respects they differed from the former societies. In so doing he was using the *negative* comparative method—identifying conditions associated with divergent outcomes. By thus manipulating the conditions and the outcomes, Weber built his case that differences in religious systems were crucial in accounting for the different economic histories of the various societies.[18] Translating Weber's comparative method into the language of scientific inquiry, we see that Weber was making parameters of those general features shared by both the West and his Oriental examples (for instance, he ruled out the influence of merchant classes by pointing out that both China and the West had these classes prior to the development of capitalism in the West); and he was making operative variables of those religious features in which they differed.

The comparative method as just outlined is a systematic attempt to come to grips with the methodological issues raised at the beginning of this essay. It takes cognizance of the variability in sociocultural context but attempts to control it by the method of systematic illustration, and by continuous transformation of parameters into operative variables and vice versa. Viewing the comparative problem in this way, it is possible to suggest a few specific research strategies that are advisable at the present state of the art of comparative analysis.

First, while it is in principle possible, given the appropriate comparative categories, to compare economies so different as the American urban-industrial complex and hunting-and-gathering tribes, it is more fruitful to compare economic variations in societies that are much closer to one another in many respects. For example, it would be a fruitful exercise to compare the different paths of development of socialist economic policies in Denmark, Norway, Sweden, Finland, and Iceland, which are similar

[17] Above, pp. 18–19.

[18] Relevant works include *The Protestant Ethic and the Spirit of Capitalism,* trans. Talcott Parsons (London: George Allen & Unwin, 1948); *The Religion of China,* trans. Hans H. Gerth (New York: The Free Press of Glencoe, Inc., 1951); *The Religion of India,* trans. Hans H. Gerth and Don Martindale (New York: The Free Press of Glencoe, Inc., 1958).

but not identical in cultural traditions and social structure. It would be less fruitful to compare the socialism of Denmark with the socialism of emerging African countries, whose cultural traditions and social structures are vastly different. The reason for adopting this research strategy can be stated in terms of the distinction between parameters and operative variables. If two societies share some important conditions in common, it is relatively more permissible to treat these common conditions as parameters, and proceed to examine the operation of other variables as if these common conditions were not operative, because their operation is presumably similar in both cases. By contrast, if two social units that differ in almost every respect are chosen for comparison, the investigator is in the disadvantaged position of having to consider all sources of difference as operative variables, because he is unable to "control" them by considering them to be similar. The more similar two or more societies are with respect to crucial variables, in short, the better able is the investigator to isolate and analyze the influence of other variables that might account for the differences he wishes to explain.[19]

Second—and related to the first—it is fruitful to replicate comparisons *between* social units by means of comparisons *within* social units. Let me illustrate this method first by reference to a noneconomic example. Durkheim's most thoroughly analyzed case of altruistic suicide was the military case. His general interpretation was that military personnel, in comparison with civilians, are more involved in a collective code of honor, and therefore are more likely to sacrifice themselves through self-destruction in the name of this code. On this basis he predicted higher rates of suicide among military personnel than among civilians. The available suicide statistics tended to support his hypothesis. Even after he corrected for marital status, the differences between military and civilian personnel stood. Still, it might be argued, it is not clear that Durkheim had isolated the salient differences between military and civilian personnel; after all, they differ in many other circumstances than in degree of commitment to a code of honor, and on the basis of the gross comparison between military and civilian personnel alone it is impossible to know that the differential value-commitment is the operative variable. By way of attempting to support his own interpretation, Durkheim turned to the analysis of *intramilitary* differences in suicide rates. First he compared those with limited terms of service with those of longer duration, finding that the latter—presumably more imbued with the military spirit than

[19] For an example of a comparative study of "close" cases, see Lipset's comparisons of differences in political structure among the four English-speaking democracies of Australia, Canada, Great Britain, and the United States. Seymour M. Lipset, "The Value Patterns of Democracy: A Case Study in Comparative Analysis," *American Sociological Review*, XXVIII (1963), 515–32.

the former—showed higher suicide rates; next he compared officers and noncommissioned officers with private soldiers, finding that the former—again more involved in the military life—showed higher rates; finally, he found a greater tendency for suicide among volunteers and re-enlisted men, i.e., those who chose the military life freely. Summarizing these intramilitary findings, Durkheim concluded that "the members of the army most stricken by suicide are also those who are most inclined to this career. . . ." [20] By this replication at the intraunit level Durkheim rendered more plausible the interunit relation (between military and civilian).[21]

The main advantage of replication at different analytic levels is to increase or decrease the investigator's confidence in a suspected association between conditions and the phenomenon to be explained. In some cases intraunit comparisons may prove more fruitful than interunit comparisons. The logic behind this assertion is the same that lies behind the assertion that it is more fruitful to compare social units that are similar to one another in important respects. Suppose we wish to carry out certain investigations on societies that differ from one another in terms of level of industrialization. Suppose further that Germany, a highly industrialized country, and Italy, a less industrialized country, are the two societies chosen for comparison. For many purposes it would be more fruitful to compare northern Italy with southern Italy, and the Ruhr with Bavaria, than it would be to compare Germany as a whole with Italy as a whole. These two countries differ not only in level of industrialization but also in cultural traditions, type of governmental structure, and so on. From the standpoint of interunit comparison these differences are not controllable as parameters. If the investigator were instead to pursue intraunit comparisons between those parts of Italy and Germany that are industrialized and those parts that are not, it is more nearly possible to hold these interunit differences constant, and thus pinpoint the factors lying behind differential industrialization more precisely. Then, having located what appear to be operative factors in the intraunit comparisons, it is possible to move to the interunit comparisons to see if the same differences hold in the large.

Important and advantageous as are the methods of comparison of similar cases and of replication at different levels for the establishment of comparative findings, the investigator must proceed judiciously in their use. He must attempt to establish empirically—not merely assume—that those conditions he treats as parameters are indeed based on similarities

---

[20] Emile Durkheim, *Suicide,* trans. by John A. Spaulding and George Simpson (New York: The Free Press of Glencoe, Inc., 1951), p. 233.

[21] For a discussion of Durkheim's study, with special reference to the problems of replication and statistical significance, cf. Hanan C. Selvin, "Durkheim's *Suicide* and Problems of Empirical Research," *American Journal of Sociology,* LXIII (1958), 607–19.

and continuities between and within social units. Otherwise his study will suffer from the methodological weaknesses that arise when incomparable units are analyzed.

I shall conclude with a few comments—ventured in the light of the methodological approach I have outlined—on the first issue I introduced: the appropriateness of asking to what degree empirical phenomena and associations are universal and to what degree variable. So long as this question is posed with the understanding that the extent of empirical occurrence of a phenomenon and its associations is a necessary pre-liminary to comparative explanation, it is a legitimate question. Insofar as the search for empirical universals becomes an end in itself, however, it can lead to relatively unproductive research and unnecessary contro-versy. I shall illustrate this point by referring to the familiar issue of the relations between the urban-industrial complex and the isolated nuclear family.

The argument for the universal association between these two social phenomena—an argument presented by the Chicago school of the inter-war period [22]—runs roughly as follows: The traditional farm or peasant family is given a shock by the development of a commercial market struc-ture, by the development of industry, or by the development of cities—usually, in fact, by some great social force involving an undifferentiated combination of all three. The immediate effects of this shock are to draw one or more family members into wage labor (separated from the house-hold), thereby destroying the traditional division of labor, making the family more mobile socially and geographically, placing the family in a generally anonymous social environment, and perhaps destroying its economic base further by flooding the market with cheap, mass-produced commodities that compete with those previously produced in the domestic setting. The result is the small nuclear family that is mobile, neolocal, and isolated from many of its previous social connections and functions. Once this assertion of the universality of the connection between the urban-industrial complex and the isolated nuclear family is made, the research problem quite appropriately becomes one of establishing the empirical strength of the relation by examining different societies at different stages of economic and urban development.

If the research question remains at this level, it is likely to lead to two unhelpful preoccupations. First, research on the degree of universality of some occurrence or association may degenerate into controversy over the

[22] Relevant works are Ernest W. Burgess and Harvey J. Locke, *The Family: From Institution to Companionship*, 2nd ed. (New York: American Book Company, 1953); W. F. Ogburn and M. F. Nimkoff, *Technology and the Changing Family* (Boston: Houghton Mifflin Company, 1955); Ernest R. Mowrer, *Family Disorganiza-tion: An Introduction to a Sociological Analysis* (Chicago: University of Chicago Press, 1927).

precise degree of "universality" that exists. With respect to the association between the urban-industrial complex and the family, "negative findings" have begun to accrue and attacks have been launched on the formulation just outlined.[23] These findings tend to show that the isolated nuclear family sometimes antedates urbanization and industrialization and that various kinds of extended family structures persist into urban-industrial development. While such findings are valuable, the research does little to specify, in a systematic way, any new conditions by which we can account for differences in the relations between urban-industrial variables and family structure. This limitation stems, I submit, from an exaggerated preoccupation with the empirical universality—or lack of it—of the association.

Second, if a sociocultural occurrence or association is to be described as genuinely universal, its characterization may have to be so general as to compress many important sources of variation into very global concepts, Certainly the variables of industrialization and urbanization should be separated from one another at the very outset for purposes of assessing their impact on the family. Furthermore, neither urbanization nor industrialization constitutes an irreducible whole; several subtypes of each should be identified before any adequate statement of the relations between each and the family can be formulated. In addition, the "isolation of the nuclear family" is not a single entity; it also displays a variation that demands classification and separate description of subtypes. If we introduce these kinds of complexity in relating the variables—though limiting the subclassifications on both sides to avoid falling into mere historical description—we are in a more advantageous position for establishing the specific conditions under which urban and industrial variables will influence family variables than if we remain at the level of highly nonspecific universals. Of course, to refine variables in this way means to sacrifice some "universals" and "invariants" in the meantime, but in this case I consider the sacrifice to be an advantage for the program of comparative analysis.

---

[23] For example, Gideon Sjoberg, "Family Organization in the Pre-industrial City," *Marriage and Family Living*, XVIII (1956), 30–36; John Mogey, "Introduction" to "Changes in the Family," *International Social Science Journal*, XIV (1962), 417; Eugene Litwak, "Occupational Mobility and Family Cohesion," and "Geographic Mobility and Extended Family Cohesion," *American Sociological Review*, XXV (1960), 9–21 and 385–94; Sidney M. Greenfield, "Industrialization and the Family in Sociological Theory," *American Journal of Sociology*, LXVII (1961–62), 312–22. See also the brief but informative discussion by William J. Goode, in *The Family* (Englewood Cliffs, N.J.: Prentice-Hall, Inc., 1964), pp. 108–16.

FOUR: Sociological History:

The Industrial Revolution and

the British Working-Class Family *

In this essay I am constrained to pursue two objectives. The first is to explore some of the general relations between sociological and historical analysis—how these are similar, how they are different, and how they might contribute something to one another. This objective raises many philosophical and methodological problems. The second objective, more empirical (it does not matter whether we call it sociological or historical for the moment), is to give an account of the causes, character, and consequences of the changes in working-class family life in Great Britain during the Industrial Revolution.

Each objective is important, and it is tempting to discuss them separately because there is a scholarly literature on each issue. There exists, on the one hand, a vast literature on the history of the working classes and their condition of life; much of this literature does not deal directly with the family, but those sources on child and female labor involve the family. There exists, on the other hand, a great proliferation of discussions on the general relations between history and sociology.[1] The first type of literature is interesting and provocative, but I shall resist the temptation to discuss the historical issues directly, if for no other reason than that as a sociologist I would like to do something more than dwell on things historians know more about than I. I shall also refrain from

* Revised version of a paper delivered at the annual meetings of American Sociological Association, Los Angeles, August 1963; and at the Pacific Coast Meetings of the American Historical Association, San Francisco, August 1963. The paper appeared in *The Journal of Social History,* I (1967), pp. 18–35.

[1] For a brief commentary on the general relations between the two disciplines, see above, pp. 34–37.

adding my bit on the general relations between sociology and history for several reasons. First, I am not sufficiently conversant with the literature of the philosophy of history. Second, that part of the literature I do know runs the danger of drifting into uninformative abstractions, and I have no good reason to believe that my own ideas would not meet the same fate. Finally, I believe that so great is the variety of activities that go under the name "sociological analysis" (and the same is probably true of what is called "historical analysis") that any general attempt to relate them to one another would have to be couched in so many qualifications that the statements would lose general interest.

What I shall try to do is to bring the two traditions of scholarship I have outlined into some new relation. I shall proceed by examining a few general problems that arose in my own attempt to apply sociological theory to history. I shall thus avoid "straight" history and explicit and methodological discussion of the relations between sociology and history. I shall discuss some general issues, but hopefully only those that came alive in conducting actual research that involved applying a theoretical model from sociology to a well-worked historical era. The results of my research have appeared in a book entitled *Social Change in the Industrial Revolution.*[2] I shall summarize parts of this work in this paper, but I shall try to focus more on general issues.

THE MODEL OF STRUCTURAL DIFFERENTIATION

The thing that set my research off most from what many historians do is that I approached the Industrial Revolution as a case illustration for an explicit, formal conceptual model drawn from the general tradition of sociological thought. Stated in very general terms, this model says that under certain conditions of social disequilibrium, the social structure will change in such a way that roles previously encompassing many different types of activities become more specialized; the social structure, that is, becomes more complex and differentiated. It was this abstract, analytic model—the details of which I shall spell out presently—that generated problems for me, not the period of the Industrial Revolution as such. I might well have chosen industrial change in another country and another period, or even an instance of rapid social change in which industrialization did not occupy a significant place.

The intellectual roots of the model of differentiation are very diverse. They can be located, for example, in Adam Smith's conceptions of the division of labor, Karl Marx's theory of the development of industrial capitalism, Herbert Spencer's principles of differentiation and integration,

² London: Routledge & Kegan Paul, Ltd., and Chicago: University of Chicago Press, 1959.

Emile Durkheim's theory of the social aspects of the division of labor, and, more recently, the work of Talcott Parsons and his associates on role differentiation and personality development.[3] In varying degree all these men were cognizant of the forces that went into the Industrial Revolution, and some of them have had something to say about this historical era. But it is important to note that many of the essential features of the model I used arose not from the analysis of the Industrial Revolution—indeed, not from the study of industrial change at all—but from the study of experimental small groups, learning, and personality adjustment, and so on.

I have implied that when posing questions sociologists and historians differ in that the former rely on models and the latter do not. This is not literally correct. The very act of posing a question about a historical period implies that the investigator—whether he be sociologist or historian—regards a certain range of facts as more relevant to his purposes than other facts. It follows from this that all historical analysis is bound to be selective. Moreover, the manner in which the investigator poses his question reveals that he brings to history certain preoccupations, hunches, hypotheses, and general notions about human conduct, however implicit these might be. Historical selectivity, viewed in this way, emerges as an essential ingredient of all historical analysis, necessary if we are to avoid writing about all aspects of all historical facts at once. A model formalizes this selectivity. As a conceptual apparatus, it states that if a given number of conditions are combined in a certain way, a definite historical outcome is to be expected. It makes as explicit as possible the exact dimensions of the historical problem, the explanations, and the underlying assumptions. In the light of these considerations, it is more nearly correct to say that both sociologists and historians employ models in their interpretations of history, but that they differ in the degree to which these are made formal and explicit.

What is the character of the model of structural differentiation? As indicated, its most general feature rests on the well known sociological principle that as a society develops, its social structure becomes more complex. This perspective is contained in Adam Smith's famous formulation that as an economy grows its division of labor increases in complexity. This principle is clear enough in the case of the economic division of labor. But as a general sociologist I was operating with an extended formulation, namely, that rapid social development involves the same

[3] The relevant works are Adam Smith, *Inquiry into the Nature and Causes of the Wealth of Nations* (1776); Karl Marx, *Capital* (1867); Herbert Spencer, *The Principles of Sociology* (1876); Emile Durkheim, *The Division of Labor in Society* (1893); Talcott Parsons, Robert F. Bales, *et al.*, *Family, Socialization and Interaction Process* (New York: The Free Press of Glencoe, Inc., 1955).

increasing complexity of structure in other institutions as well—in education, religion, politics, the family, and so on. For example, in the preindustrial family of a craftsman, the parents themselves are responsible for teaching the child minimum occupational skills, as well as for his emotional molding during his early years. When a growing economy places demands for greater literacy and more technical skills, the pressure is for this multifunctional family to give way to a new, more complex set of social arrangements. Structurally distinct educational institutions appear, and the family begins to surrender some of its previous training functions to these new institutions; having lost these functions, accordingly, the family becomes more specialized, focusing relatively more on emotional conditioning in the early childhood years and relatively less on its former economic and educational functions. This process of increasing specialization is called *structural differentiation.*

Another feature of the model is that differentiation does not happen automatically. It occasions a great deal of pain and dislocation for people, and it destroys many traditions that are likely to be held sacred; consequently it brings on a flurry of protest, uncertainty, groping, and experimentation before new, more differentiated units actually appear. Differentiation therefore produces conflict and social disorganization, which is likely to jeopardize social stability.

The model has been broken into a formal seven-step sequence which recapitulates analytically the process of structural differentiation:

Step 1 Dissatisfaction with the performance of incumbents of an institutionalized role, or with the organization of the role itself. In the economic sphere an example would be dissatisfaction with the level of profits, or with inefficiencies in a marketing system. In the family sphere an example would be dissatisfaction with a family's inability to earn a living wage in a particular occupational endeavor.

Step 2 Symptoms of disturbance reflecting this dissatisfaction, which are manifested in expressions of anxiety, hostility, and fantasy. For those sectors of society under pressure to change there is a sense of threatened loss or decay, perhaps generalized into prophecies of gloom. A great deal of scapegoating and conflict between agents of change and traditional and vested interests are also found in this stage. Finally, in the face of dissatisfactions, tendencies to glorify the past or build utopian visions of the future also flourish. Sometimes these symptoms of disturbance congeal into an ideology, in the name of which one or more social movements arise.

Step 3 Handling and channeling the symptoms of disturbance. This step is a first-line response to the disturbances just outlined. The agencies of social control—the police, the courts, the press, community leaders, etc. —are activated, in an effort to prevent the symptoms of disturbance from running to excess and threatening social stability. These handling and channeling processes constitute a holding operation before any structural change actually occurs.

Step 4 Encouragement of new ideas to deal with the supposed sources of dissatisfaction. Here the energy unleashed in the expression of symptoms of disturbance begins to be turned more in the direction of positive change. This is the stage of investigating what cultural resources might be brought to bear on the sources of dissatisfaction.

Step 5 Attempts to specify institutional forms that will ease the supposed sources of dissatisfaction. Here the process of change moves from the general to the specific, from ideas and notions to concrete proposals for innovation. In the economic sphere this might involve the proposal to reorganize labor around a new invention. In the social sphere it might involve the entertainment of legislation to ease a social problem.

Step 6 Attempts to establish new institutional forms. Here the "innovator" takes over from the "inventor"; and here the new, differentiated element of social structure makes its appearance. Attempts are now made to implement the ideas and suggestions of the previous two steps. In the economic sphere, the entrepreneur sets up new firms and thus meets the test of the market. In another sphere the legislature actually passes laws and thus meets the test of public support. In this step, successful innovations are greeted with an extraordinary burst of rewards—for example, huge profits or public goodwill.

Step 7 The new institutional forms are consolidated as permanent features of the social structure.

The general consequence of a large number of interrelated sequences of differentiation just outlined is a vast social upheaval, resulting in the emergence of a much more complex, specialized organization of the social structure. The purpose of the model is to permit the investigator of a historical period in flux to disentangle and analyze the many separate social processes that are proceeding apace.

What is the methodological status of this model? First, it is an abstract heuristic device rather than a simple empirical generalization. It may be likened to the economists' supply-demand scheme for a perfectly competitive market—a theoretical construct which is seldom if ever found in pure form empirically, but which permits us to interpret a wide variety of empirical situations. Second, it is a middle-range theory of change rather than a grand theoretical account of the history of a whole civilization. While resting on Spencer's notion of differentiation, for instance, the model lacks the concomitant of Spencer's theory—the notion that the overall direction of multiple processes of differentiation is from a military to an industrial society. The model of structural differentiation does not involve any specific claims as to a particular type of society as a point of beginning or a particular type of society as a point of termination. It is thus an "open-ended" model. Third, the model of structural differentiation is not a single-factor theory of change. Rather, it is a combination of a large number of assertions and assumptions about the relations among social phenomena (many of which do not hold universally but which are useful for purposes of analysis). The utility of this model, to repeat, is to unravel and analyze the bewildering tangle of happenings that present themselves in periods of rapid social change.

What are some of the assumptions on which the model is based? A central assumption is that, as a matter of psychological fact, people come to be disturbed about inadequate performance in roles; another assertion is that the initial manifestation of this disturbance is anxiety, anger, and fantasy. Both of these assertions, while widely applicable empirically, are certainly questionable as psychological universals. Another assumption is that the social control operations referred to in Step 3 will always "work," and that symptoms of disturbance—tendencies to violence, social movements, perhaps even threats to political legitimacy—will in fact be contained. Empirically this is a very questionable assumption; the frequency of violent outbursts and successful revolutionary movements in human history testifies to its limitations. Yet still we retain the assumption. Why? Because in the analysis of complex processes of change it is necessary to employ convenient fictions as working assumptions to simplify the multiplicity of sources of historical variation. If the convenient fictions become too fictional, of course, they lose their convenience, for they cease to apply to *any* historical situation. Furthermore, the convenient fiction (e.g., the success of social control operations) may be useful in one historical setting (e.g., parliamentary Britain) but not in another (e.g., parliamentary Iraq). Yet as I hope to indicate later, we may capitalize on this limitation. For purposes of more extensive comparative historical analysis, we may relax these rigid, limited, but workable assumptions and allow them to become a source of variation; and then we can ask, for instance, what happens when social control breaks down in different ways.

THE APPLICATION OF THE MODEL TO THE INDUSTRIAL REVOLUTION

Up to this point I have depicted the many relations that compose the model of structural differentiation in completely general terms, without reference to any definite historical period or problem. This is an important thing to do, but it constitutes only half the job of sociological history. At this analytic level, the model may be criticized logically in terms of its consistency; it may be assessed aesthetically in terms of its elegance or simplicity; and it may be viewed in terms of its imaginativeness or originality. But its utility for interpreting history is unknown. To determine this utility, the investigator must turn to the laborious tasks of historical analysis. He must translate the general concepts and relations into historically specific terms. He must track down the best historical sources to ascertain the degree to which the hypothesized connections among events hold. He must render as careful and objective a judgment as possible on whether the historical record lends support to the relations posited in the model. And if history proves embarrassing by not conforming to the model sequences, he must be prepared to return to the model and modify it in the light of his researches.

In bringing the model of structural differentiation to the Industrial Revolution, I proceeded by attempting to ascertain the degree to which the general relations of the model were replicated in many different institutional contexts. The two major spheres of application were the changes occurring in the industrial sector of society and those occurring in the family life of workers employed in industry. To make my application manageable, I chose the cotton textile industry, the leader in the British Industrial Revolution. On the industrial side, I analyzed the organizational changes in domestic and factory industry arising from the introduction of the various inventions—the jenny, the water-frame, the mule, the steam engine, and the power loom. For each I traced the course of indices such as economic organization, profits, capital investment, prices, and so on, as data to assess the workability of the model. On the family side, I traced the changes in family structure of workers in the cotton industry. In addition I applied the model to changes in other structures that were intimately tied to the family's security—friendly societies, trade unions, savings banks, and cooperative societies. I shall now summarize the application of the model to the changing structure of family life between 1770 and 1840, with particular reference to the "factory question," the agitation to limit hours, and factory legislation.

It is widely accepted that the sources of pressure on the family of the working classes lay in the demands imposed by the new urban, industrial environment of the late eighteenth and early nineteenth centuries. Yet this environment did not exert its pressure very early in the Industrial Revolution; nor did it exert its pressure in the ways commonly supposed. In fact, it appears that the traditional British working-class family survived the first fifty years of the Industrial Revolution quite remarkably intact and without much protest. Yet these were the gloomiest years from the standpoint of wages, hours, and working conditions. It was only when the industrial and urban changes began to affect the traditional relations *within* the family that really furious protest and disturbance began. Let me elaborate these points.

The typical pre-industrial textile family was an economic unit. The father normally was a weaver and he was assisted by his older sons, whom he apprenticed to the trade. The mother spun on the distaff or spinning wheel; she was assisted by the younger children, and she taught her daughters how to spin. The father was the main breadwinner, the wife and children auxiliary workers.

Between 1770 and 1790 the major technological innovations in the cotton industry were the spinning jenny and the water-frame. The jenny was initially installed in the home and run by an adult male, with the wife and children occupying subsidiary roles. The jenny raised the wage level of the family, but it did not disturb the traditional relations among its members. For the water-frame, which was set up in manufactories instead of homes, a different set of family arrangements evolved. According to the very limited information that is available, masters preferred to hire whole families as units—and actually did so—because of their more reliable work habits. Another adaptation was to set up cottages near the manufactory and put out cotton to be worked up in the home, where domestic duties kept adult women. As indicated, some of the child labor in the manufactories was supervised by parents; in addition, however, the water-frame manufactories made widespread use of parish apprentices, or children without any family, who were shipped from workhouse to manufactory to work. With the exception of parish apprentices, then, the historical record shows that the initial phase of the Industrial Revolution did not seriously alter the traditional relations between family members.

Between 1790 and 1820 a number of sweeping changes came over the cotton industry. The mule thoroughly displaced the jenny and surpassed the water-frame in production. When yoked to steam, moreover, the machines moved from mills on country streams into factories in the crowded centers of population, especially Manchester and Salford and the surrounding towns. In these decades the factories came to approximate their modern form. Yet when we examine the internal structure of the factory, we find a tenacity of the traditional family patterns. Typically the skilled spinner was allowed by the master to hire his own assistants (two or three in number in these years), and typically he hired his wife, children, or nephews, and apprenticed sons and nephews to the trade. Most of the trade union regulations of the day *required* that he restrict his apprentices to these relatives. So within the anonymous city and the impersonal factory an anchor of tradition persisted; and the working-class family, at least in this sector of industry, was not under pressure to relinquish a significant portion of its traditional functions of apprenticeship and economic cooperation.

In the middle 1820s and 1830s a number of historical trends continued and a number of new developments materialized. The centralization of industry in urban Lancashire, the concentration of population in this county, and the increase in size of the factories all proceeded apace. From the standpoint of immediate pressures on the family, however, two technological changes were apparently of much greater consequence. One was in spinning, the other in weaving. In spinning the 1820s brought a much larger and more productive variety of mule. This meant lower piece-rates but higher weekly wages for spinners; it also meant a possibility of technological unemployment because of the larger mules' greater productivity, even though the industry as a whole was continuing to expand. In addition, the larger mules called for a multiplication of assistants to the spinner. Whereas in the period between 1810 and 1820 two or three assistants per spinner were required, estimates in the early 1830s ranged from four to nine per spinner. This development immediately undermined the family-apprentice system, for a spinner would seldom have enough children of his own to fill these positions. He was forced to let in outsiders. Furthermore, the multiplication of assistants threatened in the long run to glut the market with too many skilled spinners.

The advent of the power loom aggravated these threats. For the handloom weaving family—already in a sick trade by the 1820s—the power loom brought new hardships. The advance of the power loom was most dramatic in the late 1820s and early 1830s. It drove down weavers' wages even more, and increased the pressure on weavers to send their children into the factories. But in the power-loom factories the team necessary to man the looms did not permit parental supervision of children at work. From all sides in the late 1820s, then, the pressures were to split the parent from his child, both on the factory premises and in the surviving domestic industries. It was in these years, 1825–1835, that the question of child labor became critical, not because of any deterioration in the hours and working conditions for children (indeed, these aspects appear to have been improving in that decade) but because the social environment of the child was changing.

So much for the pressures on the family life of the factory workers in the Industrial Revolution. What can now be said about the timing and content of the symptoms of disturbance arising from these circumstances?

In the first fifty years of the Industrial Revolution, 1770–1820, there were many manifestations of protest among the working classes in the textile industry. Yet most of these came from representatives of the pre-industrial order, especially hand-spinners and hand-loom weavers. In the last three decades of the eighteenth century, the new machines in the mills and manufactories were periodically attacked; the most serious outburst was the wholesale destruction of machinery in Lancashire in 1779. In all these cases the opposition came from domestic workers and was directed toward factory machinery. The hand-loom weavers participated in a long parade of disturbances beginning with petitions for support in the 1790s and ending with their active involvement in the violent aspects of the Chartist movement in the 1840s. Their history in this half-century is one of alternatively appealing for assistance, bursting into violence, embracing a variety of utopian schemes, and failing in sporadic attempts to organize into trade unions.

The new factory proletariat presents a study in contrast with the surviving domestic workers. Between 1770 and 1800 the factory workers were almost completely quiescent. Between 1800 and 1820 they engaged in a number of strikes, but these were mainly for higher wages in periods of brisk trade. As far as can be ascertained, the factory operatives were almost entirely passive with respect to the factory legislation of 1802 and 1819. Furthermore, according to the best available records, factory operatives were scarcely involved in the Luddite disturbances and played a secondary role in the popular disturbances between 1816 and 1819. According to the thesis here offered, the quiescence of the factory operatives is traceable to the persistence of certain fundamental family relations in the factory setting. In many ways their lot was hard and their adjustments many; but these family traditions were being preserved. The pressures on the surviving domestic workers, by contrast, were to abandon a total traditional way of life.

In the 1820s, however, the factory operatives were drawn into massive protest against the progress of the Industrial Revolution for the first time. Beginning about 1820, increasing in intensity through the 1820s, and culminating in the gigantic outburst in Ashton-under-Lyne in 1830–31, the Lancashire spinners launched one strike after another against the enlarged mules and their accompanying piece-rate reductions. Most of these strikes failed. The records of the Lancashire trade unions in this decade show the spinners' increasing apprehension over the apprenticeship problem. It is my interpretation that these strikes and the other efforts of the unions were aimed at halting the flood of children into the industry, at guarding against threatened technological unemployment, and at protecting the traditional economic relationship between parent and child.

This interpretation is strengthened by examining the factory operatives' role in the agitation to limit hours of labor in the cotton industry. As indicated, they were quite passive on this question in the first several decades of the nineteenth century. But toward the end of the period of unsuccessful strikes against the enlarged mules, the factory workers became embroiled in the factory agitation. This agitation reached explosive proportions between 1831 and 1833. The factory movement was accompanied by many extravagant claims concerning the effects of machinery and the factory on the health of the children, the morals of the factory population, and so on. But if we examine the more immediate aims and behavior of the factory operatives in this agitation and after the Factory Act of 1833, it becomes apparent that their objectives were very similar to what they had been in the strikes against improved machinery in the 1820s—to halt the flood of children into the industry, and to continue the link between parent and child. Let me illustrate.

Between 1831 and 1833 the factory operatives insisted on a ten-hour day for children, knowing that this would probably mean a ten-hour day for adults as well. They apparently wished to reduce their own hours and maintain the link between the labor of children and adults. In fact, when the Factory Act of 1833 was passed, limiting children's hours to eight and suggesting a relay system for young children, the operatives were not satisfied. In fact, Nassau Senior commented after the passage of this Act that the operatives were "far more vehement for a ten hours' bill [for all labor] than before." [4] Their further agitation, *after* factory legislation had been passed, makes sense according to the present interpretation. For, indeed, the Factory Act of 1833, with its relay system and its eight-hour limitation, worked to further weaken the link between parents' and children's labor (a tendency already set in motion by the enlarged mules). In short, the pressures to differentiate the economic aspects from the other aspects of family life were augmented by the Factory Act of 1833.

What form did the operatives' agitation take after 1833? In late 1833 some factory operatives formed a furtive little movement called the Society for National Regeneration, one objective of which was to call for a universal eight-hour day. This movement failed after several months of existence, terminated by a feeble strike. Then, in 1835, factory operatives began to hold meetings throughout Lancashire to call for a universal twelve-hour day, which would extend the hours of children, who had been limited to eight hours for several years. And again in 1837 the workers agitated for a universal ten-hour day, including ten hours for children. These last two agitations embarrassed the supporters of factory legislation in Parliament, for it appeared that the workers themselves were indifferent to the length of the children's working day and to their health and morals. Finally, between 1833 and 1837, despite the efforts of the government, it was apparent that both masters and operatives were willing to evade the Factory Act of 1833 by working children more than eight hours. All these signs point toward a strong desire on the part of the operatives to maintain the traditional link between parent and child on the factory premises.

We have now covered the first steps of the process of differentiation —pressures on the family generating dissatisfactions and symptoms of

[4] Nassau Senior, *Letters on the Factory Act as It Affects the Cotton Manufacture* (London: B. Fellowes, 1837), p. 19.

disturbance arising from these pressures. The remainder of the sequence of structural differentiation is found in the history of the factory legislation itself. In the period of explosive agitation for the Ten Hour Day (1831–33), the demonstrations, petitions, and the rest were permitted but contained by the authorities. And before long, the government moved to establish investigatory machinery to inquire into the factory question. The Sadler Committee of 1832, and its supersession by the Factory Commission of 1833, mark the attempts of the government to ascertain the facts of the factory question, to entertain suggestions and recommendations, and to make its proposals for action to Parliament. These parliamentary activities constitute Steps 4 and 5 of the sequence of differentiation—entertainment of ideas and suggestions for implementation.

With the Factory Act of 1833 Parliament opted in favor of pushing the family toward the future. By splitting the hours of child labor from those of adults, they augmented the pressures already being exerted by the technological improvements. In addition, the Commission recommended and Parliament adopted an educational provision—that the factories provide schools for children for several hours a day while adults presumably continued at work. This educational provision also marked a line of structural differentiation—to give a rudimentary schooling to children meant that some of the training responsibilities of the undifferentiated family were being turned over to a separate social organization.

Yet even though the Factory Act of 1833 completed, as it were, a number of pressures toward structural differentiation, the story of factory legislation was not yet finished. A number of separate forces had come to bear on the family in the 1820s and 1830s, all of which operated to remove some of its economic and training functions from it. These forces were in the technological advances of the spinning and weaving branches, the impact of these changes on the domestic hand-loom weaving population, and the legislative enactment of Parliament in 1833. Yet the success of these forces, success evident already by 1833, posed a new, serious problem for the family: if the link between parent and child on the factory premises was broken, *and* if masters still insisted on working adults the full twelve-hour day, what then became of the family? So long as many "domestic" functions such as discipline and even some recreation and play could be carried out in the factory, the length of the working day was not so critical from the standpoint of performing the various family functions. But if the children were to be separated from the parents during the working day, the home took on a new significance. This need to reconstitute the family in the home, once it was broken up in the factory, lay behind the pressures to reduce the hours of all labor and establish the "normal working day" for adults during the fifteen years following 1833. The final factory legislation of the late 1840s and early

1850s, establishing the ten-hour day, then, completed the differentiation of the working-class family—involving a clearer split between home and factory, a split between the economic and other aspects of the parent-child relationship, and a surrender of some of the family's training functions to an embryonic educational system.

SOME METHODOLOGICAL PROBLEMS

Such, in brief outline, is my account of the major events surrounding the changing structure of the family life of the cotton operatives during the first few generations of the Industrial Revolution. To conclude, I should like first to mention a few specific methodological problems that arise in applying the model of differentiation and second to raise the more general question of how necessary or helpful it is to use a formal model in interpreting history.

One methodological problem concerns the difficult task of deciding when an historical fact is an "instance" of one of the general categories of the model. For example, in applying the model to industrial growth, I classified entrepreneurial decisions as an instance of institutional innovation; in applying it to the changing structure of the family I classified certain acts of Parliament—such as the Factory Acts—as instances of institutional innovation; in applying it to the rise of new forms of trade unions I took the passage of union regulations as an instance of institutional innovation. The question that the investigator must face in these kinds of operations is the following: By what criterion are these three historical events—an entrepreneurial decision, an act of the legislature, and an enactment of a union regulation—assigned to the same general category? My answer in this case was that each involves a commitment of resources to a selected line of social action. But even this criterion is a bit vague, and in the case of other general categories, the criteria for moving from general concepts to historical events are even less satisfactory. I might add, however, that this particular methodological problem is not limited to the application of theoretical models to history; it is a problem that arises, even though not always explicitly, every time an investigator—historian or sociologist—attempts to apply a generic term to historical events.

A second methodological problem concerns the location of appropriate historical data when bringing a relatively novel approach—such as structural differentiation—to history. In many cases the investigator asks questions for which there are no data; this is particularly true for questions about the family, an intimate institution for which records are not generally kept, especially in the working classes. In other cases the investigator must revisit primary sources that have already been combed over, since other investigators have not necessarily been sensitive to data that are brought into question by the novel approach. And in still other cases, the investigator is forced to reinterpret many secondary sources radically, since the questions he is asking are so different from those asked by writers of past accounts; such reinterpretation, it goes without saying, is a very risky practice.

A third and very important methodological problem concerns what to do when the theoretical model does not seem to work. Suppose, for instance, that the investigator discovers a clear instance of differentiation that develops without any accompanying symptoms of disturbance; in this case Steps 2 and 3 are skipped. Suppose, to take another example, Step 2 brings an array of disturbances that are not contained by the agencies of social control, but generalize into widespread social conflict, leading ultimately to a collapse of the governmental regime in the face of violent revolution. Here we have a case of something that begins like differentiation, but ends as something very different; clearly the model does not apply. The temptation of the investigator, enamoured as he is with his model, is to generate some *ad hoc* explanation every time the model does not appear to fit the facts. He can say that there were special historical circumstances at hand—for example, that the Napoleonic Wars influenced the process of change, or that the factory agitation was influenced by the simultaneous agitation to reform Parliament. However tempting it is to indulge in these asides, it is illegitimate from the standpoint of the application of theory to history. For if the investigator generates *ad hoc* explanations for all the exceptions, he is making an *appearance* of applying the model, but he is in actuality appealing to all kinds of extraneous, theoretically irrelevant factors to account for instances that are potentially embarrassing for the model.

I feel the presence of historical exceptions to a general theoretical model signalizes the need for further theoretical development. The investigator should admit his embarrassment but capitalize on it. When a process that looks very much as though it is starting out as an orderly process of differentiation suddenly turns into an uncontrolled disturbance, the theoretically interesting question is the following: Given the apparent fact that the process of differentiation and the development of uncontrolled disturbance have some but not all factors in common, what are the conditions that push the process toward one outcome or the other? By asking such a question the investigator is likely to end up with a second model. But so much the better. It is more difficult, but more profitable, to build systematic accounts of exceptions than to explain each one away as it arises.

WHY APPLY A MODEL?

In closing, let me ask a few rude questions of myself. Was it necessary to use a general model for this study of labor history? Assuming for the moment that the study has some merit as a piece of historical analysis, could not the same connections have been traced by an historian without benefit of the model? If so, what are the gains, if any, that accrue from approaching history in the theoretically self-conscious way I did? These questions raise the problem of the general utility of formal, explicit models in interpreting history.

It is true that it is not essential to have a model to arrive at the empirical conclusions I did about the Industrial Revolution. A social historian, proceeding inductively and without the model of structural differentiation, might well have made similar assertions about the causes of factory agitation. His conclusions might not have been shrouded in such general terms as mine, but the content would have been the same. Any advantages that arise from applying this model—or any model—to history must be other than that a sociologist with a model can discover historical truths that an historian without one cannot. What, then, are the advantages?

A first advantage is specific to social history, and, within that, specific to the problem of explaining the content and timing of social disturbances such as violent outbursts and social movements. My impression of the work of social historians is that as a rule their explanations of these kinds of events often rest on oversimple causal assumptions—for example that economic misery or political repression alone will provoke such disturbances. For a variety of reasons such explanations are inadequate.[5] The model of structural differentiation, while acknowledging the role of these factors, incorporates them into a systematically organized framework containing other social variables. It is my conviction that the model of differentiation offers a superior explanation. But above and beyond this assertion—the validity of which can be established only on the basis of theoretical debate and empirical research—it is true that the model of differentiation introduces a number of determinants of social disturbances that have hitherto been relatively neglected by social historians. The first advantage of using a generalized model, then, is that it is likely to suggest new causal connections among historical events.

A second advantage, alluded to earlier, concerns the discipline that a formal model imposes on historical explanation. If an historical investigator is operating within a very loose and implicit interpretative framework, it is a simple matter for him to introduce new factors and explana-

[5] See *Social Change in the Industrial Revolution*, Chapter 14.

tions on an *ad hoc* basis when the main interpretative thrust appears to be losing its force. Insofar as this is done, historical analysis is weakened. If the investigator is operating with a definite model, he, too, may engage in subtly smuggling in factors and explanations that are not part of the model. But insofar as his model is formal and explicit, it is much easier to identify the lax eclecticism that arises from relying on *ad hoc* explanations as the occasion demands.

A third advantage of framing historical explanations within a general model appears when we wish to consider comparative cases. If we restrict our interest to British society in the late eighteenth and early nineteenth century, there is no advantage in using a language more general than that necessary to describe events in that setting. However, if we wish to trace the impact of industrial change more generally—in France, the United States and India, for example—it is necessary to employ categories general enough to encompass phenomena in highly diverse social settings. The use of a general model to interpret a specific historical case, then, facilitates systematic comparisons with other cases.

Finally, using an abstract model to account for specific historical changes permits the investigator to relate his results more readily to other types of knowledge. As I indicated, the model of structural differentiation has its roots partly in the study of institutional change, partly in experimental small group research, and partly in the study of personality changes. To frame the model in sufficiently general terms that it can be applied to these diverse settings allows the relations among phenomena in one setting to be translated into analogous relations in other settings. These various relations are confirmed or rejected, of course, not by analogy but by independent empirical investigations in each setting. But the presence of a model does facilitate the exchange and generalization of different kinds of empirical knowledge.

FIVE: Social and Psychological Dimensions of Collective Behavior *

The subject of this essay is that class of phenomena commonly grouped under the label "collective behavior"—including panics, crazes, fads, riots, reform movements, revolutionary movements, and religious cults. My starting point is the commonplace observation that such behavior manifests both social and psychological characteristics. On the one hand it has a social dimension, since it involves collective or group action by definition, and since many of its causes are rooted in social conditions—conditions such as economic hardship, social disorganization, and political repression. On the other hand it has a psychological dimension, since the deepest and most powerful human emotions—idealistic fervor, love, and violent rage, for example—are bared in episodes of collective behavior, and since persons differ psychologically in their propensity to become involved in such episodes.

Moreover, most theories that attempt to explain why people participate in collective outbursts and collective movements stress either the social or the psychological aspect more or less exclusively, frequently relegating the other, underemphasized aspect to the realm of implicit assumptions. For example, Karl Marx regarded political revolutions as resulting primarily from a particular convergence of economic and social forces at a given stage in the evolution of a society; accordingly, the revolutionaries' psychology was not very important for Marx, since it, like the revolution itself, is a product of overwhelming laws of social develop-

* This essay has not been published before. An earlier version was presented to the Ad Hoc Research Committee of the San Francisco Psychoanalytic Institute in January 1966.

92

ment.[1] By contrast, Willfred Trotter traced human involvement in crowds and related groupings to the workings of powerful, universal instincts;[2] he touched only incidentally on socially determinants of this involvement. Very few if any theorists, however, have attempted to develop an explanatory account that synthesizes the social and psychological causes of collective behavior. In this essay I shall explore the possibility of such a synthesis, emphasizing the psychoanalytic approach on the psychological side.

I shall proceed by the following steps. First, I shall specify the differences between explanations on the social level and explanations on the psychological level. Second, I shall present an example of each type of explanation and attempt to locate the distinctive shortcomings of each. As an instance of explicitly sociological explanation I shall outline the results of my own research on collective behavior.[3] As an instance of an explicitly psychological explanation I shall review Freud's essay on group psychology.[4] Third, I shall specify some of the theoretical and empirical problems that arise when attempting to synthesize these two approaches. Finally, as a more specific illustration, I shall outline the general characteristics of protest movements—first in terms of their typical social aims, then in terms of their probable psychoanalytic significance—and illustrate how social and psychological determinants may interact to give rise to and sustain such movements.

THE PSYCHOLOGICAL AND SOCIAL LEVELS OF ANALYSIS [5]

The study of psychological systems focuses on the individual as the unit of analysis, regarding him as a system of drives, affects, skills, defenses, and so on.[6] In this case the organizing conceptual unit is the person. The study of social systems focuses on certain relations that emerge when

---

[1] In speaking of the political reforms that led to the shortening of the working day in the nineteenth century, Marx said: "[The reform] developed gradually out of circumstances as natural laws of the modern mode of production. Their formulation, official recognition, and proclamation by the State, were the result of a long struggle of classes." Karl Marx, *Capital*, trans. Samuel Moore and Edward Aveling, ed. Frederick Engels (London: George Allen & Unwin, 1949), p. 269. For a brief account of Marx's theory of revolutionary convulsions, see below, pp. 254–57.

[2] Willfred Trotter, *Instincts of the Herd in Peace and War* (London: T. Fisher Unwin, 1922).

[3] *Theory of Collective Behavior* (New York: The Free Press of Glencoe, Inc., 1963).

[4] Sigmund Freud, "Group Psychology and the Analysis of the Ego," *Standard Edition* (London: The Hogarth Press and the Institute of Psycho-Analysis), XVIII, 65–143.

[5] Portions of the next few pages are drawn from the Introduction to *Personality and Social Systems*, ed. by Neil J. Smelser and William T. Smelser (New York: John Wiley & Sons, Inc., 1963), pp. 1–18.

[6] Above, pp. 38–39.

two or more persons interact with one another.[7] In this case the organizing conceptual unit is the relation itself.

Ultimately, the study of both psychological and social systems is based on inferences from a common body of behavioral data. The investigator of human affairs is confronted with a complex variety of phenomena: verbal and nonverbal communications, expressive movements, physiological states, and interactions of various sorts. To organize these at the *psychological* level, he infers or posits that more or less repeated patterns of behavior—e.g., restlessness, searching, eating, quiescence—can be characterized as signifying a "need" or "drive" for the person. It is convenient to use this term to describe the person's activities, because it organizes many discrete items of behavior under one construct. In addition, the investigator may generate constructs about "attitudes," "defense mechanisms," and so on. To facilitate analysis further, he may posit certain relations among such constructs, and the result is a "psychological system." [8] Thereafter, any behavioral datum interpreted in terms of this system of constructs is significant at the "psychological level."

Similarly, to make sense of behavior at the *social* level, the investigator infers that certain more or less repeated events—performances, interactions, expressions of sentiments, attempts of one person to influence another—can be characterized as signifying a "role," and, depending on the environmental context, roles may be subdivided as political, economic, religious, familial, and so on. A general term such as role simplifies the process of describing thousands of discrete events separately. Constructs such as "norm," "sanction," and "clique" also may be developed. Then, when several of these constructs are set in logical relation with one another, the result is a "social system." Thereafter, any datum interpreted in terms of this system of constructs is significant at the "social level."

Any given behavioral datum is inherently neither "psychological" nor "social"; indeed, the same event may be both, depending on the body of constructs within which it is interpreted. An outburst of anger on the job, for instance, may be "psychological" in the sense that it gives rise to recriminations of conscience and subsequent adaptations to these recriminations by the individual. The same outburst may also be "social" in the sense that it strains the social relations among employees in the office where it occurs. The status of a behavioral datum, then, is determined by the conceptual system to which it is referred for assessment and explanation.

Conceptually, these frames of reference—the psychological and the social—should be kept distinct. A description of a social system cannot be

---

[7] Above, pp. 47–48.

[8] Commonly referred to as a "personality system" when the total psychological system of the individual is involved.

reduced to the psychological states of the persons in that system; a social system must be described in terms of roles, norms, subgroups, and so on. Similarly, a description of a personality system cannot be reduced to the social involvements of the person; it must be described in terms of distinctive psychological units. Empirically, however, these two frames of reference articulate in many ways. A social role may integrate many of an individual's drives, skills, attitudes, and defenses; an individual's motivational predispositions determine in large part whether a system of roles (e.g., a network of friendship) will persist or not; a social role (for example, that of a parent) may be internalized to become part of a child's personality.

In seeking to explain any given type of behavior, both the psychological and social levels of analysis can be used as either dependent or independent variables. A dependent variable, defined briefly, is an identifiable empirical phenomenon or class of phenomena, variations in which we wish to explain.[9] Suppose we wish to explain variations in the incidence of suicide. This behavior may be described either in terms of its psychological motives to the individual victims [10] or in terms of its aggregated rates among different social groupings—for example, Protestants as compared with Catholics, young persons as compared with old persons—without reference to any personal meaning of suicide.[11] Because these illustrative descriptions of suicide are pitched at two different conceptual levels, it is apparent that the explanatory problems facing the investigator in each case are somewhat different.

Whether suicide as a dependent variable is described at the psychological or social level, however, the independent variables by means of which we try to account for this behavior lie at both the social and psychological levels. Suppose suicide is defined in terms of its psychological significance (for example, as the turning of anger upon an object that has been internalized through a process of narcissistic identification [12]); in seeking explanations for suicide, thus defined, it is appropriate to inquire what kind of family constellations (a social factor) give rise to this particular complex of self-destructive tendencies. Or suppose suicide is described in terms of its differential incidence between Negroes and whites; in seeking explanations for this social fact, it is appropriate to inquire into

[9] Above, p. 5.

[10] See, for example, Karl A. Menninger, *Man Against Himself* (New York: Harcourt, Brace & World, Inc., 1938).

[11] In his classic study, Emile Durkheim insisted on the importance of studying suicide rates as social facts, apart from any individual motivations that might give rise to self-destruction. *Suicide,* trans. John A. Spaulding and George Simpson (New York: The Free Press of Glencoe, Inc., 1951), pp. 46–53 and Part II.

[12] Sigmund Freud, "Mourning and Melancholia," *Standard Edition,* XIV, pp. 251–52.

the differential distribution of personality traits (for example, intropuni-tiveness) between the two groups that might account for the different rates. More complicated explanations call for some combination of social and psychological factors.[13] In accounting for the high suicide rates among members of certain Protestant denominations, for example, it might be discovered that the ascetic values of these denominations encourage so-cialization of children mainly by means of withdrawing love; this in turn would encourage the development of especially repressive superego structures, which would increase the propensity of individuals in this religious group to turn aggression inward. From these observations it beccmes apparent that a full explanatory account of any type of behavior must include a systematic combination and formulation of the principles of interaction between both social and psychological determinants.

Applying the two distinctions I have developed—psychological and social levels, and dependent and independent variables—to the subject of collective behavior, we may conclude the following: In describing the phenomena to be explained, it is possible to focus *either* on the psycho-logical significance of, say, riots and reform movements, for the partici-pants; or on the differential incidence of these kinds of episodes in various sectors of the social structure. But no matter at which level we choose to define the phenomena, it is apparent that a full explanatory account of this behavior will involve a synthesis of *both* social and psychological deter-minants.

SOCIAL FACTORS IN COLLECTIVE BEHAVIOR: AN EXAMPLE [14]

In my own research on collective behavior I relied on a primarily social definition. Collective behavior is defined as purposive, socially oriented activity by which people attempt to reconstitute their sociocul-tural environment.[15] Furthermore, people involved in episodes of col-lective behavior are trying to reconstitute this environment on the basis of a certain type of belief, which I call a generalized belief; in this kind

---

[13] For examples of recent attempts to combine social and psychological factors to explain differential suicide rates, see Andrew F. Henry and James F. Short, *Suicide and Homicide* (New York: The Free Press of Glencoe, Inc., 1954); and Herbert Hendin, *Suicide and Scandinavia* (New York: Grune & Stratton, 1964).

[14] The summary statement that follows is taken in part from my paper, "Theoreti-cal Issues of Scope and Problems of Collective Behavior and Conflict," *The Socio-logical Quarterly,* Vol. 5 (1964), pp. 116–122.

[15] This reconstitutive element is evident enough in reform and revolutionary movements, but it also characterizes less obvious forms such as the hostile outburst (in which behavior is directed toward harming or destroying some agent perceived as threatening) and the panic (in which behavior is directed toward withdrawing from a threatening situation).

of belief the environment is portrayed in terms of omnipotent forces, conspiracies, and extravagant promises, all of which are immanent. Uninstitutionalized action taken in the name of such a belief constitutes an episode of collective behavior. Even though generalized beliefs are involved, I focused on the social diffusion of these beliefs rather than their psychological significance for participants. I assumed that no special motive or mentality (such as psychological regression) necessarily characterizes the participants in episodes of collective behavior.[16]

Furthermore, the explanatory problem I set for myself was at the social level. I was interested primarily in why various types of collective episodes cluster in time and in certain parts of the social structure—for example, among adolescents, recent migrants, and unemployed people. This general question breaks down into several more specific issues: What distinctive conditions give rise to generalized beliefs? Under what conditions are generalized beliefs translated into collective action? Once collective episodes appear, what conditions govern their spread, duration, and intensity? These questions take the collective episode itself as the primary object of analysis. This focus differs from that of other approaches, which take the behavior of the individual participant (and his psychological state) as the primary phenomena to be explained.

In attempting to generate answers to these questions I remained mainly at the social level in identifying determinants. Even at this level, a great array of determinants bears on the occurrence of episodes of collective behavior. An intellectual apparatus is required to sort out and arrange these determinants, if one is to advance beyond eclectic identification of determinants from one case to another. The intellectual apparatus I chose to employ is the "value-added" approach. Applying this approach to the social determination of collective behavior, it provides a way of ordering its determinants on a scale from general to specific. Each determinant is seen as operating within the scope established by the prior, more general determinant. Each determinant is viewed as a necessary but not a sufficient condition for the occurrence of an episode of collective behavior; taken together, the necessary conditions constitute the sufficient condition for its occurrence.[17] Let me illustrate the several determinants of the value-added scheme with reference to the occurrence of financial panic.

The first necessary condition for the occurrence of panic is *structural conduciveness*. An example of structural conduciveness is the ability of actors to dispose of their resources rapidly at will. If property is closely tied to kinship and can be disposed of only on the death of the father,

---

[16] See *Theory of Collective Behavior*, Chapters 1, 4, and 5.
[17] For a longer summary of the value-added scheme, and an attempt to assess its theoretical significance, see below, pp. 210–11.

panic is ruled out as structurally impossible; the property is locked into the social structure and cannot be moved unless the institutional framework is altered. If, on the other hand, free and rapid disposal is permitted —as it is in the stock exchange—panic becomes possible. The word "possible" must be stressed; structural conduciveness alone does not cause panics; it merely establishes a range of situations within which panic can occur and rules out other situations in which it cannot. As a determinant, therefore, structural conduciveness is not very specific.

The second determinant is some kind of *strain*. The most obvious kind of strain in the determination of financial panic is the threat of financial loss. The threat of financial loss alone, however, can give rise to many other kinds of behavior than panic (scapegoating, reform movements, etc.); consequently this strain must be seen as operating within the context of conduciveness. It is not possible to see the logic by which the several determinants are organized; each time a new determinant is introduced, it is seen as operating within the scope of the previous determinant, and an increasingly great number of alternative behaviors are ruled out. The process of determination becomes progressively more specific.

The third necessary condition involves the growth of a *generalized belief*, in which the threat is exaggerated and seen to be imminent. The result, in the cause of panic, is a hysterical [18] belief—cognitive structuring of an uncertain threat into a definite prognostication of disaster. Various precipitating events (such as the closing of a bank) give focus to this belief, and provide "evidence" that the terrible threat is at work.

The fourth necessary condition is to *mobilize* people for action in the name of the generalized belief. In the case of the panic this may be realized by a single dramatic event, such as a rumor of a "panic sell" by a leading holder of securities. In more complicated social movements leadership may be more deliberate and highly organized.

Finally, it is necessary to mention *social control* as a determinant. In its more general sense, social control refers to the activation of counter-determinants for the conditions just listed. It is helpful, however, to distinguish between counter-determinants of a preventive sort (dealing with conduciveness and strain) and counter-determinants which appear only when the collective episode has made its appearance. In the case of panic, social control is effected, for instance, by spiking scare rumors or by actually preventing potential sellers from selling. This last measure is sometimes employed by governments attempting to stop an international flight of capital.

[18] I am using the word "hysterical" in its common sense meaning, not in its technical psychoanalytic meaning.

The value-added approach, in sum, is a logical patterning of social determinants, each contributing its "value" to the explanation of the episode. To round out the exposition of this approach, let me illustrate how three of these determinants—strain, conduciveness, and social control —operate with reference to quite a different kind of collective behavior, *viz.*, social movements that turn into violent revolutions.

The type of strain that can potentially give rise to revolutionary sentiment is so varied as to be bewildering—economic hardship, migrations of populations, defeat in war, religious persecution, value differences among different groups in the population, and so on.[19] If an investigator is interested in establishing a relation between a specific type of strain (e.g., economic depressions) and revolutionary movements, he will be able to illustrate his case extensively in the historical record, but he will also find that economic depressions give rise to many other kinds of behavior, and that endless other types of social strain give rise to revolutionary movements. In order to determine whether social strains will work their way into a revolutionary ideology or some other kind of behavior, it is necessary to turn to the variable of structural conduciveness.

The rise of many potentially revolutionary ideologies in the colonial countries during the first half of the twentieth century was preceded by a period in which the colonial powers "closed the door" on various kinds of protest against colonial domination. The colonial powers were relatively successful in "pacifying" the colonies—i.e., ruling out hostile outbursts— and they were relatively unresponsive to modest demands for institutional reform by the colonials. (The British provide an exception to this generalization in some of their colonies, e.g., Ceylon.) The history of many colonies before the appearance of aggressive nationalism is one of the colonial powers "reminding" the colonials, sometimes with force, that the colonial powers were both effective in imposing their will and inflexible in the face of demands for reform. It was in this context of closing off other alternatives—combined with a multiplicity of strains—that various nativistic and other ideological forerunners of revolutionary nationalism made their appearance in the colonies.

The appearance of a potentially revolutionary ideology, however, does not necessarily lead to an aggressive revolutionary outburst. Indeed, some of the ideological movements in the colonies experience a long existence either as underground groups harried by colonial authorities or as bizarre cults of withdrawal (the growth of the Peyote religion among the permanently repressed American Indians is perhaps the most striking example of the latter). The subsequent career of these potentially revolutionary

---

[19] For documentation, see *Theory of Collective Behavior,* pp. 338–47.

ideologies depends above all on the behavior of agencies of social control. If authorities continue to be effective in crushing opposition, unresponsive to demands, and repressive of expressions of revolutionary sentiment, the movement tends to drift toward the cult form. If, however, the agencies of control suddenly lose their effectiveness, the movement turns in an overtly revolutionary direction. It is not so much the nature of the ideology of the movement as the behavior of the authorities that determines this change of direction. The ineffectiveness of the authorities may take many forms—division among the ruling classes themselves, weakening through military defeat (the British and the Dutch defeats in Southeast Asia at the hands of the Japanese in World War II are examples), or the fraternization or defection of the rulers' military forces. In sum, then, we call upon separate combinations of determinants to account for the rise of a revolutionary ideology and its expression in revolutionary form. The rise of the ideology is accounted for mainly by a specific combination of strain and conduciveness, whereas its translation into action depends above all on the behavior of the agencies of social control.[20]

SOME SHORTCOMINGS OF THE SOCIOLOGICAL EXPLANATION

By examining different combinations of the several social determinants, it is possible to throw some light on why collective episodes cluster in time and in certain parts of the social structure. But this approach can be criticized as incomplete or erroneous, or both, on two grounds—first, that it offers an inadequate account of the social determinants themselves; and second, that it ignores, oversimplifies, distorts, or otherwise treats inadequately a number of psychological variables that must be taken into account to give a full explanation of episodes of collective behavior. Leaving the first line of criticism aside for the moment, I shall attempt to identify some of the implicit and perhaps questionable psychological assumptions upon which the social account is based.

First, the account rests on the unspoken assumption that the various social factors exert their influence on the individual human mind, indeed that they must be combined in the minds of participants in order to cause an episode of collective panic. The simultaneous existence of a stock market in New York City (structural conduciveness), the fear of economic loss on the part of the French peasants (strain), and the rumor of panicky selling of suburban real estate in Sydney, Australia (a precipitating event around which a hysterical belief crystallizes), surely will not cause a panic. These conditions must operate in roughly the same place, and in

---

[20] This principle is a very important one in accounting for the different directions taken in long-term processes of social change. Below, p. 278.

fact, must influence the same individuals, if panicky behavior is to occur.[21] So, at the very minimum, the apparently social account assumes that the external social conditions impinge on and are combined in individual minds.

Once this assumption is granted, a torrent of objections to the sociological account is unleashed. How can it be imagined, for example, that the social condition of being unemployed (strain) has the same impact on all individuals it affects? One person may experience unemployment as a minor crisis to be weathered until an opportunity for reemployment arises; another may experience it as a blow to his identity as a male; another may experience it as an occasion for rage at the economic system. If we ignore this diversity of psychological means of the same event for different individuals, we are guilty of presenting an unwarranted psychological generalization about human reactions to economic deprivation. Furthermore, if we hold to the implicit assertion that unemployment affects all equally, we discover ourselves in the questionable position of accepting the proposition that all unemployed people are predisposed to enter some episode of collective behavior if other social conditions are present. In short, the simple presentation of social factors, accompanied by the assumption that they affect everyone they touch equally, without independent psychological processing of these factors, yields little power to explain why some, not all, of those affected become participants. The social account alone is not very discriminating.

Even if a listing of social conditions could provide a degree of discrimination between participants and nonparticipants, it would do little to explain the different *types* of participation. Some participants become involved as leaders; others as activist followers; others as passive followers; others as sympathizers who do not actually engage in any overt behavior; and so on.[22] Reference to internal psychic structures and processes is necessary if we are to discriminate among individuals in terms of their thresholds for different kinds of involvement.

In some cases participation in an episode of collective behavior would appear to have little to do with social conditions at all. Certainly some of the generalized beliefs that enter collective outbursts—fear of entrapment as an ingredient of panic, a sense of religious mission as an ingredient of a religious cult, for example—exist as enduring psychological predispositions with little reference to the particular social environment of individuals. Indeed, it might be said that some individuals are more or less com-

[21] I am indebted to Roger Brown for making explicit this psychological assumption. See his *Social Psychology* (New York: The Free Press of Glencoe, Inc., 1965), pp. 731–33.

[22] See Roger Brown, "Mass Phenomenon," in Gardner Lindsey, ed., *Handbook of Social Psychology* (Cambridge: Addison-Wesley Publishing Company, 1954), II, 846–47.

pletely "programmed" psychologically to "act out" in collective episodes —certain types of phobic individuals in panics and certain types of border-line psychotic cases in bizarre religious cults, for example—and that what the social environment provides is an opportunity. A small religious cult in San Francisco, made up of several individuals from various parts of the country who have drifted into the metropolis and each of whom had a long experience of involvement in religious causes,[23] could scarcely be said to be the product of social conditions in San Francisco. Its most important determinants are to be found in the psychological life histories of the individual members.

In sum, any account of the recruitment into, the internal composition of, and the quality of participation in a collective episode must rest on a consideration of the psychological dynamics of the individual person. Furthermore, recruitment, composition, and quality of participation determine in part the content, timing, and social direction of the episode. It follows that any purely sociological account of collective behavior can offer only a limited explanation.

PSYCHOLOGICAL FACTORS IN COLLECTIVE BEHAVIOR: AN EXAMPLE

Freud's ambition in writing "Group Psychology and the Analysis of the Ego" was not to create a full-scale theory of collective behavior, but rather to raise "a few questions with which the depth-psychology of psycho-analysis is specially concerned."[24] His essay is sufficiently comprehensive, however, to merit treating it as a relatively coherent, distinctively psychological account of some aspects of collective behavior.

Freud distinguished between individual and social or group psychology, though he found the distinction to be an imprecise one. "Individual psychology," he wrote, "is concerned with the individual man and explores the paths by which he seeks to find satisfaction for his instinctual impulses."[25] Invariably, however, man's search for gratification involves social objects—parents, siblings, loved ones, and so on. But, Freud added, in speaking of social or group psychology proper, it is usual to set these intimate relations aside and treat group psychology as "concerned with the individual man as a member of a race, of a nation, of a caste, or a profession, or an institution, or as a component part of a crowd of people who have been organized into a group at some particular time for some

---

[23] For a description of such a cult, see John Lofland, *Doomsday Cult* (Englewood Cliffs, N.J.: Prentice-Hall, Inc., 1966).

[24] "Group Psychology," p. 71.

[25] *Ibid.*, p. 69.

definite purpose." [26] Within group psychology he felt it important to distinguish between short-lived groups on the one hand and "stable groups or associations in which mankind pass their lives, and which are embodied in the institutions of society" on the other.[27] Yet in his own illustrations he did not adhere consistently to the distinction. His two most striking empirical illustrations came from highly stabilized groups—the church and the army—whereas his major theoretical formulations concerned "primary groups" that "have a leader and . . . not . . . too much 'organization.'" [28] The latter types of groups—primary or uninstitutionalized—are those that usually form during episodes of collective behavior.

So much for Freud's definitions and scope of interest in social groupings. What aspects of the behavior of these collectivities did he wish to explain? In reading his essay it is possible to discern four distinct preoccupations. First and most generally, he was preoccupied with the reasons why men enter such groups and engage in such behavior at all. Second, he was interested in accounting for the resemblance between the mentality and action of these groups and that of children and primitives. Here he took as his starting point Gustave Le Bon's classic description of the crowd mentality—the crowd as impulsive, changeable, and irritable; incapable of sustained attention, criticism, or perseverance; governed by a sense of omnipotence, exaggerated feelings, magical formulas, and illusions.[29] Third, he was interested in why participants in primary groups display such adulation of and submission to leaders. And finally, he was interested in explaining why these participants experience such a sense of equality and solidarity—even identity—with their fellow participants.

Before outlining his own contributions to these issues, Freud criticized several authors who had previously attempted to account for the mentality of groups. In particular, he attacked several theories of suggestion, involving the claim that the group renders people susceptible to suggestion, and thus leads them to take leave of their critical faculties and give vent to their primitive emotions. Freud found this theory—presented by Le Bon and several others—to be a shallow one, since it gives

[26] *Ibid.*, p. 70. It is worth noting that Freud's distinction between individual and social psychology differs from the distinction between "psychological" and "social" I outlined above, pp. 38–39. He did not go beyond the *individual's orientation* to groups and institutions, whereas "social" as defined above involved aspects of regular and perhaps institutionalized *interaction among* two or more individuals or groups, without viewing any single individual as the point of reference.

[27] *Ibid.*, p. 83.

[28] *Ibid.*, p. 116.

[29] Gustave Le Bon, *The Crowd: A Study of the Popular Mind*, with a new introduction by Robert K. Merton (New York: The Viking Press, 1960). First published in 1895.

"no explanation of the nature of suggestion, that is of the conditions under which influence without logical foundation takes place." [30] In addition, he discarded as circular Le Bon's emphasis on the force of the leader's "prestige" in causing crowd behavior, since "prestige . . . is only recognizable by its capacity for evoking suggestion." [31] Finally, and more indirectly, he criticized McDougall's views on the conditions that prevent involvement in crowd behavior. McDougall had argued that if individuals are integrated into social organizations that possess a division of labor, definite traditions and customs regulating the interaction among members, and some continuity of existence, they will be less likely to be drawn into primary groups governed by emotionalism and an uncritical mentality.[32] Freud, however, changed the import of McDougall's insight. Instead ·of viewing it as an attempt to outline a set of social conditions, Freud redefined the question in more psychological terms: "[McDougall's] problem consists in how to procure for the group precisely those features [of organized participation in a structured collectivity] which were characteristic of the individual and which are extinguished in him by the formation of the [primary] group." [33]

While launching these criticisms, Freud was also changing the nature of the question he was addressing. Instead of asking, "What characteristics of groups bring out primitive mental characteristics in the individual?" Freud now wondered, "What psychological forces induce men to form and stay together in groups?" By focusing on the second question he hoped to reach an explanation of the mental qualities of group life that were not, in his opinion, well accounted for by the theorists he criticized.

Freud found the answer to his question in the concept of libido, or Eros. Indeed, his whole theory of group participation rests on a peculiar combination of instinct-object relationships in the individual. And these relationships involve not object-cathexes so much as indentifications with objects. Freud outlined three types of identification: first, the original form of emotional life with his father as an ideal in the early history of the Oedipus complex; second, a regressive form, in which the object is introjected in the Oedipal crisis; and third, identification with other persons on the basis of some common quality—for example, the identification of members of a ship's crew with one another on the basis of their common subordination to the captain's authority.

Using this classification of identifications, Freud characterized the essence of involvement in a primary group. First and foremost, a group's members are identified with the leader in the second sense of the term;

[30] "Group Psychology," p. 90.
[31] *Ibid.*, p. 88.
[32] William McDougall, *The Group Mind* (New York: G. P. Putnam's Sons, 1920).
[33] "Group Psychology," p. 86.

they "have put one and the same object in the place of their ego ideal." [34] They have regressed from the condition of having definite object-relations with the leader to the condition of introjecting the leader as their ego ideal. In addition, the group's members are identified with one another in the third sense of the term; they "have . . . identified themselves with one another in their ego" because they share in common subordination to the introjected leader.[35] This phenomenon accounts in part for their experience of solidarity and equality in the group. But the collective spirit of equality is fostered by still another mechanism. All members of the group are desirous of the leader's love and envious of one another for his love. Since all cannot possibly gain his exclusive love, however, they renounce their selfish desires and believe that the leader does and should love all of them equally. "No one must want to put himself forward, every one must be the same and have the same." [36] This attitude explains the growth of primitive social justice in groups. The total result of this combination of instinctual forces and objects is that everyone in a group is equal except the leader, and he is superior in equal degree to all the others.

By now Freud had supplied an account of the last two of his preoccupations—the relations between leaders and followers, and the relations among followers. But how to explain the primitive emotionalism and the loss of critical faculties of the group? To shed light on this question Freud turned to his theory of the primal horde, and treated all primary groups as instances of psychological and presumably historical regression:

> The uncanny and coercive characteristics of group formations, which are shown in the phenomena of suggestion that accompany them, may . . . be traced back to the fact of their origin from the primal horde. The leader of the group is still the dreaded primal father; the group still wishes to be governed by unrestricted force; it has an extreme passion for authority; . . . it has a thirst for obedience. The primal father is the group ideal, which governs the ego in the place of the ego ideal.[37]

These features—as well as the loss of consciousness, the dominance of the mind by affects, the impatience, and the impulsiveness of crowds— "correspond to a state of regression to a primitive mental activity." [38] Unlike those he criticized, Freud did not view these characteristics as products of the group's social influence over the individual, but rather

[34] *Ibid.*, p. 116.
[35] *Ibid.*
[36] *Ibid.*, p. 120.
[37] *Ibid.*, p. 127.
[38] *Ibid.*, p. 122.

as products that emerge as a concomitant of the same psychological tendencies to regressive identification that lead men to form groups in the first place.

SOME SHORTCOMINGS OF THE PSYCHOLOGICAL EXPLANATION

In criticizing Le Bon, Freud found his characterization of the crowd mentality inadequate because it rested on a rather mystical notion that the group influences people in such a way as to bring out new and unusual mental characteristics and types of behavior. And in criticizing the sociological approach, I noted that it involved a number of questionable generalizations about the effect of social situations on beliefs and behavior. In both instances the explanation regards the individual person as a kind of passive vessel through which the social forces work; or to put it another way, the individual himself is not seen as processing or modifying, much less initiating these social forces. Freud's account avoids this difficulty by specifying psychological dynamics which lead people to enter social groups and behave in certain ways.

Despite this singular advantage, Freud's theory suffers from a number of shortcomings, some of which suggest the need for a systematic synthesis with those approaches that emphasize social factors. The following problems seem most important:

1. Freud's account is incomplete on psychological grounds alone. The weakest link of his argument appears to be appeal to the logic of regression to the primal horde to account for the various psychological characteristics described so vividly by Le Bon—the impulsiveness, irritability, credulousness, emotionality, and so on. Reliance on this type of explanation can be criticized on the grounds that it involves some mystical notions about man's capacity to regress through the centuries to a primitive historical past. Leaving this line of criticism aside, however, and reading the idea of the primal horde in its metaphorical rather than its literal historical meaning, Freud's concept of regression is still subject to criticism. Basically his theory amounts to a process of regression to a pre-Oedipal state of identification with an authority figure. But two features of this kind of regression—features treated elsewhere in Freud's writings—appear to be underplayed in this account of group psychology.

First, Freud tended to overemphasize the positive side of the identification of the followers with the leader and with one another—loving the leader equally, being loved by him equally, and loving one another equally. This emphasis appears both in his empirical characterization of the church and the army, and in his more general theoretical formulation.[39] But he gave much less attention to the negative side of the ambivalent feelings toward authority figures. He did refer to the hostile attitude of members of religious groups toward outsiders who do not believe in the leader, and he did speak of the envy and hostility of followers to one another because each of them desires the exclusive love of the leader. But he did not deal with the phenomenon of hostility toward the leader himself.

Second, in characterizing the process of regressive identification, Freud tended to overemphasize impulse expression and to underemphasize the ego's defensive operations. Le Bon's description, which Freud accepted, deals almost exclusively with the expression of id impulses normally forbidden by the ego in deference to superego imperatives. The view taken by Freud is that the superego, being replaced by the object of the leader, relinquishes its controlling function. Freud's other accounts of identification, however, are more complex than this, in that they bring into play a number of other defenses—repression, projection, denial, and displacement, for example.[40] If Freud's theory of regressive identification has general validity, we should be able to account for the content of the group mentality by reference to these mechanisms as well as those of identification and regression. Freud did not explore these additional mechanisms in his essay on group psychology.

2. Because much of Freud's explanation is carried by the single mechanism of regressive identification with a leader, his account suffers from being unable to account for several aspects of group behavior. It is true that reliance on this mechanism provides a specific explanation for the relations between leader and followers and among followers. But without further elaboration this explanation shares with the sociological explanation an inability to discriminate among differential degrees of involvement in collective behavior—involvement as leader, as active follower, as sympathizer, as spectator, and so on. Presumably this would depend on the differential propensity of individuals to regress to a level of identification, but without specification of further psychological conditions under which this is likely to occur, such a statement is not very helpful. Furthermore, the mechanism of regressive identification is nonspecific with respect to the *form* of collective behavior—violent rioting, reform movement, religious cult, and so on—that may appear. All these forms manifest the general regressive relations among leaders and followers, but nothing in Freud's psychological account explains why one rather than another of these types of episodes would arise. In sum, Freud's explanatory variable of regressive identification is too general to account

[39] *Ibid.*, Chapters 5 and 10.
[40] See Freud, "Analysis of a Phobia in a Five-year-old Boy," *Standard Edition*, Vol. X, and "The Ego and the Id," *Standard Edition*, Vol. XIX.

for more than a few broad contours of collective behavior; it says little about the questions of differential recruitment into an episode of collective behavior or the directions of group behavior.

3. Finally—and related to the second line of criticism—Freud's theory, with few exceptions, leaves out of consideration the social factors that influence men to enter into group activity. It strikes me that more might be made of McDougall's insights than Freud made of them. By noting that involvement in a group with definite organization, specialization of tasks, traditions and customs, and so on, inhibits involvement in outbursts of collective behavior, McDougall was asserting also that the absence of these social-structural factors constitutes an occasion for men to be drawn into such episodes. To translate McDougall's point into psychoanalytic language, involvement in a structured social organization provides the individual with opportunities for stable object-attachments of various sorts, and this diminishes the probability of regressive identification. Correspondingly, if the social organization itself undergoes some sort of disintegration, this increases the probability that the individual will be placed under strain and, as a consequence, will reconstitute his object-world in a regressive direction. Freud declined to accept this implication of McDougall's reasoning, which identifies a typical social occasion—loosening of social attachments—that encourages individuals to enter into episodes of collective behavior.[41] To make this point in more general terms: If Freud's theory is to offer an adequate account of the content and timing of collective episodes, it cannot rest solely on the type of psychological mechanisms he specified; there must also be a systematic account of the social conditions that facilitate the activation of these mechanisms.

INGREDIENTS OF A SYNTHETIC APPROACH

In this section I shall spell out the requirements of a synthetic explanation for episodes of collective behavior which hopefully can minimize the shortcomings associated with the sociological and the psychological approaches, each considered singly. In the final section I shall illustrate some of these requirements with reference to a typical protest movement.

The first requirement of any explanation of collective behavior is to specify the aspects of this behavior that demand explanation (dependent variables). At various points in the exposition I have identified explicitly

---

[41] Yet in his own account of the outbreak of panic Freud relied on a similar kind of reasoning. A typical occasion for the military panic is the disappearance of the commander, which severs the libidinal ties between him and the followers. "The mutual ties have ceased to exist, and a gigantic and senseless fear is set free." "Group Psychology," *op. cit.,* p. 96.

or implicitly the following kinds of variation: (1) Variation in the *type* of collective behavior—panic, craze, hostile outburst, reform movement, revolutionary movement, religious cult, and so on. Why, in general terms, do these types of behavior erupt, and under what conditions should we expect one rather than another type? (2) Variations in *timing of occurrence*. Why do these types of behavior occur at one time rather than another? (3) Variations in *content*, in terms of the beliefs that accompany these types of behavior. Under what conditions do hysterical beliefs, beliefs in personal and social regeneration, etc., arise? (4) Variations in *recruitment* and *differential participation*. Why are some people more attracted to episodes of collective behavior than others, and why do they differ in their degree of involvement? (5) Variations in the *relations among participants*. How can we account for the particular types of authority relations, division of roles, etc., in groups that form during episodes of collective behavior? (6) Variations in the character of the episode *over time*. Does a collective outburst have different characteristics during its period of incipient development, its period of explosiveness, and its period of decline? If so, how do we account for these differences? Not every explanation of collective behavior need address itself to all these questions; but it is essential that the precise scope of the problems to be addressed is made explicit.

The second requirement of an explanation synthesizing the social and psychological approaches is that the dependent variables be described in two languages—one at the conceptual level of the social system, and one at the conceptual level of the psychological system.[42] The range of *social* meanings of a movement for equal feminine rights, for example, would include its significance for the traditional organization of sex roles; its significance for a political party that may wish to capitalize on such a movement to gain support in its bid for electoral success; its significance for the structure of domestic law; and so on. The range of *psychological* meanings of the same movement would include its significance for the types of sexual identification of participants with maternal figures; its significance from the standpoint of feminine envy of the male's superior advantages; and so on. A major *social* meaning of a religious cult such as the Black Muslims may lie in its challenge to traditional racial and political arrangements; a major *psychological* meaning may lie in a rebirth of personal identity for Negroes who have experienced a life of poverty and rootlessness. Any episode of collective behavior should be described, therefore, in terms of what it is for the social system and what it is for the individual.

This double description yields the following advantages for the in-

[42] See above, pp. 38–39.

vestigator of collective behavior: First, it enables him to translate social and psychological determinants, respectively, directly to the dependent variable at parallel conceptual levels, and thus to avoid reductionist or simplistic causal statements. For example, if social significance of the feminist movement—i.e., the reconstitution of traditional sex roles—is appreciated, the investigator is less likely to attribute the impetus of the movement exclusively to considerations of conflicts over sex identification, even though the involvement of some participants may be explained in these terms. Second, it enables him to avoid characterizing psychological states of individuals by reference to data at the social level, and vice versa. For example, in the literature on collective behavior it is common to assume that all the participants in a race riot are motivated by racial hostility, since conflict between the races is the dominant social characteristic of the episode. But more careful study of the participants shows that while some do appear to be motivated by racial antagonisms, others are drawn into the disorder only after social controls have broken down, their defiance being directed more toward the police and other public authorities; and still others appear to seek economic advantage through looting.[43] The motivations of the participants, then, have to be ascertained by direct psychological measures, not the gross social features of the episode. Furthermore, the social aims of an episode of collective behavior cannot be characterized by reference to the motivational states of individuals. It is erroneous, for example, to characterize a social movement exclusively in power-oriented terms on the basis of the political motivations of selected participants.

The third requirement of a synthetic explanation is to specify and show the interaction among the various social and psychological determinants of collective behavior. These determinants can be classified conveniently under four headings: structural setting, deprivation, mobilization for action in the name of a belief, and the operation of social and personal controls.[44]

1. The structural setting—both social and psychological—for involvement in collective behavior. At the *social* level this setting has two aspects —the opportunity for alternative lines of behavior other than the collective outburst, and the social moorings of potential participants that might inhibit their involvement. With respect to the first, the events leading up to the outburst of riots in American prisons in 1952 and 1953 provide an example. Prior to this time many prisons had evolved a system of informal inmate self-government, whereby leaders among the prisoners dispensed

---

[43] See *Theory of Collective Behavior*, pp. 257–61.
[44] This classification of determinants is similar to the classification of determinants to be incorporated into any theory of social change. See below, pp. 205–7.

favors among other inmates and received their various complaints about prison conditions. The informal leaders also maintained close communication with guards and warden. During a period of penal reform in the years before the early 1950s, however, "the inmate clerks and assistants were shorn of their power, and replaced by paid, Civil Service personnel." [45] Administration became more formal, more distant, and less receptive to the expression of prisoner grievances than it had been under the preceding informal system. Partly as a result of such reforms, "there appears to have occurred a marked disturbance and disruption of the channels normally established for the airing of grievances and distribution of rewards. The general resentment resulting from this condition was directed, mobilized, and heightened by inmate leaders." [46] In this case the disappearance of alternative channels of protest increased the probability of uncontrolled hostile outbursts.

One of the common background features of episodes of collective behavior is that the stable social linkages of individuals are "loosened" in various ways. Riots, for example, tend to break out on hot summer Sundays at beaches, recreational resorts, taverns, and public dance halls—in short, in those corners of the social structure where people are most likely to be away from their familial and occupational role attachments.[47] Students and adolescents generally have a high rate of participation in various types of collective outbursts; one reason for this is that they are in the age-grade "gap" between the relatively well-defined role of being a child and the relatively well-defined cluster of occupational, marital, religious, and other adult roles. As youths enter these adult roles, their predilection for involvement in both frivolous and serious episodes generally diminishes. Recent migrants to large cities, who are generally relatively unattached to trade union, voluntary association or neighborhood group, tend to be drawn disproportionately into bizarre religious cults.[48] These kinds of facts lend weight to McDougall's assertion that involvement in a social organization with definite and specialized roles, traditions, and continuity operates as a counter-influence to involvement in collective outbursts.

To view this point from the psychological side: If an individual is

[45] Frank E. Hartung and Maurice Floch, "A Social-Psychological Analysis of Prison Riots: An Hypothesis," *The Journal of Criminal Law, Criminology and Police Science*, XLVII (1956), 54–55.

[46] Lloyd E. Ohlin, *Sociology and the Field of Correction* (New York: Russell Sage Foundation, 1956), pp. 24–25.

[47] Joseph D. Lohman, *The Police and Minority Groups* (Chicago: Chicago Park District, 1947), pp. 71–73.

[48] J. B. Holt, "Holiness Religion: Cultural Shock and Social Reorganization," *American Sociological Review*, V (1940), 746–47; A. H. Fauset, *Black Gods of the Metropolis* (Philadelphia: Publications of the Philadelphia Anthropological Society, 1944), pp. 87–88, 107.

involved in a number of relatively stable role structures, this may mean a relatively stable distribution of libidinal energy. But this is not necessarily the case. The stability of an individual's psychic world of object-representations and identifications is in part independent of the stability of his actual, contemporary object-world. The reason for this is that the stability or instability of psychological structure is only in part a function of an individual's current reality involvement; they are also a function of his personal history, including his resolution of crises at various stages of development.

In explaining the differential recruitment and participation in a collective outburst, then, it is necessary to refer to the degree of structural permissiveness at both the social and psychological levels. In the case of the prison riots of 1952 and 1953, for example, a partial explanation of why the riots occurred in some prisons rather than others can be given in terms of the recent structural "reforms" that had cut off alternative opportunities for expression of grievances and hostility. The riots clustered in the reformed prisons. But within these prisons, not every inmate rioted, even though all were presumably affected in some degree by the reforms. To account for this differential involvement, recourse must be made to psychological determinants. According to some accounts, the rioters were composed mainly of psychopathic and homosexual inmate leaders, and more passive individuals who feared reprisal or loss of favor in the eyes of the riot leaders.[49] But, again, in those prisons that had not recently experienced penal reform, even these types of individuals did not often initiate and participate in hostile outbursts. This illustration reveals how the incorporation of both social and psychological factors magnifies the power of the explanation of the differential incidence of and recruitment into the riots.

2. The deprivation—defined both in social and psychological terms—that operates as an impetus to collective behavior. Up to this point I have considered only the structural oportunities for involvement in collective outbursts. These opportunities alone, however, do not guarantee that behavior will occur. There has to be some sort of more active "push" to behavior, and this normally takes the form of some real or imagined deprivation. For example, in the prisons, the inmates' grievances centered around conditions such as "poor, insufficient, or contaminated food; inadequate, unsanitary, or dirty housing; sadistic brutality by prison officials," or some combination of these.[50] These reality conditions, combined with the exaggeratedly suspicious attitudes toward authority on the part of the selected prison population, made for a high level of hostility. And

---

[49] Austin H. MacCormick, "Behind the Prison Riots," *Annals of the American Academy of Political and Social Science*, CCXCIII (May 1954), 18–20.

[50] Hartung and Floch, *op. cit.*, p. 51.

when these conditions of deprivation are combined with the structural conditions described above, the probability of overt violence is augmented.

Another example will show how social and psychological factors interact to determine the exact level of threat or deprivation. A common background condition for collective panic is the presence of some uncontrollable danger of unknown proportions, such as an approaching army or an air raid alert. When this kind of threat is combined with a structural setting of limited and closing exits, collective panic is very likely to occur.[51] But in addition to the presence of realistic danger, an individual's sense of guilt, anxiety, hostility, and especially his tendency to project these outward, are important determinants of his susceptibility to possibly dangerous situations. During the air raid drills in New York City in World War II, for instance, most people remained calm, but a small number of citizens—both adults and children—experienced seizures of acute anxiety. Clinical analysis of persons who showed this reaction revealed that they

> . . . were individuals who in their family relations experienced intense hostility together with great fear of retaliation if they expressed it. They felt that they would be precipitated into great danger if the hostility which they inhibited precariously and with great effort were to break through. This, then, was the explosion which they dreaded, the image of which became projected on the outer world. The danger of bombs exploding thus seemed imminent to them though it did not to others in the same external circumstances.[52]

An analysis of situations leading to panic would uncover some situations in which the realistic threat is so overwhelming that almost all affected individuals would be driven to panic;[53] other situations in which individuals "bring" diffuse anxieties to circumstances that are not realistically very threatening; and still other situations—presumably most—in which the threatening agent is a function of both the external environment of the persons affected and the psychological predispositions they bring to this environment.

3. Mobilization for action on the basis of a belief. On the *social* side this determinant refers above all to the appearance of a leader or leaders who have the capacity to create or assemble a rumor or ideology that defines the situation as one calling for collective action; to disseminate the

---

[51] See *Theory of Collective Behavior*, pp. 135–43.

[52] Martha Wolfenstein, *Disaster: A Psychological Essay* (New York: The Free Press and the Falcon's Wing Press, 1957), pp. 7–8. Also see pp. 37–38. See also Irving L. Janis, "Problems of Theory in the Analysis of Stress Behavior," *Journal of Social Issues*, X (1954), p. 21.

[53] Some of the "classic" panic situations, such as a sinking ship or a theater fire, would be appropriate examples.

belief; to elicit and focus the affects of followers; to stimulate them to action; and perhaps to coordinate this action. If these key elements of leadership and coordination are not present, the impetus to an episode of collective behavior will be manifested in other forms of behavior.

On the *psychological* side many individuals may be "readied" for action insofar as they are appropriately motivated, hold appropriate beliefs, and are receptive to direction from a demagogic leader. The most famous studies attempting to isolate this kind of individual are the University of California studies of authoritarianism, in which anti-Semitic and other sociopolitical attitudes were traced to typical family experiences and typical personality constellations.[54] Though the investigators in these studies limited themselves to the study of family and personality determinants of attitudes, presumably those individuals designated as "authoritarian" would be more likely to be drawn into episodes of collective behavior directed against Jews and other minority groups.

I shall discuss the questions of ideology and leadership in greater detail in the final section of this essay.

4. The operation of social and personal controls. Once a collective outburst has begun to develop, its course, direction, and intensity are dependent in large part on the social and personal controls operating on the participants. I have already indicated a number of ways in which social controls influence collective behavior.[55] Probably the type of response on the part of authorities that aggravates and intensifies an episode of collective protest is harshness and rigidity that alternates with evident weakness. Harshness and rigidity provide the participants with "evidence" of the vicious character of the authority, and thus justify extreme and militant tactics; weakness or collapse in the face of threats provides "evidence" that these extreme tactics are in fact effective, and encourages participants in protest movements to give credence to their own fantasies of omnipotence. On the other hand, an agent of control who is firm but patient, consistently prohibiting certain types of protest but consistently permitting and giving serious consideration to others, provides neither kind of evidence to participants in collective protest movements and thus tends to contain the protest.

Many who have written about collective behavior have stressed the uncontrolled and impulsive behavior of participants. But it should not be forgotten that such behavior is continuously conditioned by the operation of personal controls. At one moment in the history of the Free Speech Movement at the University of California, for example, hundreds of

[54] T. W. Adorno, *et al.*, *The Authoritarian Personality* (New York: Harper & Row, Publishers, Inc., 1950).
[55] Above, pp. 98–100.

individuals were mobilized to engage in illegal action in the name of free speech, when the question concerned the political rights of students; at another moment only a handful were mobilized for a day or two of mischief in the name of free speech, when the question amounted to the right to be obscene in public. Of course, many different conditions affected the two episodes. But one key difference is that in the one case the moral sensitivities of many were aroused to the point where they would forego certain personal controls, whereas in the other their moral sensitivities were offended to the point where they would not even sympathize with the protest, even though the leaders of both episodes justified their protest in the language of free speech.

One of the many dilemmas facing the militants within any social movement arises from the tension between their desire for extremist tactics and their fear that the moral sensitivities of the moderates will be offended by such tactics. Later I shall enumerate some reasons why protest movements attempt to provoke authorities into repressive actions. Certainly one reason for such behavior on the part of militants is to generate "evidence" for the moderates that the authority is arbitrary and cruel—evidence which, if accepted by the moderates, would justify their participation in extreme and perhaps otherwise reprehensible actions.

In this section I have discussed four sets of variables separately, considering each at the social and psychological levels as it bears on the determination of episodes of collective behavior. In closing this section, it is essential to note that in any empirical case the several sets of variables combine and interact with one another in very complicated ways. It seems to me that one of the highest theoretical priorities for the field of collective behavior is not so much to search for new variables as to generate explanatory models that incorporate the interaction and feedback relations among the several sets of known influences on collective behavior.

SOCIAL AND PSYCHOLOGICAL SIGNIFICANCE OF PROTEST MOVEMENTS

In the final section of the essay I shall probe a little deeper in describing the social and psychological characteristics of collective behavior. I shall take the protest movement as a type case. Rather than focus exclusively on a single example, however (such as a pacificist movement or the Townsend Movement), I shall describe a number of characteristics that are common to many protest movements. First I shall describe these characteristics at the social level. Then I shall outline what I consider to be a common—though by no means universal—psychodynamic significance of these characteristics. The object of this exercise is to provide the reader with more circumstantial and detailed suggestions than it was possible to give in the preceding section.

Common Elements of Social Protest Movements

Protest movements—whether reform or revolutionary in spirit—develop remarkably similar ideologies. These ideologies have both negative and positive components. On the negative side there is a sense of foreboding, of great anxiety about threats to social life, and the specification of agents in society who are responsible for these threats. In the prohibition movement which culminated in the Eighteenth Amendment, liquor became a symbol for a variety of forces—the city, the "foreign element," Catholics, and so on—which were felt to be undermining traditional values of American Protestantism. These forces were, in a rather mysterious combination with liquor, causing "disease, destitution and depravity," and were, as "the Great Destroyer of the Temple of the Soul," working against organized religion.[56] Supporters of the Townsend Plan in the 1930s found generalized economic threats in a social system which left the aged isolated and poor, and generalized moral threats in tobacco, liquor, petting, and the laziness of the young. Adherents of the movement also singled out political authorities (especially Roosevelt and the Supreme Court) whom they viewed as obstacles to the realization of their design to eradicate these evils.[57] The negative components of the ideology, then, are great anxiety, which focuses on the decay of social and moral life, and great hostility, which focuses on some individuals or groups in society. If the movement is of the reform variety, opposition tends to be directed toward "vested interests" in the society who resist reform; if the movement is revolutionary, protest tends to be directed against the ruling authorities themselves as the source of evil.

On the *positive* side, those who adhere to protest movements often endow themselves and the envisioned reconstitution of society with enormous power, conceived as the ability to overcome that array of threats and obstacles which constitute the negative side of the adherents' worldpicture. The proposed reform or social change will render opponents helpless, and will be effective immediately. Because of this exaggerated potency, adherents often see unlimited happiness in the future if only the social changes are forthcoming. For if they are adopted, they argue, the basis for threat, frustration, and discomfort will disappear. Consider the symbolism of the Townsend Plan. Meetings of adherents often produced the following chant:

---

[56] Peter H. Odegard, *Pressure Politics: The Story of the Anti-Saloon League* (New York: Columbia University Press, 1928), pp. 29–34.

[57] Richard L. Neuberger and K. Loe, "The Old People's Crusade," *Harper's Magazine* (March 1936), pp. 434–35.

Two hundred dollars a month.
Youth for work, age for leisure,
Two hundred for the oldsters,
To be spent in ceaseless pleasure.[58]

The Townsend planners not only planned to save capitalism, but also to engulf competing plans; the movement would "swallow the EPICS and Utopians . . . would gather the Technates and Continentals under its wings. Humanity marches on." [59] Symbols of omnipotence also appeared:

Nothing can stop us! (cheers and more cheers) Not even President Roosevelt and the Supreme Court can stop us (tremendous cheers—no one is afraid of that big bad wolf, the Supreme Court). The speaker can hardly go on. Higher and higher he lifts his voice in exultation— "No, not even Almighty God can stop us!" [60]

Thus normative movements frequently display a world-view of conflicting forces of good and evil which characterize many types of generalized beliefs—two omnipotent forces locked in combat.

Protest movements also display those characteristics noted by Freud— an exceptional solidarity between leader and followers; a tendency for the leader to be endowed with supernatural, superhuman, or exceptional powers; [61] a corresponding tendency for followers to subordinate themselves to the decisions of the leader because of these powers; an exceptional solidarity among adherents of the movement; and a correspondingly great antagonism to opponents of the movement and other outsiders.

On closer examination, the relations between those inside the movement and those outside are more complex. While outsiders are commonly treated as enemies, it is also important to note that protest movements often depend on public support for their success, and continuously engage in efforts to win it. The support required for success need not be universal, of course; it may only be the support of some critical constituency.[62] Necessarily, then, the relations between adherents and outsiders have a double aspect. On the one hand outsiders are viewed as unenlightened, untrustworthy, or heterodox; but on the other hand they are viewed as possible supporters if won over to the cause.

[58] L. Whiteman and S. L. Lewis, *Glory Roads: The Psychological State of California* (New York: Thomas Y. Crowell, 1936), p. 75.

[59] *Ibid.*, pp. 101–2.

[60] *Ibid.*

[61] For a classic account of the characteristics of this type of "charismatic" leader, see Max Weber, *The Theory of Social and Economic Organization*, trans. A. M. Henderson and Talcott Parsons (New York: Oxford University Press, 1947), pp. 358–63.

[62] For example, the degree of faculty support for the students and corresponding faculty opposition to the university administration was of critical significance for the fortunes of the Free Speech Movement during 1964–65 at the University of California.

One final feature of protest movements deserves mention. Once the major aim of the movement is realized—for example, when some offensive statute is removed from the books, when some desired social reforms are effected—one might normally expect the movement to dissolve. Frequently this happens. But there are other tendencies that lead many movements to endure beyond their "natural" life. Some movements persist in a "watchdog" capacity to protect and consolidate gains. Others turn to issues and reforms related to their original purpose. Still others attempt to provoke authorities into hostile actions which presumably will breathe new life into the movement. One striking feature of the Free Speech Movement during the spring of 1965—the months after its days of brilliant success in gaining various political rights during the period from September through December, 1964—was not so much its fragmentation and decline as the efforts of its fragmented sectors to bring the movement alive once again over new issues. Among these efforts were the challenge to the university authorities over the control of student government; the short-lived effort to set up a "free university" in opposition to the University of California; various efforts to defy minor University regulations in order to provoke the University into repressive action; and the attempt to push the free speech issue to a new level by insisting on the right to utter obscenities in public. It was as though the days of December had provided a particular sort of gratification for many participants, and the subsequent history of the movement witnessed a number of attempts to recreate those days, even though the particular historical circumstances were no longer the same as in that period.

Psychodynamic Meanings of the Common Elements of Social Protest Movements

As indicated in the last section, many features of protest movements are explicable by reference to the social situations in which they arise. To increase the power of our explanation of them, however, reference must be made to their psychodynamic significance. I shall conclude this essay by suggesting a number of these deeper psychological meanings. In any given situation, of course, participants may either "bring" these meanings to a protest movement or have them "evoked" by the circumstances of the movement; most situations would show a continuous interplay between internal psychic determination and external stimulation.

Let me begin by reviewing the psychic ingredients of two common childhood situations—the Oedipal situation of the child, in which he enters into competition with the parent of the same sex for the love of the parent of the opposite sex; and situations in which the child competes with his siblings for the attention and affection of his parents. Needless to say, these situations resemble one another in many respects and may be fused in various ways in the child's psychological development; but they are distinguishable conceptually.

The Oedipal situation is marked by several types of ambivalence. Toward the father the boy experiences feelings of love, affection, and direct identification; [63] yet at the same time he is filled with feelings of competition and rage toward the father because he stands in the way of the boy's sexual desires for his mother. Simultaneously the boy is afflicted with the related feelings of castration anxiety and homosexual anxiety. Toward the mother the ambivalence is between positive sexual attraction on the one hand, and his frustration and anger because she refuses to be seduced away from the father on the other.

Typically the Oedipal conflict is resolved mainly by a process of repression and identification—repression of the anxiety-provoking elements, and identification with the opposite-sex parent.[64] Most conspicuously, the repressed elements are the hostile and erotic impulses toward both the father and the mother. What remains is the internalized superego, which becomes the seat of moral anxiety, and feelings of de-eroticized affection for the mother.

With respect to the relations among siblings, similar ambivalences, both toward the sibling and toward the parents whose affection is desired, are in evidence. In addition, the mechanisms of resolving the ambivalences are similar, though not quite so dramatic or phase-specific as in the Oedipal situation. The "preferred" solution is to repress the hostile and erotic elements of the ambivalences toward the siblings; to retain the gentler feelings of brotherhood, affection, and loyalty; and to identify with them. As Freud indicated, however, the identification in this case does not involve regarding them as superordinate, but rather regarding them as equally subordinate, loved—or whatever—by the parents.

Viewing these common psychodynamic processes with reference to the common features of protest movements, it seems to me that the protest movement is typically an occasion which permits the repressed elements of these crises to emerge and be gratified, though certain other defenses continue to operate.[65]

This formulation applies most dramatically to the ambivalent attitudes toward authority figures manifested in protest movements. On the one hand there is the unqualified love, worship, and submission to the leader of the movement, who articulates and symbolizes "the cause." On the other hand there is the unqualified suspicion, denigration, and desire to

[63] "Group Psychology," p. 105.

[64] "The Ego and the Id," p. 32. Freud notes, however, that a number of different patterns of identification are possible.

[65] I hope this formulation overcomes in part the first two objections raised against Freud's theory of regressive identification, above, pp. 106–8.

destroy the agent felt responsible for the moral decay of social life and standing in the way of reform, whether he be a vested interest or a political authority. There is one important difference, however. In the Oedipal crisis the ambivalence is directed toward a single individual, the father; in the protest movement the ambivalence is split between two types of object. This splitting appears to serve a number of defensive purposes. It permits the gratification of the feelings of love and passivity as well as of the feelings of hostility toward the authority figure; but by a combination of projection and denial it also avoids the anxiety that is created when these ambivalent feelings are focused on the same object. In addition, these defenses—when combined with rationalization—permit certain kinds of behavior that might otherwise be reprehensible to the individual participants: passive dependency, now justified because of the sheer power and wonder of the leader; and destructive or even violent behavior, now justified because of the fundamental evil of the enemy. The same mechanisms of splitting, projection, denial, and rationalization also seem to operate when the hated object is not so much an authority figure as a sibling figure—such as a minority group that is perceived as gaining too many social advantages or "forgetting its proper place."

An ambivalence characterizes the relations of adherents to the movement to potential sources of outside support, but it is a different sort of ambivalence. This traces more to the child's Oedipal wish to seducing the opposite-sex parent into joining in the destruction of the same-sex parent; [66] or, in the sibling situation, his wish to seduce the parent into joining in the destruction of the sibling. It seems to me that one of the common meanings of a movement's desire for solidarity and support is often a manifestation of this kind of wish. This would account for the extraordinarily solidary, eroticized ties among "converts" who have become "committed" to the cause. At the same time these feelings are tinged with ambivalence. At the positive extreme is the joy of gratification if the seduction is accepted; at the negative extreme is the pain of bitter frustration if it is refused. Adherents to a movement must always be prepared to be disappointed with supporters who are less than totally committed. Perhaps this ambivalence lies behind the cynical disdain with which core members of a movement sometimes regard their less committed followers. Perhaps it also lies behind the attitude frequently expressed by adherents that "those who are not with us are against us," an attitude which suggests that the ambivalence toward outsiders is also subject to splitting and the associated defenses.

This kind of logic also throws some light on the future state of social

---

[66] This formulation extends the common meaning of the term "seduction" beyond the invitation to erotic stimulation to include an invitation to engage in a common attack on a hated object.

bliss, peace, and harmony that is frequently envisioned by adherents to a cause. These visions tap very vivid Oedipal and sibling-destruction fantasies of what the world would be like if only the hated objects were obliterated and the child could have the loved object to himself. This fantasy, usually subjected to severe repression, comes closer to the surface, albeit in disguised form, in the ideologies of social protest.

Finally, the tendency for adherents of protest movements to create conditions that might reactivate the movement is also highlighted by these psychological considerations. The striking feature of the protest movement is what Freud observed: it permits the expression of impulses that are normally repressed. But the participant continues to defend against the impulses involved—especially the hostile and erotic ones—by mechanisms such as projection, denial, rationalization, and splitting. The efforts—sometimes conscious and sometimes unconscious—of leaders and adherents of a movement to create issues, to provoke authorities, and even to be martyred by these authorities, would seem to be in part efforts to "arrange" reality so as to "justify" the expression of normally forbidden impulses in a setting which makes them appear less reprehensible to the participants.

CONCLUDING REMARK

By describing a protest movement at both the social and psychological levels, it is more nearly possible to see in detail how the various determinants—structural setting, deprivation, mobilization, and controls—feed into such movements from both levels. In concluding, I express the hope that I have avoided two opposing biases in this essay—first, the bias that episodes of collective behavior arise as "natural" consequences of disequilibrating social conditions, and that under these conditions any "normal" human being would be drawn into such episodes; and second, the bias that episodes of collective behavior are little more than seizures of "acting out" of impulses and conflicts that are irrelevant to existing social conditions. Some statements, lifted from context, may appear to reveal one or the other of these biases. The entire spirit of the essay, however, is to avoid the conceptual and empirical distortions that arise from either bias, and to work toward a synthetic approach.

PART II: The Sociological Explanation of Change

SIX: Toward a
Theory of Modernization *

INTRODUCTION

A thorough analysis of the social changes accompanying economic development would require an ambitious theoretical scheme and a vast quantity of comparative data. Because I lack both necessities—and the space to use them if I possessed them—I shall restrict this exploratory statement in two ways. (1) Methodologically, I shall deal only with ideal-type constructs, in Weber's sense; I shall not discuss any individual cases of development, or the comparative applicability of particular historical generalizations. (2) Substantively, I shall consider only modifications of the social structure; I shall not deal with factor-allocation, savings and investment, inflation, balance of payments, foreign aid, size of population, and rate of population change—even though these variables naturally affect, and are affected by, structural changes. These omissions call for brief comment.

Max Weber defined an ideal-type construct as a

> one-sided accentuation . . . by the synthesis of a great many diffuse, discrete, more or less present and occasionally absent *concrete individual* phenomena, which are arranged . . . into a unified *analytical* construct. In its conceptual purity, this mental construct cannot be found anywhere in reality.[1]

* This paper appeared originally under the title, "Mechanisms of Change and Adjustment to Change," in B. F. Hoselitz and W. E. Moore, eds., *Industrialization and Society* (The Hague: UNESCO-Mouton, 1963), pp. 32–54. I am grateful to William Petersen, Herbert Blumer, Reinhard Bendix, and Kingsley Davis for critical comments on an earlier version of this essay.

[1] Max Weber, *The Methodology of the Social Sciences* (New York: The Free Press, Inc., 1949), pp. 90, 93.

The analyst utilizes such constructs to unravel and explain a variety of actual historical situations. Weber mentions explicitly two kinds of ideal-type constructs—first, "historically unique configurations," such as "rational bourgeois capitalism," "medieval Christianity," etc.; and second, statements concerning historical evolution, such as the Marxist laws of capitalist development.[2] While the second type presupposes some version of the first, I shall concentrate on the dynamic constructs.

"Economic development" generally refers to the "growth of output per head of population."[3] For purposes of analyzing the relationships between economic growth and the social structure, it is possible to isolate the effects of several interrelated technical, economic, and ecological processes that frequently accompany development. These may be listed as follows: (1) In the realm of technology, the change *from* simple and traditionalized techniques *toward* the application of scientific knowledge. (2) In agriculture, the evolution *from* subsistence farming *toward* commercial production of agricultural goods. This means specialization in cash crops, purchase of nonagricultural products in the market, and often agricultural wage-labor. (3) In industry, the transition *from* the use of human and animal power *toward* industrialization proper, or "men aggregated at power-driven machines, working for monetary return with the products of the manufacturing process entering into a market based on a network of exchange relations."[4] (4) In ecological arrangements, the movement *from* the farm and village *toward* urban centers. These several processes often, but not necessarily, occur simultaneously. Certain technological improvements—e.g., the use of improved seeds—can be introduced without automatically and instantaneously causing organizational changes;[5] agriculture may be commercialized without any concomitant industrialization, as in many colonial countries;[6] industrialization may occur in villages;[7] and cities may proliferate even where there is no signifi-

[2] *Ibid.*, pp. 93, 101–3.

[3] W. A. Lewis, *The Theory of Economic Growth* (Homewood, Ill.: R. D. Irwin, 1955), p. 1.

[4] M. Nash, "Some Notes on Village Industrialization in South and East Asia," *Economic Development and Cultural Change*, III: 3 (1954), 271.

[5] W. H. Beckett, for instance, distinguishes between "technical improvement" and "organizational improvement" in agriculture. See "The Development of Peasant Agriculture," in P. Ruopp, ed., *Approaches to Community Development* (The Hague: W. Van Hoeve, 1953), pp. 138–43. For an analysis of the interplay between technological advance and productive reorganization during the Tokugawa period in Japan, see H. Rosovsky, *Capital Formation in Japan 1868–1940* (New York: The Free Press of Glencoe, 1961), Chapter 4.

[6] For example, J. H. Boeke, *The Structure of the Netherlands Indian Economy* (New York: Institute of Pacific Relations, 1942), pp. 76–89.

[7] Nash, *op. cit.*; T. Herman, "The Role of Cottage and Small-Scale Industries in Asian Economic Development," *Economic Development and Cultural Change*, IV: 4 (1955), 356–70; H. G. Aubrey, "Small Industry in Economic Development," in L. W.

cant industrialization.[8] Furthermore, the specific social consequences of technological advance, commercialized agriculture, the factory, and the city, respectively, are not in any sense reducible to each other.[9]

Despite such differences, all four processes tend to affect the social structure in similar ways. All give rise to the following ideal-type structural changes, which have ramifications throughout society: (1) Structural differentiation, or the establishment of more specialized and more autonomous social units. I shall discuss the occurrence of this process in the different spheres of economy, family, religion, and stratification. (2) Integration, which changes its character as the old social order is made obsolete by the process of differentiation. The state, the law, political groupings, and other associations are particularly salient in this integration. (3) Social disturbances—mass hysteria, outbursts of violence, religious and political movements, etc.—which reflect the uneven advances of differentiation and integration, respectively.

Obviously, the implications of technological advance, agricultural reorganization, industrialization, and urbanization differ from society to society, as do the resulting structural realignments. Some of the sources of variation in these ideal patterns of pressure and change are described in the next paragraphs.

1. Variations in premodern conditions. Is the society's value system congenial or antagonistic to industrial values? How well integrated is the society? How "backward" is it? What is its level of wealth? How is the wealth distributed? Is the country "young and empty" or "old and crowded"? Is the country politically dependent, newly independent, or completely autonomous? Such pre-existing factors shape the impact of the forces of economic development.[10]

Shannon, ed., *Underdeveloped Areas* (New York: Harper & Row, Publishers, Inc., 1957), pp. 215–25.

[8] T. Hodgkin, *Nationalism in Colonial Africa* (New York: New York University Press, 1957), Chapter 2.

[9] B. F. Hoselitz, "The City, the Factory, and Economic Growth," *American Economic Review*, XLV: 2 (1955), 166–84; K. Davis and H. H. Golden, "Urbanization and the Development of Pre-Industrial Areas," *Economic Development and Cultural Change*, III: 1 (1954), 6–26; Nash, *op. cit.*, p. 277.

[10] S. Kuznets, "Problems in Comparisons of Economic Trends," in S. Kuznets, W. E. Moore, and J. J. Spengler, eds., *Economic Growth: Brazil, Indian, Japan* (Durham, N.C.: Duke University Press, 1955), pp. 14–19; Kuznets, "International Differences in Income Levels: Some Reflections on Their Causes," *Economic Development and Culture Change*, II: 2 (1953), 22–23; A. Gerschenkron, "Economic Backwardness in Historical Perspective," and R. Linton, "Cultural and Personality Factors Affecting Economic Growth," both in B. Hoselitz, ed., *The Progress of Underdeveloped Areas* (Chicago: University of Chicago Press, 1952), pp. 3–29, 80 ff.; H. G. J. Aitken, ed., *The State and Economic Growth* (New York: Social Science Research Council, 1959).

2. Variations in the impetus to change. Do pressures to modernize come from the internal implications of a value system, from a wish for national security and prestige, from a desire for material property, or from a combination of these? Is political coercion used to form a labor force? Or are the pressures economic, as in the case of population pressure on the land or that of loss of handicraft markets to cheap imported products? Or do economic and political pressures combine, as, for example, when a tax is levied on peasants that is payable only in money? Or are the pressures social, as they are when there is a desire to escape burdensome aspects of the old order? Factors like these influence the adjustment to modernization greatly.[11]

3. Variations in the path toward modernization. Does the sequence begin with light consumer industries? Or is there an attempt to introduce heavy, capital-intensive industries first? What is the role of government in shaping the pattern of investment? What is the rate of accumulation of technological knowledge and skills? What is the general tempo of industrialization? These questions indicate elements which affect the nature of structural change and the degree of discomfort created by this change.[12]

4. Variations in the advanced stages of modernization. What is the emergent distribution of industries in developed economies? What are the emergent relations between state and economy, religion and economy, state and religion, etc.? While all advanced industrialized societies have their "industrialization" in common, uniquely national differences remain. For instance, "social class" has a different social significance in the United States than in the United Kingdom, even though both are highly developed countries.

5. Variations in the content and timing of dramatic events during modernization. What is the import of wars, revolutions, rapid migrations, natural catastrophes, etc., for the course of economic and social development?

These sources of variation render it virtually impossible to establish hard and fast empirical generalizations concerning the evolution of social

---

[11] E. Staley, *The Future of Underdeveloped Areas* (New York: Harper & Row, Publishers, Inc., 1954), pp. 21–22; W. W. Rostow, *The Stages of Economic Growth: A Non-Communist Manifesto* (Cambridge: The Clarendon Press, 1960), pp. 26–35; W. E. Moore, *Industrialization and Labor* (Ithaca and New York: Cornell University Press, 1951), Chapters 2–4; Hoselitz, "The City, the Factory, and Economic Growth," pp. 177–79.

[12] United Nations, Department of Economic and Social Affairs, *Processes and Problems of Industrialization in Underdeveloped Countries* (New York: United Nations, 1955), Chapter 1; C. P. Kindleberger, *Economic Development* (New York: McGraw-Hill Book Company, 1958), pp. 184–85, 315–16; N. S. Buchanan and H. S. Ellis, *Approaches to Economic Development* (New York: Twentieth Century Fund, 1955), pp. 275 ff.; Kuznets, "International Differences in Income Levels," pp. 21–22.

structures during economic and social development.[13] Therefore, my purpose here is not to search for such generalizations, but rather to outline certain ideal-type directions of structural change involved in modernization. On the basis of these ideal-types, we may classify, describe, and analyze varying national experiences. Factors like those indicated above determine, in part, a nation's distinctive response to the universal aspects of modernization; but this in no way detracts from their universality. While I shall base my remarks on the vast literature of economic development, I can in no sense attempt an exhaustive comparative study.

STRUCTURAL DIFFERENTIATION IN PERIODS OF DEVELOPMENT

The concept of structural differentiation can be employed to analyze what is frequently termed the "marked break in established patterns of social and economic life" in periods of development.[14] Simply defined, "differentiation" is the evolution from a multifunctional role structure to several more specialized structures. In illustration, we may cite here three typical examples. During a society's transition from domestic to factory industry, the division of labor increases, and the economic activities previously lodged in the family move to the firm. As a formal educational system emerges, the training functions previously performed by the family and church are established in a more specialized unit, the school.[15] The modern political party has a more complex structure than do tribal factions, and the former is less likely to be fettered with kinship loyalties, competition for religious leadership, etc.

Formally defined, then, structural differentiation is a process whereby *one* social role or organization . . . differentiates into *two or more* roles or organizations which function more effectively in the new historical circumstances. The new social units are structurally distinct from each other, but taken together are functionally equivalent to the original unit.[16] Differentiation concerns only changes in role structure. It must not be

---

[13] For instance, Blumer has questioned the generalization that "early industrialization, by nature, alienates and disaffects workers, makes them radical, and propels them to protest behavior." He even concludes that "industrialization . . . is neutral and indifferent to what follows in its wake." (H. Blumer, "Early Industrialization and the Laboring Class," *The Sociological Quarterly*, I: 1 (1960), 9. If one searches for specific generalizations like those Blumer has rejected, of course, he will inevitably be disappointed. One must not conclude, however, that the establishment of ideal-type constructs about the consequences of industrialization and their use in interpreting national experiences are fruitless.

[14] Kuznets, "International Differences in Income Levels," p. 23.

[15] N. J. Smelser, *Social Change in the Industrial Revolution* (Chicago: University of Chicago Press, 1959), Chapters 9–11.

[16] *Ibid.*, p. 2.

confused with two closely related concepts. The first of these involves the cause or motivation for entering the differentiated role. Someone may be motivated to engage in wage-labor, for instance, by a desire for economic improvement, by political coercion, or indeed by a wish to fulfil traditional obligations (e.g., to use wages to supply a dowry). These "reasons" should be kept conceptually distinct from differentiation itself. The other related concept concerns the integration of differentiated roles. For example, as differentiated wage-labor begins to emerge, there also appear legal norms, labor exchanges, trade unions, and so on, that regulate —with varying degrees of success—the relations between labor and management. Such readjustments, even though they sometimes produce a new social unit, should be considered separately from role specialization in other functions.

Let us now inquire into the process of differentiation in several different social realms.

Differentiation of Economic Activities

In underdeveloped countries, production typically is located in kinship units. Subsistence farming predominates; other industry is supplementary but still attached to kin and village. In some cases, occupational position is determined largely by an extended group, such as the caste.[17]

Similarly, exchange and consumption are deeply embedded in family and village. In subsistence agriculture, there is a limited amount of independent exchange outside the family; thus production and consumption occur in the same social context. Exchange systems proper are still lodged in kinship and community (e.g., reciprocal exchange) and stratification systems (e.g., redistribution according to caste membership), and in political systems (e.g., taxes, tributes, payments in kind, forced labor).[18] Under these conditions, market systems are underdeveloped, and the independent power of money to command the movement of goods and services is minimal.

---

[17] Boeke, *op. cit.*, pp. 8–9, 32–34; E. E. Hagen, "The Process of Economic Development," *Economic Development and Cultural Change*, V: 3 (1956), 195; B. K. Maden, "The Economics of the Indian Village and Its Implications in Social Structure," *International Social Science Bulletin*, III: 4 (1951), 813–21; D. F. Dowd, "Two-thirds of the World," in Shannon, *op. cit.*, pp. 14 ff. For qualifications on the degree to which caste dominates occupation in India, see K. Davis, *The Population of India and Pakistan* (Princeton, N.J.: Princeton University Press, 1951), pp. 163 ff.

[18] K. Polanyi, C. M. Arensberg, and H. W. Pearson, eds., *Trade and Market in the Early Empires* (New York: The Free Press and Falcon's Wing Press, 1957); N. J. Smelser, "A Comparative View of Exchange Systems," *Economic Development and Cultural Change*, VII: 2 (1958), 173–82; Boeke, *op. cit.*, pp. 36–39; M. R. Solomon, "The Structure of the Market in Underdeveloped Economies," in Shannon, *op. cit.*, pp. 131 ff.

As the economy develops, several kinds of economic activity are removed from this family-community complex. In agriculture, the introduction of money crops marks a differentiation between the social contexts of production and of consumption. Agricultural wage-labor sometimes undermines the family production unit. In industry several levels of differentiation can be identified. Household industry, the simplest form, parallels subsistence agriculture in that it supplies "the worker's own needs, unconnected with trade." "Handicraft production" splits production and consumption, though frequently consumption takes place in the local community. "Cottage industry," on the other hand, often involves a differentiation between consumption and community, since production is "for the market, for an unknown consumer, sold to a wholesaler who accumulates a stock." [19] Finally, manufacturing and factory systems segregate the worker from his capital and not rarely from his family.

Simultaneously, similar differentiations emerge in the exchange system. Goods and services, previously exchanged on a noneconomic basis, are pulled progressively more into the market. Money now commands the movement of increasingly more goods and services; it thus begins to supplant—and sometimes undermine—the religious, political, familial, or caste sanctions which had hitherto governed economic activity.[20] This is the setting for the institutionalization of relatively autonomous economic systems that exhibit a greater emphasis on values like "universalism," "functional specificity," and "rationality." [21]

Empirically, underdeveloped economies may be classified according to the respective distances they have moved along this line of differentiation. Migratory labor, for instance, may be a kind of compromise between full membership in a wage-labor force and attachment to an old community life. Cottage industry introduces extended markets but retains the family-production fusion. The employment of families in factories maintains a version of family production. The expenditure of wages on traditional items, like dowries, also manifests the half-entry into the more

[19] These "levels," which represent points on the continuum from structural fusion to structural differentiation, are taken from Boeke, *op. cit.*, p. 90.

[20] F. G. Bailey, *Caste and the Economic Frontier* (Manchester: Manchester University Press, 1957), pp. 4–5.

[21] M. J. Levy, Jr., "Some Sources of the Vulnerability of the Structures of Relatively Non-Industrialized Societies to Those of Highly Industrialized Societies," in Hoselitz, *The Progress of Underdeveloped Areas*, pp. 116–25. The pattern variables of T. Parsons are also relevant (discussed in *The Social System* [New York: The Free Press of Glencoe, Inc., 1951], pp. 58–67). For applications of the pattern variables to economic development, see G. A. Theodorson, "Acceptance of Industrialization and Its Attendant Consequences for the Social Patterns of Non-Western Societies," *American Sociological Review*, XVIII: 5 (1953), 477–84; and B. F. Hoselitz, "Social Structure and Economic Growth," *Economia Internazionale*, VI: 3 (1953), 52–77.

differentiated industrial-urban structure.[22] The causes of such partial differentiation may lie in resistance on the part of the populace to give up traditional modes, in the economics of demand for handmade products, in systems of racial discrimination against native labor, or elsewhere.[23] In any case, the concept of structural differentiation provides a yardstick for discerning the distance that the economic structure has evolved toward modernization.

Differentiation of Family Activities

One consequence of the removal of economic activities from the kinship nexus is the family's loss of some of its previous functions, and its thereby becoming a more specialized agency. As the family ceases to be an economic unit of production, one or more members leave the household to seek employment in the labor market. The family's activities become more concentrated on emotional gratification and socialization. While many halfway houses, such as family hiring and migratory systems, persist, the trend is toward the segregation of family functions from economic functions.[24]

Several related processes accompany the differentiation of the family from its other involvements. (1) Apprenticeship within the family declines. (2) Pressures develop against nepotism in the recruitment of labor and management. These pressures often are based on the demands of economic rationality. The intervention frequently persists, however—especially at the managerial levels—and in some cases (e.g., Japan), family ties continue to be a major basis for labor recruitment. (3) The direct control of elders and collateral kinsmen over the nuclear family weakens. This marks, in structural terms, the differentiation of the nuclear family from the extended family. (4) An aspect of this loss of control is the

[22] Examples of these compromises may be found in Moore, *op. cit.*, pp. 29–34; *idem.*, "The Migration of Native Laborers in South Africa," in Shannon, *op. cit.*, pp. 79 ff.; A. I. Richards, ed., *Economic Development and Tribal Change* (Cambridge: W. Heffer, 1952), Chapter 5; C. A. Myers, *Labor Problems in the Industrialization of India* (Cambridge, Mass.: Harvard University Press, 1958), pp. 52, 175; S. Rottenberg, "Income and Leisure in an Underdeveloped Economy," in Shannon, *op. cit.*, pp. 150–51; Aubrey, *op. cit.*, pp. 215 ff.; A. Doucy, "The Unsettled Attitude of Negro Workers in the Belgian Congo," *International Social Science Bulletin*, VI: 3 (1954), 442–51; G. Balandier, "Social Changes and Social Problems in Negro Africa," in C. W. Stillman, ed., *Africa in the Modern World* (Chicago: University of Chicago Press, 1955), pp. 60–61; Smelser, *Social Change*, Chapter 9; Herman, *op. cit.*, pp. 357–58.

[23] Noneconomic barriers are discussed at length in Moore, *Industrialization and Labor*, Chapters 2–4. On the persistence of handicrafts, see A. L. Minkes, "A Note on Handicrafts in Underdeveloped Areas," *Economic Development and Cultural Change*, I: 2 (1952), 56–58; Herman, *op. cit.*, pp. 362–65; T. Uyeda, *The Small Industries of Japan* (Shanghai: Kelly and Walsh, 1938), pp. 84–112.

[24] For case studies, see M. J. Levy, Jr., *The Family Revolution in Modern China* (Cambridge, Mass.: Harvard University Press, 1949), and Smelser, *Social Change*.

growth of personal choice, love, and related criteria as the foundation for courtship and marriage. Structurally, this is the differentiation of courtship from extended kinship. (5) One result of this complex of processes is the changing status of women, who generally become less subordinated economically, politically, and socially to their husbands than they had been under earlier conditions.[25]

In such ways, structural differentiation undermines the old modes of integration in society. The controls of extended family and village begin to dissolve in the enlarged, complicated social setting which differentiation creates. Thereupon, new integrative problems are posed. We shall inquire presently into some of the lines of reintegration.

Differentiation of Religious Systems

Because of Max Weber's monumental thesis linking ascetic Protestantism and capitalism,[26] a disproportionate amount of attention has been devoted to the initiating role that *formal* religious values play in economic development. Although much excellent work has been done in this area,[27] insufficient emphasis has been given to the important role of secular nationalism in the industrial takeoff.

> With the world organized as it is, nationalism is a *sine qua non* of industrialization, because it provides people with an overriding, easily acquired, secular motivation for making painful changes. National strength or prestige becomes the supreme goal, industrialization the chief means. The costs, inconveniences, sacrifices, and loss of traditional

[25] Kindleberger, *op. cit.*, pp. 59 ff.; Moore, *Industrialization and Labor*, pp. 29–34, 71–75; E. F. Frazier, "The Impact of Colonialism on African Social Forms and Personality," in Stillman, *op. cit.*, pp. 76–83; UNESCO, *Social Implications of Industrialization and Urbanization South of Sahara* (Geneva: UNESCO, 1956), pp. 108–9, 115–17, 187, 216–20, 369–72, and 616 ff.; K. El Daghestani, "The Evolution of the Moslem Family in the Middle Eastern Countries," *International Social Science Bulletin*, VI: 3 (1954), 442–51; B. J. Siegel, "Social Structure and Economic·Change in Brazil," and S. J. Stein, "The Brazilian Cotton Textile Industry, 1850–1950," both in Kuznets, *et al.*, *Economic Growth*, pp. 388 ff., 433–38; W. Elkan, *An African Labour Force* (Kampala, Uganda: East African Institute of Social Research, 1956), Chapter 5; Myers, *op. cit.*, p. 177; Linton, *op. cit.*, pp. 83–84; H. Belshaw, "Some Social Aspects of Economic Development in Underdeveloped Areas," in Shannon, *op. cit.*, pp. 88 ff., 191 ff.; G. St. J. Orde-Browne, *The African Labourer* (London: Oxford University Press, 1933), pp. 100–5.

[26] Weber's relevant works include *The Protestant Ethic and the Spirit of Capitalism* (London: G. Allen & Unwin, 1948); *The Religion of China* (New York: The Free Press, Inc., 1951); and *The Religion of India* (New York: The Free Press, Inc., 1958). For secondary treatments, see T. Parsons, *The Structure of Social Action* (New York: The Macmillan Company, 1937), Chapters 14–15; and R. Bendix, *Max Weber* (Garden City, N.Y.: Doubleday & Company, Inc., 1960), Parts I and II.

[27] R. N. Bellah, *Tokugawa Religion* (New York: The Free Press and the Falcon's Wing Press, 1957); C. Geertz, *The Social Context of Economic Change* (Cambridge, Mass.: Center for International Studies, MIT, 1956).

values can be justified in terms of this transcending, collective ambition. The new collective entity, the nation-state, that sponsors and grows from this aspiration is equal to the exigencies of industrial complexity; it draws directly the allegiance of every citizen, organizing the population as one community; it controls the passage of persons, goods, and news across the borders; it regulates economic and social life in detail. To the degree that the obstacles to industrialization are strong, nationalism must be intense to overcome them.[28]

In fact, nationalism seems to many cases to be the very instrument designed to smash the traditional religious systems—those like the classical Chinese or Indian—which Weber himself found to be less permissive than Protestantism for economic modernization.

On the other hand, nationalism, like many traditionalistic religious systems, may hinder economic advancement by "reaffirmation of traditionally honored ways of acting and thinking," [29] by fostering anticolonial attitudes after they are no longer relevant,[30] and, more indirectly, by encouraging passive expectations of "ready-made prosperity." [31] We can distinguish among these contrasting forces of "stimulus" and "drag" that such value systems bring to economic development by using the logic of differentiation in the following way.

In the early phases of modernization, many traditional attachments must be modified to permit more differentiated institutional structures to be set up. Because the existing commitments and methods of integration are deeply rooted in the organization of traditional society, a very generalized and powerful commitment is required to pry individuals from these attachments. The values of ascetic and this-worldly religious beliefs, xenophobic national aspirations, and political ideologies (like socialism), provide such a lever. Sometimes these diverse types of values combine into a single system of legitimacy. In any case, all three have an "ultimacy" of commitment, in whose name a wide range of sacrifices can be demanded and procured.

The very success of these value systems, however, breeds the condi-

[28] K. Davis, "Social and Demographic Aspects of Economic Development in India," in Kuznets *et al.*, *Economic Growth*, p. 294; Gerschenkron, *op. cit.*, pp. 22–25; Rostow, *op. cit.*, pp. 26–29.

[29] B. F. Hoselitz, "Non-Economic Barriers to Economic Development," *Economic Development and Cultural Change*, I: 1 (1952), p. 9.

[30] Cf., for example, the Indonesian expulsion of needed Dutch teachers and engineers. It has been maintained that the upsurge of regionalism in India has led to a deterioration of English as a linguistic medium for education in Indian universities. See S. E. Harrison, *India: The Most Dangerous Decades* (Princeton, N.J.: Princeton University Press, 1960), pp. 60–95.

[31] J. van der Kroef, "Economic Developments in Indonesia: Some Social and Cultural Impediments," *Economic Development and Cultural Change*, IV: 2 (1955), 116–33.

tions for their own weakening. In a perceptive statement, Weber notes that, at the beginning of the twentieth century, when the capitalistic system was already highly developed, it no longer needed the impetus of ascetic Protestantism.[32] By virtue of its conquest of much of Western society, capitalism had solidly established an institutional base and a secular value system of its own—economic rationality. Its secular economic values had no further need for the "ultimate" justification they had required during the newer, unsteadier days of economic revolution.

Such lines of differentiation constitute the secularization of religious values. In the same process, other institutional spheres—economic, political, scientific, etc.—become more nearly established on their own. The values governing these spheres are no longer sanctioned directly by religious beliefs, but by an autonomous rationality. Insofar as this replaces religious sanctions, secularization occurs in these spheres.

Similarly, nationalistic and related value systems undergo a process of secularization as differentiation proceeds. As a society moves increasingly toward more complex social organization, the encompassing demands of nationalistic commitment give way to more autonomous systems of rationality. For instance, the Soviet Union, as its social structure grows more differentiated, is apparently introducing more "independent" market mechanisms, "freer" social scientific investigation in some spheres, and so on.[33] Moreover, these measures are not directly sanctioned by nationalistic or communistic values. Finally, it seems reasonable to make the historical generalization that, in the early stages of a nation's development, nationalism is heady, muscular, and aggressive; as the society evolves to an advanced state, however, nationalism tends to settle into a more remote and complacent condition, rising to fury only in times of national crisis.

Hence there is a paradoxical element in the role of religious or nationalistic belief systems. Insofar as they encourage the breakup of old patterns, they may stimulate economic modernization. Insofar as they resist their own subsequent secularization, however, these same value systems may become impediments to economic advance and structural change.

Differentiation of Systems of Stratification

In analyzing systems of stratification, we concentrate on two kinds of issues.

1. Are ascribed qualities subject to ranking? Ascription focuses primarily on those aspects of the human condition that touch the biological

---

[32] *The Protestant Ethic and the Spirit of Capitalism*, pp. 181–82.

[33] E. Crankshaw, "Big Business in Russia," *Atlantic*, CCII: 5 (1958), 35–41. For discussion of the balance among political and other elements in Soviet society, see R. A. Bauer, A. Inkeles, and C. Kluckhohn, *How the Soviet System Works* (Cambridge: Harvard University Press, 1957), Part II.

and physical world—kinship, age, sex, race or ethnicity, and territorial location. To what extent is status determined by birth in a certain tribe? in a certain family? in a certain ethnic group? in a certain place—a region of the country or "the wrong side of the tracks"? Some ascription exists in all societies, since the infant in the nuclear family always and everywhere begins with the status of his parents.[34] The degree to which this ascribed ranking extends beyond the family varies from society to society. In our own ideology, we minimize the ascriptive elements of class and ethnic membership; but in practice these matter greatly, especially for Negroes.

2. To what degree are all positions in society (occupational, political, religious, etc.) consequences of status ascribed from birth? For example, the American egalitarian ideology places a premium on the maximum separation of these positions from ascribed categories; but in fact, family membership, minority-group membership, etc., impinge on the ultimate "placing" of persons. In many nonindustrialized societies, the link between ascription and position is much closer. Criteria like these reveal the degree of openness, or social mobility, in a system.

Under conditions of economic modernization, structural differentiation increases along both dimensions discussed.

1. Other evaluative standards intrude on ascribed memberships. For instance, McKim Marriott has noted that, in the village of Paril in India,

> Personal wealth, influence, and mortality have surpassed the traditional caste-and-order alignment of kind groups as the effective bases of ranking. Since such new bases of ranking can no longer be clearly tied to any inclusive system of large solidary groupings, judgments must be made according to the characteristics of individual or family units. This individualization of judgments leads to greater dissensus [sic].[35]

Of course, castes, ethnic groups, and traditional religious groupings do not necessarily decline in importance *in every respect* during periods of modernization. As political interest groups or reference groups for diffuse loyalty, they may become even more significant.[36] As the sole bases of

[34] K. Davis, *Human Society* (New York: The Macmillan Company, 1957), Chapter 14; T. Parsons, "An Analytical Approach to the Theory of Social Stratification," *Essays in Sociological Theory,* rev. ed. (New York: The Free Press, Inc., 1954), Chapter 4.

[35] M. Marriott, "Social Change in an Indian Village," *Economic Development and Cultural Change,* I: 2 (1952), 153; UNESCO, *op. cit.,* p. 152; J. S. Coleman, *Nigeria: Background to Nationalism* (Berkeley and Los Angeles: University of California Press, 1958), pp. 70–73.

[36] In some cases, these ascriptive pegs become the basis for political groupings long after the society has begun to modernize. See E. H. Jacoby, *Agrarian Unrest in Southeast Asia* (New York: Columbia University Press, 1949), pp. 27–28, 50, 76, 91–93, 123–25, and 248; Coleman, *op. cit.,* pp. 332–67. Harrison has argued that the

ranking, however, ascriptive standards become more differentiated from economic, political, and other standards.[37]

2. Individual mobility through the occupational hierarchies increases. This is indicative of the differentiation of the adult's functional position from his point of origin. In addition, individual mobility is frequently substituted for collective mobility. Individuals, and no longer whole castes or tribes, compete for higher standing in society. The phenomenon of growing individual mobility seems to be one of the universal consequences of industrialization. After assembling extensive empirical data on patterns of mobility in industrialized nations, Lipset and Bendix conclude that "the overall pattern of [individual] social mobility appears to be much the same in the industrial societies of various Western countries." [38] Patterns of class symbolization and class ideology may, however, continue to be different in industrialized countries.

THE INTEGRATION OF DIFFERENTIATED ACTIVITIES

One of Emile Durkheim's remarkable insights concerns the role of integrative mechanisms during periods of growing social heterogeneity. Attacking the utilitarian view that the division of labor would flourish best without regulation, Durkheim demonstrated that one concomitant of a growing division of labor is an *increase* in mechanisms for coordinating and solidifying the interaction among individuals whose interests are becoming progressively more diversified.[39] Durkheim located this integration largely in the legal structure; however, similar kinds of integrative forces can be discerned elsewhere in society.

Differentiation, therefore, is not by itself sufficient for modernization.

---

present significance of caste in India is "if anything, stronger than before," but that this significance appears as competitiveness in the new political arena of the country (Harrison, *op. cit.*, Chapter 4; also Davis, *Population of India*, p. 171). William Petersen has suggested that, in the advanced society of Holland, a process of "pillarization" has occurred, in which semi-ascribed religious groups have become the major focus of political and social competition ("Dutch Society vs. Mass Society," University of California Public Lecture, May 9, 1960).

[37] For a study of the cross-cultural similarity in the ranking of industrial occupations in developed countries, see A. Inkeles and P. H. Rossi, "National Comparisons of Occupational Prestige," *American Journal of Sociology*, LXI: 4 (1956), 329–39.

[38] S. M. Lipset and R. Bendix, *Social Mobility in Industrial Society* (Berkeley and Los Angeles: University of California Press, 1959), pp. 13 ff. Of course, the transition from collective to individual mobility is not instantaneous. See Marriott, *op. cit.*, p. 153; and Davis, "Social and Demographic Aspects of Economic Development in India," pp. 308–13.

[39] E. Durkheim, *The Division of Labor in Society* (New York: The Free Press of Glencoe, Inc., 1949), Chapters 3–8. A recent formulation of the relationship between differentiation and integration may be found in R. F. Bales, *Interaction Process Analysis* (Cambridge, Mass.: Addison-Wesley Press, 1950).

Development proceeds as a contrapuntal interplay between differentiation (which is divisive of established society) and integration (which unites differentiated structures on a new basis). Paradoxically, however, the course of integration itself produces more *differentiated* structures— e.g., trade unions, associations, political parties, and a mushrooming state apparatus. Let us illustrate this complex process of integration in several institutional spheres.

Economy and Family

Under a simple kind of economic organization, like subsistence agriculture or household industry, there is little differentiation between economic roles and family roles. All reside in the kinship structure. The *integration* of these diverse but unspecialized activities also rests in the local family and community structures, and in the religious traditions which fortify both.

When differentiation has begun, the social setting for production is separated from that for consumption; and the productive roles of family members are isolated geographically, temporally, and structurally from their distinctively familial roles. This differentiation immediately creates integrative problems. How is information about employment opportunities to be conveyed to working people? How are the interests of families to be integrated with the interests of firms? How are families to be protected from market fluctuation? Whereas such integrative exigencies had been faced by kinsmen, neighbors, and local largesse in premodern settings, modernization creates dozens of institutions and organizations designed to deal with the new integrative problems—labor recruitment agencies and exchanges; labor unions; government regulation of labor allocation; welfare and relief arrangements; cooperative societies; savings institutions.[40] All these involve agencies which specialize in integration.

Community

When industrialization occurs only in villages, or when villages are built around paternalistic industrial enterprises,[41] many ties of community and kinship can be maintained under the industrial conditions. Urbanization, however, frequently creates more anonymity. As a result, in expanding cities there often emerge voluntary associations—churches and chapels, unions, schools, halls, athletic clubs, bars, shops, mutual-aid groups, etc. Sometimes the growth of these integrative groupings is

[40] Smelser, *Social Change*, Chapters 12–13; T. Parsons and N. Smelser, *Economy and Society* (New York: The Free Press, Inc., 1956), Chapter 3; also Nash, *op. cit.*, p. 275; A. Mehta, "The Mediating Role of the Trade Union in Underdeveloped Countries," *Economic Development and Cultural Change*, VI: 1 (1957), 20–23.

[41] Smelser, *Social Change*, pp. 99–108; Myers, *op. cit.*, pp. 52–54; Stein, *op. cit.*, pp. 433 ff.

retarded because of the movement of migratory workers,[42] who "come to the city for their differentiation" and "return to the village for their integration." In cities themselves, the original criterion for associating may have been the common tribe, caste, or village; this criterion sometimes persists or is gradually replaced by more "functional" groupings based on economic or political interest.[43]

Political Structure

In a typical premodern setting, political integration is closely fused with kinship position, tribal membership, control of the land, or control of the unknown. Political forms include chieftains, kings, councils of elders, strong landlords, powerful magicians and oracles, etc.

As social systems grow more complex, political systems are modified accordingly. Fortes and Evans-Pritchard have specified three types of native African political systems. These, listed in terms of their respective degrees of differentiation from kinship lineages, are as follows: (1) small societies in which the largest political unit embraces only those united by kinship—thus political authority is coterminous with kinship relations; (2) societies in which the political framework is the integrative core for a number of kinship lineages; and (3) societies with a more formal administrative organization. Such systems move toward greater differentiation as the society's population grows and economic and cultural heterogenity increases.[44] In colonial and recently freed African societies, political systems have evolved much further; parties, congresses, pressure groups, and even "parliamentary" systems have emerged.[45] In describing the Indian village, Marriott speaks of the "wider integration of local groups with outside groups." [46] Sometimes such wider political integration is, like community integration, based on extension and modification of an old integrative principle. Harrison has argued that modern developments in India have changed the significance of caste from the "traditional village extension of the joint family" to "regional alliances of kindred local units." This modification has led to the formation of "new caste lobbies"

[42] Orde-Browne, *op. cit.*, pp. 112–16; Doucy, *op. cit.*, pp. 446–50; Elkan, *op. cit.*, Chapters 2–3.

[43] UNESCO, *op. cit.*, pp. 84–85, 105, 120–21, 128–30, 220–21, 373–77, and 469–73; D. Forde, "The Social Impact of Industrialization and Urban Conditions in Africa South of the Sahara," *International Social Science Bulletin*, VII: 1 (1955), 119–21; Hodgkin, *op. cit.*, pp. 85 ff.; Hoselitz, "The City, the Factory, and Economic Growth," p. 183; Coleman, *op. cit.*, pp. 73–80; Harrison, *op. cit.*, pp. 330–32.

[44] M. Fortes and E. E. Evans-Pritchard, eds., *African Political Systems* (London: Oxford University Press, 1940), pp 1–25.

[45] D. Apter, *The Gold Coast in Transition* (Princeton, N.J.: Princeton University Press, 1955); Hodgkin, *op. cit.*, pp. 115–39; G. A. Almond and J. S. Coleman, *The Politics of Developing Areas* (Princeton, N.J.: Princeton University Press, 1960).

[46] Marriott, *op. cit.*, p. 152.

which constitute some of the strongest and most explosive political forces in modern India.[47] We shall mention some of the possible political consequences of this persistence of old integrative forms later.

We have indicated the ways in which differentiation in society impinges on the integrative sphere. The resulting integrative structures attempt, with more or less success, to coordinate and solidify the social structure which the forces of differentiation threaten to fragment. In many cases, the integrative associations and parties are extremely unstable: labor unions turn into political or nationalistic parties; religious sects become political clubs; football clubs become religious sects; and so on.[48] This fluidity indicates the urgent need for reintegration during rapid, irregular, and disruptive processes of differentiation. The initial response is a trial-and-error type of reaching for many kinds of integration at once.

We have outlined some structural consequences of technological advance, agricultural commercialization, urbanization, and industrialization. We have analyzed these consequences in terms of differentiation and integration. The structural changes are not, one must remember, a simple function of industrialization alone. Some of the most far-reaching structural changes have occurred in countries where industrialization has hardly begun. For instance, colonialism or related forms of economic dominance create not only an extensive differentiation of cash products and wage-labor, but also a vulnerability to world price fluctuations in commodities.[49] Hence many of the structural changes already described, and the consequent social disturbances to be described presently, are characteristics of societies which are still technically pre-industrial.

DISCONTINUITIES IN DIFFERENTIATION AND INTEGRATION: SOCIAL DISTURBANCES

The structural changes associated with modernization are disruptive to the social order for the following reasons:

1. Differentiation demands the creation of new activities, norms, rewards, and sanctions—money, political position, prestige based on occupation, etc. These often conflict with old modes of social action, which are frequently dominated by traditional religious, tribal, and kinship systems. Traditional standards are among the most intransigent obstacles to modernization; and when they are threatened, serious dissatisfaction and opposition to the threatening agents arise.

[47] Harrison, *op. cit.*, pp. 100 ff.
[48] Hodgkin, *op. cit.*, pp. 85 ff.
[49] Jacoby, *op. cit.*, Chapter 1; R. Emerson, L. A. Mills, and V. Thompson, *Government and Nationalism in Southeast Asia* (New York: Institute of Pacific Relations, 1942), pp. 135–36; S. A. Mosk, *Industrial Revolution in Mexico* (Berkeley and Los Angeles: University of California Press, 1950), pp. 3–17.

2. Structural change is, above all, *uneven* during periods of modernization. In colonial societies, for instance, the European powers frequently revolutionized the economic, political, and educational framework; but they simultaneously encouraged or imposed a conservatism in traditional religious, class, and family systems.

> The basic problem in these [colonial] societies was the expectation that the native population would accept certain broad, modern institutional settings ... and would perform within them various roles—especially economic and administrative roles—while at the same time, they were denied some of the basic rewards inherent in these settings ... they were expected to act on the basis of a motivational system derived from a different social structure which the colonial powers and indigenous rulers tried to maintain.[50]

In a society undergoing postcolonial modernization, similar discontinuities appear. Within the economy itself, rapid industrialization—no matter how coordinated—bites unevenly into the established social and economic structures.[51] And throughout the society, the differentiation occasioned by agricultural, industrial, and urban changes always proceeds in a see-saw relationship with integration: the two forces continuously breed lags and bottlenecks. The faster the tempo of modernization is, the more severe the discontinuities. This unevenness creates *anomie* in the classical sense, for it generates disharmony between life experiences and the normative framework which regulates them.[52]

3. Dissatisfactions arising from conflict with traditional ways and those arising from anomie sometimes aggravate each other upon coming into contact. Anomie may be partially relieved by new integrative devices, like unions, associations, clubs, and government regulations. However, such innovations are often opposed by traditional vested interests because they compete with the older undifferentiated systems of solidarity.[53] The result is a three-way tug-of-war among the forces of tradition, the forces of differentiation, and the new forces of integration.[54] Under these conditions, virtually unlimited potentialities for group conflict are created.[55]

[50] S. N. Eisenstadt, "Sociological Aspects of Political Development in Under-developed Countries," *Economic Development and Cultural Change,* V: 4 (1956), 298.

[51] P. T. Bauer and B. S. Yamey, *The Economics of Underdeveloped Countries* (Chicago: University of Chicago Press, 1957), p. 64.

[52] E. Durkheim, *Suicide* (New York: The Free Press, Inc., 1951), Book II, Chapter 5.

[53] Davis, "Social and Demographic Aspects of Economic Development in India," pp. 296 ff.

[54] E.g., M. A. Jaspan, "A Sociological Case Study: Community Hostility to Imposed Social Change in South Africa," in Ruopp, *op. cit.,* pp. 97–120.

[55] E.g., the conflict between migratory workers and full-time resident workers; see Elkan, *op. cit.,* pp. 23–24.

Three classic responses to these discontinuities are anxiety, hostility, and fantasy. If and when these responses become collective, they crystallize into a variety of social movements—peaceful agitation, political violence, millenarianism, nationalism, revolution, underground subversion, etc.[56] There is plausible—though not entirely convincing—evidence that the people most readily drawn into such movements are those suffering most severely under the displacements created by structural change. For example:

> [Nationalism appeared] as a permanent force in Southeast Asia at the
> moment when the peasants were forced to give up subsistence farming
> for the cultivation of cash crops or when (as in highly colonized Java)
> subsistence farming ceased to yield a subsistence. The introduction of
> a money economy and the withering away of the village as the unit of
> life accompanied this development and finally established the period
> of economic dependence.[57]

Other theoretical and empirical data suggest that social movements appeal most to those who have been dislodged from old social ties by differentiation without also being integrated into the new social order.[58]

Many belief systems associated with these movements envision the grand, almost instantaneous integration of society. Frequently, the beliefs are highly emotional and unconcerned with realistic policies. In nationalistic movements in colonial societies, for instance, "the political symbols were intended to develop new, ultimate, common values and basic loyalties, rather than relate to current policy issues within the colonial society." [59] Furthermore, belief systems of this kind reflect the ambivalence that results from the conflict between traditionalism and modernization. Nationalists alternate between xenophobia and xenophilia; they predict that they will simultaneously "outmodernize" the West in the future and "restore" the true values of the ancient civilization; they argue for both egalitarian and hierarchical principles of social organization at the same time.[60] Nationalism and related ideologies unite these contradictory tendencies in the society under one large symbol. If these ideologies are suc-

---

[56] For theoretical discussions of this relationship between strain and disturbance, see T. Parsons, R. F. Bales, *et al.*, *Family, Socialization, and Interaction Process* (New York: The Free Press, Inc., 1955), Chapters 2, 4; Smelser, *Social Change*, Chapters 2, 9, 10.

[57] Jacoby, *op. cit.*, p. 246.

[58] Emerson, *et al.*, *op. cit.*, pp. 25–29; Eisenstadt, *op. cit.*, pp. 294–98; W. Kornhauser, *The Politics of Mass Society* (New York: The Free Press, Inc., 1959), Parts II and III; S. M. Lipset, *Political Man* (Garden City, N.Y.: Doubleday & Company, Inc., 1960), Chapter 2; M. Watnick, "The Appeal of Communism to the Underdeveloped Peoples," in Hoselitz, *Progress of Underdeveloped Areas*, pp. 152–72.

[59] Eisenstadt, *op. cit.*, p. 294.

[60] M. Matossian, "Ideologies of Delayed Industrialization," *Economic Development and Cultural Change*, VI: 3 (1957), 217–18.

cessful, they are then often used as a means to modernize the society and thus to erase those kinds of social discontinuity that caused the initial nationalistic outburst.

Naturally, early modernization does not inevitably produce violent nationalism or other social movements. Furthermore, when such movements do arise, they take many different forms. Below are listed the five factors which seem most decisive in the genesis and molding of social disturbances.

1. The scope and intensity of the social dislocation created by structural changes. "The greater the tempo of these changes . . . the greater the problems of acute malintegration the society has to face." [61]

2. The structural complexity of the society at the time when modernization begins. In the least developed societies, where "the language of politics is at the same time the language of religion," protest movements more or less immediately take on a religious cast. In Africa, for instance, utopian religious movements apparently have relatively greater appeal in the less developed regions; whereas the more secular types of political protest, like trade union movements and party agitations, have tended to cluster in the more developed areas.[62] The secularization of protest increases, of course, as modernization and differentiation advance.

3. The access that disturbed groups have to channels that influence social policy. If dislocated groups have access to those responsible for introducing reforms, agitation is usually relatively peaceful and orderly. If this avenue is blocked—because of either the isolation of the groups or the intransigence of the ruling authorities—demands for reform tend to take more violent, utopian, and bizarre forms. This is the reason that fantasy and unorganized violence are likely to cluster among the disinherited, the colonized, and the socially isolated migrants.[63]

4. The overlap of interests and lines of cleavage. In many colonial societies, the social order broke more or less imperfectly into three groupings: (a) the Western representatives, who controlled economic and political administration, and who were frequently allied with large local landowners; (b) a large native population who—when drawn into the colonial economy—entered it as tenant farmers, wage-laborers, etc.; (c) a group of

---

[61] Eisenstadt, *loc. cit.;* J. S. Coleman, "Nationalism in Tropical Africa," in Shannon, *op. cit.,* pp. 42 ff.; Hodgkin, *op. cit.,* p. 56.

[62] Hodgkin, *op. cit.,* pp. 95–150; Coleman, "Nationalism in Tropical Africa," pp. 38 ff.

[63] B. Barber, "Acculturation and Messianic Movements," *American Sociological Review,* VI: 6 (1941), 663–69; H. R. Niebuhr, *The Social Sources of Denominationalism* (New York: Henry Holt, 1929), J. B. Holt, "Holiness Religion: Cultural Shock and Social Reorganization," *American Sociological Review,* V: 5 (1940), 740–47; B. G. M. Sundkler, *Bantu Prophets in South Africa* (London: Lutterworth Press, 1948); P. Worsley, *The Trumpet Shall Sound* (London: MacGibbon and Kee, 1957).

foreigners—Chinese, Indians, Syrians, Goans, Lebanese, etc.—who fitted between the first two groups as traders, moneylenders, merchants, creditors, etc. This view is oversimplified, of course; but several colonial societies approximated this arrangement.[64] The important structural feature of such an arrangement is that economic, political, and racial-ethnic memberships *coincide* with each other. Thus, *any* kind of conflict is likely to assume racial overtones and to arouse the more diffuse loyalties and prejudices of the warring parties. Many colonial outbursts did, in fact, follow racial lines.[65] Insofar as such "earthquake faults" persist after independence has been attained, these societies will probably be plagued by similar outbursts.[66] If, on the other hand, the different lines of cleavage in the society crisscross, the society is more nearly able to insulate and manage specific economic and political grievances peacefully.[67]

5. The kind and amount of foreign infiltration and intervention on behalf of protest groups.

STRUCTURAL BASES FOR THE ROLE OF GOVERNMENT

Many have argued, on economic grounds, for the presence of a strong, centralized government in rapidly modernizing societies. Governmental planning and activity are required, for example, to direct saving and investment, to regulate incentives, to encourage entrepreneurship, to control trade and prices, etc.[68] To their arguments, I should like to add several considerations that emerge from the analysis of structural change during periods of rapid development.

1. Undifferentiated institutional structures frequently constitute the primary social barriers to modernization. Individuals refuse to work for wages because of traditional kinship, village, tribal, and other ties. Invariably, a certain amount of political pressure must be applied to loosen these ties. The need for this pressure increases, of course, in proportion to the rate of modernization desired.

2. The process of differentiation itself creates conditions demanding a larger, more formal type of political administration. Thus, another argument in favor of the importance of strong government during rapid and

---

[64] Emerson, *et al.*, *op. cit.*, pp. 136–40; Hodgkin, *op. cit.*, pp. 60–75; C. Robequain, *The Economic Development of French Indo-China* (London: Oxford University Press, 1944), pp. 79–88; J. S. Furnivall, *Colonial Policy and Practice* (London: Cambridge University Press, 1948), pp. 116–23.

[65] Emerson *et al.*, *op. cit.*, pp. 141–43; Jacoby, *op. cit.*, Chapter 8.

[66] J. M. van der Kroef, "Minority Problems in Indonesia," *Far Eastern Survey*, XXIV (1956), 129–33, 165–71; Harrison, *op. cit.*, Chapters 3–6.

[67] Lipset, *Political Man*, Chapter 3.

[68] J. J. Spengler, "Social Structure, the State, and Economic Growth," in Kuznets *et al.*, *Economic Growth*, pp. 370–79.

uneven modernization is based on the necessity to accommodate the grow-ing cultural, economic, and social heterogeneity, and to control the politi-cal repercussions of the constantly shifting distribution of power accom-panying extensive social reorganization.

3. The probability that periods of early modernization will erupt into explosive outburst creates delicate political problems for the leaders of developing nations. We shall conclude this essay on the major social forces of modernization by suggesting the kinds of government that are likely to be most effective in such troubled areas. First, political leaders can increase their effectiveness by openly and vigorously committing themselves to utopian and xenophobic nationalism. This commitment is a powerful instrument for attaining three of their most important ends. (*a*) They can enhance their own claim to legitimacy by endowing them-selves with the mission of creating the nation-state. (*b*) They can procure otherwise unobtainable sacrifices from a populace which may be com-mitted to modernization in the abstract, but which resists making concrete breaks with traditional ways. (*c*) They can use their claim to legitimacy to repress protests and to prevent generalized symbols systems, such as communism, from spreading to all sorts of particular grievances. How-ever, these political leaders should not take their claim to legitimacy too literally. They should not rely on their nationalistic commitment as being strong enough to enable them to ignore or smother grievances completely. They should "play politics," in the usual sense, with aggrieved groups, thus giving these groups access to responsible political agencies, and thereby reducing the conditions that favor counter-claims to legitimacy. One key to political stability seems to be, therefore, the practice of flexi-ble politics behind the facade of an inflexible commitment to a national mission.

CONCLUSION

I have attempted to sketch, in ideal-type terms, the ways in which economic and social development are related to the social structure. I have organized the discussion around three major categories: differentia-tion, which characterizes a social structure that is moving toward greater complexity; integration, which in certain respects balances the divisive character of differentiation; and social disturbances, which result from the discontinuities between differentiation and integration.

Four qualifications must be added to this analysis. (1) I have not tried to account for the determinants of economic development itself. In fact, the discussion of differentiation, integration, and social disturbances has presupposed a certain attempt to develop economically. However, these three forces condition the *course* of that development once it has started. (2) For purposes of exposition, I have presented the three major categories in the order restated above. However, this ordering must not be inferred to mean that any one of the forces assumes causal precedence in social change. Rather, they form an interactive system. Disturbances, for instance, may arise from discontinuities created by structural differentiation; but these very disturbances may shape the course of future processes of differentiation. Likewise, integrative developments may be set in motion by differentiation; but they, in their turn, may initiate new lines of differentiation. (3) Even though the forces of differentiation, integration, and disturbances are closely linked empirically, we should not "close" the "system" composed of the relationship among the three forces. Differentiation may arise from sources other than economic development; the necessity for integration may emerge from conditions other than differentiation; and the sources of social disturbances are not exhausted by the discontinuities between differentiation and integration. (4) The "all-at-once" character of the transition from less differentiated to more differentiated societies should not be exaggerated. Empirically, the process evolves gradually and influences the social structure selectively. This essay has emphasized various halfway arrangements and compromises in order to illustrate this gradualness and irregularity.

SEVEN: Social Structure, Mobility, and Economic Development [*]

Analysis of economic development often begins by identifying a specific dependent variable—for example, rate of growth of per capita output. The strategy of explanation is to assemble certain independent variables—consumption, investment, labor supply, for instance—and, by assigning values to these variables, to arrive at resultant rates of economic growth.[1] Sometimes a theory of economic development moves beyond the mere assignment of quantitative values to such independent variables, and takes into account changes in the *structure* of the economy, such as shifts in the distribution of industries.[2]

The same strategy of explanation can be followed in analyzing development in noneconomic spheres, though frequently it is more difficult to identify variables and specify measures for them. Take educational development, for instance. One salient dependent variable is change in the rate of literacy in a population. The immediate determinants of variations

[*] Coauthored with Seymour Martin Lipset of Harvard University. This paper appeared as Chapter I in Neil J. Smelser and Seymour Martin Lipset, eds., *Social Structure and Mobility in Economic Development* (Chicago: Aldine Publishing Co., 1966), pp. 1–50. Although the authors share equal responsibility for this article, we divided the initial drafting by sections that reflect our varying concerns. I handled the first part, dealing with matters of conceptual clarification, while Lipset dealt primarily with the second, the discussion of research problems and findings beginning on page 161. Some of the remarks in the first part grow from a memorandum entitled "The Allocation of Roles in the Process of Development," prepared jointly by Harvey Leibenstein and myself. A portion of the second part was published earlier in S. M. Lipset, "Research Problems in the Comparative Analysis of Mobility and Development," *International Social Science Journal*, XXVI (1964), 35–48.

[1] For a summary of the recent literature on such models, cf. Henry J. Burton, "Contemporary Theorizing on Economic Growth," in Bert F. Hoselitz, ed., *Theories of Economic Growth* (New York: The Free Press of Glencoe, Inc., 1960), pp. 243–61.

[2] *Ibid.*, pp. 262–67.

in this rate are the economic and political requirements of the society in question, the availability of teachers and educational facilities, and so on. These variables in their turn depend in part on the rates of change in the educational system's social environment.

Development as a whole involves a complex series of changes in rates of growth—of output per capita, of literacy, of political participation, etc. —and major changes in these rates depend on the occurrence of fundamental changes in the social structure of the developing society. To complicate the study of development even more, changes in one institutional sector set up demands for changes in other sectors. Rapid economic development, for instance, establishes pressure for adjustment in the education and training of a new type of labor force. Again, if the educational system produces a large number of literate, skilled, but unemployable persons, this often sets up demands for economic or political adjustments to assimilate these persons into socially meaningful and perhaps economically productive roles.

Viewing developing thus, we cannot escape the fact that persons must be shuttled through the social structure during periods of rapid development. Often they have to move to an urban setting. They must fill new occupational roles and positions of leadership. They must learn to respond to new rewards and deprivations and to accept new standards for effective performance. Development often requires more movement of persons than during predevelopment periods; certainly it requires different forms of movement. The ease with which this movement is effected, furthermore, depends largely on the character of the social structure of the society in question—in particular, the demands of the developing structure, the characteristics of the traditional social structure, and the emerging tension between the two.

The study of this movement of persons—either as individuals or in groups—through the social structure is the study of *social mobility*. The objective of this essay is to define and explore the relations between social mobility and social structure, especially under conditions of development. We shall first review the concepts of social structure, stratification, and social mobility; then we shall mention several dimensions of social structure that are critical for the study of mobility; finally, we shall explore the impact of rapid development on social structure and on patterns of social mobility.

SOCIAL STRUCTURE AND RELATED CONCEPTS

At the most general level "social structure" as a construct is used to characterize recurrent and regularized interaction among two or more persons. In its contemporary usage in the social sciences, however, this construct can be understood only by referring to two other sets of concepts: the *directional tendencies* of social systems, and the *resources* of social systems. Let us define each briefly, and show how the concept of social structure links them.

1. *Directional Tendencies*   One of the most fundamental sets of concepts employed in analyzing social systems concerns the general orientation of social life. Or, some put the question, what exigencies must be met if the social system is to continue functioning? Exigencies that are typically listed include the production and allocation of scarce commodities, the socialization of the young, the coordination and control of social interaction, and so on. Around these exigencies social life revolves; social resources are devoted to meeting each exigency. Some analysts maintain, moreover, that unless these exigencies are met satisfactorily, disequilibrium of the social system will result.[3]

2. *Resources*   A second set of variables that enter propositions about social systems concerns the capacities or resources available to the system. In economics the concept of capacities has been formulated as the "factors of production"; given the general objective of producing goods and services, the capacities of the economy are found in land, labor, capital, and organization. The importance of resources arises in other institutional sectors as well: the level of literacy and training of the population and its physical fitness, the level of information available for action, and so on, are always relevant to structured social action. It is useful to distinguish between two aspects of capacities: (*a*) obstacles that limit the performance of a system—examples are the limited number of hours in a day, and the limited physical energy that people can expend before becoming exhausted; (*b*) means that facilitate the performance of a system. Examples are a high level of skill of the actors, a high level of knowledge about the social situation at hand, etc.

"Social structure" refers to organized bundles of human activities oriented to the directional tendencies of a social system. The business firm, for instance, is a structure devoted primarily to the production of goods and services. The nuclear family is a set of institutionalized roles, one major function of which is to socialize the young in the cultural values of a society. In contributing to such functions, these structures utilize the resources of social systems. Firms utilize the factors of production. Families utilize some of the motivational energy of adults and some of the family income in socializing children. Thus "social structure" is an interstitial concept in that it links the basic directional tendencies of a social system and its resources.

The usual basis for classifying social structures is to return to the

[3] For further discussion of the way the concepts of directional tendencies, exigencies, functional imperatives, etc., are used, see above, pp. 10–11.

basic directional tendencies of the social system. Thus we refer to political, economic, familial, religious, educational, aesthetic, etc., structures. This type of classification involves the assignment of *primacies* only. Even though "religious structure" is the concept used to classify a cluster of rites or an organized church, the social significance of this bundle of activities is not exhausted by using this term. From an analytic point of view, this religious structure has a "political aspect," an "economic aspect," and so on. "Social structure," then, refers to concrete clusters of activities devoted primarily but not exclusively to meeting the exigencies of one major directional tendency of a social system.

The basic units of social structure are not persons as such, but selected aspects of interaction among persons. The concepts that are used to characterize this level of analysis are the familiar sociological concepts of "role," "organization," and "institution." [4] In addition, concepts concerning personnel are employed in the analysis of social structure. Here the conceptual level shifts from the relations among persons to persons themselves. Roles and organizations are always filled by persons. Accordingly, the motivation and behavior of persons in roles is extremely important in analyzing processes within social structures. Finally, sociologists make use of the concept, "sanctions," which refers to the use—both as rewards and as deprivations—of various social resources to control the behavior of persons in social structures. Aspects of this control include establishing roles, inducing individuals to enter and perform in roles, and controlling deviance from expected performance in roles. Conceptually, sanction is a very important interstitial notion that links the concept of "social structure" and the concept of "person."

Classifications of sanctions usually parallel classifications of social structures. We may speak of political sanctions (the use of power or force), economic sanctions (the use of wealth), aesthetic sanctions (condemning something as ugly or commending it as beautiful), religious sanctions (giving or withholding blessings), and so on. From one angle sanctions are the distinctive *products* of particular types of social structure. The economic structure, for instance, produces wealth, which can be used as a sanction in a wide variety of social contexts; the political structure produces power, another generalized sanction; and the educational structures produce knowledge or information, still another generalized sanction. From another angle, sanctions produced in one set of social structures are resources for other social structures. Wealth acquired by taxation and other means, is one of the basic resources for political effectiveness. Knowledge and training are important economic resources, and

---

[4] See above, pp. 9–10.

so on. The various social structures of a society are thus linked by a series of complex interchanges of resources, or sanctions.

SOCIAL STRUCTURE, STRATIFICATION, AND SOCIAL MOBILITY

Versions of Stratification   In its simplest version, stratification means that in any set of social structures, the various roles are characterized by a differential receipt of sanctions.[5] Given this phenomenon, descriptions of the distribution of sanctions in a social system result in statements of the allocation of wealth, the allocation of power, the distribution of educational benefits, the distribution of religious rewards (e.g., grace), and so on. In the first instance, then, "stratification" refers simply to the differential distribution of sanctions.

Stratification can be conceptualized in more complicated ways, which should be kept distinct from the notion just advanced. The following versions are common:

1. Stratification of *roles* themselves. This involves a summation of the various kinds of sanctions (wealth, power, esteem, etc.) that are received by the various roles in the social structure. Because it is difficult to translate one type of sanction (e.g., wealth) into precise amounts of another (e.g., cultural benefits), the ranking of roles proves to be a difficult empirical operation.

2. Stratification of *organizations*. This involves summing up the sanctions received (or resources possessed) by collectivities, such as family units, business firms, educational institution, etc. For any given sanction (such as wealth) this summation is not too difficult, but the summation of the various sanctions leads to methodological difficulties.

3. Stratification of *individual persons*. This means not only summing a number of different sanctions for a role, but also summing a number of different roles in which an individual is an incumbent. The difficulties in performing such an operation are even greater than in ranking roles or organizations alone.

4. Stratification of *classes*. This can be formulated in two ways. The first is simply to group certain classes of persons (e.g., peasants, proletarians, etc.) on the basis of some objective measures of the roles they hold or of the sanctions they receive. The second is to determine whether

---

[5] At this point we do not wish to enter the functionalist controversy as to whether in the nature of social life this differential distribution of rewards and deprivations must be so, and if so, why. We wish merely to indicate the widespread empirical fact that we take into account by using the word "stratification."

those who occupy similar roles conceive of themselves as a group and act collectively. Classes may be either special (based on the distribution of single sanctions, such as wealth) or general (based on an intermeshed system of many different positions and sanctions; an example is the "lower middle class").

Redistribution and Social Mobility [6]   Given these characterizations of social stratification, the following types of redistributive process can occur in a set of social structures.

1. Bringing sanctions to fixed personnel in fixed positions. This involves a redistribution of rewards. Examples are largesse, organized charity for the poor, distribution of groceries through a community by the ward politician, progressive redistribution of income through taxation, and so on. This process presupposes neither movement of persons from role to role nor reorganization of roles themselves.

2. Bringing personnel to sanctions. This is social mobility proper. It may take the following forms: (*a*) The movement of *individuals* upward through a hierarchy of positions. This type of mobility is conspicuously emphasized in the traditional American ideology. (*b*) The movement of *collectivities* upward through a hierarchy of positions. The most common form of this type of mobility is the movement of family units, as when the head of the household advances through the occupational hierarchy and the status of his dependent family members moves along with his. Another form of this mobility is the movement of formal organizations, as when an academic department "breaks into" the ranks of top-ranking institutions. (*c*) The movement of entire *classes*. This may occur gradually and peacefully, as in the "professionalization" of an occupation such as nursing, or suddenly and violently, as in an accession of a class to political power in a revolution.

3. Reorganizing the roles in a social structure. An example of this is a shifting balance among the primary, secondary, and tertiary industrial sectors in the economy. Such changes in the balance of roles give rise to redistributions of both rewards and personnel.

4. Introducing new *systems* of stratification. Such changes occur with great rapidity during ideological revolutions (such as the French or the Russian, which partially obliterated entire classes); or they may evolve over long periods (as in the growth of the urban-commercial complex out of the feudal, land-based patterns of stratification of medieval Europe). Since these changes involve a reorganization of the criteria for evaluating social roles, they also occasion redistributions of roles, rewards, and personnel. Most societies undergoing rapid change are characterized

---

[6] The following classification of types of mobility correspond roughly to the classification of levels of change, below, pp. 200–201.

not by a single stratification system, but by several systems of coexisting hierarchies. Social mobility in such societies is often a matter not of simply moving up or down in a single hierarchy, but of moving from one hierarchy to another.

SOCIAL STRUCTURE AND THE ANALYSIS OF MOBILITY

Three features of social structure are critical in determining the *forms* of social mobility in any society: ascription-achievement; level of differentiation of social structures; and locus of control of sanctions. We shall now discuss each of these briefly. Later we shall turn to several social determinants of *rates* of social mobility.

1. *Ascription-Achievement* Societies vary considerably in the degree to which persons are assigned to roles (occupational, religious, political, etc.) on the basis of status ascribed at birth. The basis of ascription may be kinship, age, sex, race or ethnicity, or territorial location. So far as these criteria dominate, the society emphasizes ascription. So far as assignment to roles rests on some sort of behavioral performance, the society emphasizes achievement.

The implication of ascription-achievement for the form of social mobility is this: If ascription is firmly institutionalized, mobility tends to be collective; if achievement, mobility tends to be individual.[7]

To illustrate: Classical India displays a stratification system at the ascriptive extreme. Under ideal-typical conditions, virtually every aspect of an individual's future life was determined by his birth into a particular caste: his marriage choice, his occupation, his associational memberships, his ritual behavior, his type of funeral, and so on. Choices were determined at the instant of birth. In this way the caste system discouraged individual mobility from one caste or caste-associated role to another during his lifetime. What form did mobility take, then? According to Hutton's account, mobility manifested itself as the *collective* splitting off of subcastes, or what he calls the "fissiparous tendencies in Indian castes." Members of a caste were aggregated into a subcaste, which for a time accepted wives from other subcastes but simultaneously refused to give daughters to these subcastes. This established a claim to superiority, which was fortified by some change in occupational duties. The final step was to adopt a new caste name and deny all connection with the caste of origin. Thus, in Hutton's language, "by organization and propaganda a caste can change its name and in the course of time get a new one ac-

---

[7] This argument concerns only the movement of persons. Societies that institutionalize ascription also encourage the distribution of rewards to existing "estates" or "classes," whereas societies that institutionalize achievement encourage the movement of persons to rewards.

cepted, and by altering its canons of behavior in the matter of diet and marriage can increase the estimation in which it is held." [8] This multiplication of castes over the centuries provides the clue to the distinctive form of social mobility in classical India.

American society possesses, ideally, a stratification system at the achievement extreme. An individual is able, in his lifetime, to move away from ascribed positions (based on region, ethnic background, even family of orientation) into new roles. In practice, of course, ascribed characteristics, especially racial ones, prevent the operation of this system in pure form.

One reason for the pronounced hostility toward "welfare" practices in the United States stems from this distinctive American emphasis on achievement. The introduction of welfare measures means bringing facilities and rewards to certain defined classes of persons, rather than having persons move to these facilities and rewards. One of the interesting justifications for introducing welfare measures in the United States—as opposed to continental European states, where state welfare is taken more for granted—is that such measures must presumably *facilitate* equality of opportunity for individuals in the society. If it can be argued that *not* to give welfare somehow impedes the life chances of a potentially mobile individual or class of individuals, then welfare measures are more likely to be accepted as legitimate.

Within the United States some interesting variations on the dominantly individual form of mobility are observable. When a person assumes an adult occupational role and reaches, say, age thirty, his mobility as an individual is more or less completed, except perhaps within the same occupational category. Thus adult occupational status is in certain respects an ascribed position, though this ascription is not a matter of position at birth. Under these circumstances mobility tends to become collective. Whole occupational groups try to improve their standing or guard it from erosion. Collective mobility in the American system becomes legitimate, in short, when the battle for individual mobility is in effect closed for an individual, when he becomes lodged in an ascribed group.

Great Britain constitutes a system intermediate between extreme individual mobility and extreme collective mobility. Individual mobility is emphasized but individuals carry with them certain ascribed and semi-ascribed markings—accent, habits, manners, etc.—which reflect family and educational background and operate as important status symbols. Full mobility takes place only in the next generation, when mobile individuals can give their own children the appropriate cultivation and education.

[8] J. H. Hutton, *Caste in India* (London: Cambridge University Press, 1946), pp. 41–61, 97–100.

This case is intermediate because it is the family that moves collectively upward over two or more generations.[9]

2. *Differentiation of Social Structures*   One point of contrast between simple and complex societies is the degree of differentiation of social structures. In an ideal-typical simple society, little differentiation exists between a position in a kinship group (e.g., elderly men in a certain clan), political authority (since elderly men in this clan hold power as a matter of custom), religious authority (since political and religious authority are undifferentiated), and wealth (since tributes flow to this position). The social structures are undifferentiated, and an individual occupies a high or low position in all roles simultaneously.

In complex societies, by contrast, a position in the age structure does not necessarily entitle a person to membership in specific roles in the occupational structure;[10] a position of importance in the religious hierarchy does not necessarily give an individual access to control of wealth. Thus, though some individuals *may* simultaneously receive great amounts of different rewards—wealth, power, prestige—these rewards are often formally segregated in a highly differentiated social structure.[11]

Two implications of the level of differentiation of social structures for the form of social mobility are: (a) The less differentiated the system, the more difficult it is for individuals to move with regard to a *single* role (e.g., through occupational success). The individual would have to move with regard to all roles—political, economic, ethnic, etc. This means that individual mobility is difficult, and that the distribution of rewards is effected not by movement of the individuals to positions so much as by collective competition among multifunctional groupings. In highly differentiated systems it is possible to move, for example, into a new occupational role, thereby achieving economic success without simultaneously having to become a political leader, change one's ethnic identification, etc. Segmental mobility, in short, is conducive to individual mobility. (b) The highly differentiated system leaves room for status disequilibrium (being high in one role and low in another, as in the case of the Negro doctor). This phenomenon is rare in societies with coinciding social hierarchies.

[9] This example is not meant to imply that several-generation mobility is absent in the United States. The contrast between Britain and the United States is a relative one.

[10] Very young and very old persons are generally *excluded* from occupational positions, however. The institutionalization of the seniority principle in industry and elsewhere also constitutes a qualification of the principle of separation of age and occupation.

[11] For a characterization of colonial societies, many of which were intermediate between the simple and complex societies, in that ethnic and political-economic roles frequently coincided, see above, pp. 143–44.

3. *The Locus of Control of Sanctions*   Where does the locus of power to apply sanctions reside in a society? Consider several different types of economic activity: In an ideal-typical paternalistic industrial setting, the industrial manager has at his own disposal both economic and political—and perhaps even moral—sanctions to recruit and control employees. In an ideal-typical free enterprise system, the industrial manager has only economic sanctions to recruit employees, but once they are recruited he also has limited political authority over them. In an ideal-typical totalitarian system, the industrial manager may utilize both economic and political sanctions, but for both he is held accountable to a central political source.

To compare and contrast political situations such as these, and to assess their implications for social mobility, two dimensions are particularly important: (*a*) Elitist-egalitarian, which refers to the locus of control over rewards and facilities in the stratification system itself. In the elitist case power to allocate sanctions is concentrated in the hands of a few; in the egalitarian case the origin of decisions to allocate is presumably dispersed, even though the implementation of these decisions may rest in the hands of a few. (*b*) The locus of power in territorial terms: just as the elitist-egalitarian dimension refers to the concentration of power in social space, the dimension of central-local refers to the same concentration in geographical space. (*c*) The degree to which the several concentrations of sanctions coincide. Are those classes with primary responsibility for decisions concerning economic sanctions the *same* classes that determine educational policy, religious doctrine, and so on? This last dimension, closely related to the concept of differentiation, refers to the relations among the distributions of several types of sanction.

DEVELOPMENT AND FORMS OF SOCIAL MOBILITY

What are the typical consequences of rapid social and economic development in terms of these dimensions? In a general way the answer is that rapid development sets up tensions between ascription and achievement, between differentiated and undifferentiated structures, between egalitarian and hierarchical principles, and between central and local power. Let us examine each type of tension briefly:

1. As economic and social development proceeds, various criteria of achievement—attainment of wealth, attainment of political power, etc.— begin to intrude on ascribed memberships as bases for organizing roles. This in turn gives rise to tension between ascriptive and achievement standards for ranking roles and recruiting persons into them.[12]

---

[12] Above, pp. 135–37.

2. Because of the widespread tendency for social structures to become differentiated from one another during periods of rapid development, individual mobility through occupational and other structural hierarchies tends to increase. This signifies the separation of the adult's roles from his point of origin. In addition, individual mobility is frequently substituted for collective mobility.[13] Individuals, not whole castes or tribes, compete for higher standing in society. This phenomenon of increasing individual mobility appears to be one of the universal consequences of industrialization.[14]

3. Most contemporary developing areas, emerging from colonial domination of one sort or another, are committed to egalitarian ideologies. Since most of these societies have traditional hierarchical social arrangements, yet another source of tension—between hierarchical and egalitarian principles—is introduced by rapid development.

4. Most contemporary underdeveloped countries have chosen a highly centralized approach to the management of their economy and social structure. This choice generates many tensions and conflicts, however, since most of the countries in question have strong local traditions of tribalism, community life, etc.

These several tensions frequently make their appearance in the relation between *demands* for mobility imposed by the exigencies of development on the one hand, and the *supply* of potentially mobile individuals and groups with appropriate motivations, attitudes, and skills on the other.

Issues that Arise on the Demand Side of Mobility in Developing Societies   For any society attempting to modernize we must ask which sectors of the social structure provide the developmental vanguard movement, and which lag behind. Under the combined influence of the classic British model of industrialization, as well as of lingering materialist assumptions, analysts have tended to assume that economic development leads the way, and that other sectors change in order to adjust. Parliaments are reformed, education is strengthened, etc., as a response to the exigencies imposed by economic change. This is not the only pattern of development, however. Although the *commitment* to economic change is pronounced in many African societies, for instance, these societies have moved much faster into the modern age in the political sphere (with universal suffrage, parliaments, parties, and administrative bureaucracies) than in the economic sphere. In these same societies, moreover, changes

---

[13] The degree to which this takes place depends also on the residue of ascription in industrial societies, as well as the locus of power with regard to the control of major social sanctions.

[14] Seymour Martin Lipset and Reinhard Bendix, *Social Mobility in Industrial Society* (Berkeley and Los Angeles: University of California Press, 1959), pp. 13 ff.

in the educational structure seem to be outdistancing actual economic accomplishments.

A related issue concerns the organizing principles employed in fostering development, and the ways in which such principles change the course of development. By "organizing principles" we refer to the kinds of sanctions (rewards and deprivations) used to establish roles and to induce personnel to perform in them. The following organizing principles might be considered:

1. Reliance on monetary sanctions. This refers to the system of wages, salaries, and profits that can be employed to determine the role distribution in a society, the recruitment of individuals into these roles, and the degree of effort elicited within them. Such sanctions may operate positively (e.g., the offer of high wages in industrial operations) or negatively (e.g., the "push" of agricultural wage laborers from the land into urban settings during periods of slack demand).

2. Reliance on political measures. These include physical coercion or the threat of coercion, influence, bargaining, persuasion, the promise of political power, etc. Again, these sanctions may be used to induce individuals into new roles or to force them from old ones, or both.

3. Integrative measures. One focus of integrative pressure is particularism, or membership in some ascriptive group. Membership in a kinship grouping, for instance, not only may set up expectations with respect to roles that a given member may assume, but also may determine the conditions of entry and tenure in a role. Group membership may also be important for controlling a person once he has entered a role. The key feature of particularistic sanctions of this sort is that the sanctioner appeals to the integrative ties (memberships) of the actor in question. Other foci of particularism are caste membership, tribal affiliation, membership in ethnic groups, and so on. Such integrative measures, like the other sanctions, may operate positively (e.g., in the case of particularistic hiring in the Japanese case) or negatively (e.g., in the case of escaping burdens to extended family and tribe, as reported for some African societies).

4. Value-commitments. Commitment to fundamental principles can be used as a lever to induce individuals to enter roles and behave in certain ways, once in them. Specific areas in which fundamental values operate as sanctions are in religious doctrine, nationalism, anticolonialism, socialism, and communism, or any combination of these. Again, in specific cases entry into a role may be as a result of the pull of a positive commitment to a "modern" value system, or as a result of the push of alienation from some "traditional" value system.

The *effectiveness* of these organizing principles refers in the first instance to the ability to stimulate the social mobility requisite for the society's developmental needs. In addition, however, reliance on a particular type of sanction has consequences other than merely stimulating mobility. For example, in some cases political sanctions may be the most effective means for establishing and filling roles necessary for economic production, though these same sanctions may not be the most effective means of allocating roles to foster changes in the educational sector. Furthermore, the wholesale application of political sanctions may set up inflexible political cleavages that paralyze a society, thus making these sanctions ineffective in the long run.

A final issue concerns the locus of power with respect to the organizing principles during periods of rapid development. In any empirical case a society relies on *several* of the organizing principles for development. Broadly speaking, the dominant principles of recruitment into economic roles in American society are: (1) reliance on the belief in fundamental values such as free enterprise, inculcated in potential incumbents of occupational roles during periods of early socialization and education; (2) reliance on monetary compensation, implemented through the market mechanism; (3) reliance on the outcome of political contests among interest groups, especially labor and management; (4) reliance on more centralized political machinery, usually when the second and third principles seem to be functioning inadequately. In general, the political controls over these different organizing principles are dispersed in our society; a single political agency is *not* presumed to have direct control over the education of children in the basic values of society, the operation of the labor market, the settlement of industrial disputes, etc. In other societies— e.g., theocratic, totalitarian—the political centralization of control over organizing principles is much greater.

Social mobility may be viewed as a consequence of the organizing principles involved, the capacity of the society to maintain such organizing principles, and their effectiveness in achieving the ends for the society. Mobility in turn is an important variable in determining the rate and form of development, and development in its own turn may feed back to the organizing principles and pattern of mobility by occasioning shifts in the power balance of society, changes in the distribution of wealth, and so on.

Issues that Arise on the Supply Side of Mobility in Developing Areas On this subject we may be briefer. The effectiveness of the organizing sanctions depends very much on the predisposition of the persons and groups in society to be moved by such sanctions. This depends in turn on their motivation, attitudes, and skills. The social structures that are critical in forming these characteristics are religion, education, community, and kinship, for these structures "specialize" in creating commitment and social outlook. Many of the problems that new nations face revolve around the attempt by those eager for development to undermine traditional familial, community and religious structures and establish new ones—especially in education—so as to modify the supply conditions for mobility.

Any historical case of individual or collective mobility resolves into the interplay of various demand and supply conditions for mobility. One familiar case of mobility involves immigrant groups in the United States during the past 150 years. Roughly speaking, migrants have filled the lowest economic rung—unskilled labor—upon arrival, only to be displaced "upward" by a new wave. Although most ethnic groups have remained at the very lowest level for only a short time, they have moved upward economically at different rates, and each wave leaves behind its dregs. Four factors appear to determine the relative speed of ascent:

1. Economic conditions of demand. The rise of the Negro during World War II and the postwar prosperity has resulted in large part from increased economic opportunities throughout the occupational structure.

2. The degree to which the ethnic group is "held back" through discrimination by the majority group. Every ethnic minority has experienced some discrimination; but for the Negro this has been extreme. Hence Negroes traditionally have been consigned to manual labor and servant work, and are underrepresented in professional, business, and clerical occupations. Discrimination may be direct, when employers resist employment of Negroes because they are Negroes; or indirect, when employers refuse to hire Negroes because they are less technically qualified for employment (which usually means that they have experienced discrimination elsewhere in the system, especially in education).

3. The internal resources of the ethnic group itself, both financial and sociocultural. Thus the Jews, Greeks, and Armenians, with a much more highly developed commercial tradition than the Polish, Irish, or Italian peasants, possessed an initial advantage in terms of capital and commercial skills. Also the Irish pattern of kinship and community loyalties fit Irishmen particularly for American political-party life, in which the Irish have been notably successful.

4. The continuing strength of particularistic ties. Once an ethnic group makes an inroad on a new higher-level occupation, the successful few will allocate their new talent and resources to bringing in people of their own kind to reap the advantages. This particularistic pressure applies in varying degree to every ethnic group.

A final issue arising on the supply side of mobility concerns not the *conditions* under which persons become mobile, but rather the psychological and social *consequences* of mobility once it has occurred. Two potentially disruptive consequences of mobility are: (1) The creation of individuals and groups who have moved upward rapidly according to one set of rewards, but whose advance is constricted in other spheres. The "unemployed intellectuals" so frequently found in the developing areas are an example. Sometimes groups of such persons do constitute a vocal portion of public opinion calling for changes in the pattern of development. In such a case the "supply" side of mobility begins to affect the nature of development itself and hence the "demand" side for mobility. (2) The creation of individuals and groups that are forced to move downward by virtue of the changes in the social structure. Examples are handicraft workers displaced by factory production, traditional chiefs displaced by the growth of centralized political structures, peasants displaced by programs of land reform, and so on. Both the irregularly upwardly mobile and the downwardly mobile groups in the developing societies provide many candidates for protest movements. The political stability of these societies depends in large part on the extent of this protest and on the ways in which the constituted authorities respond to such protest.

RESEARCH PROBLEMS IN THE COMPARATIVE ANALYSIS OF MOBILITY AND DEVELOPMENT

Our discussion thus far has dealt with the general relations between different elements of social structure and various patterns emerging around the creation of new roles in a developing economy. Empirical analysis of these relationships, however, requires a detailed look at the processes through which new structures, such as governments, business organizations, trade unions, the military, political parties, and so on, locate individuals to fill roles at all levels, particularly at the important summit or elite positions. An investigation of the problem of mobility must also involve an analysis of the relations between individual and collective social mobility. The first, of course, refers to the changes in position, within or between generations; the second, to changes in the relative income, power, or status of entire strata which may be occasioned by major economic or political changes.

Drastic social change on the scope of significant economic growth or social revolution must, in and of itself, result in a sizable increase in the amount of social mobility in a society. A shift from an agrarian system toward an urban and industrial one means that many who began life in peasant or artisan families must become workers, clerks, or entrepreneurs; politically a change in fundamental patterns of rule will open many positions in government and the military to those of low origin. Conversely, of course, some in stable positions, e.g., peasants and artisans, may find it difficult to retain their positions and may lack the flexibility to adjust to the requirements of the new occupational structure, while those from a more insecure background may be more willing to take the risks necessary to improve their circumstances. In major social revolutions certain classes are often downgraded as a matter of policy.

The phenomenon of "collective mobility" has been little analyzed by social scientists. A given stratum, such as skilled workers, or those possessing a certain level of education, may find its social bargaining power sharply increased when a society commits itself to rapid industrialization. This pattern has occurred in the Soviet Union and other communist countries, and probably in a number of the developing countries in other parts of the world. Social revolution may increase the status and opportunities of given classes as a consequence of the downgrading of others. In some communist countries, workers and peasants and their children were given greater opportunities to secure education and to achieve good positions as a matter of deliberate policy. The organized strength of certain classes may equalize rewards to some extent. Changes in the relative income position of the manual and white collar strata reflect differential political and trade union strength.

In the long run, however, such discrepancies between status and opportunity tend to disappear. In the Soviet case, for example, it seems clear from the available materials that being a member of a higher status stratum is a major asset in enhancing the status of one's kin. The children of the higher classes and the better-educated do better in the educational system and have a better chance to secure high status positions than do those of lowly background. The ideological commitments to discriminate in favor of the lowly are gradually downgraded or ignored under the pressures from those who control the new system and seek to maintain privilege for themselves.

The analysis of social mobility patterns in rapidly changing societies is also bedeviled by the problem of relating data concerning shifts from one role to another to assumptions concerning movements up or down the class structure. A move from the status of peasant or artisan to that of factory worker is clearly mobility, but it is not clear whether it should be regarded as upward, downward, or parallel movement. A man who has given up "control" over his pace of work, his economic independence, etc., to accept factory employment has made a drastic change in the social relationships linked to the job. From one perspective the changes may involve an increase in income or in status. Yet, from another perspective, self-employed peasants and artisans are more conservative politically, acting as part of the "have" classes, as contrasted with manual workers who develop antagonisms to their employers. And in Western society, petty businessmen and lower white-collar workers demonstrate a closer affinity to upper-middle-class values and general styles of life than do manual workers whose incomes are higher than theirs.

Many discussions of the rates, causes, and consequences of social mobility by sociologists have ignored this extremely difficult question of distinguishing between mobility that involves a change of "social setting" and mobility that clearly involves upward or downward movement. The literature assumes, on the whole, that most movement can be classified roughly as upward or downward, with the manual-nonmanual line as the main dividing point. Farm or peasant owners have been left out because it is too difficult to fit them into this dichotomous division. This approach may be plausible in advanced industrial societies where rural-urban move-ment is of relatively small importance, but it creates obvious difficulties for analysis of mobility in rapidly developing nations. Some scholars (e.g., David Glass) have attempted to surmount this problem by locating all occupations on a social status scale (social rankings given to them by a sample of the population), or by some sort of socioeconomic classifica-tion established by the researcher (differential weights to income, skill, presumed status, etc.). This latter method presents the difficulty that cer-tain kinds of movement are not counted as social mobility, since they are classified as movements within the same stratum. Thus, English students of mobility classify most shifts from skilled to lower white-collar worker or the reverse, as job changes occurring within the same class, and most rural-urban moves are also by definition not social mobility. A common change in newly developing countries—from farm laborer to manual laborer—would not be counted as mobility under some of these methods.

These difficulties must be kept in mind in evaluating the research findings and interpretation presented here. Much of what seems puzzling and contradictory, either to common or to theoretical sense, may be, in fact, a consequence of the lack of reliability of the indicators, and often the generalization under discussion cannot be tested because of the way in which the data were collected and classified. A further limitation is that the existing literature on the subject is by and large confined to analysis of patterns of total labor force movement, omitting considerations of important problems such as recruitment into elite positions.

There is a puzzling lack of association between indicators of economic development and measures of social mobility. Data assembled by Lipset, Zetterberg, and Bendix suggest considerable "upward mobility," as meas-ured by shifts across the manual-nonmanual line, even in traditionalist and preindustrial society.[15] Miller and Bryce have attempted to relate variations in nations' mobility patterns (e.g., combinations) of high up-ward and low downward movement, or high upward and high down-ward, low upward and high downward, etc.) to various indicators of economic growth drawn from Kuznets, as well as to current variations in productivity. The one significant relationship they uncovered is between

[15] Lipset and Bendix, *op. cit.*, pp. 11–75; see also S. M. Miller, "Comparative Social Mobility: A Trend Report," *Current Sociology*, IX: 1 (1960).

current national income and such patterns. There is little association between mobility patterns, percentage growth in national product, percentage growth in per capita income, or percentage growth in population.[16]
As Miller and Bryce suggest, "this finding is surprising since we would
expect a rather strong relationship between economic forces and the
patterns of mobility."

These findings so contradict the logical expectation that economic
growth should result in a pattern of high upward and low downward
mobility (one which has been suggested by the data from the Harvard
Russian refugee sample as characteristic of Soviet life before World
War II) that we wonder whether these negative results are a function of
the methodological weaknesses suggested above. Do we really have a
reliable way to estimate upward or downward mobility in developing
countries? As of now, we do not: a systematic effort must be made to
relate the data of changes, classified in different ways, to the estimates of
growth.

STATUS VALUES AND THE POTENTIAL FOR ECONOMIC GROWTH

If we can question the hypothesis that high rates of economic growth
give rise to high rates of social mobility, we can also question the frequent assumption that a strong concern for social mobility in a society
will invariably contribute to economic growth, presumably because those
most anxious to succeed will seek ways to maximize resources. Under
some conditions the desire for social mobility, inherent in the logic of any
system of social stratification, may actually serve to reduce the supply of
talent available for economic development. Thus, in cultures that emphasize the worth of occupations associated with traditional aristocratic
status, the desire for higher status may lead men out of more economically productive tasks into occupations less significant from the point of
view of the economy. Sons of the successful businessmen go to a university and enter the learned professions, the civil service, politics, the arts,
or other similar occupations. Such behavior presumably diminishes capital
investment.

The conditions under which new, socially important roles acquire the
status necessary to recruit and maintain a high level of talent must therefore be considered. Some have suggested that variations in rates of development among certain countries are partly due to differences in values
attached to entrepreneurial occupations. Thus, the emphasis on mobility
through entrepreneurship in the United States has been causally linked

---

[16] S. M. Miller and Harrington Bryce, "Social Mobility and Economic Growth
and Structure," *Kölner Zeitschrift für Soziologie*, XIII (1961), 303–15.

to the absence of aristocratic status patterns and to the "purity" of the tie between economic achievement and social status. Foreign travelers early in American history described American materialism as a reflection of the values of a new society without a traditional upper class.[17]

Conversely, the ability of the English entrepreneurial strata to recruit from the established upper class has been explained in part by pressure for downward mobility among the "younger sons" of the privileged in a society emphasizing primogeniture. To avoid downward mobility, younger sons had to find occupational roles that would give them the income appropriate to their background.[18]

Analyses of Latin societies have stressed the presumed desire of Latin Americans and Europeans to secure property, either in land or business, as a source of family solidarity and status, but they also have indicated that the traditional Latin values emphasize preservation of property once attained, and dictate an extreme unwillingness to risk capital to make enterprise more efficient.[19]

Many middle developed countries retain important elements of the status and political power structure of a pre-industrial society. Their situation has been well described by Harbison and Myers:

> Landlords, lawyers, government officials, owners of large family enterprises, and often military leaders enjoy both high status and political power. They are the elites. And access to their ranks is likely to depend largely upon political and family connections rather than demonstrated competence or high intellectual ability. The status of

[17] Seymour Martin Lipset, *The First New Nation: The United States in Historical and Comparative Perspective* (New York: Basic Books, Inc., 1963), pp. 57–59, and *passim*.

[18] Robert Ulrich, *The Education of Nations* (Cambridge: Harvard University Press, 1961), p. 95; Nancy Mitford, "The English Aristocracy," in Mitford, ed., *Noblesse oblige* (Harmondsworth: Penguin Books, 1959), pp. 36–37.

[19] On France, see various articles by David Landes, "French Entrepreneurship and Industrial Growth in the XIXth Century," *Journal of Economic History*, IX (1949), 49–61; "French Business and the Business Man: A Social and Cultural Analysis," in Edward H. Earle, ed., *Modern France* (Princeton: Princeton University Press, 1951), pp. 334–53; and "Observations on France: Economy, Society and Polity," *World Politics*, IX (1957), 329–50; see also, John E. Sawyer, "Strains in the Social Structure of Modern France," in Earle, *op. cit.*, pp. 293–312; and Roy Lewis and Rose Mary Stewart, *The Managers: A New Examination of the English, German and American Executive* (New York: Mentor Books, 1961), pp. 182–87. For a discussion of similar attitudes and behavior in Italy, see Maurice F. Neufield, *Italy: School for Awakening Countries* (Ithaca: New York State School of Industrial and Labor Relations, 1961), p. 35 and *passim*. For Quebec, see Norman W. Taylor, "The French-Canadian Industrial Entrepreneur and His Social Environment," in Marcel Rioux and Yves Martin, eds., *French-Canadian Society* (Toronto: McClelland and Stewart, 1964), pp. 271–95. For discussions of values and economic behavior in Latin America see T. C. Cochran, "Cultural Factors in Economic Growth," *Journal of Economic History*, XX (1960), 515–30; John Gillin, "Ethos Components in Modern Latin American Culture," *American Anthropologist*, LVII (1955), 488–500.

professional engineers and scientists is usually inferior, since in most cases they are employed and perhaps managed by these elites. And in some countries, a so-called "humanitarian tradition" may strengthen the tendency to downgrade agronomists, physicists, chemists, and engineers. . . . Professional managers in private enterprises, as distinguished from owners or family managers, are not very high either on the status ladder. . . .

A social structure of this kind obviously is an obstacle to growth along modern lines; and it must be drastically changed if the newly articulated goals of the partially developed countries are to be achieved. In China, of course, the required changes have been made in a completely ruthless and arbitrary fashion. There, the scientist, the engineer, the technician, and the factory worker are glorified, and other "intellectuals" who are not members of Communist ruling elites are roundly castigated.[20]

There is considerable empirical evidence drawn from studies of the behavior and attitudes of aspiring (university students) and actual elites of many underdeveloped nations which sustain the conclusions reached by Harbison and Myers.[21] There are important national variations in the propensity to sustain business careers; successful businessmen often turn to other more traditional high status pursuits on a part or full time basis. More important, perhaps, is the propensity of the economic elite of such nations to follow the values of pre-industrial society in the operation of their businesses, e.g., strong emphases on family particularism. Such behavior by the elite, however, is not reflected in major differences in occupational prestige ranking reported in various sociological studies in many nations, both developed and underdeveloped.[22]

Although much more research, both between and within nations, is needed before any definitive conclusions can be drawn concerning the factors that determine occupational prestige, the data in hand suggest that certain common underlying forces affect these rankings in all societies. And if emphasis is placed not on the descriptive content of specific occupations as such, but rather on their functions, financial rewards, and re-

[20] Frederick Harbison and Charles A. Myers, *Education, Manpower and Economic Growth* (New York: McGraw-Hill Book Company, 1964), p. 92; see also William F. Whyte and Allan R. Holmberg, *Human Problems of U.S. Enterprise in Latin America* (Ithaca: New York State School of Industrial and Labor Relations, 1955), p. 9.

[21] For a discussion of this literature in the context of an analysis of Latin American development problems, see Seymour Martin Lipset, "Values, Education, and Entrepreneurship," in Seymour Martin Lipset and Aldo A. Solari, eds., *Elites and Development in Latin America* (New York: Oxford University Press, 1967), pp. 3–60.

[22] Robert W. Hodge, Donald J. Treiman, and Peter H. Rossi, "A Comparative Study of Occupational Prestige," in Reinhard Bendix and Seymour Martin Lipset, eds., *Class, Status, and Power: Social Stratification in Comparative Perspective* (New York: The Free Press of Glencoe, Inc., 1966), pp. 309–21.

quirements, it seems evident that varying types of societies accord high status to positions that convey considerable power in key institutions, i.e., government, economy, education, religion, to those that alleviate tension, e.g., physicians, and to those requiring prolonged education, training, and intelligence.[23] Both modern and traditional roles seem to be judged according to such underlying assumptions, although the old elites strongly, and often successfully, resist according equal status to the *nouveaux riches* "materialistic" positions of the encroaching industrial society.

MOBILITY AND THE INTEGRATION BETWEEN TRADITION AND MODERNITY

One of the greatest difficulties in generalizing about mobility in the developing societies involves the relations between tradition and modernity in periods of transition. The principal socioeconomic change with which development is associated is the change from technically simple production to complicated modern production methods, a change that creates a demand for individuals who are motivated to train for or create new positions in the secondary and tertiary sectors of the economy. This change, however, is comparatively rapid in some countries and slow in others, and it does not progress at a uniform rate among various regional sectors in a single country. As a result, certain parts of a developing country, especially the industrialized urban sectors, have acquired a new stratification structure, while other sections still possess a more traditional, less differentiated structure of social relations. Though often neglected in the past, analyses of these contrasts in economic life should be related to any effort to specify the causes and consequences of social mobility in emerging societies.

Some of the first analysts of such differences emphasized the way in which the imposition of a Western modern economy, stressing a nationally centralized production-oriented system, in countries where the great majority of the population was engaged in an agricultural, consumer-oriented economy, destroyed the organic political and social unity of essentially *Gemeinschaft* societies. A "dual" society and economy results, in which the larger but weaker traditional one ultimately loses its ability satisfactorily to fulfill many functions it had handled before changes were originated from outside. Colonial domination or indigenous efforts to industrialize, by bringing in Western values, undermined the social utility of many traditional institutions for the population. Many customs were abandoned. Antisocial forces were released, hastening the disintegration

[23] For a more detailed effort to suggest such general factors, see R. Murray Thomas, "Reinspecting a Structural Position on Occupational Prestige," *American Journal of Sociology*, LVII (1962), 565; see also Hodge, Treiman, and Rossi, *op. cit.*

of organic solidarity. According to this view, the efforts of the rulers of such nations to control these antisocial forces through chiefs and tribal or other local authorities, or by establishing modern governmental rule, failed to provide a socially accepted integrative or organizing principle. Both parts of the "dual" society operated inefficiently.[24]

This thesis stresses the social dysfunctions inherent in cultural diffusion and efforts to modernize. Others have criticized its failure to recognize the positive effects an emerging cultural pluralism may have on a society, or the varying consequences of "dualism" under different conditions.[25] The contrasts between different sectors of the society and between different spheres of peoples' lives are a major factor in the alteration of the original social stratification system, helping to motivate some individuals to enter new and previously nonexistent social groups. Accordingly, intrusions may be viewed as a means of encouraging new structures of social relations which permit an increase in the standard of living, rather than as a source of the disintegration of structures that embody traditional customs and ideals, such as the family and religion.

The existence of separate social stratification systems within the disparate cultural, caste, religious, regional, and linguistic communities of many underdeveloped communities makes it virtually impossible to assess directly the relations between economic change and social mobility, especially since gross rates may conceal significant variations in the rates and patterns of various groups with different cultures. Studies do exist, however, of mobility in the urban areas of some developing societies. These indicate that in the cities, at least, mobility rates resemble those of Western societies. Thus, some observers point to the fact that a relatively unchanged agricultural and rural stratification system may exist in one country simultaneously with a high (i.e., Western) rate of mobility in the urban sectors.

A related problem concerns the effects that the intrusion of foreign political concepts into a rather undifferentiated sociopolitical system may have on mobility orientations. In many underdeveloped countries the adoption of Western (including Marxist) legalistic political ideas has produced many occupational positions, such as political party worker, toward which new vocational aspirations are directed. Knowing that the distribution of power directly influences decisions about the allocation of economic

[24] J. H. Boeke, *Dualistische Economie* (Leiden, 1930); Boeke's inaugural lecture at Leiden, "Dualistic Economics," reprinted in *Indonesian Economics: The Concept of Dualism in Theory and Policy* (The Hague, 1961); J. H. Boeke, *Oriental Economics* (New York: Institute of Pacific Relations, 1947); J. S. Furnivall, *Colonial Policy and Practice* (London: Cambridge University Press, 1948), p. 5.

[25] Manning, Nash, "Introducing Industry in Peasant Societies," *Science*, CXXX (November 27, 1959), 1456–62.

resources, we can expect that the structure of political stratification will seriously affect patterns of mobility in developing nations. Ambitious educated men are now more likely to seek to advance themselves within the powerful political-public sector as opposed to the private and production sectors than was true in Western nations while they were developing.

In general, of course, political elites are legitimated by their incorporation or evocation of sacred, traditional values. In the developing countries where new states are coming into existence, programs of modernization usually are interwoven with the goals of nationalism. Consequently, both nationalism and modernization are major conditions of legitimating the governing elites. Nationalism supported by all may encourage political pluralism by identifying traditional groups and institutions with the new state. In this sense the new nationalism may itself sustain interest in old loyalties and avenues of status mobility.[26]

Ironically, certain recent Western innovations may become "traditional" barriers to modernization because they are identified with the struggle for national independence and pride. For example, the impact of Western education on contemporary Africa has in many cases been a source of controversy because African administrators and new nationalist leaders who, as products of "academic" or general education, resist proposals for introducing widespread technical and agricultural education. Because an elitist "academic" system of education contributed to increased aspirations for political independence, and is characteristic of developed European countries, many leaders therefore contend that a "traditional" British or French type educational system is a prerequisite for economic growth. In Ghana the government finds itself in a painful dilemma, between the need to deal with advocates of African and Western "traditionalisms" and the need to open modern roads to economic development. On one hand, students and faculty at the elitist university modeled on Oxbridge have strongly resisted efforts to give the university a more vocational or utilitarian emphasis on the grounds that this will denigrate the culture of the Ghanaian elite and shame the nation before the world. On the other hand, though committed to modernization, it is forced to celebrate the virtues of traditional society while its aggressive nationalist ideology assumes that Western education in the colonial period robbed Africans of their traditional heritage. Thus, the most acculturated individuals in Ghana demand the "Africanization" of the schools.[27] The persistence of neocolonial and traditional values and practices among a political

[26] See Rupert Emerson, *From Empire to Nation* (Cambridge: Harvard University Press, 1960), p. 329.

[27] The discussion of Ghana is based on Philip J. Foster, *Education and Social Change in Ghana* (Chicago: University of Chicago Press, 1965), Chapter 9.

elite that openly rejects both, makes it difficult to establish and legitimate universalistic values, including perhaps an ideological program that formally sanctions processes and structures of social mobility.

The gap between economic aspirations and the facts of underdevelopment, brought about by the spread of modern media of communication, especially the motion picture and the transistor radio, may result in political instability, even in very backward areas with little direct exposure to modern education or to industrial-urban society. The isolated, almost totally nonurban kingdom of Cambodia has been cited as a society in which the lure of industrial civilization, reaching now even into the most remote sections, forces the peasants to change many attitudes and encourages them to want more manufactured goods.[28] The processes of change may contain the seeds of social unrest and foster support for revolutionary movements which have appeared in nations seemingly unaffected by economic or other structural changes. Peasants become receptive to varied forms of propaganda and appeals to violence as a result of upheaval of traditional patterns, the inept establishment of modern values, and perhaps premature aspirations for mobility.

EDUCATION AND ECONOMIC GROWTH

When it comes to suggesting a relationship between possible deliberate action and changes in values and behavior that might affect the emergence of a modern elite, more thought has been given to the effects of increases in educational facilities than to any other variable.[29] In spite of this, however, the various *ad hoc* generalizations that have been made in this area remain largely in the category of "unproven," and, not surprisingly, some of them contradict each other. Most writers generally accept the thesis that heavy investment in education will pay off in economic growth because it increases the amount of skill in a society and the motivation of the educated to create new development-fostering positions.[30] This positive thesis has been countered by several arguments: that a transfer of educational and research techniques from developed to underdeveloped societies sometimes results in efforts at innovation that are dysfunctional to the country; that an "overexpansion" of educational resources may create a frustrated and hence politically dangerous stratum whose political activities undermine the conditions for growth; that the

[28] Jean-Claude Eicher, "Trend Report of Studies in Social Stratification and Social Mobility in Cambodia," working paper for the Conference on Social Mobility and Stratification in East Asia, Tokyo, April 1964.

[29] Adam Curle, *The Role of Education in Developing Societies* (Accra: Ghana University Press, 1961).

[30] See T. W. Schultz, *The Economic Value of Education* (New York: Columbia University Press, 1963).

"educated" often develop diffuse elitist status and cultural sustenance demands which lead them to refuse to work in the rural or otherwise "backward" parts of their country; that the educated often resist doing anything which resembles manual employment; and that rapid educational expansion results in many being poorly educated, while reducing the opportunities available to the small minority of really bright students.[31]

Apparent evidence for the thesis that increased education makes for growth is found in the history of the United States, Japan, and the Soviet Union. In these three countries, high levels of national expenditure on education preceded industrialization.[32] North America has led the world in educational attainments almost from its establishment as a nation. There is general agreement that this investment has played a major role in its economic success. The United States Census of 1840, the first to deal with literacy, reported that only 9 per cent of the white population twenty years old and above were illiterate.[33] It is often forgotten that both Japan and Russia were strongly oriented toward popular education before they entered their modern rapid development stages, that is in the pre-Meiji and pre-Communist eras. Close to half the Japanese male population was literate at the end of the Tokugawa era,[34] and the rulers of Meiji Japan initiated a campaign of educational investment on all levels, resulting in close to 95 per cent elementary school attendance by the beginning of the present century. Similarly in Czarist Russia, the Census of 1897 indicated that 44 per cent of males aged 30–39 were able to read; in urban areas, 69 per cent were literate, including 60 per cent of the workers, while almost 40 per cent of the rural population was reported as literate.[35] A much higher percentage of school-age youth was enrolled in elementary school. Thus the Bolsheviks, like the Meiji elite of Japan, took over a country which had already gone a long way toward providing a seeming prerequisite for economic development, a literate population. And both, of course, on taking over, enlarged the national commitment toward educational growth as a means of fostering economic development.

---

[31] H. Myint, "Education and Economic Development," *Social and Economic Studies*, XIV (1965), 8–20.

[32] John Vaizey, *The Economics of Education* (London: Faber and Faber, Ltd., 1962), pp. 55–56.

[33] U.S. Bureau of the Census, *A Statistical Abstract Supplement, Historical Statistics of the U.S. Colonial Times to 1957* (Washington, 1957), p. 214.

[34] Herbert Passin, "Japan," in James S. Coleman, ed., *Education and Political Development* (Princeton: Princeton University Press, 1965), p. 276; Ronald Dore, *Education in Tokugawa Japan* (Berkeley: University of California Press, 1965), pp. 317–22.

[35] C. A. Anderson, "Footnote to the Social History of Modern Russia: The Literacy and Educational Census of 1897," *Genus*, XII (1956), 1–18; see also Arcadius Kahan, "Russian Scholars and Statesmen on Education as an Investment," in C. Arnold Anderson and Mary Joan Bowman, eds., *Education and Economic Development* (Chicago: Aldine Press, 1965), pp. 3–10.

It is obviously difficult to separate out the extent to which any given aspect of national policy has contributed to high rates of economic development. But there is no question that both Japan and the Soviet Union entered on a policy of heavy investment in education at all levels, long before any one could argue that the demand for the educated equaled the increased supply. Today, the Soviet Union spends more per capita on education than any nation except Kuwait. Similarly, Communist China has increased its educational expenditures enormously. Although in 1949 China and India were approximately at the same level of development, the Chinese have invested far more than India in expanding educational facilities, with particular emphasis on higher education.[36]

It is interesting that a report of the discussions at a conference of the International Economic Association on factors in raising productivity states "that economists from around the world believed that the educational system of the United States was the reason for its achieving by a fair margin the highest productivity of labor of any country.... The economists at the conference pointed out that what was different was that the United States was the first country to have the land grant institutions based on the idea that the university would contribute to all of society. The Communists and others at the conference shared this view: the secret of the United States was not the fact that it was a democracy or a capitalist society, or that it had the greatest physical resources, but rather that it got started very early using education largely, or at least philosophically, for political reasons, and then this turned out to be a great economic asset." [37]

A number of studies have provided evidence for the close links between the distribution of literacy and education to economic development. An analysis of the relation between levels of educational achievement and industrialization indicates that literacy and levels of industrialization correlate quite highly on an international level (.87 for seventy countries in 1950), and that these two factors have been associated historically in the development of industrialized nations. The author concludes:

> The differential rates of economic advance for the educationally retarded and the educationally advanced countries point to the importance of the dissemination of literacy and education in the transformation of peasant-agricultural nations into urban-industrial nations.... The countries that today are ahead educationally will find it easier to achieve this goal [increased industrialization] than those that are be-

[36] Adam Curle, "Education, Politics and Development," *Comparative Education Review*, VII (1963), 236–38.

[37] Clark Kerr, "Presentation," in Council on Higher Education in the American Republics, *National Development and the University* (New York: Institute of International Education, 1965), p. 10.

hind. The latter countries . . . will need to spend a great share of their goal of mass education before they can aspire to become modern industrial states.[38]

There seems to be a close association between a high degree of literacy and high per capita income, and between very low literacy rates and quite low incomes. Thus, of twenty-four nations in the early 1950s whose adult populations were over 90 per cent literate, twenty-one had a per capital income of $500 or more; conversely, of the twenty-five countries with less than 30 per cent literate, only one had an income of over $200, oil-rich North Borneo.[39] The relationship is less striking but still present for nations falling in the intermediate categories.

The relationship between levels of literacy and education and subsequent economic development is obviously much more complex than any two variable relationship statements such as those made here would indicate. Identical rates of literacy or proportions enrolled in universities will have different consequences for societies with varying values, levels of economic development, types and quality of schooling, opportunities for educational mobility, and the like. Such factors do not appear in the national parameter statistics employed in most studies of the issues. A look at gross national data, for example, indicates that for "Western and Far Eastern countries 1930, primary attendance seems to be the best of . . . three educational predictors [primary, post-primary, and adult literacy] of 1955 incomes; for Latin America, the Middle East, and Africa adult literacy best predicts subsequent income."[40] There has been no adequate effort, as yet, to account for such regional differences. The correlations between educational levels and economic development also seem to be affected by the seeming "occurrence of important, distinct stages in educational lead and lag; an early stage of education-economic breakthrough; a plateau on which diffusing education is still not sufficient to support a high-level economy; and a third stage in which another economic breakthrough is possible, based on a well-educated population."[41]

A number of recent studies do suggest high positive relationships between levels of secondary and higher education and statistical indi-

[38] Hilda H. Golden, "Literacy and Social Change in Underdeveloped Countries," in Lyle Shannon, ed., *Underdeveloped Areas* (New York: Harper & Row, Publishers, Inc., 1957), pp. 108–13.

[39] Mary Jean Bowman and C. Arnold Anderson, "Concerning the Role of Education in Economic Development," in Clifford Geertz, ed., *Old Societies and New States* (New York: The Free Press of Glencoe, Inc., 1963), pp. 251–52.

[40] C. Arnold Anderson, "Economic Development and Post-Primary Education," in Don C. Piper and Taylor Cole, eds., *Post-Primary Education and Political and Economic Development* (Durham: Duke University Press, 1964), p. 5.

[41] Bowman and Anderson, "Concerning the Role of Education in Economic Development," pp. 266, 277.

cators of economic development.[42] Harbison and Myers, in fact, conclude that in moving from one stage of economic development to a higher one the investment in secondary and higher education increases about three times as fast as productivity.[43] Such relationships, of course, do not indicate which is cause and which effect. However, a study comparing rates of technological growth between 1952 and 1958 (as indicated by changes in use of electric power), and higher educational enrollments, found that those countries that had relatively high levels of university enrollment in 1950 had much higher rates of technological growth during the 1950s than did the nations with relatively low levels of enrollment.[44] It is significant that "higher education enrollments bear an even closer relation to rates of economic growth in the 1950s than secondary education does." [45]

These findings are clearly relevant for specifying the ways in which education, particularly higher education, is related to the role of the elite in contributing to political modernization and economic growth. First, as Arthur Lewis has suggested, there is some reason to suspect that the status concomitants that are linked to education should vary with the proportion and absolute size of the population that is educated. A relatively small higher education establishment will encourage the retention or even development of traditional diffuse elitist values among university graduates, while where a large proportion of the university age population attends school, the pressures should be in the opposite direction.[46] In much of Latin America, university students almost automatically "become part of the elite. It matters little whether a student is the son of a minister or the son of a workman. His mere enrollment at the university makes him one of the two per thousand most privileged in the land." [47] Conversely in the United States, with its mass educational system, few university graduates may expect to attain high status; many of them will hold relatively low nonmanual positions, and a certain number will even be employed in manual occupations. Where comparatively few attend university, as in Britain, graduates who fail to achieve a status comparable to that of most of their fellow graduates will feel discon-

[42] J. Tinbergen and H. Correa, "Quantitative Adaption of Education to Accelerated Growth," *Kyklos*, XV (1962), 776–86; Curle, *op. cit.*, pp. 227–29; for a somewhat different result see Anderson, *op. cit.*

[43] Harbison and Myers, *op. cit.*, pp. 23–49, 182–87.

[44] David McClelland, "Does Education Accelerate Economic Growth?" (unpublished dittoed paper), p. 23.

[45] *Ibid.*, p. 22.

[46] For a discussion of the consequences of moving from a small elite system to mass higher education in Japan, see Herbert Passin, "Modernization and the Japanese Intellectual: Some Comparative Observations," in Marius B. Jansen, ed., *Changing Japanese Attitudes toward Modernization* (Princeton: Princeton University Press, 1965), pp. 478–81.

[47] Rudolph P. Atcon, "The Latin American University," *Die Deutsche Universitätszeitung*, XVII (February 1962), 16.

tented, for their reference group will be a more highly successful group. The same analysis may be applied to the different implications of education for status concerns in the Philippines as contrasted, say, with Senegal. A Filipino who attends the massive University of the Far East must know that few of his fellow students can expect an elite position; Senegalese students, however, know that among their classmates at the University of Dakar are the future economic and political leaders of the nation.

Some further evidence that the reality of the opportunity structure also affects the aspiration level of students in developing countries on a lower level may be found in a study of Ghanaian secondary school students. Contrary to many assumptions about the unrealistic elitist aspirations of African students, those in Ghana, though aspiring to high-status positions, have adjusted their career expectations to the actual structure of opportunities, which favors white-collar employment for the large majority of graduates. Over two-thirds of the 963 questioned were found to prefer a career in the natural sciences and their related technology in physics, chemistry, meteorology, and engineering, while the remainder indicated a preference for biology and agricultural science. But the number who expect to enter scientific and technical fields if they should not be able to proceed with full-time study beyond the fifth form drops to 7 per cent, and virtually no students believe that it will be possible for them to enter professional or semiprofessional employment. In fact, 84 per cent of all students *expect* to enter low-level clerical employment or primary and middle school teaching, and the bulk of secondary school graduates are employed in clerical positions. Graduates, then, tend to obtain precisely the jobs which they expect. While the Ghanaian students would like to have various professional positions, their perception of the occupational value of a secondary school education is realistic. And most of them realize that a secondary education has become increasingly terminal, given the small numbers admitted to higher education.[48]

There is good reason to believe, however, that growth in the numbers who attain higher levels of education should result in an increase in the amount of high achievement orientation in a population. Studies of the occupational goals of college students in nations with tiny systems of higher education suggest that the large majority of them expect positions in government work.[49] Since some form of white-collar employment must be the goal of college and secondary students, a sharp increase in their numbers should make talent available for a variety of technical and entrepreneurial roles. As Tumin and Feldman have indicated: "From the point

[48] Foster, *op. cit.*

[49] See K. A. Busia, "Education and Social Mobility in Economically Underdeveloped Countries," *Transactions of the Third World Congress of Sociology,* V (London: International Sociological Association, 1956), 81–89.

of view of a theory of stratification, education is the main dissolver of barriers to social mobility. Education opens up the class structure and keeps it fluid, permitting considerably more circulation through class positions than would otherwise be possible. Education, further, yields attitudes and skills relevant to economic development and such development, in turn, allows further opportunity for persons at lower ranks."[50] These assumptions are borne out in a comparative analysis of the relationship between national rates of social mobility and various characteristics of nine western European nations, plus Communist Hungary, Japan, and the United States; this analysis reports that the education variable emerges as the individually most important and ostensibly reliable determinant of manual outflow mobility. "Higher levels of upward mobility are associated with higher levels of education. . . ."[51] School enrollment correlated more highly with upward mobility than did other parameter items, such as gross national product per capita or population in localities over 20,000. However, investment in education affects only the amount of *upward* mobility; the relationship between rates of downward mobility and education was insignificant, lower than with any of the other variables examined. Although there are some contradictory reports, the weight of the available evidence supports the thesis that increased expenditure for education increases the number of individuals available and motivated to seek new and more prestigious roles.[52]

Educational expansion, however, has been criticized for impeding economic growth by fostering dysfunctional values in some countries, by reinforcing "status values and/or special privileges that are incompatible with economic advance."[53] "It has been suggested that the labour-shortage for sugar-cane cutting in some of the West Indian islands may be due to the spread of primary education among the younger people."[54] There is no doubt, of course, that a rapid expansion of an educational system may result in an oversupply of persons with relatively high ex-

[50] Melvin Tumin with Arnold S. Feldman, *Social Class and Social Change in Puerto Rico* (Princeton: Princeton University Press, 1961), p. 7.

[51] Thomas Fox and S. M. Miller, "Economic, Political, and Social Determinants of Mobility: An International Cross-Sectional Analysis," *Acta Sociologica*, IX (1966), 76–93.

[52] See C. Arnold Anderson, "A Skeptical Note on the Relation of Vertical Mobility to Education," *American Journal of Sociology*, LXVI (1961), 560–70. Anderson indicates that in countries in which many received prolonged education, the level of an education does not affect mobility. But an opposite finding is reported in a detailed analysis of the relationship between education and mobility in the United States. Otis Dudley Duncan and Robert W. Hodge, "Education and Occupational Mobility: A Regression Analysis," *American Journal of Sociology*, LXVIII (1963), 629–44.

[53] Bowman and Anderson, *Education and Economic Development, op. cit.,* p. 227.

[54] Myint, *op. cit.,* pp. 18–19.

pectations of employment, salary, and status. The increase in the numbers of educated people in a developing economy necessarily means that as education becomes less scarce it should command less status and income. The process of adjusting expanded levels of education to reduced rewards is obviously a difficult one, and often results in political unrest. And as W. Arthur Lewis has pointed out, "upper classes based on land or capital have always favored restricting the supply of education to absorptive capacity, because they know the political dangers of having a surplus of educated persons." [55] One must, however, separate the problem of the possible political consequences of educational expansion from the economic ones. As Lewis indicates, "as the premium for education falls, the market for the educated may widen enormously. . . . The educated lower their sights, and employers raise their requirements. . . . As a result of this process an economy can ultimately absorb any number of educated persons. . . . One ought to produce more educated people than can be absorbed at current prices, because the alteration in current prices which this forces is a necessary part of the process of economic development." [56] The argument against expansion is largely a political rather than an economic one, and calls for a detailed examination of the sociological consequences. The history of a rapidly growing postrevolutionary country, Mexico, affords an example of the way in which economic growth and emphases on new values may reduce the tensions inherent in rapid educational expansion. William Glade contends that though the educated were often frustrated in prerevolutionary Mexico, "the more or less steady expansion of the private sector activity since the mid-1920's" has meant a continuing demand for trained persons. "Secondly, . . . with the over-all expansion of the social, economic, and political structure there came a widening range of socially approved channels for the realization of achievement." [57]

The main criticisms of educational growth, however, have usually not involved so much opposition to expansion, *per se,* but rather have raised questions as to the *type* of education provided. There is considerable controversy as to the relative value of varying amounts of concentration on the elementary, secondary, and higher levels, an issue which we do

[55] W. Arthur Lewis, "Priorities for Educational Expansion," *O.E.C.D. Policy Conference on Economic Growth and Investment in Education, III. The Challenge of Aid to Newly Developing Countries* (Paris: O.E.C.D., 1962), p. 37.

[56] *Ibid.,* pp. 37–38.

[57] William P. Glade, Jr., "Revolution and Economic Development; Mexican Reprise," in Glade and Charles W. Anderson, *The Political Economy of Mexico: Two Studies* (Madison: University of Wisconsin Press, 1963), pp. 44–46; for a general discussion of the conditions which affect student participation in various forms of politics see S. M. Lipset, "University Students and Politics in Underdeveloped Countries," *Minerva,* III (1964), 15–56, and the special issue on "Student Politics," *Comparative Education Review,* X (June 1966).

not want to treat here in any detail; or the suggestion is made that under-developed nations are more in need of semiprofessional trained talent—e.g., nurses, technicians, and the like—than of university graduates, but that institutions designed to fulfill these needs are rarer than universities. And a considerable amount of the sociological and political analysis has concentrated on the supposed dysfunctions inherent in the "elitist" educational systems common in these societies. Such critics argue that the humanistic emphases which were introduced by the English and French into their African and Asian colonies, or developed on European models in Latin America, are to a large extent dysfunctional for a society seeking to modernize its economy. The American, Japanese, and Communist university systems, with technical and vocational courses within the university, would seem more appropriate for developing nations. As one of the foremost students of comparative higher education concludes, once universities have been separated from "their upper class associations," once they have been viewed as agencies of training for a wide variety of occupations, rapid expansion need not lead to unrest.[58]

Although western European universities, from which the emphasis on a humanistic orientation derived, are changing rapidly in this respect, many in the "third world" resist. Statistics provide a clear picture of this. As of 1958–59, 34 per cent of all west European university students were studying science or engineering, in contrast to 23 per cent in Asia (excluding Communist China and India), 19 per cent in Africa, and 16 per cent in Latin America.[59] The comparable figure for the major communist countries, including the Soviet Union and China, is 46 per cent.[60] China now trains more engineers per year than any country except the two leading ones, the Soviet Union and the United States. And 90 per cent of all China's scientists and engineers have been trained since 1949.[61] In 1958, by contrast, 58 per cent of Indian students were enrolled in faculties of humanities, fine arts, and law.

The rulers of Meiji Japan have provided an excellent example of the way in which a development-oriented elite consciously used the educational system both to provide the needed cadre of trained and highly motivated people and to enhance the status of those occupations that were needed for modernization. Shortly after the restoration, technical education was introduced at the university and middle-school levels, and it covered a broad range of theoretical science and practical instruction

---

[58] Joseph Ben-David, "Professions in the Class Systems of Present-Day Societies," *Current Sociology*, XII (1963–1964), 276–77.

[59] J. Tinbergen and H. C. Bos, "The Global Demand for Higher and Secondary Education in Underdeveloped Countries in the Next Decade," *O.E.C.D. Policy Conference . . . , op. cit.*, p. 73.

[60] Harbison and Myers, *op. cit.*, p. 179.

[61] *Ibid.*, p. 88.

in agriculture, trade, banking, and, above all, industrial technology." [62] In addition to the various government schools in these fields, Japanese businessmen helped start private universities such as Keio and Hitotsubashi designed to train for executive business positions students who could absorb the norms of modern business rationality as part of their education.[63]

The problem, therefore, is not so much the number of graduates as such, but the content of education and the status orientations and curricula that encourage vast numbers to work for degrees in subjects that are not needed in large quantity. Educational policy often encourages such maladjustments by making it much easier to secure a degree in subjects like the law or the humanities than in the sciences or engineering. Clearly the policy to pass students in the former fields for less and easier work than in the latter is an implicit policy decision, a decision which says, in effect, "We will overtrain and overencourage a section of our youth." An analysis of these problems in Egypt points out that while the numerous graduates in the humanities and in law contribute to revolutionary forces, those in fields in which employment may be found "have by contrast a vested interest in what the regime is already accomplishing and are hence its conservative supporters." [64] The Egyptian system is like many in other less developed societies, in that it rations admission to engineering, medicine, and the sciences, which are costly, but permits unrestricted enrollment in the others. Malcolm Kerr's comment about these policies applies to many countries:

> The passively accepted assumption is that in these fields, where tuition fees are very low and nothing tangible is sacrificed by increasing the attendance at lectures, freedom of opportunity should be the rule. In reality, of course, a great deal is sacrificed, for not only does the quality of education drop, but a serious social problem is made worse, and thousands of students beginning their secondary schooling continue to be encouraged to aim for the universities rather than for the secondary technical education which would be more useful to themselves and to the economic progress of the country.[65]

As we have previously noted, the many studies of occupational prestige in both developed and underdeveloped countries suggest that occupations that are perceived as "academic" or intellectual in character are quite universally highly valued. To a considerable extent, the difference in the relative attractiveness of technical or managerial positions in various

[62] Johannes Hirschmeier, *The Origins of Entrepreneurship in Meiji Japan* (Cambridge: Harvard University Press, 1964), pp. 127, 128–31.

[63] *Ibid.*, pp. 164–71.

[64] Malcolm H. Kerr, "Egypt," in James S. Coleman, ed., *op. cit.*, p. 190.

[65] *Ibid.*, pp. 190–91.

countries may be a function of the extent to which these occupations have been incorporated into the university system, and have taken over some of the aura of that system. Even in the United States, a study based on interviews with business executives in the largest corporations and with leading intellectuals, designed to learn how they perceived each other, reported that the executives were disturbed concerning their low status with intellectuals. Many of them argued that their jobs required a high order of creativity, a quality which intellectuals presumably valued but did not realize was as much an aspect of managerial as of intellectual work.[66] The various efforts to professionalize business occupations through the establishment of graduate business schools in leading universities, and other devices, testify to the continuing tribute which American business-men pay to the attainment of "academic status."

Seemingly a general problem of many underdeveloped societies is the desire of students to use university training as a means of attaining diffuse high status, most often affirmed through the free professions or govern-mental position, rather than through achievement in business.[67] Even in the second most developed Latin American country, Argentina, a report on national values points out that the traditional landed aristocratic dis-dain for manual work, industry, and trading continues to affect the educa-tional orientations of many students. When an Argentine seeks to move up, "he will usually try to do so, not by developing his manual skills or by accomplishing business or industrial feats, but by developing his *in-tellectual* skills. He will follow an academic career typically in a field that is not 'directly productive' from an economic point of view—medicine, law, social sciences, etc." [68]

North American, Japanese, and Russian experiences indicate that the introduction directly into the university curriculum of such vocational subjects as animal husbandry, accounting, elementary school teaching, engineering, and so forth, as well as the wide dispersion of colleges and universities in provincial and small communities, can have the effect of creating a trained stratum of talent that is motivated to work outside of metropolitan centers, willing to accept employment that has little appeal to college graduates in more elitist systems. To create a mass system of higher education that includes highly vocational subjects may lower the status of university graduates as compared to their status in a society

[66] See "The Intellectual's Challenge to the Corporate Executive," *Public Opinion Index for Industry* (September 1961).

[67] Joseph Fisher, *Universities in Southeast Asia* (Columbus: Ohio State University Press, 1964), pp. 6, 81–82, 96.

[68] Tomas Roberto Fillol, *Social Factors in Economic Development: The Argen-tine Case* (Cambridge: The M.I.T. Press, 1961). For a detailed discussion of many of these problems in a Latin American context see Lipset, "Elites, Education and Entrepreneurship in Latin America," *op. cit.*

with a small, elitist university system, but it may also raise the status of positions that do not require university training in elitist systems. The contrast between Puerto Rico and Jamaica may be relevant here. Many occupations that involve university education in Puerto Rico are held in Jamaica by men who did not go to university. It may be suggested that both the level of competence and, perhaps more significant, the achievement motivation of the former will be higher.[69] Similarly in the Philippines, which has absorbed the American emphasis on the worth of a massive higher educational system, and has the second highest percentage of the relevant age cohort in universities in the world, there is some evidence that the investment is worthwhile. "While the quality of education is low by Western standards the system produces an impressive flow of graduates with minimum technical and professional skills. . . . Enrollment in technical and agricultural courses is increasing rapidly." [70]

Concern with fostering egalitarianism and achievement through manipulation of the educational system is often perceived as necessarily involving a reduction in the class recruitment bias, which denies many of the potentially most able the opportunity to enter the elite. In all societies, the higher one goes in the educational system, the larger the proportion of students from privileged backgrounds. Many talented youth from less well-to-do families lack the opportunity or motivation to attend a university. To some extent, the discrimination against the lowly is associated with size of the educational establishment. The larger the system in relation to the relevant age cohort, the greater the relative proportion from lower-class backgrounds who can go on. But this varies by country, in part reflecting the extent of conscious concern and efforts to create opportunities for the brighter lower-class students, and in part reflecting aspects of the pre-university system, for example, whether it is costly or not. The proportions in education at various levels will, of course, also be related to the size of the national income, and to its distribution. Where most families have no possible economic reserve to sustain a student through school, he will not go. And the evidence indicates that less developed countries give financial aid to a much smaller proportion of secondary and university students than do developed ones.[71] In Latin

---

[69] "In almost all underdeveloped countries, there is still too great an emphasis on literary-historical and narrowly legal training." Bert Hoselitz, "The Recruitment of White-Collar Workers in Underdeveloped Countries," in Shannon, *op. cit.*, p. 188.

[70] Frank H. Golay, *The Philippines: Public Policy and National Economic Development* (Ithaca: Cornell University Press, 1961), pp. 201–3; Curle, *op. cit.*, p. 54; "A high emphasis in the Philippines is placed on mass education, and education accounts for nearly one-quarter of the nation's total governmental expenditures." Edward A. Tiryakian, "Occupational Satisfaction and Aspiration in an Underdeveloped Country: The Philippines," *Economic Development and Cultural Change*, VII (1959), 442.

[71] Frank Bowles, *Access to Higher Education*, I (Paris: UNESCO, 1963), 188–89.

America, about two-thirds of all secondary school students attend fee-charging private schools, a factor that undoubtedly operates to increase class discrimination. Latin America has done little to "identify and encourage able students . . . to provide programmes for part-time students, although it is known that a sizable proportion of the students in higher education support themselves through employment, and there is no programme for external or correspondence students. Perhaps most important of all, the number of students who receive financial assistance must be discounted as negligible." [72] This situation, of course, means that the overwhelming majority of students at Latin American universities are from quite privileged backgrounds. [73] The distribution of class backgrounds may become more rather than less discriminatory in the future, if higher education does not expand rapidly. For greater selectivity, brought about by a more rapid increase in demand than in places, will increase the relative advantage of those from well-to-do, culturally privileged homes, who can prepare for admission examinations with the advantage of having attended good private schools or having had private examination tutors. [74]

It is important to note that a universalistic and achievement-oriented educational system does not necessarily produce an egalitarian society. In fact, given the cultural, economic, and other advantages that go with higher status, the more emphasis a society places on locating people in the occupational hierarchy through educational attainments, the less equal will be the origins of those above the working class unless the educational system expands greatly. In Japan, very few elite university students are from lowly background. The latter simply cannot compete in the rigorous entrance examinations. Similar findings and conclusions are reported in a recent survey of the backgrounds of university students in the Soviet Union which, like Japan, has a universalistic competitive admission system:

> According to the survey, the children of white-collar workers have a far better chance for higher education than have the children of industrial workers and farmers. A sample survey showed that 90 per cent of the youngsters living on farms went to work after graduation from high school and only 10 per cent went on to higher schools.
>
> Of the children of white-collar workers, 15 per cent go to work after high school and 83 per cent continue their studies. The remaining 3 per cent combine work and study.
>
> The investigators point out that the larger graduating classes of

[72] *Ibid.*, p. 148.

[73] Robert W. Burns, "Social Class and Education in Latin America," *Comparative Education Review*, VI (1963), 230–38.

[74] Robert J. Havighurst and J. Roberto Moreira, *Society and Education in Brazil* (Pittsburgh: University of Pittsburgh Press, 1965), pp. 104–5.

the postwar generation will increase the competition for admission to college and further handicap the children of workers and peasants who usually are less prepared for college than the children of the so-called urban intelligentsia.[75]

"OTHER-DIRECTEDNESS," VALUE ORIENTATIONS, AND ECONOMIC GROWTH

Much of the analyses of the social requisites for economic development has suggested that a highly industrialized society requires the breakdown of traditional ties, a considerable degree of flexibility in role relationships, the willingness to treat market forces and individuals impersonally, and a system of recruitment to important positions that is based largely on universalistic and achievement criteria. A brief look at the fulfillment of these requisites in different societies suggests some additional complexities in the ways in which education contributes to development.

It has been suggested that "other-directedness," sensitivity to the opinions of others, contributes to economic growth. This thesis rests in part on the assumption that concern with general opinion facilitates a breakdown of traditional loyalties. "The transition to the new order is certainly likely to be helped if people can learn to listen to what 'other people' say is the right thing to do." [76] An analysis of the correlation between estimates of the relative emphasis on "other-directedness," as reflected in the content of children's readers, for several nations, and their economic growth in two different time periods, reveals that the two variables are related to each other, that an emphasis on other-directedness "predicts" growth. It may be noted further that the association with rates of growth is increased greatly when nations are ranked on measures of achievement-orientation as well as other-directedness.[77]

It may seem curious to argue that "other-directedness" serves to rein-

[75] Theodore Shabad, "Job Lack Faces Young in Soviet," *New York Times*, June 30, 1965. This article summarizes a report by a group of sociologists of the Economic-Mathematical Research Laboratory of Novosibirsk University, published in the journal *Voprosy Philosofii* (Problems of Philosophy). Similar results have been reported for Poland. See Jerzy Janicki, "Choice of Vocation by Warsaw School Pupils," *Polish Sociological Bulletin*, I (June-December 1961), 88–89; and Slowzimierz Michajlow, "Higher Education," *Twenty Years of the Polish People's Republic* (Warsaw: Warszawa Panstwowe Wydawnictwo Ekonomiczne, 1964), p. 199.

[76] David C. McClelland, *The Achieving Society* (Princeton: D. Van Nostrand Co., Inc., 1961), p. 194. See pp. 192–203 for a comprehensive discussion of other-directedness and economic development. Albert Hirschman argues that the ability to "engineer agreement," to deal with others, officials, subordinates, and the like is a key component of entrepreneurship. Albert Hirschman, *The Strategy of Economic Development* (New Haven: Yale University Press, 1958), pp. 17–18.

[77] McClelland, *op. cit.*, pp. 201–2.

force strong achievement drives in stimulating individual initiative, since many have linked "inner-direction" to a strong emphasis on technological development and capital accumulation.[78] Before coining the term "inner-direction," David Riesman referred to those so oriented as having a "Protestant Ethic" personality type, thus reflecting a common interpretation of Max Weber's analysis of the role that Protestantism played in fostering economic growth in northern Europe. This interpretation rests on the assumption that Calvinism produced a thoroughly inner-directed individual. In fact, however, Max Weber did not make this case. Rather, he urged that one of the significant components distinguishing ascetic Protestantism, and particularly Calvinism, from other religious groups was precisely its pressure to conform to the judgment of others:

> The member of the [Protestant] sect (or conventicle) had to have qualities of a certain kind in order to enter the community circle. . . . In order to hold his own in this circle, the member had to *prove* repeatedly that he was endowed with these qualities. . . . According to all experience there is no stronger means of breeding traits than through the necessity of holding one's own in the circle of one's associations. . . . The Puritan sects put the most powerful individual interest of social self-esteem in the service of this breeding of traits. . . . To repeat, it is not the ethical *doctrine* of a religion, but that form of ethical conduct upon which premiums are placed that matters. . . . The premiums were placed upon "proving" oneself before God in the sense of attaining salvation—which is found in *all* Puritan denominations—and "proving" oneself before men in the sense of socially holding one's own within the Puritan sects.[79]

A key difference between the Puritans who fostered economic initiative and the Lutherans and Catholics who did not, in Weber's judgment, lay in the extensive use of an appeal to "social self-esteem" or the power of group opinion by the former, and imposing religious discipline "through authoritarian means" and punishing or placing premiums on "concrete individual acts," by the latter two.

It is interesting to note in this connection that the educational system of Communist China, in addition to strongly stressing individual achievement, has also initiated changes from aspects of pre-Communist China which correspond to the differences between the mechanisms of control of the Protestant sects and Catholicism. It emphasizes the role of "public opinion or 'other directedness' rather than institutional norms." [80] And

[78] David Riesman, *The Lonely Crowd* (New Haven: Yale University Press, 1950), p. 115.

[79] H. H. Gerth and C. Wright Mills, eds., *From Max Weber: Essays in Sociology* (New York: Oxford University Press, 1946), pp. 320–21 (emphases in the original).

[80] John Wilson Lewis, "Party Cadres in Communist China," in Coleman, *op. cit.*, p. 424.

the Chinese Communists have established a system of social control that resembles the Protestant sects, as described by Max Weber, in which there is a strong emphasis placed on securing "the personalized approval of one's group." [81]

An effort to account for the seeming presence of "other-directedness" early in American history (as indicated by the comments of many "foreign travelers") indicates that this quality has been a consequence of the fluidity of the American status system.[82] That is, where there is a general emphasis on achieved status, and a reduction in ascribed status, participants in a social system are much more likely to be concerned with the opinion of others. Status in an open and egalitarian society depends largely on others' judgments. If this be true, then the massive introduction of institutions that upset normal status definitions should increase the amount of other-directedness in the culture. The *arrivistes* are the other-directed *par excellence*. The quickest way to create a large group of other-directed is to enlarge the higher educational system.

If egalitarianism and consequent "other-directedness" contribute to economic growth, then egalitarianism and investment in education should be positively correlated. A comparison of the nations of Latin America, Africa, the Middle East, and Europe, which divided countries within each area into "egalitarian" and "nonegalitarian" groups according to the extent to which they emphasized ascribed qualities in determining opportunity for high position, reports that within each region the more egalitarian nations spend much more on education per capita and have a higher average income.[83] Separating out the factors indicated the "egalitarianism, rather than national wealth, is the important corollary of high per capita expenditure on education." [84] Of course these findings do not demonstrate that a presumed increase in other-directedness is the principal intervening variable between egalitarianism, education, and economic development. A greater commitment to egalitarian values is usually also associated with greater emphasis on universalism as opposed to particularism, and on specificity, particularly in role definition, as opposed to diffuseness.[85] And these values, together with egalitarianism and achievement, constitute a large part of what we mean by modern as distinct from traditional values.

Relating the strength of national emphases on achievement to educational investment and economic development shows the independent strength of this variable also. When comparing technological growth

[81] *Ibid.*, p. 429.
[82] Lipset, *The First New Nation*, pp. 101–39.
[83] Curle, *op. cit.*, pp, 232–44.
[84] *Ibid.*, p. 244.
[85] See Lipset, *The First New Nation*, pp. 209–13.

rates for 1929–1950 and 1952–1958, McClelland finds that "achievement motivation [as measured by content analyses of children's readers] facilitates economic growth; knowledge (as represented by more education) facilitates economic growth, but motivation plus knowledge has a significantly greater effect than motivation or knowledge alone." [86]

The assumptions that economic development is fostered by emphases on "other-directedness," egalitarianism, universalism, and achievement appear to be congruent with the success of the major protagonists in today's world, the United States and the Soviet Union. The ideologies and practice of both Americanism and Communism, as well as their stress on education, subsume these orientations and values. Many have pointed to the relatively low emphases on these factors in much of Latin America and the other less developed regions as among the principal inhibitions on economic development.

DOWNWARD MOBILITY

Analyses of the problem of mobility and motivation in developing nations have usually assumed that these societies emphasize the maintenance of high-status nonmanual positions more than in the developed nations because the demand for such positions is higher, and consequently the gap in the rewards between manual and nonmanual status is much larger. Presumably, therefore, it is much more difficult to get people who have a claim to a higher-status position to accept a lower one. As Bert Hoselitz has put it:

> Very low prestige . . . is attributed to manual work which "dirties one's hands." . . . Some employees endure their economically unenviable position, because being a white-collar worker gives the illusion . . . that one is above the ordinary crowd of common labourers. . . .
>
> In many underdeveloped countries the relative social prestige which attaches to white-collar jobs is even greater, and that is in close correlation with the relatively greater scarcity of literate persons. . . .[87]

Attitudes toward manual work in underdeveloped as compared with developed nations, particularly the United States, probably are very different. But the evidence does not justify the conclusion that those with a claim to white-collar status in underdeveloped societies view manual work with such abhorrence that they will refuse to accept such positions if they are more readily available or if they pay more than nonmanual jobs. The rates of movement from nonmanual to manual positions in a number of these countries are similar to those reported for various industrialized

[86] McClelland, "Does Education Accelerate Economic Growth," p. 22.
[87] Hoselitz, *op. cit.*, p. 183.

nations. Thus, in a recent survey of labor mobility in Taiwan, based on data from the files of those who registered for a job or a change in position at the Taiwan Employment Office, 22.6 per cent of those whose job experience had been limited to one "high white-collar" position stated as their preference a manual position. Among those who had been salesmen, 27 per cent asked for a manual job. If we look at the actual shifts in job status among those who had had at least two jobs, we find that 7 per cent of those who began in white-collar work and 18 per cent who started in sales took a manual job as their second position. Conversely, among those who began in low manual jobs, 27 per cent secured a white-collar position as their second job, and 22 per cent shifted to sales work.[88] A survey of mobility in Poona, India, which compared intergenerational mobility, reports that one-quarter of those whose fathers were in nonmanual positions had become manual workers, while 27 per cent of those of manual origin had risen into the middle classes.[89] In São Paulo, Brazil, similar data indicate that 19 per cent of those of nonmanual origins were in manual positions when interviewed, while 30 per cent of those with manual family backgrounds had secured white-collar positions.[90]

The most comprehensive analysis of social mobility in a developing nation, Tumin's study of stratification in Puerto Rico, indicates that the Commonwealth has the highest rate of downward mobility ever reported. Over half the sons (58 per cent) of middle-class fathers, urban and rural, were in manual jobs when interviewed; among the sons of the urban middle-class, the proportion who had fallen in occupational status is 44 per cent.[91] This downward mobility is not primarily a result of movement from low-status nonmanual to manual occupations: Tumin reports a high rate of movement into the working class from "elite" middle-class status.[92] Thus, 42 per cent of the sons of "elite" fathers were in manual occupations when interviewed. And, significantly, a comparison with rates in eleven other European nations and Japan indicates that the two countries with the highest rate of downward mobility from the "elite" strata are the two among them that are currently in the process of emerging industrially— Italy, with 36 per cent moving downward into manual positions from the elite strata, and Japan, with a downward rate of 27 per cent.[93]

[88] Wolfram Eberhard, "Labor Mobility in Taiwan," *Asian Survey*, II (May 1962), 38–56.

[89] V. Sovani and Kusum Pradhan, "Occupational Mobility in Poona City Between Three Generations," *The Indian Economic Review*, II (1955), 23–36.

[90] Robert J. Havighurst, "Educação, mobilidade sociale e Mundança social em quatro sociedadas—estudo comparativo," *Educação e Ciencias Socias,* II (1957), 103–31.

[91] Tumin with Feldman, *op. cit.*, p. 441.

[92] The elite groups are professionals, semiprofessionals, and owners of businesses other than "one-man enterprises at very low levels of capitalization." *Ibid.*, p. 428.

[93] *Ibid.*, p. 443.

The phenomenon of extensive "downward" mobility occurring within emerging industrializing societies is a feature of European history as well. Sorokin amassed considerable evidence from a variety of studies in late nineteenth- and early twentieth-century Europe indicating that sizeable proportions of the manual work force had been recruited from the offspring of middle-class and even elite fathers.[94]

One structural cause of downward mobility has been suggested in an interesting paper by the Argentinian sociologist Di Tella. His data indicate that in the early stages of industrialization economic growth may decrease the percentage of the labor force in middle-class occupations rather than increase it. Within Chile he finds that the more developed a province is, the smaller the proportion of its middle class will be. He suggests that in underdeveloped areas, urban areas are largely centers of trade with a middle-class composed of merchants and government workers, including teachers. With the growth of industry, the artisans and petty traders find it difficult to compete for workers or to compete in the market. Consequently there is an absolute or relative decline in the numbers of such establishments.[95]

The presence of high rates of upward mobility in emerging societies has never struck observers as surprising since it has always been assumed that industrial expansion results in a rapid increase in the proportion of higher status as contrasted with lower status positions. (Di Tella, of course, has thrown this assumption into doubt.) The assumption that particularistic and ascriptive values are emphasized in traditionalist and underdeveloped societies more than in industrialized nations implied that low rates of downward mobility should occur in such nations as they began to develop economically. Those with a privileged background, and a strong motivation to retain high status, should in an expanding economy find it relatively easy to retain or improve their status. The fact that many actually fall in status suggests that the skills and orientations necessary to adapt successfully to the new roles of an industrializing society may be at variance with those linked to "middle-class" status in pre-industrial society. The offspring of such strata who seek to preserve or advance status

[94] Pitirim Sorokin, *Social and Cultural Mobility* (New York: The Free Press of Glencoe, Inc., 1959), pp. 435–40, 447–49. First published in 1927, this work, which is rarely cited today, is not only a rich source of comparative data, but contains highly sophisticated analyses of both the causes and consequences of social mobility. Much of the recent work in this field touches precisely on the issues Sorokin dealt with, and often "rediscovers" processes he specified. Unlike some of the more recent writers, Sorokin recognized the difficulties involved in trying to be overprecise in comparative research, and did not try to draw precise conclusions from what was and is only roughly comparable data.

[95] Torcuato S. Di Tella, "Economía y estructura ocupacional en un pais subdesarrollado," *Desarrollo Económico,* I (1961), 123–53.

using traditional methods may be at a disadvantage with the ambitious sons of low-status families who more readily reject or do not even know of the customary behavior patterns associated with privileged status.

These findings also suggest consequences for the behavior of the industrial work force in emerging societies if we assume that it includes a significant proportion of workers who have been downwardly mobile in status terms. The downwardly mobile may provide a reservoir of potential leadership for class organization (union or leftist party), or conversely, they may contribute heavily to the ranks of those who serve as work force leaders, e.g., foremen and supervisors. As yet, we know little about the consequences of downward mobility in such situations. Studies of this phenomenon in developed nations suggest that the downwardly mobile remain oriented toward middle-class values and behavior with respect to politics (they are much more conservative and less likely to join unions than workers of lower-status background) and work habits (they are more likely to possess a commitment to steady work).[96]

Wilensky and Edwards report, in the most comprehensive study of downwardly mobile American workers, that as compared with nonmobile workers they are more likely to "reject identification with the working-class . . . ; believe in an open class system and in ability as a proper basis for promotion . . . ; aspire to middle class position for themselves, attach importance to promotion opportunities, and say they would accept the job of foreman if offered . . . ; anticipate leaving the factory soon . . . ; and expect their children to achieve middle class position." [97] And in suggesting consequences for the larger social structure of the presence of a large group of downwardly mobile among the workers, they suggest that these men "with their adherence to the free mobility ideology, constrain tendencies toward political extremism among two-generation workers, who, sharing the same grievances and perspectives, if unexposed to the deviant views of skidders would be more susceptible to totalitarian solutions." [98]

Wilensky and Edwards thus cast doubts on the argument that an excess of middle-class ambitions caused by changes in various structural

[96] See Lipset and Bendix, *Social Mobility in Industrial Society*, pp. 64–71; Seymour Martin Lipset and Joan Gordon, "Mobilty and Trade Union Membership," in Reinhard Bendix and Seymour Martin Lipset, eds., *Class, Status and Power: A Reader in Social Stratification* (New York: The Free Press of Glencoe, Inc., 1953), pp. 491–500; Arnold Tannenbaum and Robert Kahn, *Participation in Union Locals* (Evanston: Row, Peterson, 1958), pp. 142–48; Harold Wilensky and Hugh Edwards, "The Skidder: Ideological Adjustments of Downward Mobile Workers," *American Sociological Review*, XXIV (1959), 215–31; and Alain Touraine and Bernard Mottez, "Classe ouvrière et société globale," in Georges Friedmann and Pierre Naville, eds., *Traité de sociologie du travail*, II (Paris: Librarie Armond Colin, 1962), 238–41.

[97] Wilensky and Edwards, *op. cit.*, p. 226.

[98] *Ibid.*, p. 230.

factors—e.g., education, urbanization—is a major source of political tension.

Recent research has also raised questions about the general validity of the proposition that the sharp discontinuities in social relationships and values occasioned by the rapid recruitment of an industrial labor force from rural areas predisposes the "new workers" to accept radical ideologies or theologies.[99] A comparative study of Indian, American, and English textile mills during the period of rapid industrial growth concludes these causal analyses are wrong:

> Scholars have spent a good deal of effort describing the profound adjustments that were required by the shift of workers into factory employment and the violence of the reactions to that new discipline. The striking feature of the Bombay pattern is that there was no violent reaction to factory work. . . . Similarly, in New England, no violent antagonisms manifested themselves among those who worked in the mills during the early phase.[100]

A similar argument based on Brazilian experience has been presented by by Herbert Blumer.[101] He suggests that the growth of an industrial work force in the expanding petroleum industry had increased social integration rather than reduced it among the workers recruited from rural environments. And Japan is, of course, the classic case of a nation that has endured the strains inherent in rapid industrialization without the emergence of significant working-class protest. Explanations for some of these variations have been offered, referring to the extent to which a new working class retains strong links to the rural communities from which it was recruited, or the relative difference in economic standard and living conditions between pre-industrial and industrial positions. The fact remains, however, that a systematic analysis of the variations in reactions to the dislocations inherent in rapid industrialization has not been accomplished.

[99] See Walter Galenson, "Scandinavia," in Walter Galenson, ed., *Comparative Labor Movements* (Englewood Cliffs, N.J.: Prentice-Hall, Inc., 1952), esp. pp. 105–20; Val Lorwin, "Working-Class Politics and Economic Development in Western Europe," *American Historical Review*, LXIII (1958), 338–51; Reinhold Niebuhr, *The Irony of American History* (New York: Charles Scribner's Sons, 1952), pp. 112–18; Seymour Martin Lipset, *Political Man* (Garden City, N.Y.: Doubleday & Company, Inc., 1960), pp. 68–71; William Kornhauser, *The Politics of Mass Society* (New York: The Free Press of Glencoe, Inc., 1959), pp. 150–58.

[100] Morris David Morris, "The Recruitment of an Industrial Labor Force in India, with British and American Comparisons," *Comparative Studies in Society and History*, II (1960), 327.

[101] Herbert Blumer, "Early Industrialization and the Laboring Class," *The Sociological Quarterly*, I (1960), 5–14.

CONCLUSION

In this essay we have explored the problems of social structure and social mobility—with reference to economic development—at two levels, theoretical and empirical. In the first section we advanced definitions of social structure and social mobility, and suggested some of the broad consequences of social structure for the overall pattern of social mobility in any society. In the second portion, we selected certain research areas about which scholars and policy makers have definite opinions and judgments, but on which the empirical evidence is far from clear. In particular we examined the general relations between rates of growth and rates of mobility, the relations between education and patterns of mobility; and the relations between economic development and downward mobility.

EIGHT: Toward a General
Theory of Social Change *

INTRODUCTION: THE ASSESSMENT OF KNOWLEDGE
ABOUT SOCIAL CHANGE

The Setting for This Essay

In attempting to evaluate knowledge in the social sciences, it is essential to pose three different kinds of questions:

1. Substantive questions. Such questions deal with the content of a theory. What aspects of social life does it concern? For example, does it focus on explaining changes in institutional patterns over long periods of time? If so, what particular institutional patterns—political, religious, or educational—does it treat as most important? And what are the causes of change? For example, are they geographical, psychological, cultural, or some combination of these? By posing a series of such questions we learn what a theory is about.

2. Methodological-empirical questions. Given certain substantive assertions or hypotheses about social life, what degree of confidence may we have in them? How are they to be tested? By what means do we decide whether these assertions are to be accepted, modified, or rejected? The term "methodology," as it is commonly employed in the social sciences, refers to these kinds of questions. It includes a concern with the logic of drawing inferences from data, and the various ways in which data must be arranged in order to permit reliable inferences to be drawn.

* This essay has not been published elsewhere. Parts of it derive from a working paper prepared for Human Sciences Research, Inc., entitled "Theories of Social Change and the Analysis of Nuclear Attack and Recovery." Other parts derive from the chapter entitled "Processes of Social Change," which appeared in Neil J. Smelser, ed., *Sociology* (New York: John Wiley and Sons, Inc., 1967).

Among these ways of arranging data the most conspicuous is the classical experimental method, which exercises certain situational controls over data; but various approximations to the experimental method have also been devised—approximations involving statistical and other manipulations of data that cannot be controlled experimentally.[1] Methodology in the empirical sense also includes a concern with detailed techniques of measuring and recording data.

3. Methodological-theoretical questions. An additional kind of methodological assessment refers not to the empirical verification of hypotheses, but rather to the *conceptual* relations among hypotheses and other ingredients of systematic explanation. This assessment involves the following kinds of questions: What are the basic definitions of the variables in the explanation? Are the definitions precise and unambiguous? Are the variables conceptually distinct from one another, or do they overlap in various ways? What are the relations among the various hypotheses about social life? Are they derived from a coherent theoretical model? If so, what are the features of this model? Is it represented as some kind of equilibrium system, and if so, what kind? Does the process of derivation yield a consistent pattern of hypotheses, or does the theoretical model generate contradictory hypotheses? Are theoretical models stated as economically as possible, or are they burdened with excess conceptual baggage? Upon what kind of broader theoretical perspectives are models and hypotheses based? What kinds of assumptions regarding society and human nature underlie the theory? Are these assumptions justified? These kinds of questions concern the logical structure of explanations, and are commonly grouped under the heading, "the logic of theory construction."

In this essay I shall focus mainly on methodological-theoretical issues. I shall outline the criteria for assessing any theory of social change. Then I shall present a skeletal outline of a number of different theories of change; sometimes this operation will involve filling in gaps and elaborating portions of these theories. I shall criticize the theories with respect to the general canons of scientific logic. And finally, I shall attempt to develop a synthetic statement on the theory of social change, based on the foregoing analysis and criticism of the several theories.

This task is a formidable one for several reasons. First, most exciting theories of social change are lacking in scientific adequacy, so I shall have to speculate about many loosely implied theoretical connections in these bodies of thought. Second, existing theories of social change have been generated within a wide range of intellectual traditions and conceptual frameworks; to ask a common set of methodological-theoretical questions of these theories always involves the danger of distorting them from their

---

[1] Above, pp. 16–20, for an outline of these several methods.

original form. And third, because the various theories of change have been directed toward very diverse kinds of historical situations, it is very difficult to consider them as general theoretical statements, apart from the specific historical situations they are meant to characterize. Despite these obstacles, I am convinced of the usefulness of extracting the explicit and implicit theoretical frameworks from a number of different theories, and attempting to synthesize them.

The Program of This Essay

To work toward the objectives just outlined, I shall divide the essay into three sections: a section specifying the criteria for any theory of social change; a section reviewing a number of theories with respect to their formal structure; and a section setting forth a synthetic statement.

Section I: The Criteria for a Theory of Social Change   This section will begin with a discussion of the general issues that must be faced by any theorist of social change, regardless of the subject matter of his theory. In this section I shall raise such issues as the formulation of scientific problems, the definition of basic concepts, the organization of concepts into theoretical systems, and the derivation of models and hypotheses from such theoretical systems. In this discussion of the logic of theory construction, I shall simultaneously be laying down the criteria by which to evaluate theories of social change.

Section II: Review of Existing Theories of Change   The history of sociological theory, to say nothing of the history of social thought in general, abounds in notions concerning the causes, courses, and consequences of social change. Some of these notions have been only vaguely formulated, whereas others have been developed within relatively formal conceptual frameworks. Furthermore, these ideas about social change vary greatly in the degree to which they are helpful for the scientific understanding of processes of adjustment and change. By what criteria should theories of change be selected for review?

In scanning the literature and selecting theories of change for analysis, I have been guided by three considerations:

1. Since I intend to emphasize the methodological-theoretical aspects, I have limited my selections to theoretical statements that are relatively systematic—or, if they are not systematic themselves, they are sufficiently explicit to lend themselves to elaboration and systematization.

2. Since I intend to stress the internal logic of theory, I have restricted the number of theories selected; if the number were too large, it would not be possible to go beyond superficial summaries of their content.

3. Most important, I have attempted to choose a diversity of theoretical approaches, so that the concluding synthetic statement will be at a general level. More particularly, I have chosen theories that vary with respect to two dimensions: constructive versus deteriorative changes, and short-term versus long-term changes.

With respect to the first dimension, it is possible to distinguish between those theories that focus on explaining the augmentation of social outputs or the construction of social arrangements on the one hand, and those that focus on the decline of social outputs or the deterioration of social arrangements on the other. Examples of the former are theories concerning economic development, the formation of organizations, institutional growth, and the rise of civilizations. Examples of the latter are theories of economic decline, breakup of organizations, institutional disintegration, and the stagnation and deterioration of civilizations. In one sense the distinction is an artificial one, since any historical period of flux manifests both constructive and deteriorative types of change; but for analytic purposes the two types of change can be distinguished, and approaches to social change can be classified in terms of their primary focus on each type.

Both the constructive and deteriorative features of social change, furthermore, can be viewed in their short-term and long-term aspects. Though this distinction is also a relative one, it is possible to distinguish between more or less short-term changes (such as adaptation to crisis conditions, explosive collective outbursts, and so on) and long-term changes (such as the growth of a legal tradition, the gradual decline of a maritime power, the rise of systems of higher education, and so on).

These two dimensions yield a four-fold table, shown in Figure 8–1, which outlines the requirements for selecting theories for review. A mini-

	Short-Term Processes	*Long-Term Processes*
Disintegrative processes	Theory of social collapse in crisis conditions	Theory of decline, decay, or "death"
Reconstructive processes	Theory of recovery from crisis conditions	Theory of development or "growth"

FIGURE 8–1

mum condition to be met in this essay is that at least one theory be selected for each of the four cells.[2]

As an example of a theory of short-term social collapse in the face of crisis, I have chosen an analysis of the deterioration of Japanese morale toward the end of World War II, an analysis based on intelligence data about Japanese society in this period and on subsequent interview data. The research, conducted by the Foreign Morale Analysis Division in the Office of War Information, was subsequently written in book form by Alexander H. Leighton.[3] While the original context of the research was to guide American war policy, and while Leighton did not frame his analysis in formal theoretical terms, the findings presented are at a sufficiently general level to permit their elaboration into a statement of some of the determinants of collapse under crisis conditions.

The reader should note that the notion of "collapse" as used in this particular historical case—and, no doubt, in many others as well—is quite time-bound, and judged to be a "collapse" largely because the end of the war is taken as the endpoint of analysis. If we were to study changes in Japanese society in the decade following World War II, a theoretical framework focusing on the reconstructive aspects of social change would have to be employed.[4] The more general point here is that the identical empirical instance of change may be analyzed as several different types of change, depending on the time-perspective adopted by the investigator. What may be crisis or collapse in the short run may also be an episode integral to longer-term growth; what may be constructive activity in the short run may be a brief lull in a longer-term process of social disintegration.

As an example of a theory of short-term social recovery from crisis, I have chosen Anthony F. C. Wallace's analysis of disaster based on the Worcester, Massachusetts, tornado of 1953.[5] While Wallace did discuss

[2] It should be noted that the literature on social change is very uneven in providing good examples of the theories called for by the table. In particular, theories of social decline are very sparsely represented in the literature. It should also be noted that in selecting theories I made no effort to be "representative" of schools of thought or theoretical approaches in the area of social change.

[3] *Human Relations in a Changing World: Observations on the Use of the Social Sciences* (New York: E. P. Dutton & Co., Inc., 1949).

[4] For a characterization of the remarkable recovery of the Japanese economy after World War II, seek Jack Hirshleifer, *Disaster and Recovery: A Historical Survey* (Santa Monica, Calif.: The RAND Corporation, 1963).

[5] *Tornado in Worcester: An Exploratory Study of Individual and Community Behavior in an Extreme Situation* (Disaster Study Number 3 of the Committee on Disaster Studies Division of Anthropology and Psychology) (Washington, D.C.: National Academy of Sciences—National Research Council, 1956). See also Anthony F. C. Wallace, *Human Behavior in Extreme Situations: A Survey of the Literature and Suggestions for Further Research* (Disaster Study Number 1 of the Committee on Disaster Studies, Division of Anthropology and Psychology) (Washington, D.C.: National Academy of Sciences—National Research Council, 1956).

various nonconstructive aspects of behavior in crisis situations, he also stressed the reconstructive aspects of change under the heading of the "counter-disaster syndrome." Furthermore, the endpoint of Wallace's analysis is the reestablishment of some sort of "steady state" or new equilibrium, indicating that the social system, while changed by the crisis, has been rehabilitated and reconstructed.[6] A final reason for selecting Wallace's work is that his discussion is explicitly couched in theoretical terms, and thus readily lends itself to formalization.

Finding an appropriate example of a theory of long-term decline proved to be very difficult. The scholarly literature yields, on the one hand, a number of traditional historical treatments of specific cases, such as the Roman Empire, which are, however, devoted mainly to historical detail; and, on the other hand, a number of grand theories of social growth and decline, which are, however, more social-philosophical and prophetic than scientific in character.[7] In the absence of a clear body of systematic theory in this area,[8] I decided to present a theory fashioned mainly from Oswald Spengler's classic comparative study of civilizations.[9] In treating this work I have had to be liberal in my interpretations, since it is far from anything like social-scientific theory. Yet I feel it important to include serious discussion of the long-term process of social decline.

As an example of a theory of long-term social development I have chosen not a single theory but rather a theoretical tradition. For lack of a better term I shall call this tradition the "differentiation-integration" analysis of social change. As a starting point I shall take Herbert Spencer's statement of social differentiation and integration in his classic, *The Principles of Sociology*.[10] I shall also consider Emile Durkheim's criticisms, modifications, and elaborations of Spencer.[11] In addition, I shall attempt to incorporate various modern extensions of the theory, to be

---

[6] *Tornado in Worcester*, p. 12.

[7] A number of these theories are summarized and criticized in Pitirim A. Sorokin, *Modern Historical and Social Philosophies* (New York: Dover Publications, 1963).

[8] The absence of systematic theory on social decline is a striking phenomenon in contemporary social science. It would be an instructive exercise in the sociology of knowledge to explore the reasons for this phenomenon. My own speculation is that social scientists have ignored decay and decline because of the persistence of two traditions—first the ideology of progress inherited from the eighteenth-century Enlightenment, and second the tradition of active mastery of the social environment as conditioned by the Protestant reformation and other cultural traditions. These traditions have led social scientists to focus on situations of social growth on the one hand, and on situations about which it is possible to "do something," in a policy sense, on the other.

[9] Oswald Spengler, *The Decline of the West*, authorized translation with notes by Charles Francis Atkinson (New York: Alfred A. Knopf, Inc.), I: *Form and Actuality* (1962); II: *Perspectives of World-History* (1928).

[10] (New York: D. Appleton and Company, 1897).

[11] Emile Durkheim, *The Division of Labor in Society*, trans. George Simpson (New York: The Free Press of Glencoe, Inc., 1949).

found especially in the work of Talcott Parsons and his associates,[12] and in my own theoretical work.[13] Together these can be regarded as an accumulation of theory relating to the growth of institutional structure and the processes accompanying this growth.

As indicated, each of the four bodies of theory emphasizes one direction of social change more than another—short-term collapse, short-term recovery, long-term decline, and long-term development, respectively. As we shall see, however, all of them give at least some attention to other aspects of change than that of their primary focus. This internal complexity of each theory will provide a number of suggestions as to how these theories complement one another and how they might be synthesized. To facilitate my effort at synthesis further, I shall examine selected aspects of two additional long-term theories of social change, each of which systematically incorporates both the deteriorative and constructive aspects of social change. The first of these is found in the works of Karl Marx, whose social theories include not only an account of social characteristics of industrial capitalism (and other types of society) but also an account of the mechanisms by which these characteristics are destroyed and superseded. The second theory is found in the last major work of the functional anthropologist, Bronislaw Malinowski.[14] Basing his theory on the colonial societies of Africa, Malinowski focused attention on the conflict between modern Western forms of social organization and traditional African forms; in addition, he tried to explain how the former came to dominate the latter in many ways, and how new, qualitatively different forms of social organization emerged from the conflict. These two additional theories raise a number of problems not contained in the first four, and will provide further guidelines for the synthetic statement in the final part of the paper.

Section III: Statement of Theoretical Synthesis In Section II, I shall have outlined the skeletal features of six theories of social change; in addition, I shall have indicated some of the sources of strength and weak-

[12] Relevant works include Talcott Parsons, R. F. Bales, *et al., Family: Socialization and Interaction Process* (New York: The Free Press of Glencoe, Inc., 1955); Talcott Parsons and Neil J. Smelser, *Economy and Society* (New York: The Free Press of Glencoe, Inc., 1956); and Talcott Parsons, "A Functional Theory of Change," in Amitai Etzioni and Eva Etzioni, eds., *Social Change: Sources, Patterns, and Consequences* (New York: Basic Books, Inc., 1964), originally as "Some Considerations on the Theory of Social Change," *Rural Sociology,* XXVI (1961), 219–39.

[13] Neil J. Smelser, *Social Change in the Industrial Revolution* (Chicago: University of Chicago Press, 1959); *Theory of Collective Behavior* (New York: The Free Press of Glencoe, Inc., 1963); *The Sociology of Economic Life* (Englewood Cliffs, N.J.: Prentice-Hall, Inc., 1963).

[14] *The Dynamics of Culture Change: An Inquiry into Race Relations in Africa,* ed. Phyllis M. Kaberry (New Haven: Yale University Press, 1945).

ness of each. Using this as a starting-point, I shall attempt, in the final section of the essay, to specify the general requirements of a theory of change, and to indicate the substantive characteristics of such a theory, insofar as this is possible. In short, my efforts in the final section will be guided both by the statement of ideal criteria for a theory of social change (Section I) and by the critical treatment of several substantive theories of change (Section II).

More particularly, I shall attack the following problems in the final part of the essay:

First, I shall identify the variables that require specification in a theory of social change. This statement will involve not only a classification of the elements that are subject to change but also a classification of the types of influence by which a balance between the forces of social stability and the forces of social change is determined.

Second, insofar as is possible, I shall indicate the major kinds of interactions among these variables. I shall attempt to identify various principles of equilibrium by which the determinants of social change can be organized. In this task it will be necessary to specify a number of different kinds of equilibrium, depending on the predicted direction of change and on the phase of development of change. A different type of equilibrium model should be employed, for example, to characterize a society in an advanced state of social decline, from that employed to characterize a society in the early stages of reconstruction. I shall also attempt to say something about the relations among the different types of equilibrium.

Finally, I shall speculate about some of the general perspectives on society that underlie this synthetic statement.

I. THE CRITERIA FOR A THEORY OF SOCIAL CHANGE [15]

Specification of Dependent Variables   The first [16] task facing any investigator of social change—indeed, any social scientist—is to specify adequately *what he wishes to explain*. To put it another way, he must raise *a scientific problem about one or more dependent variables*. The following are sample problems: Why has the divorce rate in America shown a steady upward climb during the past century? Under what conditions should rapid economic recovery from a depression be expected?

[15] In some respects this section represents an application of the general criteria spelled out in Chapter One, above, to the special problems of analyzing social change.

[16] In using the term "first" I am merely indicating that I shall examine the components of a theory of social change in a certain logical order. I do not mean to imply that specifying a scientific problem about a dependent variable or set of variables is the *most important* ingredient of a theory of change from every standpoint, or that its specification is the initial thing (in time) that an investigator must do.

What social conditions are associated with the rise of totalitarian social movements? In these questions the dependent variables—changes in which we wish to explain—are the divorce rate, economic recovery, and totalitarian movements, respectively. The first component of a theory of change, then, is a scientific problem, or a "why" question about some change in one or more dependent variables. Without adequately specifying such a question, the investigator is in the embarrassing position of not knowing what he wishes to explain. Accordingly, any subsequent explanation or theory of change he might devise may be legitimately criticized as scientifically inadequate.

Analysts of social change typically focus their interest on temporal variations of one or more of the following kinds of dependent variables:

1. Changes in *aggregated attributes* of the population of a social unit. Examples of these attributes are the proportions of persons of different ages in a population, persons holding various occupations, persons professing various religious beliefs, illiterate persons, and so on. To pose scientific questions is to ask under what conditions changes in these aggregated attributes may be expected.

2. Changes in *rates of behavior* in a population over time. Here I have in mind variations in rates of voting, religious attendance, crime, suicide, collective protest, and so on. To pose scientific questions is to ask under what conditions changes in these rates may be expected. While questions of this sort deal with the aggregated properties of individual members, they are conceptualized as a *flow* of behavior within a specified period of time rather than a *stock* of attributes characterizing the population at a given point in time. The difference between the two types of variables is illustrated by the following: To enumerate the proportion of Ph.D.s in a population is to identify an aggregated attribute; to calculate the number of graduate students attaining Ph.D.s in 1968 is to identify a behavior rate.

3. Changes in *social structure*, or patterns of interaction among individuals. To pose scientific questions is to ask under what conditions changes in structure may be expected. In one sense the notion of social structure is very close to the first two variables, since we often identify social structure by pointing to regularities in attributes and rates of behavior. In using the term, "family structure," for instance, we refer to the empirical facts that the same people—adult male categorized as husband and father, adult female categorized as wife and mother, and several young people categorized as son, daughter, brother, and sister—regularly sleep under the same roof, share economic goods, and otherwise behave in repetitive ways. Social structure, however, differs from the other two variables in that it is characterized on the basis of the *relations* (for

example, authority relations) among members of a social unit, not on some aggregated versions of attributes or behavior of its individual members. Moreover, in conceptualizing social structure, we assume that the relations among members are not merely fortuitous or statistical, but are regulated by two types of social forces: *sanctions*, including both rewards and deprivations, and *norms*, or standards of conduct that indicate the occasions on which various sanctions are applied.

4. Changes in *cultural patterns*. Cultural patterns—including values, world-views, knowledge, expressive symbols, and so on—supply systems of meaning and legitimacy for patterned social interaction. Examples of cultural patterns are the Judeo-Christian religious heritage, the values of democratic constitutional government, and the Baroque musical style. To pose scientific questions is to ask under what conditions changes in these kinds of patterns may be expected.

It is necessary for the investigator to set some limits on the scope of the dependent variables in question. Surely the student of changes in social structure cannot hope to explain all such changes everywhere. He first must indicate the type of social structure to which his theory applies —whether political, religious, economic, educational, medical, or some combination of these. This requirement of theory raises two critical issues —namely, the problems of *definition* and *classification* of dependent variables.

Let me approach the problems of definition and classification by focusing on a single dependent variable—the prevalence of divorce, changes in which we wish to explain.[17] Suppose divorce is defined simply as the "dissolution of the marriage relation." The function of such a definition seems clear—to circumscribe the boundaries of the dependent variable in question, and to set it off from other phenomena (in this case, intact marriages and nonmarital relations) that are not to be regarded as cases of the dependent variable. Viewing the problem of definition in this way, it immediately becomes evident that every time an investigator defines a phenomenon, he is simultaneously establishing a system of classification containing at least two classes—the class including the variable on the one hand (divorce) and the class of events and situations that are to be considered as excluded from that class on the other (nondivorces). Sometimes the class excluded by the definition may be further classified, for example, when nondivorced persons are divided into persons with intact marriages and persons never married. But the general point remains that the very process of defining a variable entails the operation of classifying it relative

---

[17] This would be an example of a change in rate of behavior in a population over time. But the same general points about definition and classification could be made as conveniently with respect to any other kind of variable.

to phenomena falling outside the scope of the definition. Indeed, definition and classification must be regarded as parts of the same conceptual operation.

In defining any variable, it is essential that its boundaries be clearly demarcated. On closer examination, for example, the definition of divorce as "dissolution of the marriage relation" is likely to be ambiguous and therefore inadequate for many purposes. Such a definition does refer commonly and unambiguously to legally dissolved marriage relations, but it does not reveal whether two other classes of relations should be included or excluded from the definition—first, legal separations (such as arrangements for temporary maintenance and interlocutory decrees) that are not, in the strict sense, finally dissolved marriages; and second, desertions and other informal separations that have no special legal status as dissolutions. Furthermore, the definition does not specify whether the rate should be based on all persons divorced or only on those who are divorced and not remarried. The investigator may wish to exclude or include various of these categories, depending on the problems guiding his research, but whatever his decision, the boundaries of the definition should be made precise and unambiguous.

Suppose, finally, that the investigator wishes to focus on dissolved marriages, but that for purposes of analysis he wishes to distinguish among the four categories implied in the preceding paragraph: (1) legally divorced persons who have never remarried; (2) legally divorced persons who have remarried; (3) persons legally separated but not divorced; and (4) persons informally separated. In this case he would be dividing the major dependent variable into several subclasses, each of which receives a definition and is set off from the other subclasses. This operation once again reveals the intimate connection between classification and definition: Each time an investigator divides a variable into a number of classes, he simultaneously establishes a number of subdefinitions; and each time an investigator defines a variable, he simultaneously classifies it relative to a larger class of phenomena.

Description of Change

So much for some of the general issues involved in identifying and defining variables. Suppose the investigator has met these issues more or less satisfactorily. He next confronts a number of problems involved in describing changes in these variables. The most immediate problem involves the specification of a context in social space and time in which the variables are to be studied. The investigator must, for example, specify the kind of social unit about which his problem is being posed—an experimental small group, a formal organization, a community, a society, or an international order. Of course, he may frame his problems in very general terms so his theory will apply to many kinds of social units; but if this is the case, they must be translated into more specific terms each time he desires to study problems in a particular social setting.

In addition, the investigator must decide on the establishment of beginning and end points for any given process of change. In order for there to be any theory of change, Parsons notes, "there must be an initial and terminal pattern to be used as points of reference." [18] If the investigator is interested in accounting for changes in the American family system over the past 100 years, for example, he has to choose some kind of family arrangement (e.g., the typical frontier family) as a starting point and another kind of family arrangement (e.g., the urban family) as a terminal point. And sooner or later, if he is going to be able to explain what happened historically, he has to make a judgment about when these respective family arrangements were predominant. But unfortunately history does not provide many obvious clues. If only it could be said that the nineteenth-century frontier family gave way to the twentieth-century urban family on New Year's Day in 1900, the investigator's problems would be relatively easy. History is very stingy in providing such obvious transition points; in the main, it rolls along in continuous flux. The result is that the investigator is often forced to select his own initial and terminal points and thus artificially "freeze" history by describing social arrangements as though they existed in fixed form at these moments. [19]

In connection with depicting the states of affairs at the initial and terminal points—as well as at intermediate stages between them—three related methodological problems arise. The first deals with the necessity of having proper concepts to characterize the initial and terminal states. The definition of concepts must be sufficiently general so as to include (and *not* to exclude) instances of the concepts in different historical periods. This is the familiar "problem of comparability"; for the student of social change, however, it often appears as the problem of comparing the same social system at two different points in time, as contrasted with comparing two different social systems. [20]

The second problem deals with the adequacy of indices or measures of variables at the beginning, intermediate, and terminal points of change. In tracing the course of a divorce rate over the past 100 years, suppose the

---

[18] Talcott Parsons, *The Social System* (New York: The Free Press of Glencoe, Inc., 1951), p. 483.

[19] A discussion of the many methodological problems involved in describing unique historical situations in general terms is found in Max Weber, " 'Objectivity' in Social Science and Social Policy," in *The Methodology of the Social Sciences*, trans. and ed. Edward A. Shils and Henry A. Finch (New York: The Free Press of Glencoe, Inc., 1949), pp. 49–112.

[20] For a more general discussion of the problem of comparability, see Chapter Three, above.

investigator decides to rely on court records as a measure of dissolved marriages. For some purposes this measure may be adequate. But, still speaking hypothetically, suppose that while the incidence of legal divorce showed a steady increase by this measure, informal separations showed a corresponding decline (as social groups formerly relying on desertion made increasingly regular use of the divorce courts). In this case, an apparent index of marital dissolution would actually reveal only a change in the *form* of marital dissolution, and would therefore be inadequate as a true index. To take another example, suppose an investigator wishes to trace the course of the crime rate during the past fifty years, using court convictions as data. Is this obvious measure an adequate one? Surely the rate of detection and conviction of crime has changed in the past fifty years. Surely the social definition of a crime has also changed, since criminal laws themselves and attitudes of judges and juries toward criminals have been modified. Is this investigator justified, then, in using the same measure for crime in 1915 as he does in 1965? If not, what sort of measure should he use? To put this point in terms of the problem of definition discussed above, the indices used to measure a variable should represent or otherwise correspond as closely as possible to that which is included in the initial conceptual definition of the variable.

The third problem deals with the necessity for concepts to describe the direction of change over time. When the investigator is dealing with readily quantifiable variables such as a population's attributes or rates of behavior, his task is relatively easy. He is usually interested in either increases and decreases, or some distinctive combination of these, such as a cycle. When he attempts to characterize changes in social structure and cultural patterns, however, his task is more complex. It is not very helpful —in fact it may even be nonsensical—to say that a society has quantitatively *more* social structures or *fewer* aesthetic symbols than before. It is necessary instead to turn to qualitative indicators of change. For example, in considering the modernization of traditional societies, it is important to trace the ways in which social structures grow more complex and specialized—the ways, say, that local tribal political arrangements give way to complex central national governments. To measure this process, however, involves more than simple counting; it requires a detailed account of the kinds of activities performed in various roles and organizations. To characterize directions of cultural change poses even greater difficulties. Some changes in culture—for example, the rise of the Renaissance—bring qualitatively new cultural contents. Sometimes, too, the investigator may be interested in judging whether one cultural item or pattern is of higher quality than another.[21] Or he may be interested in describing the break-

---

[21] Gertrude Jaeger and Philip Selznick, "A Normative Theory of Culture," *American Sociological Review*, XXIX (1964), 653–69.

down or disintegration of cultural patterns. The systematic description and classification of these qualitative directions of change—to say nothing of their explanations—is one of the least developed aspects of the study of social change.

Specification of Independent Variables and Formation of Hypotheses

Now let us suppose that the several problems of definition and empirical representation have been attacked more or less satisfactorily, and the investigator is able to describe and measure the beginning, intermediate, and end states of change adequately. We are still far from a complete theory of change. We know only the beginning, middle and final scenes of the drama, but we do not know how or why the plot unfolded the way it did. Or, to put it in the language of social change, we have a comparative picture of a number of static states, but we have little knowledge of the dynamics of change. To gain access to the latter we have to ask about the independent variables (or causes, or determinants, or factors) in change, and the ways these can be organized into explanatory models and theories.

In the literature of social change, the determinants of changes in social variables often fall into one or more of the following broad classes: [22]

1. The structural setting for change. What implications does the existing structure of a social unit have for future changes of the unit? The concept of structural setting includes both an "opportunity" and an "obstacle" aspect. Suppose we wish to estimate the probabilities of a speculative boom and collapse on the stock market. If 90 per cent of the securities are possessed by individual holders who can dispose of them quickly, the opportunities for rapid fluctuations in the market are great. If, however, 90 per cent of the securities are held by trust companies, the managers of which must clear large transactions with their boards of directors before undertaking them, the obstacles to wild buying and selling sprees are considerable. To take another example, suppose we wish to estimate the probabilities of orderly change through reform in a society. If, like contemporary Great Britain, the society possesses numerous channels for the effective expression of grievances—channels such as elections, petitions, demonstrations, etc.—the probabilities for this kind of

---

[22] In connection with the distinction between dependent and independent variables, it should be made clear that the distinction is a relative one, and that any social variable may be considered as either a dependent or an independent variable, depending on the formulation of the original scientific problem. Thus, while I shall be giving concrete examples of the "causes" or "independent variables" in processes of social change, it should be remembered that these examples themselves can be treated as items of change that demand explanation.

change are high. If, like contemporary South Africa, the society possesses few such channels, the probabilities of repressive perpetuation or violent revolutionary overthrow of the *status quo* are higher. In considering the structural opportunities and obstacles to change, it is also important to take account of the power balance among different social groups, including vested interests, in the society.

2. The impetus to change. A conducive structural setting alone does not guarantee that change will occur. The social unit has to be under some kind of pressure (which is called by many names, such as strain, tension, imbalance, or disequilibrium) that provides a definite push toward change. The origins of such pressures for change are numerous. Pressure may accumulate in a social system simply by virtue of the fact that people go about their business in normal ways. For example, the fact that thousands of commuters pour in and out of a metropolis every day may create such problems of congestion that changes in public transport policy may result. Or pressures to change may result from events external to the society itself, such as foreign wars and natural catastrophes, which influence the internal balance of the society. Or a social system may generate pressure through different rates of change in its different parts. For example, the fact that underdeveloped countries, upon achieving national independence, institute some version of universal suffrage tends to create a crisis in education—a need to create a responsible mass electorate—in these countries.

3. Mobilization for change. If the structural setting is conducive and pressures have accumulated, the probability that *some* sort of social change will occur is high. But these two determinants by themselves are too general to indicate what specific direction change will take. This depends on the ways resources are mobilized and brought to bear on modifying the elements of social action. For some kinds of change, this may involve only a very routine operation. For example, suppose that the executives of a business firm perceive that a potential demand exists for some new product. After a period of planning, they decide to invest some financial reserves in manufacturing and marketing the product, to take on a number of new employees, and perhaps to create a new subdivision of the research branch to develop it. As these decisions are implemented, the firm undergoes a number of changes in finance, personnel, and social structure. For other kinds of change the agents may not be so well "programmed" as to the direction of change and may not have such immediate access to resources. Consider, for example, how an effective demand for social reform comes to be translated into a concrete, effective proposal for change. Before change can be effected, it is necessary for some sort of belief in a specific kind of reform to be crystallized and disseminated; for leaders to form an organization or pressure group; and for

workers to collect funds, publish propaganda, and organize demonstrations. As these examples show, leadership plays a very important role in the processes of mobilization for change.[23]

4. The operation of social controls. As leaders of reform movements well know, their efforts to mobilize do not automatically result in change, but encounter a variety of resistances. Various authorities—governmental officials, courts, community leaders, religious agencies, the press, etc.— are not indifferent to efforts of groups to change society. They may be hostile to the aims of the reform movement, or they may be exposed to counter-movements to the proposed change. Moreover, the behavior of these agents of social control determines in part the direction of change. For example, if governmental authorities are persistently hostile and repressive toward modest demands for reform, those desiring reform may be driven into underground organizations, may become more extreme in their demands for change, and may even begin to challenge the legitimacy of the political authorities. If this happens, the agents of social control themselves will have been influential in transforming a *reform* movement into a *revolutionary* movement.

In characterizing these types (or any types) of independent variables, the investigator must observe the scientific canons governing definition, classification, description, and empirical identification that were discussed in connection with dependent variables.[24] In addition, a number of methodological rules govern the conceptual and empirical relations between independent and dependent variables as these are combined to form *hypotheses*. Let us review these rules before turning to the problem of organizing hypotheses into formal models and theories.

A simple example of an hypothesis in the social sciences is the following: "The incidence of labor violence (e.g., rioting, terrorization, destruction of machinery and plant) is a direct function of the level of unemployment." The independent variable is unemployment and the dependent variable is violent behavior.[25] Regardless of whether the hypothesis is valid empirically, it does have the merit of maintaining a *conceptual and empirical independence* of the two classes of variables.

[23] In discussing "mobilization" and other purposive activities as integral parts of social change, I do not mean to imply that processes of social change are completely or even predominantly "rational" processes—that is, the products of consciously planned and executed programs. Some types of change are of this conscious and planned variety; but many other types unfold by the complex logic of social events and their consequences—a logic that lies beyond the consciousness and control of individuals and groups.

[24] Above, pp. 201–5.

[25] It is possible to break this hypothesis into a number of subhypotheses if the psychological variables that intervene between unemployment and violence are considered. These would take the following form: "Unemployment gives rise to anxiety"; "anxiety gives rise to hostility"; "hostility gives rise to violent behavior."

That is to say, those classes of events subsumed under the definition of "unemployment" do not overlap with those classes of events subsumed under the definition of "violence." The two classes evidently are mutually exclusive. For this reason, it is unlikely that the same or even similar empirical indices will be chosen for both variables. If the investigator can guarantee such a conceptual and empirical separation between independent and dependent variables, he can be assured that any association that may obtain between the two variables is genuine, and not merely a function of the fact that the two variables have common conceptual properties and are therefore associated by definition.

When the conceptual and empirical separation of variables is not observed, the association between them is said to be "contaminated." This contamination can take a number of forms, but I shall give only a few examples. Suppose we are entertaining the hypothesis that the probability of successful revolution from below is increased by the presence of a divisive conflict among the ruling classes.[26] If, in attempting to illustrate this hypothesis historically, the evidence for (or index of) a divided and weak ruling class is found in the presence of successful revolutionary overthrows, this would not constitute a true test for the hypothesis. Rather, it would be identifying the presumed cause by reference to an index of the presumed effect, thus establishing the association by faulty conceptualization and operationalization rather than by independent measures of concepts.

Again, suppose we are entertaining the hypothesis that the probability of occurrence of a revolutionary political movement is a direct function of the level of social disorganization. Suppose further that the investigator is able to avoid the simple error of assigning cause by identifying effect, and seeks independent measures for the independent and dependent variables. Presumably the indices of revolutionary political movements would be located in historical evidence relating to collective political activity. And the investigator, following the lead of Durkheim, might wish to represent the degree of integration of society by some quantitative index such as the suicide rate.[27] Clearly the measure of political activity and the measure of suicide are empirically independent. But using these two measures raises another question of conceptual contamination. On the basis of a variety of traditions of research in the social sciences, it is reasonable to assume that both political protest and suicide fall in a larger class of behavioral responses to social stress (this larger class would also include criminal activity, alcoholism, mental disorders, and religious con-

[26] For an examination of this hypothesis, see Smelser, *Theory of Collective Behavior,* pp. 364–79.

[27] Emile Durkheim, *Suicide,* trans. George Simpson (New York: The Free Press of Glencoe, Inc., 1951).

version). Insofar as this is the case, the investigator, in the example given, would be estimating the strength of the presumed independent variable (social disorganization) by reference to a behavioral alternative (suicide) to the dependent variable (political protest), thus measuring the association between two dependent variables rather than between the independent and dependent variable. In order to improve the test of the hypothesis, a more direct and conceptually independent measure of social disorganization (such as role conflict or ethnic cleavage) would have to be employed.

Organization of Hypotheses into Models

Simply to list the variables influencing the course of social change is not sufficient to create a theory of change. The most such a listing can provide is a discrete number of hypotheses. The variables must also be organized into some sort of explanatory model. A model, simply defined, is a conceptual apparatus that states that if a given number of determinants are combined in a certain way, a definite outcome (type of change) is to be expected. In one sense a model is nothing more than an explanation: but it differs from *ad hoc* explanations of particular historical situations in that it is organized into more explicit, formal, and general terms. Because the field of social change is not scientifically very mature, however, many of its models are incomplete, implicit, and not properly validated. Nevertheless, it is possible to identify several types of models, differing in degree of formality and empirical adequacy.

One of the simplest types of model explanations in the field of social change goes under the name of the "natural history" approach. This approach involves the claim that a particular kind of social change unfolds according to a distinct number of stages. A classic model of the natural stages of a social movement is that developed by Carl A. Dawson and Warner E. Gettys. The movement begins with a "preliminary stage of social unrest," passes through a "popular stage of collective excitement" and a "stage of formal organization," and finally reaches a kind of terminal point of "institutionalization." The entire sequence introduces some new institutional form—a religious sect, a law, a new kind of family structure, or a political reform.[28] A comparable model for revolutions is found in Crane Brinton's analysis of the French Revolution of 1789, the American Revolution, the British Revolution of 1642, and the Russian Revolution of 1917. The first stage finds the society in a state of general prosperity, but with a government suffering from economic troubles and political weakness. In this atmosphere various groups, especially intellectuals, become progressively disaffected with the old regime. The next stage involves

[28] Carl A. Dawson and Warner E. Gettys, *An Introduction to Sociology* (New York: The Ronald Press, 1929), pp. 787–803.

the actual revolution, and a transfer of power takes place. For a while the moderates among the revolutionaries hold power, but thereafter the extremists seize the reins of power and institute a period of bloody terrorism. This period is also limited in duration, and after a time the excesses of the revolution diminish; some of its aims are institutionalized, but in many other respects the society returns to its prerevolutionary ways.[29]

The basic organizing principle of the natural history model is *time*— the principle that, as a matter of historical fact, the various phases follow one another in temporal order. Such a principle does organize the variables of an episode of social change in a simple way, and thus reduces the randomness of their occurrence. But the model provides a general description rather than an explanation, since writers taking the natural history approach seldom inquire explicitly into the reasons why one stage gives way to the next, or why one particular sequence of stages rather than another should be expected.

Another, more formal way of organizing the determinants of change is what I have termed the "value-added" approach.[30] An analogy will reveal the logic of this approach. In the manufacture of automobiles, iron ore is converted into finished cars by a number of stages of processing. Relevant stages are smelting, tempering, shaping, combining the steel with other parts, painting, delivering to retailer, and selling. Each stage "adds its value" to the final cost of the finished product. The key element in the value-added sequence is that no single stage can contribute its particular value until the prior stages are finished. It is of no use, for example, to paint iron ore; to be effective, painting has to "wait" for the completion of the earlier processes. Every stage, therefore, is a necessary condition for the final production of the automobile, but no single stage can be effective unless it occurs at a single point in the sequence. Viewing the production process in this way, it is clear that the variables do not constitute a mere list, but have to be organized.

Apply this analogy to a process of social change. Suppose we are interested in explaining the rise of the industrial method of production. Clearly one of the necessary conditions for this is adequate technological know-how. But unless the know-how is applied in a certain structural setting—a setting that includes an allocation system for resources and products, a medium of exchange, a requisite level of skill in the labor force, and so on—it cannot possibly become effective as a determinant of the industrial method of production. Or, to take an example mentioned

---

[29] Crane Brinton, *The Anatomy of Revolution* (New York: Vintage Books, 1958).

[30] This approach is spelled out in my book, *Theory of Collective Behavior*, pp. 12–21. An earlier statement of the approach, with references to the causes of industrial development, is found in my book, *Social Change in the Industrial Revolution*, pp. 60–62. Also, see above, pp. 97–100.

earlier, a sense of opportunity and profit is a necessary determinant for a speculative craze in the stock market; but unless this occurs in a setting in which it is possible to acquire and dispose of financial assets rapidly, it cannot be effective as a determinant of a craze. A value-added model is created when a number of these variables are combined in a systematic way to produce an explanation for a particular type of social change.

One feature of the value-added explanatory model is that, while it brings a number of necessary conditions into relation with one another, this relation is not closely specified. At best the conditions are arranged in a scale of increasing specificity with respect to a given outcome. Less is known about the interaction among the determinants—i.e., the degree to which they influence one another and the degree to which they are influenced by other factors. In short, the value-added model would be improved if greater attention could be given to specifying the principles governing the relations among the independent variables.

Among the most highly organized explanatory models in the social sciences are those that incorporate various principles of equilibrium. The principles of equilibrium are most developed in the analysis of economic systems,[31] but equilibrium models are also employed—though not always under that name—in the other behavioral sciences. To conclude the discussion of the general criteria for a theory of change, I shall devote some attention to the notion of equilibrium. Before proceeding, however, I should like to note that the principle of equilibrium is not something qualitatively different from other types of explanatory model, but is simply one alternative method of generating explanations and predictions of variations in empirical phenomena.[32] In its most general sense, the notion of equilibrium refers to the principle that a given set of variables constitutes a system—that is, that they have definite and identifiable relations with one another, and that these relations persist or change in definite ways over time by means of certain processes of adjustment.

The ingredients of an equilibrium system can be grasped by following a simple hypothetical example. Let us suppose that our field of interest is municipal politics, and we wish to explain the mutual relations among three variables—the level of political corruption, the average municipal tax rate, and the turnover of elected municipal officials. Let us suppose further that the problems of defining and establishing valid and measurable empirical indices for those variables have been more or less successfully overcome. According to the hypothetical model being advanced here, the following relations hold among the three variables: When elected

---

[31] For a comprehensive survey of general equilibrium models in economics, see Robert E. Kuenne, *The Theory of General Economic Equilibrium* (Princeton: Princeton University Press, 1963).

[32] *Ibid.*, pp. 3–4.

officials achieve a reasonably secure tenure through repeated reelection (i.e., when there is low turnover), these officials will begin to feel free to dip into public funds to reward relatives, friends, political supporters, and cronies. As these practices increase, moreover, pressures on public funds begin to accumulate, and the officials find it necessary to hike various taxes to meet these pressures. The tax increases, however, infuriate those portions of the local populace that are not receiving patronage benefits. In succeeding elections, therefore, the electorate begins to turn against the local officials, and the rate of turnover in office increases. As new officials are elected, they "clean up" corruption by a series of reforms and are thereby enabled to reduce taxes. In this way they gain the continued support of the electorate, and tend to be retained in office in succeeding elections. Having been granted this security in office, however, the new crop of officials begins to indulge in corrupt practices, and this initiates once again the complex sequence just described.

In this simple model the three basic variables—corruption, tax rates, and turnover of officials—are in an equilibrium relation with one another, since a change in any one initiates changes in the others, and since these changes in their turn feed back and produce changes in the initiating variable. These particular relations, moreover, produce a series of interrelated cyclical movements among the three variables. These movements can be represented graphically as in Figure 8–2. The rate of turnover of officials is represented by the solid line; the level of corruption by the dashed line, and the average tax rate by the dotted line. Continued tenure in office (the level solid line) permits a rise in corruption. After a lag, the tax rise begins, and this in turn precipitates a turnover of officials at

CYCLICAL MOVEMENTS AMONG THREE VARIABLES

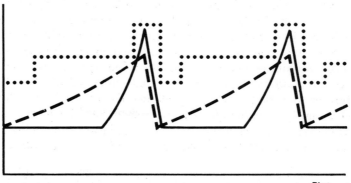

FIGURE 8–2

election time. Subsequently all three variables decrease sharply, but after a time the level of corruption begins to creep upward again, thus initiating the cyclical pattern for each variable. The *contour* of each cycle varies, however, because the units of each variable differ in their degree of divisibility. It is possible, for example, to represent corruption as smoothly rising and falling, since it can be increased or decreased by very small increments. The tax rate, by contrast, since it can be changed only by discrete legislative acts, must be represented in a more irregular contour. The rate of turnover of officials shows an even more irregular course, since it can be changed only at election time (say, every two years). Despite these different contours, it remains the case that the cyclical movements are determined primarily by the equilibrium principles governing the relations among the three variables.[33]

Using this example, it is possible to identify the ingredients of equilibrium systems in general. The first and most obvious ingredient is the *variables* themselves. In the example the variables are three well known types of political phenomena, but, in general, variables may be drawn from any of the classes listed previously.[34] Variations in the empirical indices representing these variables are sometimes referred to as *outputs* of the equilibrium system. A second ingredient of an equilibrium system is the *relations* among the variables. In the example, the tax rate is seen at one time to be a direct function of the level of corruption, at a later time a direct function of the rate of turnover of officials. The level of corruption is seen as a direct function of the rate of turnover of officials. And the rate of turnover of officials is a direct function of the tax rate. From these relations emerge specific *hypotheses*. (It might be noted that in this type of equilibrium system the distinction between independent and dependent variables becomes completely relative, since each variable is represented as a function of the others. Each variable is assessed as independent or dependent, depending on the point at which entry is made into the system; moreover, each variable may be considered independent or dependent, or simultaneously both.)

A third ingredient of any equilibrium system is the *given data* or *parameters*. These are phenomena which are known or suspected to influence the relations among the variables—and hence the outputs of the system—but variation in which is "assumed to be frozen by analytic controls." In this way their influence on the variables is held constant or otherwise neutralized. These given data, then, "lie beyond the analytical

[33] In this example I have used cyclical movements to illustrate the change in outputs of an equilibrium system. The illustration is not meant to imply, however, that cyclical adjustments are essential ingredients in the general definition of equilibrium. They are, rather, one of several types of outputs of equilibrium systems. Below, pp. 216–21.

[34] Above, pp. 200–201.

ambition of the model, in the sense that they are determining rather than determined." [35] Furthermore, the nature and extent of their determining influence is controlled by analytic assumptions.[36]

The parameters, or given data, of an equilibrium system may be broken into three subclasses:

1. Certain assumptions of stability are made about aspects of the empirical world lying beyond the limits of the model. For example, the illustration above contains a great many unspoken but important assumptions—that no major economic depression hits the municipalities whose political behavior is being studied; that no major changes in criminal law affecting corrupt practices occur; that no major international war occurs; that the municipalities are free from natural catastrophes and famines; and so on. Any equilibrium model—indeed, any model—rests on an almost interminable list of assumptions about the "rest of the world." It would be pedantic to attempt to list all such assumptions for every equilibrium model; but, notwithstanding, it should be remembered that significant variations in the phenomena ruled out by these assumptions would influence if not overwhelm the relations posited in the equilibrium model.

2. Certain features of the environment of the system are assumed to influence the behavior of the variables, but in a constant manner. For example, the fact that municipal elections are held only every two years makes for a very irregular rising and falling of the curve representing turnover in office, though the causes of the rising and falling movements themselves are found in the interactions among the primary variables. To take another example, the investment curves for industries such as railroads or shipbuilding—which must make their investments in indivisible amounts—are more irregular or "lumpy" than the investment curves of, say, a chain of retailers. Such environmental influences do intrude on the equilibrium system—and thus differ from the first type of given data, which are assumed not to influence the system—but this intrusion is of a constant, not a variable character.[37]

3. Equilibrium models incorporate assumptions concerning variables that "intervene" between the primary variables. In the example, length of tenure in office is associated positively with the level of corruption. This association rests on certain psychological assumptions about political officials—namely, that in a secure position their sense of daring will be-

---

[35] Kuenne, *op. cit.*, p. 5.

[36] For a discussion of the distinction between parameters and operative variables in the context of research design and the methodological aspects of drawing inferences, see above, pp. 16 ff. and 71 ff.

[37] Alternatively, however, these potential environmental intrusions may be assumed simply not to be problematical, as in some economic models, in which the factors of production are assumed to be continuously divisible and perfectly mobile.

come greater, and they will begin to feel that they can engage in quasi-legitimate political activities with impunity. Moreover, if these psychological assumptions are modified, the relations between the primary variables also will be modified. For example, if it is postulated that position in office increases the official's integrity and sense of public obligation, the relations between tenure in office and level of corruption will be reversed. To select another example, the relations among prices, consumers' income, and consumers' expenditures that are posited in various economic models rest on the assumption that the consumer will maximize his utility according to a definite principle. If such an assumption is modified or discarded, the relations among the primary economic variables also are altered accordingly.

The assumptions that intervene between the primary variables "make sense" of the relations among these variables. If it is asked why tenure of office is positively correlated with increasing corruption, the answer is found in the psychology of elected officials. If it is asked why a consumer changes his buying habits when the price of one product goes up and the price of another goes down, the answer will be found by reference to the kind of psychological assumptions built into his utility function. In addition, these intervening assumptions provide at least a partial account of the mechanisms by which the primary variables influence one another. In the example it is assumed that one primary variable (continuity in office) has certain psychological consequences for officials, that the officials behave in accord with these consequences, and that their behavior results in a change in another primary variable (corruption). Thus, even though the intervening assumptions do not vary—and for this reason they fall into the category of "given data"—they provide considerable service in linking the primary variables to one another.

Having specified these ingredients of an equilibrium system—variables, relations, and several categories of given data—we may now see what is involved in the *derivation of hypotheses* within an equilibrium system. Derivation consists of systematically and exhaustively specifying the implications of both the given data and the relations for the behavior of the variables. Part of a variable's variation can be predicted by virtue of its relations with other variables; and part can be predicted by virtue of the ways in which the various given data constrict or intrude upon the system. Or, to put it more formally, "the variables of the model . . . are determined in value by the constraining interaction of the data and the interrelationships that exist among the data and variables by virtue of the natural or behavioral assumptions of the model, or both." [38]

The distinction between variables and given data (parameters) is a

---

[38] Kuenne, *op. cit.*, p. 5.

relative one. By relaxing the analytic assumptions that "freeze" given data, these data may become variables, to be considered in relation to the other variables in the equilibrium system. For example, in a general economic equilibrium model, it is possible to relax various restrictive assumptions— such as perfect mobility of resources, perfect knowledge of the market on the part of the actors, and maximization of utility—and trace the consequences for the system. Alternatively, variables can be converted into given data by changing the assumptions regarding them. The refinement of equilibrium theory consists in part in the selective and systematic relaxing of assumptions—that is, treating new kinds of data as variables, and adding to knowledge about the principles governing the working of the system. Of course, there is a limit to this operation; as more and more assumptions are relaxed—and as more and more variables are simultaneously created—the equilibrium system becomes conceptually more unwieldy.

A theorist's perspectives on human nature and society are revealed primarily in his assumptions regarding given data. For example, in linking tenure of office directly with the occurrence of corruption, I introduced a view of office holders as primarily cynical and opportunistic. On the other hand, in linking the tax rate directly to the rate of turnover of officials, I introduced a view of the electorate as righteously indignant. A critic of my model might well ask whether I have adopted one psychological perspective for political leaders and another for political followers; and, if so, why; and whether either perspective is justified. To choose another example: in characterizing the response of the electorate to increasing tax burdens, I assumed that they would express their dissatisfaction only at the polls, and would not resort to violent assault on political officials or to attempts to seize the reins of municipal power. A critic might well ask why I chose to view the citizenry as so respectful of law and order; he might suggest further that if I viewed them otherwise, I would create a very different kind of model. Such criticisms should not be regarded simply as the ideological or philosophical implications of scientific explanation. As we have seen, the derivation of hypotheses relating the primary variables rests in large part on these kinds of given data; and insofar as the psychological, social, moral, and ideological perspectives of the theorist are vague, contradictory, or empirically incorrect, this detracts accordingly from the scientific adequacy of the model itself.

Types of Equilibrium Models

Equilibrium models are organized according to a number of different criteria, and this results in diverse types of models, each of which finds some use in the behavioral sciences.

One criterion concerns the degree to which the ingredients of equilibrium—variables, parameters, and relations—are assumed to constitute a system that is entirely self-determining, i.e., free from outside influences. Insofar as the system is viewed in this way, it is a *closed* equilibrium system; insofar as outside influences are viewed as determining in part the values of and interactions among the variables, it is an *open* equilibrium system. An example of closed equilibrium is the classic Walrasian model in economics:

> Walras' system was a closed one, with no impact from the outside. Consumers sold their services and bought the output of firms, while the latter bought factor services and raw materials to make products for sale to both consumers and firms. Within this general framework, the major problem was to determine the conditions of equilibrium for the entire economy, for it was only then that the prices of products, factor services, output, and costs could be established. . . . The system was described by several sets of equations. There were the demand equations which expressed consumer bids not only as functions of the price of the goods in question, but of all other consumer goods as well. Then came the cost equations, and on the assumption that prices varied directly with costs, one could obtain a series of equations in which price was equal to the outlays for productive services. Quantity equations then described the relation between the stock of available productive services and the quantity utilized for each good. The prices of the productive services also established the technical coefficients, or the production function, so that the lowest cost combinations would be employed in working up a firm's output.[39]

Most equilibrium systems in the social sciences do not approach this degree of tightness. Parsons' assessment of his own conception of a "system of action" is that it is not sufficiently developed to permit "deductive transitions from one aspect or state of a system to another, so that it is possible to say that if the facts in A sector were W and X, those in B sector must be Y and Z." [40] His own "structural-functional level of theoretical systematization" is conceived of as a "second best type of theory" to a closed system. Within such a framework, structures are described by categories that are developed as systematically as possible, and variations in structures are assessed in terms of their functional significance for the system as a whole, and in terms of the motivational processes that maintain structures in relation to one another, or operate in the process of transition from one structural pattern to another.[41] Since the concepts of "structure," "function," and "motivational process" are not derivable

[39] Ben B. Seligman, *Main Currents in Modern Economics: Economic Thought Since 1870* (New York: The Free Press of Glencoe, Inc., 1962), pp. 376–77.

[40] Talcott Parsons, *The Social System* (New York: The Free Press of Glencoe, Inc., 1951), p. 20.

[41] *Ibid.*, pp. 20–22.

from one another, the system of action as characterized by Parsons must be considered as a relatively open equilibrium system.[42]

The degree to which any equilibrium system should be represented as relatively closed or relatively open depends on several considerations: (1) In the interests of formal adequacy, the system should be represented as nearly closed as possible; insofar as it is left open, it suffers from theoretical indeterminacy. (2) If sufficiently precise language to describe a system is lacking, it cannot profitably be represented as closed. If there are appropriate mathematical techniques—e.g., simultaneous equations—available to describe a system, it can be represented as a closed system. Insofar as the variables, relations, and given data must be described in vaguer terms—e.g., common language—it is likely that the terms will overlap with one another, so that the precise character of the system cannot be known. (3) If the empirical knowledge on the basis of which a given system is assumed to be closed off from outside influences is inadequate, closing the system may result in the production of invalid empirical hypotheses. The degree to which an equilibrium system is conceptualized as open or closed should represent a compromise involving these several considerations.

A second criterion for classifying types of equilibrium concerns whether the equilibrium system is presented in *general* or *partial* terms. In economics the general equilibrium model treats the entire economy [43] by a very complex series of equations, whereas a partial equilibrium model treats only an isolated aspect of the economy—for example, consumer demand for a single good. In the latter case, the remaining elements of the economy are treated as given data, constant for purposes of analyzing the limited aspect. In sociology and anthropology most studies of the relations among different types of social structure—e.g., between religious structures and economic structures—are carried out under approximate conditions of partial equilibrium analysis, i.e., *as if* other structures in society are given data and do not intrude. To my knowledge no rigorous formulations of general equilibrium conditions for an entire society are available in the social sciences. Furthermore, until much more knowledge

[42] Alexander Gerschenkron has criticized Parsons for speaking of the social system in equilibrium terms. "The Parsonian system is presented as a social-equilibrium system, thus evoking comparisons with the general-equilibrium concept in economics. But time and again it appears that the concept of equilibrium is extended so far as to become coterminous with that of organized society; what, then, is actually discussed is not so much a set of equilibrium conditions as a set of minimum conditions of social existence, which would mean that most important and most variegated social processes might take place without any change in the basic variables that enter into the system." "Social Attitudes, Entrepreneurship, and Economic Development," in *Economic Backwardness in Historical Perspective: A Book of Essays* (Cambridge: The Belknap Press of Harvard University Press, 1962), p. 55, fn. 6.

[43] Even this "general" equilibrium is "partial" from the perspective of viewing the entire society (economy and other social systems) in equilibrium. This observation underscores the relativity of the concepts "general" and "partial."

of specific institutional relations—knowledge based on more limited, par-tial-equilibrium types of analysis—accumulates, it is probably not fruitful to attempt such a general formulation.[44]

A third criterion for characterizing equilibrium systems concerns the degree to which the given data are considered as frozen, and, correspond-ingly, the degree to which the values of the variables are specifically de-termined. If the given data are assigned a specific set of values, the value of the variables can be predicted more precisely. In this case the equilib-rium system is described as *specific*. If, on the other hand, the theorist assigns an entire range of possible values to the different kinds of given data, the system's outcomes must also be expressed as a range of possi-bilities rather than as specific predictions. In this case the equilibrium sys-tem is described as *nonspecific*.

A fourth criterion for distinguishing types of equilibrium systems is *time,* insofar as it is systematically incorporated into the system. If the system is presented simply as a resultant of forces emerging from the relations among the given data and variables, the equilibrium system is *static*. Time does not enter a static equilibrium. If, however, the system is considered as moving in time, and attention is given to the continuous interaction of data and variables to produce a distinctive path over time, the equilibrium system is *dynamic*. An intermediate type of equilibrium analysis between static and dynamic is *comparative static* analysis, ac-cording to which the system is described at different points in time, but no attention is given to the mechanisms by which the passage from one point to another is effected.

A fifth way of classifying equilibrium systems is to characterize typical *paths* taken by the outputs of the system. Actually, this method applies only to dynamic systems, since movement through time is always in-volved. One of the most familiar types of dynamic equilibrium is the *stable* or *homeostatic* type. The characteristic feature of a stable system is that when some influence disturbs the relations among the variables, certain mechanisms are thrown into operation to restore the system to its original state. In a classic work, Walter B. Cannon outlined the ways in which bodily processes are governed by this type of equilibrium principle:

> One of the most striking features of our bodily structure and chemical composition . . . is extreme natural instability. Only a brief lapse in the coordinating functions of the circulatory apparatus, and a part of the organic fabric may break down so completely as to endanger the exist-ence of the entire bodily edifice. . . . [We] have noted the frequency of such contingencies, and we have noted also how infrequently they bring on the possible dire results. As a rule, whenever conditions are

[44] For an argument of the case that general equilibrium in economics is cumber-some unless simplified in the direction of partial equilibrium analysis, see Kuenne, *op. cit.,* pp. 22–39.

such as to affect the organism harmfully, factors appear within the organism itself that protect it or restore its disturbed balance. . . . If water is needed, the mechanism of thirst warns us before any change in the blood has occurred, and we respond by drinking. If the blood pressure falls and the necessary oxygen supply is jeopardized, delicate nerve endings in the carotid sinus send messages to the vasomotor center and the pressure is raised. If by vigorous muscular movements blood is returned to the heart in great volume, so that cardiac action might be embarrassed and the circulation checked, again delicate nerve endings are affected and a call goes from the right auricle, that results in speeding up the heart rate and thereby hastening the blood flow.[45]

Cannon distinguishes two principal ways in which the body maintains homeostasis: by the storage of excess supplies that are partially run down to stabilize bodily imbalances, and by processes that are triggered by some bodily excess or deficit. In both cases the indices (or outputs) of bodily functions show small deviations from the rapid return to a set of relations between variables and parameters.

Other types of equilibrium emerge when the path is viewed as *moving* in some way. An example of a moving equilibrium is a model of a trade cycle, in which income fluctuates according to some more or less definite principle.[46] Another example is a model of an economy in which production is increasing at a steady, continuous rate, but in which the relations among population, investment, and savings remain the same. Combining the two examples, the economy could be viewed as growing at a given rate, but as experiencing cyclical fluctuations around the trend line of growth. In many models the path of the moving output is described according to some mathematical function, such as a sine curve.

With respect to *unstable* equilibrium systems, it seems fruitful to distinguish between two meanings of this concept. The first refers to wild fluctuations of some system-output (for example, the price level in a model of runaway inflation), under conditions which do not involve changes in the principles governing the relations among the variables and given data in the system. The second meaning refers to some sort of qualitative change, or breakdown of the equilibrium system itself—i.e., of the relations among variables and data—and the establishment of some new kind of equilibrium system. Examples of the latter would be the

---

[45] Walter B. Cannon, *The Wisdom of the Body* (New York: W. W. Norton & Company, Inc., 1939), pp. 286 ff.

[46] It should be noted, however, that the distinction between a stable equilibrium and a cyclical moving equilibrium is not always a clear one, and a given movement can be described in both ways in some cases. For example, the illustration concerning corruption, tax rates, and political turnover above could be described as cyclical, since the movement of the outputs conform to a regular up-and-down path; but it could also be described as stable, since the mechanisms involved tend to restore a balance among the several variables.

death of an organism, the regression of an individual into a psychotic episode, the overthrow of an existing social order by revolutionary means. Whether a system is judged to be unstable in this second sense depends in part on the level of generality of the concepts employed to characterize the relations among the variables and the given data; for example, at a very general level a postrevolutionary society can be described in terms of the same kinds of relations as the prerevolutionary society. But for many purposes it is useful to employ models of discontinuous movement from one qualitatively different type of equilibrium system to another.

If these several classificatory criteria are applied, a substantial number of types of equilibrium system results. It should be stressed, however, that no one type of equilibrium model is inherently superior to another, and that the type of model chosen depends on the analytic purpose and the scientific problem at hand. The acceptability of an equilibrium model rests on its capacity to account for variation in some specified empirical phenomenon, its internal consistency, and its economy of formulation. In short, the criteria used to assess an equilibrium model are no different from those used to assess any theory of social change; for, indeed, the principles of equilibrium are but one of the several ways of formulating theories of change.

II. REVIEW OF EXISTING THEORIES OF SOCIAL CHANGE

I have outlined a number of criteria by which theories of change may be assessed—the statement of a scientific problem about dependent variables, the description of change, the explanation of change by the use of independent variables, and the organization of these ingredients into models and theories. These criteria, however, were formulated in general terms, without reference to any particular type of change or historical situation. Now I shall review a number of specific theories of change, each of which was originally formulated with respect to a different type of historical situation. I shall be assessing these theories with respect to the criteria just outlined, though I shall not be absolutely explicit in the application of these criteria in every case. I shall first review four theories with different emphases—short-term collapse, short-term reconstruction, long-term deterioration, long-term development—then turn to the theories of Marx and Malinowski.

Social Collapse in the Face of Crisis: Japanese Morale in World War II

One of the applied uses of social science during World War II was the effort of the Foreign Morale Analysis Division in the Office of War Information to trace and analyze changes in Japanese morale, both among the fighting forces and on the home front. Consisting mainly of trained behavioral scientists, the Division supplied information and advice to the State, War, and Navy Departments, to the Office of Strategic Services, and to outposts in Asia and the Pacific. The data used by the Division included "prisoner-of-war interrogation reports; captured diaries, letters and official documents; reports from neutral observers in Japan; Japanese newspapers and periodicals; . . . radio broadcasts . . . background descriptions and analyses . . . prepared from prewar sources such as novels, histories, travel and anthropological books, movies and interviews with Japanese living in the United States." [47]

On the basis of these data as well as postwar interview material, the Division was able to trace an increasingly rapid deterioration of Japanese morale from about the middle of 1944, when military reversals and bombing of Japanese cities began to give clear evidence that the tide of war was turning against the Japanese. In the course of its work, the Division not only worked out a number of indicators of morale—such as capacity for sustained collective effort—but also developed a conceptual framework that permitted some insight into the cause of changes in morale and related behavior patterns. This framework is not a full-scale theory of behavior but rather a "limited number of assumptions concerning the nature of man derived chiefly from psychiatry, psychology, and cultural anthropology." [48] I shall summarize this partially developed theory of behavior in crisis situations, formalizing and elaborating it somewhat.

Stress and Reactions to Stress   The outline of the conceptual framework underlying the work of the Foreign Morale Analysis Division is relatively simple. It rests on the master assumption that definite types of stress are disturbing to people, and that when stress reaches a certain threshold, people will react in definite ways. The basic types of stress are:

1. Threats to life and health;
2. Discomfort from pain, heat, cold, dampness, fatigue, and poor food;
3. Loss of means of subsistence, whether in the form of money, jobs, business, or property;
4. Deprivation of sexual satisfaction;
5. Enforced idleness;
6. Restriction of movement;
7. Isolation;
8. Threats to children, other family members, and friends;
9. Dislike, rejection, and ridicule from other people;
10. Capricious and unpredictable behavior on the part of those in authority upon whom one's welfare depends.

[47] Leighton, *Human Relations in a Changing World*, p. 44.
[48] *Ibid.*, p. 45.

When several of these basic types of stress combine, they create additional disturbances of the following sort:

1. Frustration of expectations, desires, needs, intentions, or goals;
2. The dilemma of conflict between mutually incompatible desires and intentions ("ambivalence" or "multivalence");
3. Circumstances creating confusion and uncertainty as to what is happening in the present and what can be expected in the future ("disorientation").[49]

These types of stress constitute the independent variables. The dependent variables are reactions to stress, which are manifested in some combination of the following patterns of behavior:

1. Integrated and efficient action directed toward overcoming the source of stress;
2. Random, trial-and-error activity, implicit and overt;
3. Suspiciousness, hatred, hostility, destructive action often directed at substitutes rather than at the actual causes;
4. Apathy, withdrawal from effort to cope with the situation actively.[50]

In the analysis of Japanese morale during the last year of the war, the Division found an increase in various types of stress—traceable mainly to the adversities of the worsening war situation—and an increase in the various reactions to stress, particularly apathy.[51] As a framework for describing the general course of morale, then, this series of assumptions had some usefulness.

As a formal theory of social collapse, however, the framework leaves room for improvement. In the first place, it appears that the classification of both the independent variables (types of stress) and dependent variables (reactions to stress) might be reworked. For example, it might be desirable to compress the types of stress into a few more general categories; most of the items seem to be manifestations of either (1) deprivations or threats of deprivation, or (2) uncertainty or ambivalence. And on the side of reactions to stress, it seems desirable to specify a number of subtypes of constructive activity; and instead of "apathy," the category of "withdrawal" might be substituted, and subsequently subdivided into "panicky or hysterical behavior," [52] "resignation," and "fantasy solutions." Furthermore, the category of "trial-and-error" might be discarded as an

---

[49] *Ibid.*, pp. 76–77.
[50] *Ibid.*, pp. 77–78.
[51] *Ibid.*, Chapter 3 and Appendix B.
[52] The Foreign Morale Analysis Division did in fact note an increase of panicky and hysterical behavior during the last months of the war (*ibid.*, p. 70), but Leighton did not include this type of behavior in his more formal classification of reactions to stress (pp. 77–78).

independent reaction, and be treated as a combination of the other re-actions in rapid sequence. Such reclassifications, however, would depend not only on questions of logical coherence and completeness, but also on the types of scientific problem under consideration and the degree of theoretical refinement desired.

A more serious theoretical shortcoming of the conceptual framework is its indeterminacy. As it stands it provides only unorganized lists of in-dependent variables and dependent variables. The present listings provide little basis for expecting one rather than another type of reaction to stress. Thus the theoretical framework is not very specific in its predictive power, yielding only the very general hypothesis that some pattern of types of stress will give rise to some pattern of responses to stress.

There are three ways to reduce this theoretical indeterminacy:

1. To impose some internal organization on the respective lists of variables. For example, the following—to my mind plausible—assertions could be made about the relations among the various reactions to stress. Given a certain level of stress, the initial reaction is constructive activity; if this fails to reduce the stress, the next response is some kind of aggres-sion or scapegoating; and if this in turn fails to reduce the stress, some kind of withdrawal behavior will appear. Regardless of the validity of these assertions, they do state some definite relations among the responses, and allow for much more specific hypotheses to be formulated.

2. To establish more direct links between specific independent vari-ables and specific dependent variables. For example, "capricious and un-predictable behavior on the part of those in authority" may be more closely associated with "scapegoating" than it is with other reactions to stress. Such links, regardless of their empirical validity,[53] provide more determinate hypotheses than the simple lists of different classes of vari-ables.

3. In cases when the direct association between specific independent and dependent variables is not strong, to introduce intervening variables that specify the conditions under which such an association is strength-ened. One such intervening variable is some sort of "opportunity factor," which predisposes people under stress to opt for certain responses to stress and not for others.

A certain cultural or modal personality pattern may, for example, "favor" a certain type of response to adversity. A cultural tradition em-phasizing environmental mastery, for example, may predispose people to opt for "integrated and efficient action" under conditions of stress; but

[53] With respect to the connection between specific types of stress and specific collective reactions to stress, there is some evidence that efforts to establish such con-nections are not very fruitful. See Smelser, *Theory of Collective Behavior*, Chapter 3.

if this fails, it might be suggested, such people would be relatively "defenseless," and would fall quickly into some sort of disorganized behavior. A cultural tradition emphasizing stoicism might show a higher incidence of apathetic responses in the face of stressful circumstances. Or again, in societies that exert close police supervision we would expect a lower incidence of violence and scapegoating in the face of adversity and a higher incidence of other reactions to stress, since the former is "ruled out," at least in the short run, by the agents of social control. By combining independent and intervening variables, more determinate hypotheses are produced.

In the paragraphs that follow I shall limit my elaboration of Leighton's theoretical framework to the third strategy—specifying intervening variables. Furthermore, I shall limit the elaboration to variables suggested by the Foreign Morale Analysis Division's empirical research on Japan but not formally incorporated into the theoretical framework. These variables fall into two broad classes: the influence of differential vulnerability on the response to stress; and the influence of differential opportunities for reaction to stress, and more particularly the ways that authorities' behavior influences these alternatives.

Differential Vulnerability to Stress and the Response to Stress   When the Foreign Morale Analysis Division broke down the component factors of Japanese troop morale, it was found that certain aspects of morale were very resistant to change, whereas others were more vulnerable and tended to deteriorate over time. Among the former were faith in the Emperor, his divine power, and the way of life he symbolized; faith in the rightness and justice of the war; and faith in the Japanese people and their spiritual strength. Furthermore, Allied propaganda emphasizing these themes was not only ineffective in lowering the troops' morale, but often seemed to toughen their resistance. Among the factors that tended to lower Japanese morale were various kinds of physical and medical hardships, lack of faith in Japanese weapons and productive capacity, and a lack of confidence in Japanese news and information; similarly, Allied propaganda proved most effective when it dwelt on "lack of coordination in the Japanese forces, failures of reinforcement and support, lack of accurate information, blundering and cowardice on the part of officers, lack of food, lack of weapons and supplies, and a hopeless military position." [54] In short, morale held steadfast in the face of attacks on *personal and cultural identity* and on *symbols of cultural unity;* but morale was much more vulnerable when it came to inadequacies of *situational facilities* and the *social coordination* of the war effort. The implications of this finding for the original conceptual framework dealing with stress and

[54] *Human Relations in a Changing World,* pp. 50–55.

reactions to stress is that types of stress that are situationally based are more likely to give rise to the nonconstructive reactions to stress (resignation, apathy, aimless behavior) than other types of stress. With the incorporation of this finding, the relations between stress and responses to stress become somewhat more determinate.

Differential Opportunities for Reaction to Stress   The paragraph above indicates that if the Allied propaganda emphasized certain points of vulnerability in the Japanese war effort, it was more likely to be effective—that is, to increase stress, lower morale, and thus diminish Japanese fighting efficiency. But in addition, the Allies discovered that it was important to emphasize that some honorable alternative—other than continuing to fight desperately—was available to the Japanese troops if the propaganda was to be effective. Thus the Division paid attention to the way surrender to the Allies was pictured in the propaganda:

> . . . It was of first-rate importance to convince the Japanese that prisoners were not maltreated or tortured. It was worth while to make them understand that they would have an opportunity to work and would not be forced to live, as many pictured it, "idly on the enemy's charity." It would be still better, if it could be done truthfully, to tell them they would not have to go back to Japan unless they wished, but could settle in Allied countries.[55]

With respect to morale on the home front in 1945, the Division concluded that "there is very great fear of what the Americans will do when they land. It is therefore important to reassure the Japanese and try to prevent them fighting vigorously from terror."[56] It is difficult to assess exactly how important or effective such measures were to Japanese troops and civilians. But insofar as they were successful, they illustrate that responses to stress are in part a function of the differential access to alternative types of response. If the Japanese were convinced that there was no acceptable "way out" through surrender, they were more likely to fight to the finish or fall into apathy and disorganization; if they could be convinced that surrender was a viable alternative, they would be less likely to persist to the bitter end.

Another finding reported by the Division is that internal conflict and scapegoating increased rapidly in Japan, especially in 1945. This was evident among governmental and military officials as well as in the general populace. Among the former, there was evidence of an aggravation of political cliques and factions; declining prestige of the Army and Navy; an increased tendency for the various branches of the military to criticize one another and the government; heightened tensions between business,

[55] *Ibid.*, p. 55.
[56] *Ibid.*, p. 59.

military, and governmental elites; and conflicts between military com-
manders and local authorities. In the populace at large there was evidence
of mounting resentment between rural and urban residents, between intellectuals and politicians, and between women and men. Scapegoating
of minority groups like the Koreans was also noted; and various groups
blamed one another for the unsuccessful conduct of the war.[57] While the
Division did not attempt to link the conflict at these two levels in any
causal way, there is a considerable body of historical evidence which
suggests that an increase of conflict among the ruling classes or agencies
of social control encourages the hostility, scapegoating, and rebellious
activity in the society at large.[58]

Though the discussions of these two sets of intervening variables—
differential vulnerability to stress and differential access to responses to
stress—are not developed theoretically in Leighton's work, it is possible
to expand the simplified model in the following way:

stress ————▶ reaction to stress

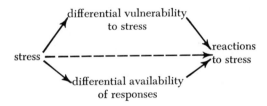

The introduction of these intervening variables makes the connections
between stress and reactions to stress more determinate, even though the
elaborated model is still a fairly crude one.

Social Recovery in the Face of Crisis: The Worcester Tornado

Not long after World War II the Division of Anthropology and Psychology, National Academy of Sciences—National Research Council, established a Committee on Disaster Studies in response to a request by the
Surgeons General of the Army, Navy, and Air Force. Specifically, the request was that the Committee "conduct a survey and study in the fields
of scientific research and development applicable to problems which
might result from disasters caused by enemy action."[59] In the years fol-

[57] *Ibid.*, pp. 244–50.
[58] Smelser, *Theory of Collective Behavior*, pp. 231–36, 261–69.
[59] Wallace, *Human Behavior in Extreme Situations*, introduction.

lowing its establishment the Committee conducted and supported research on disaster situations resulting from floods, storms, fires, explosions, and so on. From the standpoint of the present analysis, the most important of these studies is Anthony F. C. Wallace's study of the 1953 tornado in Worcester, Massachusetts, since he attempted to interpret his empirical findings within a fairly general theoretical framework.

In specifying the desiderata for a model of disaster behavior, Wallace called for an exhaustive description of the disaster, "leaving blank no major portions of time or space, nor any dimensions of social structure or individual emotion and behavior which can be observed." [60] First he outlined the major space coordinates—to which the other variables are related—according to concentric geographic circles surrounding the point of impact. Figure 8–3 shows this array. Second—using the scheme sug-

SPACE COORDINATES OF A DISASTER
WALLACE'S MODEL

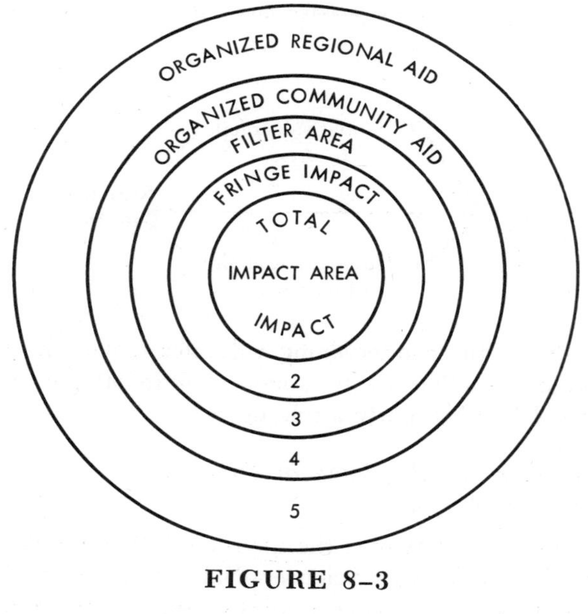

FIGURE 8–3

gested by Powell, Rayner, and Finesinger [61]—Wallace suggested a series of time phases, divided according to the kinds of behavior of persons involved in the disaster. This series is outlined in Table 8–1.

[60] *Ibid.*, p. 18.
[61] John W. Powell, Jeannette Rayner, and Jacob E. Finesinger, "Responses to Disaster in American Cultural Groups," in *Symposium on Stress* (Washington: Army Medical Service Graduate School, 1953).

TABLE 8-1

TIME PHASES OF DISASTER *

Stage		Disaster-Related Behavior and Disaster Behavior: Wallace
0	Predisaster conditions	Determining, to some degree, the effect of, and response to, impact
1	Warning	Precautionary activity
2	Threat	Survival action
3	Impact	"Holding on"
4	Inventory	Diagnosis of situation and decision on action
5	Rescue	Spontaneous, local, unorganized extrication and first aid; some preventive measures
6	Remedy	Organized and professional relief, medical care, preventive and security measures
7	Recovery	Individual rehabilitation and readjustment; community restoration of property and organization; preventive measures against recurrence.

* Anthony F. C. Wallace, *Tornado in Worcester: An Exploratory Study of Individual and Community Behavior in an Extreme Situation* (Disaster Study Number 3 of the Commmittee on Disaster Studies Division of Anthropology and Psychology) (Washington, D.C.: National Academy of Sciences—National Research Council, 1956), p. 2.

Up to this point, Wallace's scheme is a simple natural-history model, characterizing disaster as a number of events and situations, and locating these in space and time.[62] But Wallace went beyond this point, and attempted to organize each time phase in terms of an equilibrium state of the system. At any given stage the system can be characterized in terms of a balance of two sets of forces—one tending toward disorganization of the system and the other tending toward recovery of the system.[63] Let us trace the state of the system in its various phases:

In the period preceding warning, Wallace characterized the social system as being in a "steady state or in [stable] equilibrium, or nearly so." By "equilibrium" he meant that "the cultural system, and the personalties of the population, are operating sufficiently smoothly to obtain stress reductions for the population, such that the total quantity of stress in the

[62] For a brief characterization of a natural-history model, see above, pp. 210–11.
[63] This statement, as well as the characterization of the equilibrium system in the various stages, follows Wallace's work closely, but elaborates it in places.

area at large is not systematically increasing or decreasing...." [64] The description of this steady state, moreover, reads almost like a description of a society:

> Elements in this system ... are: terrain, topography, climate; the culture of the population involved (including their security agencies designed to protect them from disaster); certain non-cultural characteristics of this population, including the distribution of various demographic factors, and the distribution of personality types ("national character").[65]

While the state of the system may vary from moment to moment because of random incidence of stress and various cyclical phenomena (such as the alternation of night and day), the balance of forces is assumed to be weighted overwhelmingly in the direction of stability.

The warning period effects little change in the balance of equilibrium forces, since, according to Wallace's characterization, warning refers to a very generalized cue, and is not specific as to how, when, where, or even whether impact will occur. Consequently only some individuals may take protective or precautionary action against impact.[66] In the period of threat, however, many people become aware that a certain kind of impact is going to occur and take various kinds of emergency action.[67] This action can be broken down into two types of behavior—that which is adaptive with respect to the impact (e.g., moving to the closest shelter) and that which is maladaptive (e.g., attempting to leave the area, and thus being exposed at the time of impact).

In the several phases after impact, the system is best understood as a balance of two sets of forces: the "disaster syndrome" of emotions and behavior displayed by those immediately affected, and the "counter-disaster syndrome" of emotions and behavior displayed by others unharmed by but concerned with the disaster. The disaster syndrome breaks into three stages, corresponding roughly with the "inventory," "rescue," and "remedy" stages, respectively:

> During the first stage, the person displaying [the disaster syndrome] appears to the observer to be "dazed," "stunned," "apathetic," "passive," "immobile," or "aimlessly puttering around"... (random movement stage) ...
>
> The second stage is one of extreme suggestibility, altruism, gratitude for help, and anxiousness to perceive that known persons and places

[64] Wallace, *Tornado in Worcester*, p. 7.
[65] *Ibid.* Note that Wallace's notion of equilibrium is very close to what Gerschenkron referred to as "coterminous with ... organized society." Above, fn. 42, p. 218.
[66] *Ibid.*, p. 8.
[67] *Ibid.*

have been preserved; personal loss is minimized, concern is for the welfare of family and community . . . (suggestible stage) . . .

In the third stage, there is a mildly euphoric identification with the damaged community, and enthusiastic participation in repair and rehabilitation enterprises; it sometimes appears to observers as if a revival of neighborhood spirit has occurred . . . (euphoric stage).[68]

As recovery begins, a fourth stage—the ambivalent stage—sets in; "the euphoria wears off, and 'normally' ambivalent attitudes return, with the expression of criticism and complaints, and awareness of the annoyance of the long-term effects of the disaster." [69]

The "counter-disaster syndrome," which Wallace described in less detail, is mainly rescue behavior on the part of those near the disaster. In the early phases such behavior is likely to be performed in a hyperactive, spontaneous, even frantic manner. The impact area is swarmed with individuals and agencies who attempt to assume responsibility for the welfare of the injured. Though Wallace did not divide the "counter-disaster syndrome" into such definite phases as the disaster syndrome, it, too, appears to be marked by more or less random activity in its early stages, which gives way to more organized activity by organizations later, and then to a period of ambivalence and squabbling among the individuals and agencies involved in rescue behavior.[70]

The phases between threat and rescue (phases 2–5) can also be characterized in terms of the space coordinates (see Fig. 8–3). During the period of threat, areas 1–3 are differentiated from area 4 and parts of 5, since the former are clearly a "threat area" and the latter a "continuation of warning area." During the impact period, areas 1 and 2 constitute the "impact area," whereas area 3 constitutes a "filter area" which experiences a "near miss." During the "inventory" period the impact area is isolated from areas 3, 4, and 5, since personnel and equipment have not yet arrived from these outlying areas. And finally, during the "rescue" period, individuals, organizations, and equipment move in from the outer areas to concentrate on bringing relief to the impact area.[71]

The last two stages, after the emergency rescue and relief operations are more or less completed, are characterized by an "effort . . . to bring the system back to the original state." New organizations—such as the Red Cross, government relief agencies, and insurance companies—assume greater responsibility. While Wallace saw the rehabilitation period as lasting indefinitely in a very general sense, he set an approximate time period of one year after impact, at which time the system returns to some

[68] *Ibid.*, pp. 109–10, 125–26.
[69] *Ibid.*, p. 110.
[70] *Ibid.*, pp. 142–46.
[71] *Ibid.*, pp. 8–11.

new "steady state." The new equilibrium position is not identical to the original one, but is marked by certain "irreversible changes," such as a change in the population pyramid, or in the occupational and organizational structures of the community.[72]

Such are the broad outlines of Wallace's theoretical model, which can be summarized in capsule form as a sequence of equilibrium states, each of which manifests two sets of forces, one tending toward stability and one tending toward instability of the system. The whole sequence can be viewed as an application of the stable-dynamic type of equilibrium model: The system begins in a steady state, is given a shock by the impact of a disaster, but recovers to something like its original state by virtue of various mechanisms set in motion by the impact itself.[73]

Both the Leighton and the Wallace theories share two limitations from the standpoint of their relationship to a more general theory of social change. (1) Both theories deal mainly with social-psychological states and behavioral reactions, and tend to neglect social-structural variables. Leighton's theory is concerned mainly with changes in morale, and with behavioral responses such as scapegoating, trial-and-error behavior, and so on. And while Wallace includes cultural and social-structural variables in his initial characterization of the equilibrium system, and while he speaks of certain "irreversible" structural changes after a disaster, he touches on these variables very lightly; his main focus is on psychological variables (such as the emotional states of survivors) and on behavioral responses (such as rescue). Clearly any general theory of social change must incorporate these psychological and behavioral variables. But it is also evident that a general theory will have to consider social-structural and cultural variables as themselves changing. (2) The time span of both the Leighton and Wallace theories is limited. The empirical situation analyzed by Leighton extended barely more than a year, and Wallace set a somewhat arbitrary time limit of one year after impact for the period of rehabilitation to be completed. Yet it is clear that any investigator interested in general processes of social change has to consider phenomena that extend over much longer periods of time. With these observations in mind I now consider several theories of long-term social and cultural change.

Long-Term Social Disintegration: The Theory of Oswald Spengler

Problems in the Literature of Social Disintegration   The scientific study of social disintegration is among the least adequately developed areas of social change. Most studies are either quite specific historical

---

[72] *Ibid.*, pp. 11–12.
[73] See above, pp. 219–20, for a characterization of this kind of equilibrium model.

case studies with little effort to formalize or generalize the results or very general prophetic diagnoses of the "total state" of culture in its declining phases. More specifically, the second type of literature on disintegration presents the following difficulties:

1. The subject matter itself—social disintegration—is not sufficiently specified. Without attempting an exhaustive classification, it is clear that social disintegration could take one or more of the following forms: (a) a *social-psychological* change, such as the mass demoralization of a population over a long period; (b) a decrease in important *aggregate social indices*, such as population or wealth, in a society's history; (c) the decline, or loss of function, of particular *social roles*; (d) the disintegration of particular *collectivities*, as in divorce or bankruptcy; (e) the decline of *institutional structure*, such as a system of property law or the authority structure of a society; (f) the decline in quality of *cultural productions*, such as artistic traditions or systems of philosophical thought. Once the investigator identifies these several types of disintegration, he is in a position to uncover the combinations of determinants for each type, and to study the empirical and theoretical relations among the types. Unfortunately, most students of social disintegration have tended to view the process as a kind of undifferentiated whole, which implies that total societies undergo decline in all aspects more or less simultaneously. As we shall see, Spengler saw the rise and fall of cultures as a series of virtually fixed phases, each phase displaying simultaneous and parallel movements in several social and cultural aspects. Needless to say, this notion greatly oversimplifies the several processes of disintegration and their relations to one another.

2. The terms used to describe processes of disintegration are laden with value judgments. While Spengler, for example, viewed the historian's business as "not to praise or to blame but to consider morphologically," [74] his own language betrays this ideal of objectivity. Consider his characterization of the populations of cities, for example: "In place of a type-true people, born of and grown on the soil, there is a new sort of nomad, cohering unstably in fluid masses, the parasitical city dweller, traditionless, utterly matter-of-fact, religionless, clever, unfruitful, deeply contemptuous of the countryman...." [75] In addition, the language of "growth," "fulfillment," "the great crisis of the present," and "decay" carry implications of the moral superiority or inferiority of certain types and phases of cultural development—implications which fly in the face of the scientific canon that concepts should be as free as possible from the value preferences of the theorist.

[74] *Decline of the West*, I, 34.
[75] *Ibid.*, I, 32.

3. The number of "great cultures" on which the study of social disintegration is based is very limited, so valid comparative generalizations are difficult to establish. Spengler, for example, based his general comparative study of the modern West on eight other cultural traditions, and drew detailed comparisons mainly with the Greco-Roman culture (called the Apollonian by Spengler) and the pre-Christian Middle Eastern cultures (called the Magian by Spengler).

I have identified these problems in the literature on social disintegration, especially Spengler's work, to indicate the kinds of qualifications that should be observed in the subsequent discussion, and to underscore the extremely speculative character of this part of the essay.

General Themes in Spengler's Work   *The Decline of the West* is an enormously complex work, opening moral and epistemological as well as scientific and historical issues. No justice can be done to this complexity in a few pages. My summary and interpretation of Spengler's position will be highly selective. I shall discuss neither his philosophy of history nor the adequacy of his own historical research. Rather I shall concentrate on the substance of what he referred to as his "narrower task"— "primarily to determine from . . . a world survey, the state of West Europe and America as at the epoch of 1800–2000—to establish the chronological position of this period in the ensemble of Western culture-history, its significance as a chapter that is in one or another guise necessarily found in the biography of every Culture, and the organic and symbolic meaning of its political, artistic, intellectual, and social expression-forms." [76] More particularly, I shall be interested in Spengler's view of "Civilization"— or that phase of cultural development that marks the beginning of decline —and the course of events from Civilization to total deterioration.

One of the central unifying themes in Spengler's work is the notion of culture as an organism. "*Cultures are organisms,* and world-history is their collective biography. Morphologically, the immense history of the Chinese or of the Classical Culture is the exact equivalent of the petty history of the individual man, or of the animal, or the tree, or the flower." [77] According to this analogy, cultures possess an organic unity, an "inner structure of . . . organic units through and in which world-history fulfills itself." [78] In addition—and this is the most important aspect of the organismic analogy—each culture passes through a "childhood, youth, manhood and old age," which take the following form:

> A Culture is born in the moment when a great soul awakens out of the proto-spirituality of ever childish humanity, detaches itself, and becomes a form from the formless, a bounded and mortal thing from

[76] *Ibid.,* I, 26.
[77] *Ibid.,* I, 104. Italics in original.
[78] *Ibid.,* I, 105.

the boundless and enduring. It blooms. . . . It dies when this soul has actualized the full sum of its possibilities in the shape of peoples, languages, dogmas, arts, states, sciences, and reverts into the proto-soul. . . . The aim once attained—the idea, the entire content of inner possibilities, fulfilled and made externally actual—the Culture suddenly hardens, it mortifies, its blood congeals, its force breaks down, and it becomes Civilization.[79]

Thus far, it appears that every culture is *similar* to every other culture in its internal organization and life cycle. The *differences* among cultures, however, arise from the prime symbols, or central premises on which each culture is based. The prime symbol of Egyptian culture, for example, is "stone"; the prime symbol of Classical culture is "the sensuously present individual body as the ideal type of the extended"; the prime symbol of Western (or Faustian) culture is "pure and limitless space." [80] The prime symbol infuses into the various cultural forms—mathematics, art expression, architecture, music, philosophy—and gives its social institutions a distinctive stamp. The prime symbol gives content and integration to the culture at the various stages of its life-cycle. The growth and efflorescence of a culture involves the creative exploration of the possibilities inherent in the prime symbol, and its decline involves the exhaustion and petrification of these possibilities.

The life-cycle of any given culture is determined by a sort of inner destiny based on the prime symbol itself. Sorokin summarizes Spengler's theory of cultural immanence as follows:

> After its emergence, the whole life-cycle of a High Culture, with all the numerous changes involved, is immanently determined by the Culture itself. Like an organism immanently passing from childhood to old age, the Cultures go through their spring-summer-autumn-winter stages by virtue of their own natures. Even their death is due to their own nature and is not caused by external conditions. It is the Culture's natural death. . . . The role of external factors consists essentially in favoring or hindering, accelerating or retarding the immanent unfolding of the life-cycle of the Culture; now and then the external conditions can distort and, in exceptional cases, kill the Culture's organism. But they cannot pattern the Culture's form, or the stages of its life-cycle, or change its essential traits. . . . The external forces can distort and hinder the development of a given Culture, but they cannot transform, say, the Classical into the Egyptian or the Arabian into the Western Culture, just as the external conditions cannot change a bird into a cow, though they can mutilate and even kill it.[81]

[79] *Ibid.*, I, 106.
[80] *Ibid.*, I, Chapter 6.
[81] *Modern Historical and Social Philosophies*, pp. 107–8. We shall consider the role of "external factors" when we assess the relevance of Spengler's scheme for analyzing post-attack society.

Thus an inner destiny governs the history of the different aspects of a given culture. With respect to the history of *fine arts* in the West, for example, Spengler treats the Merovingian-Carolingian era (A.D. 500–900) as a "Pre-cultural" period characterized by a primitive art based on mystical symbolism and naive imitation. The period of "Culture" itself extends from 900 to 1800, and is divided into two phases. In the early period of Culture, the basic style expressive of the Idea of the Culture emerges. In the West this early period is best symbolized by the rise of the Gothic style (900–1500). In the late period this style reaches a mature form, becomes intellectualized, and finally reaches a point at which creativity ends and the grand forms begin to dissolve. In the West this late period is symbolized by the rise of the Baroque style, its transformation into the classical style, and its termination in romanticism (1500–1800). At this point the cycle enters the phase of Civilization, which is characterized by "existence without inner form; megalopolitan art as a commonplace; luxury, sport, nerve-excitement; rapidly changing fashions in art (revivals, imitations, borrowings, pseudo-discoveries)." In the nineteenth- and twentieth-century West is symbolized by Liszt, Berlioz, and Wagner in music; impressionism in art; and the American style in architecture. For the future (from A.D. 2000) Spengler sees the degeneration of art into "meaningless, empty, artificial, pretentious architecture and ornament" before the final demise of Western culture.[82]

With respect to the *sociopolitical* history of the West, Spengler identified the same basic stages, though the concrete historical manifestations differ for each stage. The "Pre-cultural" period (again A.D. 500–900) is characterized by a sort of prehistoric peasant existence, with no "politics" or "state," but only primitive folk, tribes, and their chiefs. The early period of Culture (900–1500) is characterized initially by feudalism; the two major classes are the nobility and the priesthood; the city has made its appearance, but is not dominant, since it serves mainly as a market, a feudal stronghold, or a religious center. Toward the end of this early period the localism of the feudal system begins to wane, and the beginnings of the aristocratic state become evident. The later period of Culture (1500–1800) involves the emergence and consolidation of the state itself. In its early phases it is marked by conflict between localities and the state power; in its middle phases the state becomes absolute and victorious over local political forces; and in its later phases the aristocratic state begins to wane as it is displaced by the forces of bourgeois society. During this later period of Culture the city comes to dominate the countryside, and money values begin to assume predominance over land. As the cultural cycle enters the phase of Civilization (1800–2000),

<hr>

[82] *The Decline of the West,* Table II at the end of Vol. I.

the bourgeoisie first rise to absolute predominance, and begin to dictate the political policies of the society through their constitutions and legal systems (nineteenth century). But this bourgeois phase is short-lived, and gives way to a society based on totalitarianism, imperialism, and wars of annihilation. Force-politics come to hold sway over money-politics, and the culture experiences a period of crude despotism over the formless mass of the population ("Caesarism" from A.D. 2000 to 2200). As a tragic finale, Caesarism itself will succumb to a period of barbarism, localism and tribalism in politics, plunder, and war (after 2200). The final phase also witnesses the rise of a "second religiosity," or chaotic floundering about for new cultural ideas, which will eventually become the basis for a new cultural life-cycle.[83]

Such, in brief outline, are the characteristic phases of the development of the West as envisioned by Spengler. From this description, as well as its comparisons with other major civilizations, the West is apparently well into the phase of Civilization at the present time, and either has entered or is on the brink of entering that phase of totalitarian despotism followed by a decline into localism and chaotic religiosity. To continue the selective summary of Spengler's themes, I shall now examine several cultural and social aspects of Civilization and its decline.

Civilization and Its Further Decline   According to Spengler, the story of any culture is dominated in many respects by its ecological history—the balance between *rural and urban forces.* "[We] cannot comprehend political and economic history at all unless we realize that the city, with its gradual detachment from the final bankrupting of the country, is the determinative form to which the course and sense of higher history generally conforms. *World history is city history.*" [84] And the period of Civilization is "that of the victory of city over country, whereby it frees itself from the grip of the ground." [85] Spengler predicted that "long after A.D. 2000, cities [will be] laid out for ten to twenty million inhabitants, spread over enormous areas of country-side, with buildings that will dwarf the biggest of to-day's and notions of traffic and communication that we should regard as fantastic to the point of madness." [86] What are the characteristics of cities in the period of Civilization? Physically they are concentrated and crowded to the point of being "demonic creations," but still people flood into them and refuse to return to the land. Spiritually cities display "tension without cosmic pulsation"—tension of the intellect. Consequently the forms of relaxation are sensual—geared to relieving hard, intensive brainwork—and take the form of "Cinema, Expressionism, boxing

---

[83] *Ibid.,* Table III, end of Vol. I.
[84] *Ibid.,* II, 95. Italics in original.
[85] *Ibid.,* II, 107.
[86] *Ibid.,* II, 101.

contests, nigger dances, poker, and racing." [87] In the advanced stage of Civilization there develops a "sterility of civilized man," which is a kind of "metaphysical turn towards death." People are no longer concerned with having children. "Instead of children, [the modern woman] has soul-conflicts; marriage is a craft-art for the achievement of 'mutual understanding.'" Because of these forces in the city of Civilization, Spengler argues that

> . . . all Civilizations enter upon a stage, which lasts for centuries, of appalling depopulation. The whole pyramid of cultural man vanishes. It crumbles from the summit, first the world-cities, then the provincial forms and finally the land itself. . . . We find everywhere in . . . Civilizations that . . . the giant cities . . . at the end of the evolution, stand empty, harbouring in their stone masses a small population. . . .[88]

With the decline of the great world-cities, the culture crumbles into a state of localism, reminiscent of the precultural period that existed before the flowering of the cities.

As the world-city comes to dominate a culture in its phase of Civilization, so a world-city economy becomes its characteristic *economic* form. The whole of cultural history is, for Spengler, a history of "a desperate conflict waged by the soil-rooted tradition of a race . . . against the spirit of money." In the phase of Civilization the money markets become centralized in a few urban centers, such as London, New York, Berlin, and Paris. The remainder of the world is a "starveling provincial economy." In addition, "money is the form of intellectual energy in which the ruler-will, the political and the social, technical and mental, creative power, the craving for a full-sized life, are concentrated. . . . At the beginning a man was wealthy because he was powerful—now he is powerful because he has money. Intellect reaches the throne only when money puts it there. Democracy is the completed equating of money with political power." [89] In the Western or Faustian culture this dominance of money has been compounded by the rise of machine technology. Faustian man, Spengler argues, has become "the slave of his creation. His number, and the arrangement of life as he lives it, have been driven by the machine on to a path where there is no standing still and no turning back." [90]

The ultimate defeat of the money-machine complex, however, is as inevitable as its domination of Civilization. The defeat occurs in what Spengler dramatically terms "the conflict between money and blood," which results in the victory of political over economic forces. "The coming

[87] *Ibid.*, II, 102–3.
[88] *Ibid.*, II, 105, 107.
[89] *Ibid.*, II, 484–85.
[90] *Ibid.*, II, 504.

of Caesarism breaks the dictature of money and its political weapon democracy." [91] While Spengler does not explicitly characterize the post-Caesarian era, presumably the economy returns to primitive peasant forms when the totalitarian dictatorships finally crumble.

With respect to *political forms* and the *relations among social classes,* Spengler envisions a similar set of transitions in the period of Civilization and its decline. Civilization appears as the bourgeoisie assume predominance and displace the State based on a land-bound aristocracy. The political philosophy of the bourgeoisie is liberalism, which Spengler views as intellectual and economic freedom—"freedom from the restrictions of the soil-bound life, be these privileges, forms, or feelings—freedom of the intellect for every kind of criticism, freedom of money for every kind of business." [92] The political forms of the bourgeoisie are Parliamentarism, emphasizing freedom, equality, and civil rights; and a civil service emphasizing orderly procedure and producing a large class of bureaucratic functionaries.

Spengler saw the phase of bourgeois Parliamentarism as a "brief transition." [93] This political system soon reveals that only those with money can enjoy the fruits of freedom and equality under liberalism. It soon shows that money, not reason, governs the political machinery. It soon produces a system of mass education and mass media that lull the population into an unthinking, formless mass.[94] Unparliamentary methods of gaining political ends—bribery, economic pressure, direct political action such as strikes—begin to undermine the democratic forms. And the new Fourth Estate, the Mass,

> . . . rejects the Culture and its matured forms, lock, stock, and barrel. It is the absolute of formlessness, persecuting with its hate every sort of form, every distinction of rank, the orderliness of property, the orderliness of knowledge. It is the new nomadism . . . for which . . . anything and everything that is merely human, provide an undifferentiated floating something that falls apart the moment it is born, that recognizes no past and possesses no future.[95]

At this juncture, Civilization enters the "age of gigantic conflicts, in which we find ourselves to-day." [96] This in turn sets the stage for "Caesarism," a period of anti-economic and anti-intellectual despotism. Caesarism is also a period of exploitation, plunder, political intrigue, and wars. Political leadership degenerates from nations and governments to

[91] *Ibid.,* II, 506–7.
[92] *Ibid.,* II, 403.
[93] *Ibid.,* II, 415.
[94] *Ibid.,* II, 461–63.
[95] *Ibid.,* II, 358.
[96] *Ibid.,* II, 416.

"bands and retinues of adventurers, self-styled Caesars, seceding generals, barbarian kings, and what not." [97] Beneath this chaos the elements of "Pre-culture" begin to appear:

> Man becomes a plant again, adhering to the soil, dumb and enduring. The timeless village and the "eternal" peasant reappear, begetting children and burying seed in Mother Earth—a busy, not inadequate swarm, over which the tempest of soldier-emperors passingly blows. In the midst of the land lie the old world-cities, empty receptacles of an extinguished soul, in which historyless mankind slowly nests itself. Men live from hand to mouth, with petty thrifts and petty fortunes, and endure. Masses are trampled on in the conflicts of the conquerors who contend for power and the spoil of this world, but the survivors fill up the gaps with a primitive fertility and suffer on.[98]

In connection with the decay of political forms in the Caesarian era and afterward, it is instructive to examine a few of the political and administrative features of the Roman Empire in its latest years—the fourth and fifth centuries A.D.—as traced by the historian, Samuel Dill. Dill did not attempt to analyze all the factors that give rise to increasing localism and the decline of the Imperial government, but he did de-emphasize the barbarian invasions and emphasize certain processes of internal petrification in Roman society. He argued that the barbarian invasions of the fifth century were "not more formidable" than those of the third and fourth centuries, which were repelled by the Romans. The more important question is "why the invasions of the fifth century succeeded, while the earlier failed." [99]

Dill argued further that Roman society was made vulnerable in the fourth and fifth centuries by the tendency of landowners to refuse to supply military recruits to the emperors; the decline of the trading classes, which meant among other things a dwindling of the sources of recruiting talent into municipal government; and the related tendency for municipal government to decline. In response to these tendencies, the Imperial government came to rely more and more on slaves and barbarians to staff the military, and attempted to enforce a rigid system of occupational inheritance. In the meantime, the power of the large landowners increased at the expense of the smaller landed proprietors and the trading classes. The landowners were able successfully to resist the power of the Imperial government and to corrupt its civil service. The tax officials, on their part, proved to be corruptible by the powerful landowners and to be capable of inflicting infinite hardships on the weaker classes in the community. While this picture of Roman society in this era does not

---

[97] *Ibid.*, II, 435.
[98] *Ibid.*
[99] *Roman Society in the Last Century of the Western Empire,* 2nd ed., revised (London: Macmillan & Co., Ltd., 1905), p. 245.

correspond in every detail to that sketched by Spengler, it does show the decline of a once strong central government into localism.

Dill's account also reveals a more detailed account of some of the dynamics of this decline than Spengler's broad characterization. As just indicated, the locus of political power began to shift toward the large landed estates in the later centuries of the Roman Empire. One response of the Imperial government to this change—and to the other forces of deterioration—was to issue harsh but unenforceable decrees with increasing frequency. Since these decrees proved to be ineffective, this further undermined the power and legitimacy of the central government, and forced it ultimately to deal with the local powers by means of bribery, cajoling, and outright conflict. A vicious circle was thereby established: The weaker the central government became, the more it tended to multiply its unenforceable decrees; and the more it issued such decrees, the weaker the easy violations made its position. So the government was driven into making moment-by-moment situational "deals" with the other political forces in the society. The exercise of power, instead of resting in large part on the legitimacy of an established government, now rested on the day-by-day processes of political bargaining. This kind of decline parallels the vicious circle that results when governments issue floods of paper currency in times of financial crisis. Inflation sets in, currency becomes depreciated, and, as a response, economic agents begin to deal with one another on a situational basis, e.g., by barter. Both processes are a kind of political depreciation, in which faith in the legitimacy and trust in the authority of the political leadership is greatly reduced.

Finally, let us sketch Spengler's view of the changes in *religion* during the phase of Civilization and its further decline. Civilization itself is dominated by rationalism and materialism, which regards the world as "a dynamic system, exact, mathematically disposed, capable down to its first causes of being experimentally probed and numerically fixed so that man can dominate it." The notion of the supernatural, so important in earlier religious forms, is relegated to the status of mere "want of knowledge." To ease the "intellectual tension" of materialism, Civilization also permits certain manifestations of "the irrational, the unnatural, the repulsive, and ... the merely silly" in religion, such as Christian Science, drawingroom Buddhism, and so on.[100]

Like Parliamentary politics, however, the period of materialism in religion is temporary. It gives way to what Spengler calls the Second Religiousness, which is the desperate attempt of the masses, oppressed and downtrodden in the era of Caesarism, to find meaning and salvation. The Second Religiousness is anti-urban, anti-intellectual, anti-rationalistic, and aims to reestablish the most primitive religious forms. The era of

[100] *The Decline of the West,* II, 309–19.

Second Religiousness thus brings a wave of cults, sects, saviors, and messiahs.[101] All this signifies the end of one cultural life-cycle and perhaps the beginning of another.

For several reasons, Spengler's theory of the decline of civilization does not appear to lend itself readily to the understanding of long-term cultural changes. Most obviously, the empirical demonstration of his forecasts about Western culture rests on what is necessarily limited evidence from a few other great cultures; consequently it is hazardous to place much confidence in his extrapolations.

But in addition, his theory does little to identify specific historical causes of disintegration of the social and cultural elements in the phase of Civilization, or to identify the specific mechanisms of this disintegration. The brunt of his account rests on two intellectual constructions—first, the notion of the "morphological relationship" in cultural integration, a relationship "that inwardly binds together the expression-forms of all branches of a Culture"; [102] and second, the notion of the organismic life-cycle of a culture with regular stages of birth, growth, maturation, and decay. These two constructions depict a set of inner cultural forces that solve—in a rather mystical way—the problems of sociocultural integration and sociocultural change, and render the search for specific causes and mechanisms of historical change unimportant.

More specifically, since Spengler saw the processes of sociocultural change as determined by immanent causes, it is difficult to assess the importance of specific events in history. Cultures appear to flow inexorably through their various phases, and external factors can hinder, facilitate, and deflect, but cannot determine the course of the cultural life-cycle. The only "external" force that occupies Spengler's attention is his notion of an "epoch." It is an historic event in that "it marks in the course of a Culture a necessary and fateful turning-point." The French Revolution was an epoch-making event because its thrust was "the transition from Culture to Civilization, the victory of the inorganic megalopolis over the organic countryside." An epoch may take several forms—a great individual person (Luther, Napoleon), "an almost anonymous happening of powerful inward constitution" (the Thirty Years' war), or "a feeble and indistinct evolution" (the Interregnum in Germany). An epoch, however, does not influence the "inward logic" of an age, which is bound to be fulfilled because of the force of the cultural life-cycle itself; but it can influence the form and timing of the transition from one phase to another, and thus affect the course of history.[103]

Spengler's theory is not scientifically adequate, in short, because it is based on a number of questionable analogies to the morphology and the

[101] *Ibid.*, II, 310–15.
[102] *Ibid.*, I, 6.
[103] *Ibid.*, I, 148–49.

life-cycle of organisms, and is, in effect, a series of crude generalizations based on the broad sweep of history in a few other cultures. Therefore, in attempting to relate his theory to other approaches to social change —as I shall do below—it will be necessary to elaborate Spengler's theory freely and "fill in" various mechanisms that might account for the long-term social changes that result in depopulation, political and economic localism, and primitive religious ferment.

Long-Term Social Development: The Differentiation-Integration Theory

The idea of "social progress" or "social growth" has enjoyed great vitality in Western thought for several centuries. The ideal of progress occupied a prominent place in the eighteenth-century Enlightenment; reformulated as a principle of evolution, it dominated the theories of most nineteenth-century social thinkers; and in the twentieth century the concept has reappeared under headings such as "economic development" or "modernization." From this vast history I shall select a single theoretical tradition—the tradition that treats social development as a continuous interplay between increasing differentiation and higher-level integration of the social structure. Within this tradition I shall consider the work of only a few of the many scholars who have contributed to it—in particular, the work of Herbert Spencer, Emile Durkheim, Talcott Parsons, and some aspects of my own work.

The Work of Herbert Spencer   The organizing principle in Spencer's work is the same as it is in Spengler's: the analogy between organism and society. Spengler, as we have seen, focused on two features of the analogy—structural morphology and the life-cycle from birth to death. Spencer, on the other hand, focused on one part of the life-cycle—the process of growth, and the rearrangement of parts during this process Because of this initial difference in emphasis, Spencer's approach differs greatly from Spengler's; though, as we shall see, some of Spencer's empirical conclusions and implied predictions resemble Spengler's.

Spencer began by asserting flatly that "growth is common to social aggregates and organic aggregates." Both "conspicuously exhibit augmentation of mass."[104] This process was called "integration" by Spencer, and takes two distinct forms. The first is "increase by simple multiplication of units, causing enlargement of the group"; an example would be an increase in population. The second is "by union of groups, and again by union of groups of groups"; an example would be the joining of tribes, cities, or states into a common political unit.[105] This process of growth, or integration, is habitually accompanied by a progressive differentiation of structures in society. As small tribal groups become consolidated into

[104] *The Principles of Sociology*, I, 449.
[105] *Ibid.*, I, 465.

larger political units, we find an increasing political complexity with the appearance of king, local rulers, and petty chiefs; at the same time, the stratification system begins to display more marked divisions—into military, priestly, slave, and so on.

"Clearly," Spencer concluded, "complication of structure accompanies increase of mass." [106] Furthermore, increasing differentiation of structures brings an increasing differentiation of activities (or functions) among the structures. Because they are unlike in activity, patterns of reciprocal aid and mutual dependence arise. "The mutually-dependent parts, living by and for one another, form an aggregate constituted on the same general principle as an individual organism." [107] A corollary is that simple social aggregates permit greater mutual substitutability of parts, since the various parts resemble one another more than in complex aggregates. As a consequence, "division or mutilation causes small inconvenience" for primitive social organisms, but it causes "great perturbation or death" in advanced ones, because of the greater mutual dependence of unlike parts. Complex societies are thus more vulnerable when their individual parts are attacked.[108]

Pursuing the organismic analogy further, Spencer identified the major social exigencies around which systems of structures specialize. The first and most urgent has to do with the relations of the society to its environment, especially the "offensive and defensive activities" dealing with "environing enemies and prey." [109] The second exigency is "inner activities for the general sustenation." In some simple hunting tribe structural specialization along these lines is very crude, but as agricultural systems arise, the differentiation between warriors and cultivators becomes more distinct. The third exigency appears as structures relating to the first two become more differentiated from one another; this gives rise to a system of "distribution" which facilitates exchange among the differentiated parts. This third system itself is subject to varying degrees of internal differentiation, ranging from very occasional meetings for bartering to highly complex market and credit systems. Fourth and finally, as the mutual dependence of parts of a society grows, there arises a "regulating system" designed to facilitate the cooperation among the differentiated parts. This system itself is subject to further specialization, and may evolve subsystems for regulating protective and warlike activities, sustenance activities, and distributive activities.[110]

From this list of exigencies emerges a basis for classifying societies. Spencer relied on two classificatory criteria—the degree of complexity to

[106] *Ibid.*, I, 473.
[107] *Ibid.*, I, p. 462.
[108] *Ibid.*, I, 489.
[109] *Ibid.*, I, 493, 547.
[110] *Ibid.*, I, Chapters 6–9.

which the social structure has evolved, and the "kinds of social activity which predominate, and on the resulting unlikenesses of organization." [111] With respect to the former, Spencer identified simple, compound, doubly compound, and trebly compound societies, though he admitted that empirically the lines between these types are difficult to draw. With respect to the latter, Spencer did not present an exhaustive classification, but emphasized two contrasting types, the militant and the industrial society. The former is based on a predominance of structures for carrying on conflict with other societies, whereas the latter is based on a predominance of structures for carrying on sustenation. As a consequence of this difference, each type is coordinated by a different principle. For the militant society, the characterizing trait is that

> . . . its units are coerced into their various combined actions. As the soldier's will is so suspended that he becomes in everything the agent of his officer's will; so is the will of the citizen in all transactions, private and public, overruled by that of the government. The co-operation by which the militant society is maintained, is a *compulsory* co-operation. The social structure adapted for dealing with surrounding hostile societies is under a centralized regulating system, to which all the parts are completely subject; just as in the individual organism the outer organs are completely subject to the chief nervous centre.[112]

The industrial type of society is

> . . . characterized throughout by that same individual freedom which every commercial transaction implies. The co-operation by which the multiform activities of the society are carried on, becomes a *voluntary* co-operation. And while the developed sustaining system which gives to a social organism the industrial type, acquires for itself, like the developed sustaining system of an animal, a regulating apparatus of a diffused or uncentralized kind; it tends also to decentralize the primary regulating apparatus, by making it derive from more numerous classes its deputed powers.[113]

Spencer viewed these two principles as "diametrically opposed . . . when . . . evolved to their extreme forms." Furthermore, he saw "the contrasts between their traits as among the most important with which Sociology has to deal." [114] Accordingly, Spencer described in great detail

[111] *Ibid.*, I, 556.
[112] *Ibid.*, I, 564.
[113] *Ibid.*, I, 569.
[114] *Ibid.*, I, 574. Spencer also envisioned the possibility of, but did not describe in detail, a possible future type of society, which had a very highly developed sustaining system, the products of which would not be used for war and conflict, but for "carrying on higher activities." This society would have a "multiplication of institutions and appliances for intellectual and aesthetic culture, and for kindred activities not of a directly life-sustaining kind." *Ibid.*, I, 575.

the ways in which the two different types of societies may be contrasted. I have extracted these points of contrast from his text, and have presented them in Table 8–2. Lest the table appear oversimply dichotomized, it should be recorded that Spencer qualified his descriptions by noting that all societies—except the lowest types that show no differentiation at all—

TABLE 8–2

THE CONTRAST BETWEEN MILITANT AND INDUSTRIAL SOCIETIES [*]

Characteristic	Militant Society	Industrial Society
Dominant function or activity	Corporate defensive and offensive activity for preservation and aggrandizement	Peaceful, mutual rendering of individual services
Principle of social coordination	Compulsory cooperation; regimentation by enforcement of orders; both positive and negative regulation of activity	Voluntary cooperation; regulation by contract and principles of justice; only negative regulation of activity
Relations between state and individual	Individuals exist for benefit of state; restraints on liberty, property, and mobility	State exists for benefit of individuals; freedom; few restraints on property and mobility
Relations between state and other organizations	All organizations public; private organizations excluded	Private organizations encouraged
Structure of state	Centralized	Decentralized
Structure of social stratification	Fixity of rank, occupation, and locality; inheritance of positions	Plasticity and openness of rank, occupation, and locality; movement between positions
Type of economic activity	Economic autonomy and self-sufficiency; little external trade; protectionism	Loss of economic autonomy; interdependence via peaceful trade; free trade
Valued social and personal characteristics	Patriotism; courage; reverence; loyalty; obedience; faith in authority; discipline	Independence; respect for others; resistance to coercion; individual initiative; truthfulness; kindness

[*] This table has been constructed from Herbert Spencer, *The Principles of Sociology* (New York: D. Appleton and Company, 1897), I, Chapter 10, and II, Chapters 17 and 18.

display a mixture of structures for carrying on conflict and structures for carrying on sustenance, and that the classification results from the *relative* dominance of each type.[115] Spencer also noted that degree of complexity is independent of the militant-industrial dichotomy. Small, relatively un-differentiated societies may be industrial (i.e., based on voluntary coopera-tion), and large complex societies—such as the communistic—may be militant (based on compulsory cooperation).[116]

In analyzing patterns of social change—or "social metamorphoses" as he termed them—Spencer identified two primary types of processes: first, increasing differentiation, or the movement from simple to complex struc-tures; and second, the movement from militant to industrial and from in-dustrial to militant. Spencer treated the first as determined mainly by the propensity for social organisms to increase in size (integration), whether this be by way of population increase or the unification of smaller group-ings. Basing his argument on the organismic analogy, he seemed to believe that the tendency to increases in integration and structural differentiation is the product of inner forces; though he did qualify his view of immanent causation by pointing out that the inherited customs of traditional societies can inhibit the processes of social development.[117]

What determines whether a society—independently of its level of com-plexity—will move in the militant or the industrial direction? In addressing this question Spencer laid greatest stress on the presence or absence of war and conflict. "[Political] institutions . . . will be moulded in this way or that way according as there is frequent war or habitual peace." [118] If the coercive structure of society does not become too rigid as a result of the pursuit of warlike activities, "the noncoercive regulating system proper [to industrial society] begins to show itself as industry flourishes un-checked by war." As an example Spencer pointed to the great liberaliza-tion of the political structure in the century of peace in Europe following 1815. But, he cautioned, "belligerent habits re-develop the militant type of structure." Writing at the beginning of the twentieth century, he fore-cast that "in the present state of armed preparation throughout Europe, an untoward accident may bring about wars which, lasting perhaps for a generation, will re-develop the coercive forms of political control." [119] Thus in the end both Spengler and Spencer envisioned the likelihood of war and coercive totalitarianism in the twentieth century and thereafter. The difference is that Spengler predicted both war and political despotism as a result of immanent forces of disintegration in the cultural life-cycle;

---

[115] *Ibid.*, I, 574.
[116] *Ibid.*, II, 604–5.
[117] *Ibid.*, I, 577–79.
[118] *Ibid.*, II, 648. This is a specific formulation of Spencer's more general point that structures change as the dominant activity of a society changes. *Ibid.*, I, 587.
[119] *Ibid.*, I, 479; II, 648.

whereas Spencer saw political despotism more specifically as a result of the threat of war and of war itself—in short, the "belligerent habits" of mankind.

Durkheim's Critique and Reformulation of Spencer   In summarizing his views on social change, Spencer reaffirmed that social evolution involves both integration (increase in mass) and differentiation (the change from structural homogeneity to heterogeneity). Continuing the summary, he introduced the concept of *coherence,* which appears to be a sort of integration distinct from a simple increase in mass:

> With progressing integration and heterogeneity goes increasing *coherence.* We see the wandering group dispersing, dividing, held together by no bonds; the tribe with parts made more coherent by subordination to a dominant man; the cluster of tribes united in a political plexus under a chief with subchiefs; and so on up to the civilized nation, consolidated enough to hold together for a thousand years or more.[120]

In another place he maintained that with the increasing complexity of society arises a "dominant [political] centre and subordinate centres," and "increasing size and complexity of the dominant centre." [121] In these statements Spencer appears to have been arguing that with differentiation arises increased internal regulation of parts.

These statements, however, raise a confusion in Spencer's work. On the one hand, one would expect—on the basis of the preceding paragraph —to find a proliferation of political and regulatory agencies in modern industrial society, since it has such a complex and extensive division of labor. On the other hand, Spencer's characterization of industrial society, as sketched earlier, indicates that political regulation is almost unnecessary in such a society, since social coordination is guaranteed by the principle of voluntary cooperation and contractual arrangements among individuals. Extensive political controls arise in such societies only if they become involved in war or conflict. Spencer's arguments thus seem to have produced a double, contradictory result for complex industrial societies.

Durkheim took issue with Spencer precisely on the point of the regulation of complex societies. Before reviewing his criticism, however, let me sketch Durkheim's views on the differences between segmental and complex societies, and the process of evolution from the former to the latter.

For Durkheim, the segmental society is a homogeneous society, similar to Spencer's simple society. The social division of labor is minimal, limited in the extreme case to that between the sexes and among persons of different ages. Durkheim compared his simple segmental society to the earthworm. It is composed of structurally identical units, which resemble

120 *Ibid.,* I, 596.
121 *Ibid.,* I, 528.

the worm's rings; if some of these units are removed, they can be replaced by the production of new and identical parts. In this way the segmental society differs from the complex society with qualitatively different role specializations—removal of some of which would leave the society without certain vital functions.[122] Durkheim argued that the principle of homogeneity in segmental society is based on the principle of like kinship units.

How are segmental societies integrated? Durkheim described this by the term "mechanical solidarity." Any disruptive act is met by a passionate and cruel reaction of vengeance by society against the offending party. This punishment reflects the collective values of the segmental society. These values, moreover, are more or less identical for all members; this identity follows from the basic homogeneity of segmental societies. The most striking instance of mechanical solidarity is found in repressive law (e.g., laws against rape, kidnapping, and murder, even in complex societies). Mechanical solidarity, then, consists in the subordination of the individual to the undifferentiated collective conscience of the society.[123] There are thus resemblances between Durkheim's concept of mechanical solidarity and Spencer's concept of compulsory cooperation. However, Spencer traces compulsory cooperation to the involvement of the society in warlike activities, whereas Durkheim traces the origin of mechanical solidarity to the undifferentiated structure of segmental societies.

Durkheim's view of the differentiated society is similar to Spencer's notion of the highly compounded society. Both possess highly specialized role structures. Both encourage the emergence of individual differences, freed from the total domination of homogeneous segmental societies. But Durkheim saw a special form of social integration arising in highly differentiated societies, which he termed "organic solidarity." It is best symbolized in restitutive law, which contrasts with the repressive law of mechanical solidarity. It is less immediate and passionate in its execution, resting on complex legal procedures; it expresses a relation between the total society and the individual; and it aims to restore the relations between parties rather than punish an offender against society.[124] Durkheim viewed the history of evolution as the progressive weakening of mechanical solidarity and the progressive advance of organic solidarity. "[It] is an historical law that mechanical solidarity, which first stands alone, or nearly so, progressively loses ground, and that organic solidarity becomes, little by little, preponderant." [125] Durkheim argued further that the basic source of increasing structural differentiation—and its derivative, organic

[122] Spencer makes the same point when he refers to the replaceability among parts of the simple society. Above, p. 244.

[123] *The Division of Labor in Society*, pp. 70–110.

[124] *Ibid.*, pp. 111–32.

[125] *Ibid.*, p. 174.

solidarity—is the increasing competition among individuals as the population density of a given society increases; specialization is a more effective kind of social organization which mitigates the pressure of increasing population on existing resources.[126]

Having laid this groundwork, Durkheim brought a fundamental criticism against Spencer's notion of social integration in highly differentiated industrial societies. The only viable principle of integration permitted in Spencer's view of such a society, he argued, is the principle of contract or free exchange. No independent integrative action, above and beyond negative controls to prevent persons from hurting one another, is necessary. Durkheim doubted the possibility of stability in such a society, which would hang together only on the basis of momentary contacts among individuals. He agreed with Spencer that as social differentiation increases, "contractual relations, which originally were rare or completely absent, multiply." But "what Spencer seems to have failed to see is that [integrative] non-contractual relations develop at the same time." [127] These noncontractural concomitants of contract are the laws and other norms that govern contractual agreements. Contract law is more than a product of individual agreements, renewed from moment to moment. Rather,

> It constitutes the foundation of our contractual relations. We cannot evade it, except partially and accidentally. The law confers its rights upon us and subjects us to duties deriving from such acts of our will. . . . The law of contracts exercises over us a regulative force of the greatest importance, since it determines what we ought to do and what we can require.[128]

Durkheim also pointed to administrative law and less formalized traditions and customs as examples of noncontractual concomitants of contract. Durkheim's major difference with Spencer, then, is that he gave independent analytic significance to the issue of internal integration of complex industrial societies, an issue which Spencer treated, by and large, as unproblematical.

In connection with this criticism, Durkheim also attacked Spencer's assertion that involvement in war and conflict is the fundamental cause of regulation and coercion by a governmental center. Durkheim maintained that the extent of the governmental organ is "more or less considerable, not because the people are more or less pacific, but rather because its growth is proportional to the progress of the division of labor, societies comprising more different organs the more intimately solidary

---

[126] *Ibid.*, Book Two, Chapter 2.
[127] *Ibid.*, p. 206.
[128] *Ibid.*, pp. 214–15.

they are [from an organic point of view]." [129] Spencer, Durkheim argued, was in error because he traced the importance of political regulation solely to society's conflicts with its outside environment.

From the confusion in Spencer's theory and the controversy between Durkheim and Spencer, the following moral emerges: It is important to distinguish clearly among three different facets of the differentiation-integration complex. The first is the problem of the *level of structural differentiation itself*, which is discovered by ascertaining the degree of proliferation of unlike, mutually dependent units in a society. The second facet is the type of integration traceable to the problem of *regulating the interaction of structurally unlike parts;* this is the problem of organic solidarity stressed by Durkheim, and deals with the operation of laws, customs, and other types of norms. The third is the type of integration required when the different agents and units in a society have to be mobilized and coordinated *for pursuing a common cause,* such as conflict with a political enemy; this problem deals with the political autonomy of social units, and was stressed by Spencer in his discussion of coercion in the militant society. *Both* types of integration—that stemming from the exigencies of structural differentiation and that stemming from the exigencies of mobilization for collective action—are important, and they should be treated as conceptually independent. Spencer's error was to fail to give sufficient recognition to the first type; and Durkheim, stressing organic solidarity, underemphasized the importance of the second type in the political life of a society.

Modern Alterations of Differentiation-Integration Theory Since the late nineteenth century, when Spencer and Durkheim made their contributions, the principle of structural differentiation as a central process in social development has continued to occupy a salient place in the literature on social change. But the theory has not remained static. In particular the past two decades have witnessed a number of modifications, refinements, and extensions of this theoretical tradition. I shall summarize and comment briefly on four lines of theoretical development.

1. The account of the conditions giving rise to the process of differentiation has been modified and expanded. Spencer, it will be remembered, stressed the tendency for social organisms to increase in mass as a source of structural differentiation; and Durkheim stressed the pressure of increasing population as a source of differentiation. These explanations have been discarded, by and large, as both oversimple and erroneous. In their place has arisen a more complex account of the social and psychological factors that, when appropriately combined, constitute a starting point for the process of differentiation. These factors include: first, some

[129] *Ibid.,* p. 226.

sort of structural strain in the social system, manifested psychologically as a sense of dissatisfaction with the performance of actors and with the allocation of resources in the system; second, the presence of a value system or other standard by which the expression of dissatisfaction and the desire for change can be legitimized; third, a sense of "opportunity," or the availability of facilities by means of which some change can be effected; and fourth, the inability of the system to relieve the strain significantly by means of simple adjustments within the existing structure.[130] The major types of strain have been classified systematically;[131] and more particularly, it has been shown how the process of differentiation itself can—if it proceeds at an irregular rate in different sectors of the society—create new strains and integrative imbalances that set the stage for even further differentiation.[132] In short, the process of differentiation is no longer regarded either as an immanent tendency of social organisms or as the product primarily of a single causal factor; the origins are much more complex and variable, depending on the strength and types of combinations of several social and psychological factors.

2. The process of differentiation itself has been further analyzed. Both Spencer and Durkheim laid stress on differentiation, but they were interested mainly in contrasting less differentiated with more differentiated societies, and did not explicitly consider the *process* of moving from one state to another. Recently a model of this process has been developed and applied to empirical phenomena as diverse as decision-making in small groups, socialization of the child, and the emergence of social structures during economic and social development.[133] The sequence begins with some sort of dissatisfaction with social functioning. This gives rise to certain symptoms of disturbance, which are manifested in expressions of anxiety, hostility, and fantasy, and which may spill over into scapegoating and conflict between those desiring change and those representing traditional vested interests. As the sequence proceeds, these symptoms of disturbance are "handled and channeled" by various agencies of social control. This holding operation is followed by encouragement of new ideas, attempts to specify new institutional forms, and actual attempts to estab-

[130] These initiating conditions are spelled out with reference to structural change at the personality level in Talcott Parsons, Robert F. Bales, *et al.*, *Family, Socialization, and Interaction Process*, pp. 202–3. The scheme was applied to the problem of economic development in Parsons and Smelser, *Economy and Society*, pp. 255–67, and further elaborated in Smelser, *Social Change in the Industrial Revolution*, pp. 32–38.

[131] Smelser, *Social Change in the Industrial Revolution*, pp. 36–37; *Theory of Collective Behavior*, Chapter 3.

[132] Smelser, *Social Change in the Industrial Revolution*, Chapter 9; *The Sociology of Economic Life*, pp. 106–12.

[133] Parsons, Bales, *et al.*, *Family, Socialization and Interaction Process*, Chapters 2, 4, 7; Parsons and Smelser, *Economy and Society*, Chapter 5; Smelser, *Social Change in the Industrial Revolution*.

lish the new forms. The sequence is terminated as the new forms are consolidated as permanent features of the social structure.[134]

The general consequence of a large number of interrelated sequences of differentiation is a vast social upheaval, resulting in the emergence of a more complex, specialized organization of the social structure. As the summary indicates, the model incorporates a number of variables—disturbances and social control, social conflict, leadership in social innovation, etc.—not systematically treated by Spencer and Durkheim.

3. Some further work has been done on the concept of integration, though this has not been developed so extensively as the work on differentiation. Further relations between the rise of differentiated structures and changes in integrative structures—such as markets, political controls, and interstitial organizations—have been specified, mainly in connection with economic development.[135] A modest amount of theoretical work has been done on the role of government in initiating, mobilizing resources for, and guiding processes of differentiation, particularly in the communist societies and the new nations.[136]

The main extension of the concept of integration, however, has concerned the role of social control *during* a process of differentiation. In the model just summarized, social control is significant primarily in the "handling and channeling" of disturbances. In this model, furthermore, it is assumed that social control will be relatively effective and that the system will not experience a breakdown of authority. But when this assumption is relaxed—and the effectiveness of social control is made a variable rather than a constant—the model of differentiation is "opened" to a number of outcomes other than the rise of new, more specialized social units. Depending on how authorities react, the outcome might be more or less continuous eruptions of hostile outbursts and violence, the development of religious sects or political clubs, the development of a value-oriented revolutionary movement, or—in the event of persistent ineffectiveness over long periods—social decline. My own work on collective behavior focuses on the influences of social control on different outcomes.[137]

4. As a result of these several theoretical alterations, the notion of differentiation-integration has become, as compared to the formulations of Spencer and Durkheim, less determinate in some respects and more determinate in others. The concept of differentiation is less determinate in that it is no longer so closely linked to any specific typology of societies—

[134] For a step-by-step summary of the sequence, see above, pp. 79–80.

[135] Smelser, *Social Change in the Industrial Revolution,* Chapters 12–13; *The Sociology of Economic Life,* pp. 110–12.

[136] Parsons, *Structure and Process in Modern Societies* (New York: The Free Press of Glencoe, Inc., 1960), Chapters 3 and 4.

[137] *Theory of Collective Behavior,* pp. 261–68, 306–10, 364–79.

e.g., militant and industrial, segmental and complex—or any specific evolutionary scheme; rather, it is a more abstractly stated process of change. It is more determinate, however, in that it has focused on the detailed process of differentiation—rather than being limited to a statement of its structural results—and has brought a number of new, hitherto neglected variables to bear on this process. Furthermore, the principles of differentiation and integration have been related more closely to alternative paths of change; this has been accomplished by outlining the causal factors in terms of a delicate combination (changes in any of which can influence the direction of change) and by attempting to assess the causal role of agents of social control (whose behavior can alter the process of differentiation). Differentiation-integration, in short, is no longer considered as a kind of fixed principle of social change, but more nearly as an important process that can be related empirically and theoretically to other processes of change.

Elements of Marxian Theory

Every theorist reviewed thus far has referred to the presence of social hostility and group conflict in the processes of social disintegration and social reconstruction. Leighton singled out "suspiciousness, hatred, hostility and destructive action" as one of the major responses to stress.[138] Wallace spoke of an "ambivalent stage" that appears toward the end of the recovery process, a stage marked by complaints, criticisms, and group conflicts.[139] Spengler found some form of group conflict at almost every phase of the rise and fall of cultures; and, in particular, he described the latter stages of the decline of Civilization as situations of political localism, exploitation, and war.[140] Spencer isolated conflict as the main basis for his "militant society"; and modern differentiation-integration theorists view scapegoating and conflict as salient features of the early phases of the process of differentation.[141] If we may take the recurring preoccupations of these diverse theorists as evidence, it can be said that social change under crisis conditions cannot be understood without grasping the many roles that conflict plays in the process. With this general observation in mind, I turn now to a brief consideration of elements from two theories of social change—those of Karl Marx and Bronislaw Malinowski—who organized their theories primarily around conceptions of conflict, and whose conceptions differ from those of the authors heretofore considered.

[138] Above, p. 223.
[139] Above, p. 231.
[140] Above, pp. 239–40.
[141] Above, pp. 247, 252.

Marx's View of Society and the Historical Process   According to Marx, every society, whatever its stage of historical development, rests on an economic foundation. Marx called this foundation the "mode of production" of commodities. This mode of production in turn has two components. The first is "the forces of production," or the physical and technological arrangements of economic activity. The second component of the mode of production is "the social relations of production" or the indispensable forms of human cooperation men must engage in when they carry on economic activity. The mode of production as a whole Marx called "the economic structure of society."

But society is composed of more than its productive arrangements. Resting on the economic structure is what Marx referred to as "superstructure," or a complex of legal, political, religious, aesthetic, and other institutions. Furthermore, the general character of the social, political, and spiritual aspects of life is determined by the economic structure of society. This is what is meant by the materialist conception of society. As Friedrich Engels summarized materialism,

> . . . the production of the means to support human life—and, next to production, the exchange of things produced—is the basis of all social structure; . . . in every society that has appeared in history, the manner in which wealth is distributed and society divided into classes or orders is dependent upon what is produced, how it is produced, and how the products are exchanged. From this point of view the final causes of all social changes and political revolutions are to be sought not in men's brains, not in man's better insight into eternal truth and justice, but in changes in the modes of production and exchange. They are to be sought not in the *philosophy*, but in the *economics* of each particular epoch.[142]

This determination might work out in the following way: The most fundamental set of social relations that emerge from the process of production is a class structure, or the division of society into a powerful wealthy class and a weak poor class. Under the capitalist mode of production—Marx analyzed the capitalist system in greatest detail—the two classes are the bourgeoisie and the proletarians. The bourgeoisie con-

[142] Friedrich Engels, "Socialism: Utopian and Scientific," reprinted in Lewis S. Feuer, ed., *Basic Writings on Politics and Philosophy: Karl Marx and Friedrich Engels* (Garden City, N.Y.: Doubleday & Company, Inc., 1959), p. 91. Other, more extensive statements of Marxian materialism are found in Marx and Engels, "Feuerbach: Opposition of the Materialistic and Idealistic Outlook," in *The German Ideology* (New York: International Publishers, 1947), pp. 3–78; and Marx, *A Contribution to the Critique of Political Economy* (Chicago: Charles H. Kerr, 1904), pp. 265–312. Marx and Engels qualified this simplified materialist notion in many ways, but space does not permit an account of these qualifications in this essay.

stitute the class that owns the means of production, directs productive process, and reaps the profits from it; the proletarians are wage-workers who perform the actual labor but who do not receive full rewards for their labor. Given these relations of production, we would expect the state, the church, the community—in short, the superstructure—to operate in the service of the bourgeoisie by helping to subordinate the workers. For instance, politicians and the armed forces would keep down worker discontent, and religious leaders would feed ideologies to the masses to convince them that they are not oppressed or that they will be saved in a future life.

For a time, this conflict between opposing classes is very one-sided. Marx assumed that in capitalist society the bourgeoisie have access to power because of their position in the economic system; they own the means of production, and they buy the laborers' services. The workers, on the other hand, have only their labor to sell, and only wages in return. Because of their superior position, the capitalists are able to exploit the worker by lengthening the work day, forcing his wife and children to work, speeding up the machinery, and displacing the worker by installing more productive machinery.[143] The capitalists' power is buttressed, furthermore, by the existence of political authorities who pass laws detrimental to the workers and put down their rioting, striking, and demonstrating. Under such circumstances the political forces in society work in the service of the economic forces.

This one-sided conflict, however, is temporary. Marx maintained that each type of economic system contains "the seeds of its own destruction." Under capitalism, for instance, the bourgeoisie, driven by competition and other forces to maintain and increase their profits, gradually drive the workers more into misery and desperation. Other minor classes—tradespeople, shopkeepers, handicraftsmen—are driven into similar proletarian misery. These conditions are exaggerated by the occurrence of increasingly severe economic depressions. How do the workers respond? At first they are an "incoherent mass," capable of only isolated individual or localized action against the capitalist class; furthermore, their attacks are directed not at the capitalist system itself, but against the instruments of capitalism —the machines and the factories. After a time, however, they begin to become more aware politically, and to unite into organized groups such as trade unions. As they become more powerful, they are able to extract concessions from the ruling forces in society—such as legislation limiting the length of the working day. The final stage in the development of worker protest is the formation of a revolutionary proletarian party, which, in league with a small section of the ruling class that joins the revolu-

---

[143] Marx, *Capital* (London: George Allen and Unwin, 1949), Chapters 7–15.

tionary movement, destroys the capitalist system in a mighty worker revolution, and ushers in the communist system.[144] All this means that as the workers become more and more threatening, the political forces are no longer working in the service of the economic order. In the end, in fact, it is by means of political revolution, not economic action, that the workers accomplish the destruction of capitalism.

With the destruction of the capitalist system the building of the communist system begins. The essence of the communist revolution is the destruction of private property, which means that the bases for social division and social conflict will disappear. But Marx is careful to assert that communist society cannot be created in a single instant. "Between capitalist and communist society lies the period of the revolutionary transformation of the one into the other. There corresponds to this also a political transition period in which the state can be nothing but *the revolutionary dictatorship of the proletariat.*"[145] Also, complete equality does not exist in the early stages of the development of communism, since individuals receive an amount of social product precisely equal to their contribution; this will involve a residue of inequality, since there will be differential contributions from individuals. In the "higher phase of communist society," however, even this limited inequality disappears, and the principle of "from each according to his ability, to each according to his needs" is realized. This complete equalization of the social product removes finally all social bases for the domination of man over man, and, as a consequence, the system of social classes and government by the state will wither away.[146]

Malinowski's Conception of Culture Change

Like most of the early functional anthropologists, Malinowski devoted little of his scholarly attention to the systematic study of social and cultural change. In his last book, however, edited posthumously by Phyllis M. Kayberry, he turned to culture contact and change in the African colonial societies.

Malinowski defined the subject of his interest—culture change—very broadly at the outset: "the process by which the existing order of a society, that is, its social, spiritual, and material civilization, is transformed from one type to another."[147] To supplement this extremely general definition, he added a very inclusive conception of culture—including as ingredients

[144] The development of worker protest is sketched in "Manifesto of the Communist Party," reprinted in Feuer, *op. cit.*, pp. 15–18.

[145] Marx, *Critique of the Gotha Programme* (New York: International Publishers, 1938), p. 18.

[146] *Ibid.*, pp. 8–11. These themes are further elaborated by V. I. Lenin, *State and Revolution* (New York: International Publishers, 1932), Chapter 5.

[147] *The Dynamics of Culture Change*, p. 1.

a society's economic organization, normative system, political constitution, mechanisms and agencies of education, and systems of knowledge and religion.[148] On the basis of these two notions, Malinowski would appear to be interested in every kind of change of every cultural trait.

Actually, however, Malinowski's focus of interest in change was narrower, both by virtue of a further definition and by virtue of his particular empirical preoccupation. The study of change, he implied, should not be the study of scattered individual cultural elements or "traits," since these do not manifest themselves as a mere "medley of words, implements, ideas, beliefs, customs, myths, and legal principles." Rather, these elements are "always integrated into well-defined units," for which Malinowski reserved the term "institution." Formally defined, an institution is "a group of people united for the pursuit of a simple or complex activity; always in possession of a material endowment and a technical outfit; organized on a definite legal or customary charter, linguistically formulated in myth, legend, rule, and maxim; and trained or prepared for the carrying out of its task." [149] An implication of this definition is that change occurs in patterns of elements, not single elements alone. With respect to subject matter, Malinowski selected a specific social setting: those African societies which had come under the influence of the Western colonial powers, and which were in transition.

How did Malinowski conceptualize change in this particular setting? First he admonished against treating the colonial society as a "well-integrated whole," simply because it is a society with a multiplicity of contrasting and conflicting cultural elements. Any conception of a well-integrated community in the contact situation would "ignore such facts as the color bar, the permanent rift which divides the two partners in change and keeps them apart in church and factory, in matters of mine labor and political influence." [150] Rather, he proposed a model of society which might be termed an "equilibrium-in-tension" model, depicting the elements of society as in conflict and continuously discarding, modifying, transforming, and producing new institutions.

Malinowski developed his conception of the colonial society in transition by a series of increasingly complex approximations. Stated in its simplest form, it is a situation involving an "impact of a higher, active culture upon a simpler, more passive one." [151] But, he insisted, it is not appropriate to view the institutions of colonial societies simply as mixtures or assortments of "partially fused elements" from Europe and Africa; it is true that the colonial institutions contain elements from the two

[148] *Ibid.*, pp. 1, 43–49.
[149] *Ibid.*, pp. 49–50.
[150] *Ibid.*, p. 15.
[151] *Ibid.*

cultures, but these are integrated according to an interactive principle. Consider, for example, the African industrial enterprise:

> It cannot be understood either as a whole, or yet in any of its component parts, in terms of European or African prototypes. There is no European prototype for color-bar legislation or practice; for recruiting on reserves; for the method of unemployment insurance by throwing back superfluous labor onto the tribal areas in times of slump. The remuneration of labor, based on the differential discrimination between the races, the type of contract with unilateral criminal sanctions current in Africa, the inducements to sign—all this is new to both Europe and Africa. It is determined by the fact that we have two races and two cultures influencing each other. The concept of the mechanical incorporation of elements from one culture into another does not lead us beyond the initial preparatory stages, and even then on subtler analysis breaks down. What really takes place is an interplay of specific contact forces: race prejudice, political and economic imperialism, the demand for segregation, the safeguarding of a European standard of living, and the African reaction to this.[152]

Accordingly, Malinowski viewed colonial societies in terms of what he called his "three-column approach," delineating three kinds of social forces:

1. "the impinging culture with its institutions, intentions, and interests";
2. "the reservoir of indigenous custom, belief, and living traditions"; and
3. "the processes of contact and change, where members of the two cultures cooperate, conflict or compromise." [153]

Subsequently he added two other kinds of social forces that influence the processes of change—the "reconstructed past," or the view of cultural history which is held by members of the society (and which, though necessarily incomplete and distorted, influences their actions), and new forces of spontaneous African reintegration or reaction, including African nationalism, syncretic social movements, and so on.[154] Though Malinowski never formalized the relations among these several variables, it seems clear that he viewed each of the first three as possessing a certain "autonomous cultural determinism," i.e., a tendency to perpetuate itself; that the last two are not of the same order of magnitude as the first three, and may, indeed, possibly be reactions to the conflicts generated among the first three; but that the five variables constitute a set of social forces that,

---

[152] *Ibid.*, p. 23.
[153] *Ibid.*, p. vii. Wording by Phyllis Kayberry.
[154] *Ibid.*, pp. 32–34.

in complex interplay, determine the direction of change in colonial societies in transition.[155]

Malinowski viewed the relations among the several forces as unstable,
for two reasons. First, the intruding European culture and the surviving
African culture are not evenly matched. He described the European culture as "higher" and "active" and the African culture as "simpler" and
"passive." These terms, as well as phrases such as the "impact of Western
civilization and the reaction thereto of indigenous cultures" [156] makes it
clear that Malinowski viewed European culture as the dominant agent of
change. Second, the coexistence of conflicting institutional patterns makes
for cultural contradictions and pressure for change:

> ... the African in transition finds himself in a no-man's land, where his
> old tribal stability, his security as to economic resources, which was
> safeguarded under the old regime by the solidarity of kinship, have
> disappeared. The new culture, which has prompted him to give up
> tribalism, has promised to raise him by education to a standard of life
> worthy of an educated man. But it has not given him suitable and satis-
> factory equivalents. It has been unable to give him rights of citizenship
> regarded as due an educated Westerner; and it has discriminated
> against him socially on practically every point of the ordinary routine
> of life.[157]

Malinowski predicted that by virtue of the incessance of the pressure of
European culture, the various forces of culture contact and change would
"sooner or later ... gradually ... engulf and supersede the whole of [sur-
viving African tradition]." [158] He expressed the hope that this process
would unfold according to a principle of the "Common Factor," or the
adoption of changes that would accommodate both the common interests
of European intentions and African institutions.[159] But he ventured this
principle as a possible guide to policy, rather than as an empirical prediction of the future direction of change.

III. TOWARD A THEORETICAL SYNTHESIS

Up to this point I have followed two lines of discussion: (1) to outline the criteria necessary for developing any theory of social change;
and (2) to summarize and criticize a group of theorists who developed
their ideas on the basis of diverse time spans, historical situations, and
conceptual frameworks. Despite the diversity of the various theoretical

[155] *Ibid.*, pp. 73–80.
[156] *Ibid.*, p. 17.
[157] *Ibid.*, p. 60.
[158] *Ibid.*, p. 81.
[159] *Ibid.*, 66–72.

approaches, I am convinced they can be brought in closer relation to one another. In the final section of this essay, I shall attempt to work toward this common theoretical framework for studying social change.

Before proceeding I should like to indiciate briefly what I shall not be doing in this final section. I shall not be attempting an inventory of propositions about social change, an inventory developed by examining the various theories of change and extracting these portions that seem to be established most nearly on a scientific basis. There is nothing intrinsically wrong with developing such an inventory; indeed, much valuable codification has been done by this procedure in the social sciences.[160] But for several reasons this kind of enterprise is not appropriate for the present essay. In the first place, the present emphasis is on the conceptual *relations* among the ingredients of theories of social change, relations that are established in part by conducting inventories of reviews of existing research, but in greater part by logical analysis of theoretical explanations. Second, it is doubtful that the scholarly research on historical change, which has been conducted under such a multiplicity of different frameworks, would yield clearly established propositions. Hopefully, of course, propositions to be tested in the light of comparative data will emerge from the kind of theoretical framework I am attempting to develop. But I am using the avenue of theoretical formulation more than the avenue of inductive inspection of masses of research as the main route to these propositions.

Despite the fact that my emphasis is theoretical, I shall not be attempting to derive, in a formal sense, a common theoretical framework from those theories of change I have reviewed. If those theories had been formulated on the basis of a common language and a common logic, logical derivation might have been possible. But as the exposition and critique of the theories reveal, they are formulated too loosely, couched in language too diverse and noncomparable, and addressed to too many different historical problems to make this a feasible effort. Any apparent elegance of strict "derivation" would be marred by distortion of the original formulations.

As I have done in other places in this essay, I shall have to settle for less than "pure" method of arriving at scientifically reliable knowledge. In this case I shall have to compromise between purely inductive generalization and purely theoretical derivation as a basis for propositions. What I shall do first, then, is attempt to frame the variables, assertions, and assumptions of the limited number of theories I have reviewed in a common language; this will involve some selective interpretation, but I shall attempt to adhere to the theorists' dominant preoccupations as faith-

[160] See, for example, Bernard Berelson and Gary A. Steiner, *Human Behavior: An Inventory of Scientific Findings* (New York: Harcourt, Brace & World, Inc., 1964).

fully as possible. I shall also state the relations among these variables, assertions, and assumptions in the language of equilibrium theory outlined above; in this way I shall be attempting to bring the theorists into a more inclusive theoretical framework. Finally, I shall consider various types of outcomes that can be illuminated by this framework. In these ways I hope to achieve a modest theoretical advance in organizing concepts and theories about social change.

The Variables in a Theory of Change   All the variables of sociological analysis are relevant to the analysis of social change. These variables include the various types of dependent variables (aggregated attributes of population, rates of behavior, social structure, and cultural patterns) and independent variables (structural setting, strain, mobilization for change, and social control) discussed above.[161] Furthermore, it is evident that the anaysis of social change itself—especially long-term sequences of change—demands the consideration of many variables that can be considered "given" for many other kinds of analysis.[162] In fact, it would be possible to find instances of these variables in each of the six theories reviewed. To take the simplest theory—Leighton's theory of demoralization under crisis conditions—his dependent variables ("responses to stress") fall into the general category of "rates of behavior" and his independent variables ("types of stress") fall into the general category of "strain." But in addition, his point that cultural and personality factors influence the thresholds of stress indicates that he considers "structural" setting an important determinant as well. Other theorists—notably Marx and some of the recent differentiation-integration theorists—focus (though not exclusively) on social structure as the major dependent variable, and the interaction among strain, mobilization for change, and social control as the independent variables of change. From all standpoints, then, any general theory of change must include many different types of variables.

These observations, however, do not contribute anything very positive to such a theory. Indeed, the observations are almost anti-theoretical. Theory involves, above all, enforcing a *determinate* logical order on a *determinate* number of variables, and I have just stressed the need for the inclusion of many variables (and the concomitant problems of conceptual unmanageability and indeterminacy). It is now necessary to suggest the means by which theoretical and empirical indeterminacy can be reduced.

The Organization of Variables into Equilibrium Systems to Analyze Social Change   In confronting the core theoretical task—to organize salient variables into different types of conceptual models, by means

[161] Above, pp. 200–201, 205–7.
[162] Above, p. 232.

of which conditional outcomes can be predicted—I shall proceed by three steps. First, I shall describe each of the theories reviewed in Section II in terms of the principles of equilibrium outlined earlier. Second, I shall specify a number of principles by which these different types of equilibrium models can be related to one another, and to different phases in a long-term process of social change. And third, I shall sketch a hypothetical series of phases of change, indicating how the different types of change feed into one another. These three operations should yield a modest increase in our theoretical understanding of social change.

Leighton's theory of change can be classified as a rather simple *shock-and-ramifications* model. The basic outcome in this model (as applied to the Japanese case) is the deterioration of morale, as indicated by a decreased incidence of efficient collective action, and an increase of nonrational responses such as scapegoating, trial-and-error behavior, hysterical behavior, and apathy. The basic determinant of this demoralization was the incessant burden of the war situation, from which, it became increasingly evident to the Japanese, there was no escape. As I reformulated Leighton's discussion, the variables of "differential vulnerability to stress" and "differential opportunities for reaction to stress" proved to be important in determining the direction and extent of the responses to stress, but these variables were intervening in the sense that they inhibit or divert the stress, but do not function as an impetus to behavior in the same way that stress does. Furthermore, Leighton's model, as presented, does not allow for much "feedback." It is plausible to assume, for example, that widespread group conflict (one of the "responses to stress") is itself generative of further stress under many circumstances. This assumption would suggest further that if the response to stress is mainly group conflict, a vicious or stress-producing sequence could be easily created, thus accelerating the deterioration of morale. But as it stands, the Leighton model does not incorporate these kinds of refinements, so it can legitimately be characterized as a very simple model of pressure that reverberates through the system, with minimal intervention of other variables and with minimal feedback.

The Wallace model is an equilibrium model, since it involves a complex interplay and feedback among several sets of variables. Furthermore, it is best described as a *stable dynamic equilibrium*, which involves an initial steady state subjected to a severe shock that disturbs the basic equilibrium, but then recovers a basically steady state (though with some "irreversible changes") by the operation of mechanisms set into motion by the shock itself. The restorative mechanisms depend above all on the "counter-disaster syndrome" which unfolds by several stages and operates to counteract the tendencies toward disorganized and nonconstructive behavior on the part of those afflicted by the shock. The strength of the "counter-disaster" forces, moreover, depends ultimately on a "cornucopia" of assistance from outlying areas. While the outcome of Wallace's model is "restoration," presumably other outcomes could be generated by dropping the assumption that the resources necessary for the counter-disaster actions are available. Finally, as far as absolute time is concerned, both the Leighton and the Wallace models were applied to historical situations of less than one year's duration.

Spengler's model of cultural cycles is best described as a *series of unstable equilibrium states*, each giving way to the next in the cycle of birth-growth-maturity-decay. The part of this cycle of most interest here is the deterioration from an advanced state of maturity (Civilization) to a qualitatively different type of society. In one sense, however, it is difficult to conceptualize Spengler's theory in equilibrium terms, because he did not state specific *relations* among the various sectors of society, nor did he identify specific *mechanisms* by which the society passes from one phase to the next. Such relations and mechanisms are only implied in Spengler's notions of organismic unity and growth, notions which suggest that the various sectors of society—economic, political, religious, city-country—rise and fall in parallel. My introduction of the notion of the "vicious circle" of social disintegration—as illustrated in the work of Dill—was an effort to supply at least the kernel of some mechanism that might account for the phenomenon of political deterioration in a society.

The Spencerian and Durkheimian versions of structual differentiation amount to a *stable moving equilibrium*. The successive states in the moving trend are states of increasing structural complexity of the system. The accounts that the two theorists gave of the reasons for the stability of the system differ, however; Spencer, in his account of the growth of industrial society, stressed the importance of voluntary cooperation, whereas Durkheim emphasized the growth of a new form of organic solidarity, symbolized by the rise of restitutive law. More recent differentiation-integration theorists, who have inquired into the processes and mechanisms that operate in the movement from a less differentiated into a more differentiated state, can be said to have constructed a *series of short-term stable (or cyclical) equilibrium models superimposed on a long-term moving stable equilibrium*. In the short term, the system is subjected to dissatisfaction with the performance of roles or allocation of resources. The system reacts initially to the strain by symptoms of disturbance, but these are contained and channeled in the direction of structural innovation. In this way the system returns to a more stable state, but possesses a more complex structure than before. The net effect of many such short-term sequences is the steady growth of a more highly differentiated system.

Marx's dialectic, by contrast, can be characterized as a *stable dynamic equilibrium in the short run* and an *unstable dynamic equilibrium in the long run*. In the short run the society is organized around a given mode of production, which in turn yields a definite kind of social stratification, government, religion, philosophy, and so on. All these social institutions operate in the service of the dominant class, and when any threat to social stability arises, it is countered, and the order of the dominant class prevails. In the long run, however, this type of social order gives way to another. Two general types of mechanism make for the change. The first is the aggravation of contradictions in the society, contradictions which trace ultimately to economic changes. The second mechanism is the increasing political awareness of the subordinate class, and its subsequent mobilization into a revolutionary movement that destroys the old and establishes a new social system.

Finally, Malinowski's conception of culture change can be characterized as a *series of unstable equilibrium states superimposed on a long-term trend toward stable equilibrium*. In the initial period the traditional society exists in a relatively stable state. But exposure to the European colonial societies creates a dominant-subordinate relation and internal contradictions that make for a long period of continuous instability and change. The ingredients of the sequence of unstable equilibrium systems are the five basic forces outlined by Malinowski—traditional culture, dominant European culture, emergent culture, the reconstructed past, and spontaneous reintegration. These forces are in continuous conflict, and the result is a cauldron of change. In the long run, however, the outcome is a domination by European culture and a subordination of the traditional elements.

Phrasing the theories in terms of equilibrium principles allows us to compare them with one another more directly than before, because they are now described by a common language. But to establish these conceptual relations among the different theories is barely to begin. Even when stated in a common language the several types of equilibrium system present a list of disparate outcomes. It is necessary to relate these several types of equilibrium to one another in a more determinate way.

The essence of this task is to divide the subject matter of change into units which can be described and related to one another in terms of the different equilibrium models. The task is a difficult one because of the fact that the flow of history appears to be "uncontrolled," and that for any given historical epoch, the impression is one of ubiquitous flux, in which everything seems to be changing at once. From a formal standpoint, this circumstance would appear to require the investigator to obliterate the distinction between given (unchanging) data and vari-

ables, and to treat the society as a completely open (and therefore conceptually unmanageable) equilibrium system.[163] Given this circumstance,
the following dilemma arises: How is it possible simultaneously *both* to
take cognizance of this seemingly inevitable requirement for theoretical
indeterminacy in the analysis of historical change *and* to organize our
thinking about change in scientifically determinate ways? To this dilemma
the next several paragraphs are addressed.

An initial task is to come to terms with the variable of time. This
involves the establishment of an initial point, a number of intermediate
phases, and some terminal point—a number of points around which the
interplay of variables is to be analyzed.[164] This division into phases is
necessarily an arbitrary operation for several reasons. First, the number,
length, and descriptive labels of the several stages vary according to the
final outcome that is envisioned. For example, the phases leading to
long-term decline envisioned by Spengler (the phases of growth, maturity, stagnation, and decline) differ radically in content and time span from
the phases leading to short-term recovery envisioned by Wallace (warning, impact, rescue, recovery, etc.). Nevertheless, each theorist was constrained to construct *some* version of initial, intermediate, and terminal
stages. Second, the phases are not actually identifiable empirically, each
beginning and ending abruptly, and giving way to the next. Empirically
they fuse indistinguishably into one another. The establishment of phases
freezes the flow of historical process. Third, any effort to assign absolute
time units—days, weeks, months, years—to the phases is bound to be
arbitrary, because the phases do not have the empirical visibility to
permit such precision. Sometimes it is necessary to settle for a relatively
indeterminate "before-after" characterization.

What is the theoretical significance of dividing any given episode
of social change into phases? Let us suppose we take as the starting point
of analysis some impetus to change—a war, a depression, a group conflict, a mass influx of migrants, or whatever. In the initial phase we wish to
estimate a variety of behavioral responses to this impetus—responses such
as changing morale, the formation of new groups, various constructive
efforts, and so on. These responses constitute the outcomes of the initial
phase. Moreover, this initial phase can be characterized in equilibrium
terms. The independent variables are the impetus to change itself. The
dependent variables are the behavorial responses. And the "given data,"
which condition the relations between the independent variables, is found
in the state of the social unit before the appearance of the impetus.
These "given data" include its resources, its institutional structure and
cultural values, and so on. The outcome of the initial phase, then, is

[163] Above, p. 218.
[164] Above, p. 203.

determined by the ways that the variables and given data interact with one another.[165] In this essay we have examined two contrasting models of outcomes in the short run—the model of Leighton, which leads to a collapse of morale and social organization, and the model of Wallace, which leads to recovery and reestablishment of a steady state.

After generating a number of conditional predictions about the short-term response to an impetus to change in the initial phase, the social unit can be described—at the termination of this phase—in terms of its salient aspects: its social structure, its level of conflict, its cultural values, the morale of its population, and so on. These descriptions, considered as "outcomes" of the initial phase, *now become given data for the subsequent phase,* much as the state of the social unit before the appearance of the initial impetus constitutes given data for the initial phase. The subsequent phase may deal with different outcomes than the initial phase; it may concern the growth of new organizations, the appearance of new units of social structure, new values, and so on. The variables that determine these outcomes will be the usual sociological variables, such as the level of social disorganization, the level of social resources, the ability of the social unit to mobilize for and guide change, and so on. But the status of these variables at the beginning of the subsequent phase—as well as the status of the constraints within which they operate— will be inherited from the initial phase. In this way the first phase provides the "given data" that influence the processes of the second phase. In possession of this set of variables, given data, and relations for the subsequent phase, the investigator is in a position to generate a number of conditional predictions about the outcomes of this phase.

Furthermore, the equilibrium principle characterizing subsequent phases may be very different from that characterizing the initial phase. For example, Japanese society toward the end of World War II experienced a kind of short-run deterioration of morale and social organization that is best understood as a kind of social collapse—or in equilibrium terms, it is best understood in terms of a model of unstable dynamic equilibrium leading to a new, more primitive type of social organization. Japanese society inherited this outcome at the end of the war. Taking the longer-term view of the society, however, this inheritance constituted a new impetus for change and a new set of constraints on change. Partly because of this inheritance, and partly because of the massive inputs of new economic and political resources, Japanese society experienced a recovery that could best be described—in the longer run—in terms of an equilibrium model geared to the analysis of social growth and differentiation.[166] A total episode of change, then, may present a

[165] Above, p. 215.
[166] Above, p. 264.

picture of "equilibria-within-equilibria," and, in addition, the "inner," or "within-phase" models of equilibrium may differ both from one another and from the equilibrium model governing the total episode.

This formulation yields a kind of cumulative or branching-tree model of successive outcomes, the outcomes of each phase building on the outcomes of the previous ones. What is outcome for one phase may become condition for the next; what is variable in one phase may become given data for the next. In addition, it is important to note that *within* each phase the problem of handling a multiplicity of variables also arises. In actuality, changes will be evident in every phase at many levels (biological, psychological, social, and cultural) and in many aspects at each level (for example, in the many different institutional aspects—educational, economic, familial, etc.—at the social level). It is evidently not possible to construct models that designate all these as simultaneously in flux. It is necessary to treat some of the changes as "given" for purposes of analysis. Conditional predictions have to be formulated about, say, the kind of political adjustment in any given phase. Hopefully these predictions can be made on the basis of carefully formulated theories and the best available data. After they are made, however, their results should be treated as given data for the analysis of processes in the economic, educational, and other spheres. The operation here described is directed toward the same objective as the specification of given data for a given stage on the basis of the outcomes of previous stages. This objective is to render our descriptions and explanation of social change more manageable conceptually.

Let me now summarize how I have addressed the dilemma of the apparent inevitability of theoretical indeterminacy and the evident desirability of generating scientific explanations of change. As I have formulated it, social change is best analyzed as a complicated sequence of different kinds of equilibrium processes; whether one type or another predominates depends both on the phase in the social-change sequence under consideration and on the interaction of variables in each phase. Furthermore, these various equilibrium processes can be related in such a way that given data and variables are systematically transformed, both within and between phases. The resulting formulation constitutes an attempt to steer between the danger of creating determinate but oversimplified explanations and the danger of creating statements so completely indeterminate as to be useless scientifically.

A Hypothetical Sequence of Phases of Change

I have now described six theorists in the language of equilibrium analysis; I have also suggested a few formal principles by which the different kinds of equilibrium systems can be related to one another in the analysis of an episode of social change. At the risk of some repetition, I shall now attempt to combine these two kinds of statements, and apply the logic of the theories reviewed to a few hypothetical phases of change. I shall consider only three phases: (1) the appearance of some impetus to change and the immediate response to this impetus; (2) an intermediate phase; and (3) a period of long-term structural and cultural change. For many purposes it would be desirable to subdivide these three phases. In the present context, however, since the main objective is to illustrate rather than to carry out full analyses, it is not necessary to go into such detail.

1. Let us begin with some kind of impetus to change. Every one of the theorists considered in this essay refers to some sort of initial impetus. Leighton referred to the bombing and other pressures resulting from the Allied war effort on Japanese society; Wallace referred to the crisis created for the community of Worcester by the impact of the tornado; Malinowski referred to the multiplicity of pressures resulting from colonial domination; Marx took the historical contradictions emerging from the economic arrangements of society as the major impetus to change; Spengler and Spencer saw the impetus to change as emanating from the organic potentialities of society for growth or decay; and contemporary differentiation-integration theorists have attempted to specify a number of different types of strain as the impetus to change. We may conclude, then, that any general theory of social change must come to terms with the problem of impetus—whether this be represented as internally generated, as externally imposed, or as a combination of internal and external pressures; and whether it be considered as a single type of pressure, or as a combination of a variety of types of pressure.

The outcomes of this initial phase are constituted by the psychological reactions and the behavioral responses of the population subjected to the impetus; the effect on structured social interaction; the gains and losses of various groups in the population, and so on. The social unit in question may emerge from the first phase in more or less the same condition as it was when the impetus was experienced (in this case it would presumably not be necessary to trace this particular episode of change into subsequent phases), or it may emerge with a condition of improvement or impairment of its social functioning, a condition that "sets the stage" for the subsequent phases of change.

The impetus to change, as well as the social unit's capacity to absorb it, varies according to the following factors:

(*a*) The extent of the effect of the impetus. Clearly a small economic recession is not so severe an impetus—nor so likely to generate subsequent change—as a major depression. Clearly a tornado that affects a few communities is not so severe an impetus, nor so likely to generate subsequent change, as a major war.[167]

(b) The suddenness of onset of the impetus. A natural disaster, such as a flood or gas explosion, is more likely to set up pressures to change than a gradually developing impetus, such as erosion or air pollution, even though the latter may ultimately be more "damaging" to the social unit in question. Similarly, a gradual decline of the stock market is less likely to set up pressures for change than a sudden collapse.

(c) The psychological and cultural vulnerabilities of the population of the social unit. Leighton singled out certain factors in the Japanese population that seemed to provide a focus for resistance to strain. In particular, he noted that faith in the Emperor and faith in the spirit of the Japanese people were important in preventing demoralization and its associated behavioral responses. Clearly, the psychological vulnerability of a population, revealed in the personality patterns of its members, intervenes between the impetus and the immediate reactions to the impetus.

(d) The structural vulnerability of the social unit. Here the work of Spencer and Durkheim provides a lead. Both these theorists stressed that the greater the extent of structural differentiation into specialized parts, the greater the interdependence among these parts, and the greater the vulnerability of a society to an assault on one of these parts.[168] A family, for example, whose whole economic welfare is dependent on the specialized employment of one member, would suffer more from his unemployment than if the family income were generated by a variety of different economic activities, on which they could "fall back" as a cushion in difficult times. A society which is highly specialized regionally, and very dependent on the maintenance of communication and exchange among its specialized parts, is more vulnerable to damage to one of its regions than if the society were not so specialized.

(e) Finally, the severity of the impetus is influenced by a variety of considerations concerning the preparedness of the social unit for the impetus. For example, if the impetus is understood and expected, and the members of the population are "programmed" to react in specified

---

[167] Wallace, for example, noticed the importance of the fact that outside communities were able to come to the aid of Worcester, thus lessening the probability of long-term crisis in that community. Wallace's theory rested on the assumptions that "any given disaster will not destroy the cornucopia itself, and that any given disaster or combination of disasters will be unable to exhaust the cornucopia before adequate relief and rehabilitation can be produced." Wallace doubted whether such assumptions apply to "disasters . . . produced by atomic or hydrogen explosions." *Tornado in Worcester*, p. 157.

[168] Above, pp. 244, 249.

ways to it, the less likely is the occurrence of extreme reactions when the impetus appears.

The outcome of the initial phase depends on the interaction among these several factors, and can be described in terms of the incidence of the various types of behavioral reactions, the psychological state of the population, and the state of several aspects of the social unit that will be operative in determining patterns of change in succeeding phases —the level of resources, the patterns of social interaction, the functioning of agencies of social control. Furthermore, these outcomes provide a set of "values" to be assigned to the variables that will be operative in the succeeding phase. In short, the description of the outcome of the initial phase constitutes the starting point of the analysis of the given data and the initial values of the variables of the second phase.

2. The initial phase of strain is characterized as a kind of impetus-and-ramifications model, with a variety of factors affecting the severity of the impetus and the responses. The second phase stretches over a longer time span, and involves various efforts to "recover," both from the initial impetus as well as from the effects that the responses to the initial impetus might have created. These attempts to recover, however, stop short of structural or cultural change, which are considered as longer-term responses. Outcomes of this phase may range from one extreme (in which social functioning is more or less restored, group conflict minimized, and the original impetus overcome or assimilated) to the other extreme (with continued social disorganization, conflict, and potential for further change). A first approximation to the kinds of processes that occur in this second hypothetical phase is indicated by the "euphoric" and "ambivalent" stages of Wallace's theory. In these stages the disaster syndrome includes a revival of neighborhood spirit, various kinds of participation in repair and rehabilitation activities, but subsequently the rise of criticisms, complaints, and group hostility; the counter-disaster syndrome involves similar kinds of behavior on the part of individuals and organizations that were initially unaffected by the disaster.[169] In this subsequent phase, in short, the social unit is seen as still dealing with the initial impetus, but, in addition, confronting the additional complications that have arisen out of responses to the initial impetus.

The outcomes of the second phase depend on the interaction among the following factors.

(*a*) The extent of social strain. If the initial impetus is still in effect —as would be the case, for example, with a prolonged period of unemployment—this is inherited from the initial phase. In addition, the second

[169] Above, pp. 231–32.

phase also must deal with a variable level of "derived" strain—for example, various impairments of the social structure that might have developed as a consequence of the initial impetus.

(*b*)   The resources available to overcome the strain.

(*c*)   The ability of the public authorities to mobilize persons and resources to overcome the sources of strain. If the public authorities in a society are themselves impaired, or do not enjoy the cooperation and support of the population, then the assault on the strain inherited by the second phase will be less effective.

(*d*)   The level of socially disruptive and unstabilizing responses to stress. Wallace referred to the fact that as efforts to rehabilitate proceed, there also develops a heightened tendency for group conflict, scapegoating, complaints about injustices, and so on. These kinds of conflict, which can be considered as reactions both to the original stress and to the processes of change involved in rehabilitation, are only a few of the many possible forms of disruptive behavior that can be expected in the first year after attack. Violence, looting, black-marketeering, rebellious and revolutionary activity, uncontrolled rumors and hysteria—all must be considered as likely reactions to a situation of continued strain and social disorganization.

(*e*)   The ability of the public authorities to resist and contain disruptive and unstabilizing behavior. One of the key variables in predicting the kind and extent of these kinds of behavior is the response of public authorities to it. For example, if authorities firmly put down displays of violence but react patiently and responsively to the grievances associated with the violence, the probability of the spread of violence is typically low. If, however, authorities prove ineffectual in containing violence and/or remain inflexible in the face of demands for reform, the probability of widespread rebellious and revolutionary activity is increased. Depending on the power of public authorities, and depending on the effectiveness with which they exercise this power, the tendencies to social and political instability could be reasonably effectively contained at the one extreme, or could result in repeated overthrows by groups claiming political legitimacy at the other.

These five sets of variables stand in complex relation to one another. The incidence of socially disruptive responses to strain, for example, is in part a function of the level of strain itself, the level of resources and organizational ability available to overcome the strain, and the reaction of public authorities to social outbursts and social movements. The level of strain is inherited in part from the first phase, but it can also be augmented by the failure of coordination of reconstructive efforts and by the ravages of uncontrolled group conflict and deviance. The ability of public authorities to contain disruptive behavior depends on the way social strain is affecting *them*, and on the resources they posses. Though not all the relations among these variables are known precisely, it is clear that they can, in principle, be organized according to the principles of equilibrium. Whether the outcome of the equilibrium process be stagnation, disorganization, reasonably effective recovery, or something else, depends on the values of the variables and their interaction during the second phase.

3. The outcome of the second phase itself leaves an inheritance for the third phase of long-term structural and cultural change; and, indeed, this inheritance determines in part the direction of these long-term processes. For example, if a reasonably effective recovery has occurred, the probability of institutional stability or growth in the long run is increased. If the society has wallowed in stagnation or disorganization in the second phase, the probability of instability or decline in the long run is augmented. In short, the outcomes of the second phase provide given data that "load the dice" for future phases, but the independent principles of long-term social change, in interaction with these given data, determine the ultimate outcomes of these subsequent phases.

For these reasons, it is advisable to envision a number of possible outcomes for the long run, and to attempt to specify the conditions under which each is likely to occur. These conditions are similar to those that operate in the second phase, except that they are now to be read in terms of a long-term theory of social and cultural change rather than a theory of short-term recovery. Briefly, the variables that combine in different ways to produce long-term outcomes are:

(*a*) The level of strain. Again, the residue from the original impetus is still relevant, but the strain resulting from irregularities and social discontinuities of the on-going processes of change is more important.

(*b*) The availability of resources to foster institutional and cultural change.

(*c*) The ability of agents of change, whether in the government-and-control apparatus or outside it, to mobilize and coordinate social action in the interests of change. (In referring to the "governmental-and-control" apparatus I am referring not only to the political authority of the state, but also other social organizations, such as welfare agencies, educational institutions, and community leaders, which are not "political" in the governmental sense.)

(*d*) The ability of persons opposed to the government-and-control apparatus to mobilize and coordinate collective action.

Using these sets of variables as the basic ingredients of long-term equilibrium analysis, the following kinds of outcomes can be envisioned:

First, social stagnation and decline. This outcome approximates the

Spenglerian model of social decline more closely than any other out-come. The combination of variables fostering this continuously down-ward spiral is the following: First, there would be a high and continuing level of strain. This would not necessarily be manifested in the inherent tendencies for a Civilization to become internally amoral and exploita-tive—as Spengler would have it—but would result from the social dis-organization that developed through the earlier phases. Second, the level of resources available to foster institutional innovation would prob-ably be low. Third, agents of change would be unable to mobilize and control people and resources to foster social and cultural change. And, fourth, persons opposed to the government-and-control apparatus would likewise be relatively unable to mobilize and coordinate collective action. The combination of these four conditions would produce decreasing levels of economic production and continuous and spasmodic social move-ments; of the latter, some would be repressed by governmental action, others would arise to topple a government and seize its reins. But even these successful movements would enjoy only a brief and ineffective hegemony, because of their lack of resources and mobilizative effective-ness. In the end, any government would prove ineffective, and efforts to make it so would augment the vicious circle of increasing defiance and increasingly futile efforts to curb the defiance. The ultimate result of this deteriorative process would be the localism envisioned by Speng-ler, and any tendencies toward social reconstruction would have to take root in the localities.

Second, the deflection of social decline through revolutionary con-vulsion. This outcome results from a particular combination of elements from the Spenglerian and Marxist theories. The initial stages of this process would be identical to the model of stagnation and decline just reviewed. Rather than deteriorating into localism, however, the process would be reversed by the development of a revolutionary group outside the government-and-control apparatus that could mobilize sufficient numbers on the basis of an appropriate ideology to topple the ineffectual existing government. This revolution would be followed by a period of repression, under which resources and people would be forcibly mobilized to reverse the trend toward stagnation to one of sociocultural development. All the variables in this model except one would be the same as the "social stagnation and decline" model: the ability of persons opposed to the government-and-control apparatus to mobilize and co-ordinate collective action, which would be the main operative force in deflecting the process of decline.

Third, social development of a continuous nature. This outcome ap-proximates the differentiation-integration model of social change, from the standpoint of both results and dynamics. Emerging from the second phase, the society would still be experiencing much strain, and this strain would continue to be generated by the discontinuous processes of social change associated with the occurrence of many simultaneous processes of differentiation and integration. Furthermore, disruptive tendencies would also be present. But in this model it is assumed that the government-and-control apparatus would be able to handle social disturbances more or less effectively, and to channel them in the direction of institutional change. A corollary of this assumption is that the ability of persons opposed to the government-and-control apparatus to mobilize and co-ordinate collective action would be limited by the effectiveness of the government and allied agencies of control. The result of the interaction among these variables—in keeping with the relations posited—would be a process of rebuilding a complex and interdependent social structure.

Fourth, social development of a discontinuous nature. One of the background assumptions of the differentiation-integration model is that structural change unfolds in a context of relatively unchanging cultural values, which serve to legitimize expressions of dissatisfaction and to operate as guiding criteria for structural change.[170] Accordingly, the depth of social conflict and social turbulence is not so great as when cultural values and standards themselves come to be the basis of conflict and change. Malinowski's work provides a case of the latter. As the reader will recall, he posits a traditional culture as the starting point of his analysis. This comes under the influence of some new culture, and the two stand in fundamental conflict with one another. Other ingredients of culture conflict are added when an "emergent" culture arises as a complex function of the conflict of the first two; and when various forces making for a "reconstructed past" and "spontaneous integration" also arise.[171] Conceived this way, Malinowski's view of society reveals a hive of conflict and instability. However, since one set of cultural forces—the "emergent"—is assumed in the end to be dominant, agencies of social control are implicitly assumed to be sufficiently strong to assure that the uncontrolled upsurge of the forces of tradition or revolution will not overthrow the government and alter the basic directions of social change. If such mechanisms can be incorporated into it, Malinowski's theory of change provides a model of relatively discontinuous social and cultural development.

Fifth, social development deflected by revolutionary convulsion. Whether social development be continuous or discontinuous, it was assumed in the third and fourth examples that the government-and-control apparatus is able to contain the social forces opposed to this apparatus. However, it may be advisable to relax this assumption. If

[170] Smelser, *Social Change in the Industrial Revolution,* Chapter 2.
[171] Above, pp. 259–60.

this is done, it is apparent that the diverse strains and social discontinuities occasioned by social reconstruction can give rise to a successful revolutionary movement that will overthrow the government-and-control apparatus. Thereafter the new government would continue the process of reconstruction under a different system of legitimacy, or would otherwise redirect the pattern of social change. In terms of the theories I have reviewed, relaxing this assumption involves a combination of a view of social development (whether continuous or discontinuous) with the Marxian conception of revolutionary dynamics.

Summary Observations In representing the three hypothetical phases of social change, Figure 8–4 summarizes this section. The initial phase begins with an impetus to change in a social unit, and traces the short-term ramifications of this impetus. A variety of outcomes are possible, ranging from the accumulation of strains at one extreme to an assimilation of the impetus at the other. If the former, the system is disposed to further change; if the latter, the initial impetus has no further implications for change. In the second phase efforts are made to come to terms with the accumulated strains. A number of variables— the level of strain, the level of resources, the responses to strain, and so on—determines whether this second phase leads to full recovery, further accumulation of strains, or some intermediate outcome. If anything but the former, the system is disposed to enter into the third phase. The third phase itself envisions a number of longer-term outcomes, the determination of which depends mainly on the level of accumulated strain, the resources of the system, and the capacities of the government-and-control apparatus.

To this summary must be added a number of observations and qualifications:

1. The representation of processes of social change in Figure 8–4 is completely abstract, and is not meant to characterize any particular historical situation. The "initial impetus" may be located at any historical time. The objective of the representation is to provide a basis for understanding and explaining change *once the initial impetus has been selected and identified.*

2. Each outcome at each phase is analyzed not as the product of a unique set of determinants, but rather as the product of different *combinations* of the same general variables. For example, the long-term outcomes, "continuous development" and "stagnation and decline," may have their historical origins *in precisely the same outcomes produced in the first two phases.* The divergent directions of change are determined only at a later stage. Thus the various long-term outcomes all may have a common historical root, much like the branches of a tree. The deter-

SCHEMATIC REPRESENTATION OF HYPOTHETICAL PHASES AND OUTCOMES OF SOCIAL CHANGE

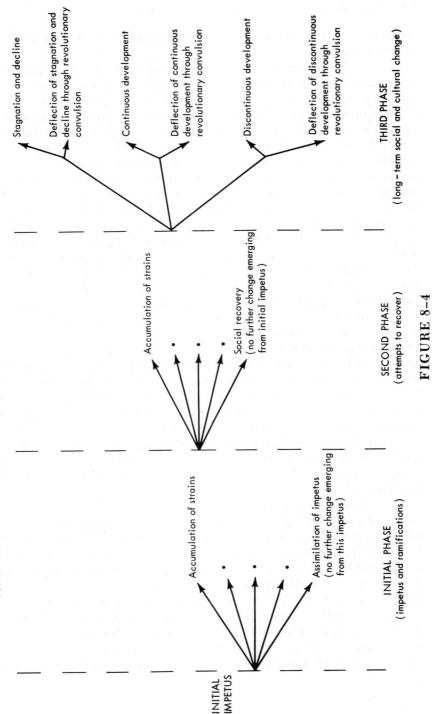

FIGURE 8–4

mination of an outcome is viewed as an accumulation of causes, not as a set of initial causes.

3. The longer-term processes of structural and cultural change can be related to the short-term processes of adjustment and change in still another way: The equilibrium models appropriate to the latter can serve, if appropriately modified, as *mechanisms* in the longer-term processes. For example, the first two steps in the model of structural differentiation [172] are dissatisfactions followed by a number of symptoms of disturbance. Considered in isolation, these two steps constitute a sort of stress and response-to-stress model reminiscent of Leighton's scheme, though the formulation of types of stress and types of responses differ in the two versions. Again, the Marxist model of development of a revolutionary movement is also a stress and response-to-stress model, though the stress in this case is manifested in historical contradictions, and the response to stress is a specific kind of revolutionary protest. In both these examples, the short-term process is an integral part of the longer-term process of social and cultural change. These illustrations underscore a general principle of social-change theory: What can be analyzed as a discrete process of change in the short term often can be treated as a mechanism of longer-term change.

4. If any variable were to be singled out as determining the long-term direction of change (i.e., type of outcome), this would be the status of the social system's government-and-control apparatus. As we have seen, the initial impetus disposes the social system to some kind of change, but this disposition is very indeterminate. The direction of change depends at every stage and in large part on the activities of the government-and-control apparatus—its planning, its ability to mobilize people and resources in periods of strain, its ability to contain and respond to protest, and its ability to guide and control institutional innovations.

5. The preceding point raises a more general observation concerning the conception of society that emerges from this essay. Modern social theory is dominated by two general and opposing conceptions of society. The first, tracing mainly to the classical functionalist position, tends to treat society either as a static equilibrium with fixed interdependence of parts or as a stable dynamic equilibrium with built-in restorative mechanisms that return it to its previous state whenever disturbances threaten its stability. While this characterization oversimplifies the views of those who have delineated society in functional terms, it is clear that the variables of government-and-control and social integration are often rendered nonproblematical, since they are assumed to swing into opera-

[172] Above, p. 79.

tion automatically, quickly, and effectively when social disruption threatens. Furthermore, this conception of society has been frequently criticized for its inability to accommodate analyses of major social disintegration and radical change.

The second conception of society, tracing primarily to the Marxist tradition, tends to treat society as subject to definite institutional contradictions, based ultimately on the evolutionary phase of economic and social development. In the long run these contradictions lie at the root of fundamental and revolutionary change and the creation of a new social system. But this conception, while more congenial to the analysis of conflict and radical change, also appears to render the problems of government-and-control and social integration nonproblematical, since the status of these factors is, in the long run, dependent upon the nature of the underlying contradictions and conflicts; governments, laws, and customs change because the economic structure changes, and in the broad sweep of history these are at the mercy of the unfolding economic and class relations.[173] The general direction of social change in the Marxian conception of society is dictated by the logic of historical materialism.

In a recent publication,[174] Wilbert Moore has suggested an intermediate conception of society, which he labels "society as a tension-management system." Like a Marxist, he views conflict and tension as normal and ubiquitous; but unlike a Marxist, he sees this as stemming from a variety of sources—imperfect socialization, role-conflict, etc.—rather than from the institutional contradictions of a specific stage of social and economic development. Like a classical functionalist, he sees social adjustment as responsive to disruptive influences; but unlike a classical functionalist, he does not assume that the adjustments necessarily reduce the tension—indeed, changes may generate even greater conflict and tension. Furthermore, Moore sees society as resilient or flexible to a degree, being able to absorb certain tensions, conflicts, and changes in some of its parts without necessarily calling for an adjustment or change of the whole system.

On most grounds Moore's reformulations seem to be more realistic than either the extreme stability or the extreme conflict model of society. But one of the costs that Moore appears to have paid is a certain loss of determinacy with respect to accounting for the precise directions or outcomes of change, a definiteness possessed by both the other models.

---

[173] In his writings on revolutionary dynamics, however, Marx conceives a political process—revolution—to be the actual engine of overthrow of one system and establishment of another; in this respect Marx endows the political aspect of society with a more independent role than would be anticipated from the perspective of radical materialism.

[174] *Social Change* (Englewod Cliffs, N.J.: Prentice-Hall, Inc., 1963), Chapter 1.

In the view of society that underlies the analysis in this essay, I have accepted Moore's view that society is subject to more or less chronic tension and potential for change. But as indicated in this final section, I have attempted to attack the problem of direction of change in part by referring to the disposition and activities of the government-and-control apparatus, broadly conceived. The fact that society is always subject to forces of internal strain and conflict guarantees that it may be always disposed to change, even change radically. But in addition, the society is seen as possessing a political apparatus, which, among other things, orients itself to these points of conflict and their consequences. The direction of social adjustment and change depends in part on the type and extent of the strains and conflicting forces, but also on the posture and behavior of the integrative and mobilizative forces. In short, I have attempted to make the latter forces problematical, and to employ variations in these factors as ways to account for different directions of change. Hopefully this strategy may work toward overcoming the explanatory shortcomings of the classical functionalist and classical Marxist approaches, as well as the explanatory indeterminacy of Moore's intermediate conception.